Inequality in the Portuguese-speaking World

Global and Historical Perspectives

The Portuguese-Speaking World

ITS HISTORY, POLITICS AND CULTURE

The Series Editors
António Costa Pinto (University of Lisbon)
Onésimo T. Almeida (Brown University)
Miguel Bandeira Jerónimo (University of Coimbra)

This new series will publish high-quality scholarly books on the entire spectrum of the Portuguese-speaking world, with particular emphasis on the modern history, culture, and politics of Portugal, Brazil, and Africa. The series, which will be open to a variety of approaches, will offer fresh insights into a wide range of topics covering diverse historical and geographical contexts. Particular preferences will be given to books that reflect interdisciplinarity and innovative methodologies. The editors encourage the submission of proposals for single author as well as collective volumes.

The Lusophone World: The Evolution of Portuguese National Narratives
Sarah Ashby

The Politics of Representation: Elections and Parliamentarism in Portugal and Spain, 1875–1926
Edited by Pedro Tavares de Almeida & Javier Moreno Luzón

Inequality in the Portuguese-Speaking World: Global and Historical Perspectives
Edited by Francisco Bethencourt

Marcello Caetano: A Biography (1906–1980)
Francisco Carlos Palomanes Martinho

Inequality in the Portuguese-speaking World

Global and Historical Perspectives

Edited by Francisco Bethencourt

SUSSEX
ACADEMIC
PRESS
Brighton • Portland • Toronto

2 4 6 8 10 9 7 5 3 1

First published 2018, in Great Britain by
SUSSEX ACADEMIC PRESS
PO Box 139
Eastbourne BN24 9BP

Distributed in the United States by
SUSSEX ACADEMIC PRESS
ISBS Publisher Services
920 NE 58th Ave #300, Portland, OR 97213

British Library Cataloguing in Publication Data

A CIP catalogue record for this book is available from the British Library.

Library of Congress Cataloging-in-Publication Data

Names: Bethencourt, Francisco, editor.
Title: Inequality in the Portuguese-speaking world : global and historical perspectives / edited by Francisco Bethencourt.
Description: Brighton ; Portland : Sussex Academic Press, 2018. | Series: The Portuguese-speaking world: its history, politics and culture | Includes bibliographical references and index.
Identifiers: LCCN 2017036280 | ISBN 9781845198466 (alk. paper)
Subjects: LCSH: Equality—Portuguese-speaking countries—History. | Portuguese-speaking countries—Social conditions. | Portuguese-speaking countries—Economic conditions. | Portuguese-speaking countries—Politics and government.
Classification: LCC HN995 .I54 2018 | DDC 303.48/217569—dc23
LC record available at https://lccn.loc.gov/2017036280

MIX
Paper from responsible sources
FSC® C013056
FSC www.fsc.org

Typeset & designed by Sussex Academic Press, Brighton & Eastbourne.
Printed by TJ International, Padstow, Cornwall.

Contents

Series Editors' Preface

This is a timely contribution to one of the most important debates of contemporary societies: the historical production and reproduction – some say resolute aggravation — of social, political and economic inequality. Edited by a well-known historian, who offers a comprehensive introduction and authors two chapters, and gathering an impressive group of scholars from different disciplinary backgrounds and mastering specific expertise, this volume places the Portuguese-speaking world in the field of studies about inequality. It does so by bringing history, interdisciplinarity, and comparison to the table. It ponders the weight of historical dynamics, emphasizing the centrality of imperial and colonial processes in historical production and reproduction of inequality, on many levels and meanings. It sponsors an interdisciplinary assessment of the topic, aiming to illuminate its numerous and multifaceted undercurrents and manifestations. The multiple faces of inequality require multidimensional approaches, benefitting as much as possible from what the humanities and the social sciences have to offer. As Francisco Bethencourt stresses in his Introduction, "The Portuguese-speaking world has a special place in the history of social inequality since it was shaped by colonialism and imperialism". One of the innovations of this book is to integrate that world in the comparative study of social inequality (although most of the chapters focus on Brazil, Portugal, Angola, and Mozambique). The editor and contributors engage with this challenge, showcasing distinct analytical frameworks, methodologies, and topics of concern. As a result, the work is a polyhedric approach to the causes, instances, mechanisms, and dynamics of inequality. Finally, it explores the analytical and heuristic virtues (and limitations) of comparative reasoning. The multiple geographies of inequality in the Portuguese-speaking world — their connections, similarities, and specificities — are duly explored, in different chronologies and specific trajectories, through diverse problems and angles. The combination of these aspects, among other important ones, turns *Inequality in the Portuguese-Speaking World* into a groundbreaking, thought-provoking, analytically challenging and empirically rich book. Naturally, the editors of this series are pleased to see it published by Sussex Academic Press.

António Costa Pinto (University of Lisbon)
Onésimo T. Almeida (Brown University)
Miguel Bandeira Jerónimo (University of Coimbra)

Introduction

Francisco Bethencourt

The Portuguese-speaking world has a special place in the history of social inequality, since it was shaped by colonialism and imperialism, although different local conditions produced divergent historical trajectories. The study of Portuguese-speaking independent countries on different continents has not previously been developed from this perspective; and this will certainly contribute to the growing debate on historical and comparative developments in social inequality. All countries where Portuguese has been the official language, and territories touched by Portuguese expansion, are included in this book; but the chapters concentrate mainly on Brazil, Portugal, Angola, and Mozambique. These countries are positioned in different political and economic inter-regional areas, reacting in different ways to the impact of globalisation. The contributors writing about them were chosen for their particular expertise. The purpose is to present an up-to-date book with deep analysis of recent economic, political and cultural trends, as well as long term historical analysis.

The first section of this volume concerns modern social inequality. The issue of race is raised by Lilia Moritz Schwarcz in a chapter in which she looks at the heavy legacy of slavery and how this is implicated in the current social inequality between white and black people in Brazil. She uses all the main indicators – those for education, employment, distribution of income, health, and poverty – to show a consistent gap in all areas. Her conclusions highlight an amnesia concerning slavery and the contradiction between cultural inclusion and social inequality. Celia Kerstenetzky looks at the improvement of the welfare state in Brazil between 2004 and 2014, based on a redistributive model of development that created growth with reduced poverty and inequality; but she points out the resilient phenomenon of a concentration of wealth at the top of income distribution, and the weaknesses of the system and the threats that it faces. Carlos Farinha Rodrigues analyses the reduction of poverty and inequality in Portugal from the mid-1990s to 2009, and the subsequent reversal of this during a period of recession. Gini coefficients and other methods of estimating distribution of income are used to place Portugal in the context of the wider range of European Union countries. Tiago Fernandes discusses social inequality during and after this period of recession, which lasted from 2008 to 2015, contrasting the policies of austerity imposed by the European Union and the International Monetary Fund, through first a Socialist and then a Right government, with the anti-austerity policies implemented by a new, minority Socialist government and its Communist and Left

Block supporters. Pedro Ramos Pinto goes back to the period of the *Estado Novo* in Portugal (1926–1974) to understand the impact of the complex mixture of traditional and modern elements of that political regime on social inequality. The extraordinary rise of inequality in the 1930s is pointed out as an anomaly, while policies towards a welfare state and a relative opening of the economy from the 1950s on did not significantly change the picture.

The second part of the volume is dedicated to postcolonial identities. Speed is at the core of the study by Laurent Vidal of life in the ports of nineteenth century Brazil. Inspired by the celebrated geographer Milton Santos, who talked about "slow men" as a metaphor for political and economic exclusion, Laurent Vidal focuses on slaves, freedmen and poor unskilled European migrants, and includes a discussion of the ways in which, while they were waiting for work, these men engaged in creative cultural activities. Vinicius Mariano de Carvalho addresses another crucial issue: how Brazilian literature presents the issue of social inequality in its different dimensions, dealing with the stereotypes that have shaped external and internal perceptions of the country from colonial times to the present. The dualism between exoticism and social criticism is analysed through two centuries of literary output; but in the end, the inherent inequality of the field is underlined by looking at the authors, the overwhelming majority of whom are white and male. The vision of women as figures of mediation between times and places of transition is analysed by Hilary Owen through two Mozambican films directed by men, *Virgem Margarida* by Licínio de Azevedo (2012) and *O jardim de outro homem* by João Luís Sol de Carvalho (2007). The extraordinary case of a virgin who is arrested without papers, and is mistakenly sent to a post-independence location for the re-education of prostitutes, is contrasted with the dreams of becoming a medical doctor of a pupil sexually harassed by her teacher. The historical and cultural contexts of Mozambique after independence are drawn on to show the extraordinary richness of these films. Literary descriptions of the capitals of Angola and Mozambique, Luanda and Maputo, are the object of Margarida Calafate Ribeiro's chapter. Reflection on the colonial urban heritage, with its spatial segregation, is the key to reconstituting conflictive, colonial visions of space and postcolonial reflections of social inequality extended into the present day.

The third section of the book, organised in a retrospective and thematic way, concerns the colonial period. Laura de Mello e Souza links violence and inequality in her study of slavery, freedmen and vagrants in the colonial period. Violence is a crucial issue that is here developed from an economic, social and political point of view. The debate among historians and anthropologists around slavery and its consequences is also brought into this analysis. Francisco Bethencourt then addresses the issue of colonialism from the points of view of both the coloniser and the colonised, stressing the opportunities for the former and the imposed conditions for the latter (dispossession of economic, political and cultural resources), who nevertheless promoted their agency and negotiated their daily life, which changed over time and place. Filipa Lowndes Vicente and Inês Vieira Gomes address here the crucial issue of gender inequality in the colonial world through an analysis of the trial of Captain Jose Veloso de Castro, administrator of Luanda and police commander of Angola, in 1919. The story of Veloso de Castro's long career highlights continual micro-conflicts involving soldiers, policemen, merchants and natives, mainly women. These were the people who, at his trial, accused him of abuse and rape of minors. Miguel Bandeira Jeronimo tackles an understudied issue: the rise and institutionalisation of the welfare colonial state in the post-war period of emerging liberation movements. Here, social programmes, private and public, are placed in a comparative perspective and related to counter-insurgence visions of the European empires.

Finally, I would like to thank the series editor, António Costa Pinto, for the enthusiastic way he welcomed the proposal for this book, and the anonymous reviewers for their pertinent suggestions. As in other volumes I have organised, Helen Hancock played an important role as a competent and committed copy editor, and also as proof reader for those authors who are not native English speakers. The book started with a symposium at King's College London organised by the Charles Boxer Chair, King's Camões Centre and King's Brazil Institute, and the main discussion on theoretical and methodological perspectives took place at that event. The engagement with different disciplinary viewpoints was very productive, as was the reflection on precise case studies. In this resulting volume, the variety of forms of inequality is better identified and analysed than has previously been the case; and the work can be classified as pioneering for its comparative and historical scope. The symposium and the book could not have been organised and produced without the consistent support of the Camões Institute in Portugal.

CHAPTER

1

Social Inequality: A Comparative and Historical View

FRANCISCO BETHENCOURT

Interpretations of inequality

The notion of inequality means disparity in size, number and quality; it has been developed in mathematics to signify differences in weight, value or properties, and also irregularity, variance and inconsistency.[1] The notion is also applied to society, having been at the core of social and political thought since classical antiquity. It led to discussion of difference in rank or social standing, superiority and inferiority, and unfairness or inequity concerning the treatment of people. In different European languages, the use of inequality with these meanings has been in evidence since the Late Middle Ages.[2]

Social and economic inequality has become a hot political issue in the last 30 years. The reduction of unequal distribution of wealth in the Western world during most of the twentieth century has been reversed since the 1980s. The ideal of an inclusive society, in which the gap between rich and poor is limited, thus contributing to equal opportunities for all, seemed to fade away after a period of economic and social improvement. The issue of the accumulation of riches was discussed in moral terms by Buddhists, Jains and Hindu reformers in India, Taoist and Confucian thinkers in China, and early Christians in the Middle East and Europe.[3] Now the issue is discussed in economic terms, as a waste of resources, responsible for low demand and stagnation.[4]

The Kuznets bell curve of increased social inequality due to technological change and economic growth, followed by diffusion of knowledge and reduction of disparities, has been discussed by many authors, particularly by Thomas Piketty.[5] It seems that the period of significant reduction of social inequality, from the 1910s to the 1970s, was mainly due to wars and economic crises, which triggered heavy taxation of rich people and redistribution of wealth to the poorer strata of the population by the state, not to a spontaneous economic dynamic.[6]

The enlargement of the discussion to the entire world has emerged in recent decades. The latest data reveal that the extent to which poverty affects the world has been receding dramatically, from 42 percent of the world population in 1981 to 12 percent in 2013.[7] Life expectancy has also been increasing significantly all over the world, showing that sanitary conditions and health have improved, although the African countries are still at the bottom of the list (average: 80 years in the developed countries; 58 in Africa).[8] However, increases in economic output have been significantly appropriated by the upper classes. In 2015 the top eight percent of adults owned 85 percent of wealth (more than $100,000 per person), while the bottom 71 percent owned only three percent of total wealth (under $10,000 per person).[9] The richest one percent now own around half of the total wealth in the world. By contrast, around 40 percent of the world population live on less than $2,50 a day.

World inequality now exhibits a Gini coefficient of 0.7 after taxes, way above the average in Asia (0.6) Latin America (0.56) and Africa (0.55), the United States (0.41), and Europe (0.31). Regional differences are also significant. In the United States social inequality is increasing, but the differences between states are minimal (1.5:1). These differences are more significant in Latin America (5.4:1), in Europe (7:1) and in Asia (32:1).[10] If we concentrate our comparison in two regions of the world, Latin America and Asia, class is the crucial explanation for social inequality in the former case, while location is the main factor in the latter case. In general, however, location provides the main explanation for the world's extraordinary levels of social inequality based on income.

Discussion of the Kuznets curve has demanded the collection of historical data, in order to clarify the main economic trends related to environmental and political impact. We now have significant databases, organised by Thomas Piketty and Branco Milanovic, which go back as far as the early nineteenth century; but it has been difficult to collect data before 1800.[11] Jeffrey G. Williamson has also engaged in the collection of data from different historical periods and parts of the world, contributing to the analysis of discrepancies and calling into question deductive claims, as we will discuss later.[12]

From a historical perspective, it is interesting to note that the estimate for Europe in 1900 indicates that the top 10 percent typically owned 90 percent of all wealth, mainly rural and urban property, but also shares in trade, while the top one percent alone owned 50 percent of all wealth. There was clear progress up to 2010, due to the rise of the middle class — the top 10 percent owned 60 percent and the next 40 percent owned 30 percent of all wealth — but the concentration of wealth in the United States has been overwhelming.[13]

In the meantime, the structure of capital, as Piketty pointed out, shifted from rural property to housing, industry and services, while high wages became a major source of income.[14] The appropriation of gains by the technostructure, define as such by John Kenneth Galbraith as early as the 1950s, has increased dramatically in recent decades, contributing to an acceleration in the development of inequality.[15] Average CEO pay, compared to that of average workers, reached a ratio more than 240:1 in the United States in 2010, while in Japan that ratio was six times smaller.[16] Work ethic, organisational culture and levels of solidarity in corporations explain the gap related to appropriation of wealth by the top earners within developed countries.

There are three problems with these approaches: first, they concern only inequality of income and assets (Piketty has played a major role shifting attention to assets). I believe there are other issues of historical inequality, particularly the divide between free and slave labour, ethnic groups, gender and generation.[17] Second, these studies do not engage much with the colonial world, with the exception of Latin America, and even there within a relatively short period of time. Third, the environmental impact of plagues and diseases is only now starting to be taken on board, while the impact of political violence is still to be fully understood, pushed to the forefront by Walter Scheidel in his recent book *The Great Leveller. Violence and the History of Inequality*.[18]

Colonialism and imperialism

The inclusion of the colonial world in the history of inequality is crucial to the creation of a minimum depth of historical analysis. But we have a theoretical inheritance to overcome. John Atkinson Hobson, in his influential book on imperialism, published in 1902, opposed the concept of early modern colonialism, implying migration from the mother country to create colonies, and modern imperialism, developed after the 1870s, with the beginning of investment in foreign dependent countries. He focused on imperialism, defined as financial development based on the exploitation of colonial people by the European powers, and on increasing concentration of capital and trade fluctuations framed by military constraints. He also pointed out Western parasitism, which drew vast tribute from Africa and Asia in what would more recently be called extractive policies. Finally, he denounced the appropriation of the imperial state by private financial capitalists, eager to have their protection costs covered.[19] This dissociation between state and financiers was rightly criticised by Christopher Bayly, who considered that nationalism and imperialism developed hand in hand.[20]

John Hobson had a profound influence on Lenin, Hannah Arendt and, more recently, Jürgen Osterhammel, who defined modern imperialism as a worldwide connection of economic areas and protection of financial interests.[21] These ideas are pertinent, but I refuse to discount the importance of early imperialism, subsumed in colonialism, since some of its modern features were developed earlier than the period discussed by Osterhammel. I argue that the difference between colonialism and imperialism is not as radical as supposed. I accept that there is a difference of scale concerning the concentration of capital, a new importance of financial capital, and a much higher level of connection between different regions of the world; but I think that we need to acknowledge continuities and overlaps between colonialism and imperialism concerning plunder, extraction, investment and the subjugation of local populations.

Branko Milanovic highlights the increased opportunities for extraction related to growing income in a society. If the vast majority of the population lives at or below subsistence level, tiny elites cannot extract much: if the average income of a society is twice the subsistence level, then the maximum Gini Coeficient is 0.5; if it is three times, it increases to 0.66; and so on. He calls this curve the Inequality Possibility Frontier, or Frontier of Inequality. If a society is close to the maximum feasible inequality, it means that the elite is extremely exploitative. Its Inequality Extraction Ratio is the relationship between the actual Gini Coeficient and the Inequality Possibility Frontier. In a sample from different periods and places in history, from Roman times to the present, he identifies six cases of societies where the extraction ratio was around 100 percent: Moghul India in 1750, New Spain (Mexico) in 1790, Maghreb in 1880, Kenya in 1914 and 1927 and India in 1947. He claims that the common feature of these six cases is that they were all colonies.[22] Moghul India is a complicated case of colonialism, since it was conquered by Mongol descendents based on what is nowadays Afghanistan; but he has a point.

The hypothesis that colonial societies could reach higher levels of extraction of wealth is attractive: foreign elites, in theory, did not have a direct tie with local subject populations, while the conditions of conquest, when this occurred, facilitated a new level of political inequality. These elites could be more extractive, having massively expropriated land and/or having control of the labour force.

It is still a big issue in historical debate whether or not colonialism and imperialism represented a major boost for economic growth in Europe. Marx's vision of the use of colonies for primitive accumulation of capital is still the backdrop to these discussions. Patrick O'Brien challenged this view, trying to prove that the impact of colonialism and imperialism on British economic growth was minimal. Basically, the data he gathered indicated that colonies had a very modest impact as sources of raw material, opportunities for investment capital, and demand for home manufactured goods.[23] These findings had an impact, but more recent studies have recognised that colonies did make a significant difference to metropolitan countries.

The case of Portugal in the period from 1500 to 1800 has been the subject of research by Leonor Freire Costa, Nuno Palma and Jaimes Reis, who have shown that "eliminating the economic links to the empire would have reduced Portugal's per capita income by at least a fifth"[24]. They compared their results with more recent data on other European empires, arriving at the conclusion that the exceptional amount of benefit accruing to England and the Netherlands from their empires was followed in size by that accruing to Portugal, which was much larger than the benefit received by France and Spain, although Portugal's capacity for extraction was not translated into economic convergence with its rivals.

The case of Latin America was analysed by Stanley Engerman and Kenneth Sokoloff some time ago.[25] These two economic historians concluded that the region was more unequal than other parts of the world, pointing to colonial extraction as the major historical factor in growth underachievement during the two centuries following independence. Colonial political power would have supported extraordinary levels of income inequality, based on the existence of a class of rich landlords and rent-seekers that would have hindered economic growth with long-term consequences.

This thesis was contested by JeffreyWilliamson through comparison of data collected in pre-industrial Western Europe and Latin America. He showed that the average Latin American Gini Coeficient of 0.48 was behind the average Gini Coeficient of Western Europe (0.53). His conclusion: Western Europe was more unequal precisely because the economic output was much higher.[26]

This should not come as a surprise. A study by Lee Soltow and Jan van Zanden of *Income and Wealth Inequality in the Netherlands, 16th–20th Century* shows the impact of urban society on inequality due to specialisation and increased surplus. This study revealed an extraordinary increase of inequality between 1580 and 1650, an increase that continued until 1740, followed by the relative stabilisation of an income structure dominated by capital, while real wages declined in the early modern period and pauperisation increased in the second half of the eighteenth century, especially after 1780. The study also showed the decline of the Netherlands nobility, in favour of burghers and peasant freeholders, when it came to share of wealth (40 percent in 1675, less than 20 percent in 1758).[27]

Returning to Latin America, Jeffrey Williamson showed that in some cases, such as those of Brazil and Peru, increased inequality occurred after the 1870s, becoming significantly more pronounced in the following years, up to the 1920s, but with a long-term impact, continuing up to the present, that has been higher than any during the whole colonial period. It is to be said that research by Leandro Prados has nuanced this vision, since he showed that the impact of independence wars, followed in some cases by civil wars, which dramatically lowered inequality, had been dissipated by the 1840s and 1850.[28] However, Jeffrey Williamson proved that extraction rates in pre-industrial Latin America were considerably higher than in Western Europe, confirming the importance of political inequality already pointed out by Daron Acemoglu and James Robinson.[29] Williamson also suggested that the reasons for less-than-expected inequality in colonial Latin America lay in the area's relatively equal pre-Colombian background, accepting that the colonial impact would have meant an increase in the Gini Coeficient of around 12–13 percentage points.[30]

Colonialism certainly did not reduce inequality in Europe, but did contribute to increased social mobility among the 4.8 million Europeans who emigrated overseas in the period up to 1800, more than 3.5 million of them to the New World. The mortality rate was very high in Africa, and significant in Asia, partly due to the long trip and military activity; but those who made their living in the New World were mostly integrated in the local elite, controlled their areas' main assets, and supervised labour. Data collected in Java, Kenya and other parts of the world has shown how the European colonists received much more income than native populations.[31] Emigration contributed to alleviating Malthusian pressure in Europe and created markets that fuelled European industrial revolutions, partly explaining the great divergence between Europe and China in the nineteenth century, well analysed by Kenneth Pomeranz.[32] European emigrants contributed to increasing inequality in other parts of the world.

The impact of colonialism

The main effect of colonialism was to dispossess natives of their land. It happened in the early modern period, in the New World, mostly in areas of nomadic or semi-nomadic populations, which did not have extensive agriculture. The distribution to colonists of land in Brazil or in North America, by the Portuguese and English kings, supposed a void that did not correspond to reality, since the land was used by natives in different ways. The English acknowledged this situation through regular treaties with local tribes and even the formal acquisition of territory, although illegal collective and private occupation in successive violations of treaties became the norm. The contrast between these practices and theory based on the assumption of void, as expressed by John Locke, is striking.[33]

The Spaniards found settled populations in what is now Mexico and Peru, which brought about a shift from expropriation of land to control of labour. The *conquistadores* (conquistadors) received *encomiendas* (distribution of native labour) and then *repartimientos* (control of communities) of natives, meaning that they were responsible for them, with, in theory, a responsibility for protecting their way of life. In return, they could expect to benefit from periods of forced labour as a form of taxation. Previously existing collective labour, called *mita*, in Inca Peru, was diverted for mining. Native villages were, however, relatively protected by Spanish legislation, since they contributed to sustaining colonial society. However, communal land became depleted, due to a massive decline in the native population as a consequence of epidemics. Privatisation of land followed, but it was in the late eighteenth and nineteenth centuries that vast programmes of privatisation of land were implemented.[34]

The consequences of these policies were twofold: a patronage system was established, in which native communities became subordinated to colonists; while vast portions of land ended up privately controlled by Spaniards or Creole elites. Collaborative native elites were promoted and special schools were created for them; but the outcome was limited, since civil and ecclesiastic jobs, even the priesthood, were largely controlled by the Spaniards and their descendants.[35] However, the Spanish policy of forced conversion gave some opportunity for negotiation to the native population, which became relatively integrated into colonial societies, contrary to what happened in British America, where natives were considered alien until the late nineteenth century.[36]

Slaves brought from Africa constituted the bottom social layer of colonial societies in the New Wold, although in the Portuguese and Spanish cases forced conversion gave them a minimum status as vassals of the king. They could petition the king, and they used this possibility.[37] They managed to have their grievances discussed, and sometimes these were decided in their favour. Conversion brought with it the organisation of black people in confraternities, which provided legal and financial support for their manumission. It can be said that Iberian legislation on manumission was more permissive than that of the English or the French after the turn of the seventeenth, into the eighteenth, century. The number of emancipated men and women, especially in Brazil, became quite important, forming a relative majority of the population by 1872: 4.2 million free coloured people against 3.8 million white people and 1.5 million slaves, the last in clear decline.[38] In urban areas, free coloured people had a major outlet for their economic activities in crafts and trade. Massive urbanisation, mainly in Spanish America, but also in Brazil, contrasted with the predominance of rural life in British America until 1800, contributing to increase inequality.

In Africa, the Portuguese created enclaves along the coast to access the gold trade and the slave trade, and they occupied the islands of Cape Verde and São Tome, where they established plantations. An annual mortality rate of 66 percent for Europeans in West Africa explains the low numbers of Europeans who migrated to the continent. Until the end of the eighteenth century, there were no more than 4,000 Portuguese in different parts of Africa.[39] These migrants were mainly in Angola and Mozambique, drawn by two projects of colonization from the 1560s onwards which took more than three centuries to implement. Dispossession of native land occurred in part of the valley of the Kwanza river and in Luanda: to be precise, at the periphery of the kingdom of Congo, where the valuable extraction of cowries took place. In Mozambique, the Portuguese also controlled ports and the Zambezi valley, in which a hybrid network of Portuguese and African institutions consolidated a system of matrilineal control of land for three generations. Although the impact of the Portuguese was felt in the hinterland from the sixteenth century on, the occupation of these territories only occurred after the Berlin Conference of 1884–5, involving long wars from the 1890s to the 1920s. Dispossession became a reality in the late nineteenth and twentieth centuries, paralleling similar processes developed by French and British colonial powers, although, in their case, private acquisition of land followed a late presence. The Dutch were the only European power which competed with the Portuguese for settlement in the early modern period, securing South Africa because of its importance to the Dutch East India Company route to Asia. Direct territorial impact in this area only became significant in the eighteenth and nineteenth centuries.[40]

In Asia, the Portuguese possessed urban land inside the forts and became overlords of communal land in the areas surrounding the main cities. They occupied a stretch of land from Bombay to Daman, in which they absorbed taxes from communities. In Sri Lanka, where they controlled most of the island from the 1590s to the 1620s, they organised the first systematic register of land, in order to define legal property and rent titles, a practice in which they preceded both the Dutch and the British.[41] The occupation of the Philippines by the Spanish took a long time, involving wars and alliance with natives, a decline in local populations due to epidemics (not as harsh as in the Americas) and the subordination of local elites.[42]

The Dutch replaced the Portuguese in Sri Lanka, and in several Asian forts, such as Cochin, Malacca and Ambon, from 1605 to 1663. By doing this they came to control a good part of trade in the Bay of Bengal in that period, and expanded within Java during the nineteenth century. Their intervention in the Moluccas was more significant than that of the Portuguese, since they managed to organise plantations. However, their impact was essentially on trade, diverting to Europe part of the profits from Asian interregional maritime commerce. In what became Indonesia, Dutch control of land rents only became a reality in modern times.[43] Finally, the British had a major intervention in India, due to effective territorial conquest from the 1750s onwards, and thus shifted part of their interests from trade to land rent.[44] The long-term impact of the Europeans on Asia was to open up markets, divert trade profits and extract land rents, and was only disrupted by independence. The impact on inequality only became visible during the nineteenth and the first half of the twentieth centuries. The growing population of Bombay and Calcutta became a sign of the divide between urban and rural populations with consequences beyond independence.

Dispossession of political resources reached its peak in the New World during the early modern period, due to the military strength of the colonial powers. Political inequality was established by colonization, with the native population being placed in a subordinate position. In Spanish America, the Nahua and the Quechuas suffered from having resisted the Spanish conquest, and were forced to pay taxes, thereby carrying the burden of building a colonial society. In nomadic and semi-nomadic environments, the British pushed the frontiers of their territory to the Appalachian Mountains, before the extraordinary expansion of the United States to the West during the nineteenth century. In Brazil, the expansion of the Portuguese colony in the seventeenth, and mainly in the eighteenth, centuries, with the discovery of gold, had similar consequences. Native Americans were forced to migrate, and finally lost their way of living, being confined to reserves across the continent, though even these reserves were systematically shrunk by colonists' greed.[45]

In the other continents, nothing similar occurred until the end of the nineteenth century. The conquest of Africa was partly due to the diffusion of quinine, which protected Europeans from malaria. But while in the Americas colonial societies were built almost from scratch through absolute control of political resources and the imposition of new institutions, in Africa the European institutional framework was only imposed during 80 or 90 years, and without the same systematic character, which in many cases involved indirect rule. In Asia, political dispossession was implemented in Dutch Indonesia and British India from the eighteenth century onwards, but the size of the territories in these places required the application of forms of indirect rule and a search for legal traditions in order to accommodate and subordinate native agency.[46]

Dispossession of native religion and culture by colonial powers represented a major form of inequality that has not been sufficiently taken on board. This process was especially brutal in Spanish America, where the conquistadores dealt with settled populations. The Portuguese in Brazil, and in their enclaves in Africa, imposed the same Christian monopoly of faith; but they had to compromise in Asia, and only in Goa did they manage to exclude other religions from the mid-sixteenth to the mid-eighteenth century. The Dutch and the English never tried to impose a monopoly for the Anglican and the Calvinist confessions: there was a conscious strategy of allowing religious diversity in order to avoid any resistance and disruption of trade.[47] In the Iberian case, dispossession of religion and culture triggered hybrid forms of worship among the natives, but Christianity became rooted in the long-term. This process was labelled by Robert Ricard as "spiritual conquest", and by Serge Gruzinski as "Colonisation of the imaginary"; but what they really meant was that natives were stripped of their gods, their rituals and their ways of living.[48] Natives became exposed to the colonisers, who controlled religion as a means of communication between humans, a channel for relationships between men and god, a crucial framework of symbolic meanings. Under these circumstances, dispossession of religion played a major role in colonisation, promoting allegiance under oppression, while in the British and Dutch empires relative religious freedom facilitated commercial relations.

Long-term consequences

The reification of the colonised by the coloniser was a central theme in the analysis by Aimé Césaire of the process of European expansion and empire building.[49] His radical critique of the consequences of colonialism was shared by Franz Fanon, who pointed out that the colonist shaped the colonised within a compartmentalised world in which the schools and hospitals for the colonists were not shared with the natives, creating a double dynamic of destruction of native cultures while the European culture was imposed as distinctive. The separation between colonisers and colonised was interpreted by Fanon in a psychoanalytic way, since he highlighted the interiorization of the mentality of the oppressor by the oppressed, with the latter the subject of oppression but at the same time absorbing the values of the oppressor.[50] It is this deeply traumatic historical experience that is at the core of postcolonial literature and multidisciplinary research. It highlights the problems of double identity already raised by Frederick Douglass and William Du Bois: problems which are at the centre of the work of many authors on postcolonial emancipation, such as the Brazilian Paulo Freire, the Kenyan Ngûgî Wa Thiong and the Maori Linda Tuhiwai Smith.[51]

The consequences of colonialism and imperialism in the impoverishment of continents is an important issue. The case of Africa is the most visible, since the slave trade, which was part of millennial African practices, was dramatically increased by European demand and reached a staggering number of close to 13 million transported to the Americas, to which we have to add around 8 million transported to North Africa and the Middle East.[52] The impact of the slave trade meant demographic stagnation, limited demand, reduced initiative, the draining of talent. The erosion of political power based on the trading of slaves from the hinterland had long-term consequences. The impact of imperialism in the modern period meant extensive control of land and mining by the Western powers; the export of profits as tribute paid; and political interference that led to coups d'état, the imposition of leaders, and the disruption of steady efforts for national unity. Mechanisms of price and production control created by the colonial powers were replicated and sometimes intensified after independence, as shown by Daron Acemoglu and James Robinson, namely in the case of Sierra Leone.[53] By the same token, mechanisms of territorial control were also replicated after independence in certain countries, for instance in Mozambique.[54] Political mismanagement after independence, including the creation of patrimonial states, certainly did not contribute to alleviating these problems.

Structural poverty is the main issue highlighted by various authors on this topic, particularly John Iliffe, who pointed out the reinforcement of these problems as a consequence of communitarian disruption, which left more exposed, incapacitated and aged people, not to mention unsupported women, as landless and isolated peasants, and stigmatised ethnic groups of outcasts, many of them with a background as slaves. By far the greatest incidence of poverty is in rural areas; urban areas, although surrounded by extensive slums in many cases, manage to produce minimal survival conditions.[55] However, the growing poverty of the 1970s and 1980s has been reduced in the last two decades, with infant mortality declining and life expectancy improving. In Asia, colonialism did not have the same long-term impact on poverty, due to its less rooted presence: a presence in which societies were not really reshaped, although the impact of the Western world concerning values and life style became more visible after independence.[56] In general, the globalization of poverty can be related to the long-term consequences of colonialism and imperialism, since it started then, with the creation of large cities, as a result of the breakdown of communitarian structures.

To sum up, colonialism and imperialism certainly had (and continue to have) a major impact on political and economic inequality, mainly in the Americas. They contributed to stagnation of population in Africa, where in several areas dispossession of land became a long-term issue. In Asia, extractive policies were pursued for two centuries in crucial regions and left their marks in unequal trade exchanges. Globalization of poverty can be defined as a long-term effect of colonialism; and it is now being reversed. The international division of labour, which embodies racial discrimination, still hinders global development. Religious and cultural dispossession, which assumed extreme features in the Americas, offer another area of visible, long-term consequences. The tension between financial extraction and the levelling power of production and the market is perhaps the main issue for social movements in the future. The gap between developed countries and countries in development will continue to grow in the near future; and while the former face long-term stagnation partly due to unsolved inequality, the latter face both improved standards of living and increased inequality.

Notes

1 *Oxford English Dictionary*, 7th edn.

2 Alain Rey, ed., *Le Dictionnaire Historique de la Langue Française*, vol. 1 (Paris: Le Robert, 1992), pp. 1195–6.

3 Alexus McLeod, *Understanding Asian Philosophy: Ethics in the Analects, Zhuangzi, Dhammapada and Bhagavad Gita* (London: Bloomsbury, 2014); *The Book of Chuang Tzu*, trans. Martin Palmer, Elizabeth Breuilly, Chang Way Ming and Jay Ramsay (London: Penguin, 1996); Paul Dundas, *The Jains* (London: Routledge, 2002); Peter Brown, *Through the Eye of a Needle. Wealth, the Fall of Rome, and the Making of Christianity on the West, 350–550 AD* (Princeton: Princeton University Press, 2012).

4 Joseph E. Stiglitz, *The Price of Inequality* (London: Allen Lane, 2012).

5 Simon Kuznets, "Economic Growth and Income Inequality", *American Economic Review* 45 (March 1955): 1–28; Thomas Piketty, *Capital in the Twenty-First Century* (Cambridge, Mass.: Belknap, 2013), pp. 11–27.

6 Anthony Atkinson, *Inequality. What Can Be Done?* (Cambridge, Mass.: Harvard University Press, 2015); Branko Milanovic, *Global Inequality. A New Approach for*

the Age of Globalization (Cambridge, Mass.: Belknap, 2016); François Bourguignon, *The Globalization of Inequality*, trans. Thomas Scott-Railton (Princeton: Princeton University Press, 2015).

7 http://data.worldbank.org/topic/poverty, accessed 22 June 2017.

8 *Global Health Observatory*, accessed 22 June 2017. http://gamapserver.who.int/gho/interactive_charts/mbd/life_expectancy/atlas.htm.

9 *Global Wealth Report 2015*, accessed 9 April 2017, http://inequality.org/global-inequality.

10 Branko Milanovic, *The Haves and the Have-Nots. A Brief and Idiosyncratic History of Global Inequality* (New York: Basic Books, 2011), pp. 75, 176–186.

11 See "World Wealth and Income Database" at wid.world; and "All the Ginis Dataset" at http://data.worldbank.org/data-catalog/all-the-ginis.

12 See *The Cambridge History of Capitalism*, Volume 2, *The Spread of Capitalism*, ed. Jeffrey G. Williamson (Cambridge: Cambridge University Press 2014), among numerous books, articles and working papers on inequality and globalization.

13 Piketty, *Capital in the Twenty-First Century*, pp. 237–303.

14 Piketty, *Capital in the Twenty-First Century*, pp. 113–163.

15 John Kenneth Galbraith, *The Affluent Society* (Boston: Houghton Mifflin, 1958); *idem*, *The New Industrial State* (Boston: Houghton Mifflin, 1967).

16 Stiglitz, *The Price of Inequality*, p. 3.

17 Francisco Bethencourt, "Humankind: From Division to Re-composition", in *Humanity — a History of European Concepts in Practice from the Sixteenth Century to the Present* eds. Fabian Klose and Mirjam Thulin (Goettingen: Vandenhoeck and Ruprecht, 2016), pp. 29–50.

18 Walter Scheidel, *The Great Leveller. Violence and the History of Inequality from the Stone Age to the Twenty-First Century* (Princeton: Princeton University Press, 2017).

19 John Atkinson Hobson, *Imperialism: A Study* (1902), revised edn. (London: G. Allen and Unwin, 1938)

20 Christopher Bayly, *The Birth of the Modern World, 1780–1914* (Oxford: Blackwell, 2004), pp. 227–228.

21 Vladimir Il'ich Lenin, *Imperialism: The Highest Stage of Capitalism* (1917) (London: Penguin, 2010); Hannah Arendt, *The Origins of Totalitarianism* (1948–51) (New York: Schocken Books, 2004); Jürgen Osterhammel, *Colonialism: A Theoretical Overview*, trans. Shelley L. Frish (Princeton: M. Wiener, 1997).

22 Milanovic, *The Haves and the Have-Nots*, pp. 198–202.

23 Patrick O'Brien, "The Costs and Benefits of British Imperialism, 1846–1914", *Past and Present*, 120, 1 (1988): 163–200.

24 Leonor Freire Costa, Nuno Palma and Jaimes Reis, "The Great Escape? The Contribution of the Empire to Portugal's Economic Growth", *European Review of Economic History*, 19 (2014), 1–22 (quote page 1).

25 Stanley Engerman and Kenneth Sokoloff, "Factor Endowments, Institutions, and Differential Paths of Growth Among New World Economies" in *How Latin America Fell Behind*, ed. S. Haber (Palo Alto: Stanford University Press, 1997), pp. 260–304.

26 Jeffrey G. Williamson, *Latin American Inequality over Five Centuries*, working paper 15305 (Cambridge, Mass.: National Bureau of Economic Research, 2009). See also Leandro Prados de la Escosura, "When Did Latin America Fall Behind?", in *The Decline of Latin American Economies: Growth, Institutions and Crises*, ed. Sebastian Edwards, Gerardo Esquivel and Graciela Marquez (Chicago: University of Chicago Press, 2007), pp. 15–58.

27 Lee Soltow and Jan Luiten van Zanden, *Income and Wealth Inequality in the Netherlands, 16th–20th Century* (Amsterdam: Het Spinhuis, 1998).

28 Leandro Prados de la Escosura, "Lost Decades? Economic Performance in Post-Independence Latin America", *Journal of Latin American Studies*, 41, 2 (2009).
29 Daron Acemoglu and James A. Robinson, *Why Nations Fail. The Origins of Power, Prosperity and Poverty* (London: Profile, 2012).
30 Jeffrey G. Williamson, "Five Centuries of Latin American Income Inequality," *Revista de Historia Económica/Journal of Iberian and Latin American Economic History* 28, 02 (2010), p.16.
31 Milanovic, *The Haves and the Have-Nots*, pp. 201–202.
32 Kenneth Pomeranz, *The Great Divergence: China, Europe and the Making of the Modern World Economy* (Princeton: Princeton University Press, 2000).
33 Anthony Pagden, "The Struggle for Legitimacy and the Image of Empire in the Atlantic to c. 1700", in *The Oxford History of the British Empiure*, vol. 1, *The Origins of Empire*, ed. Nicholas Canny (Oxford: Oxford University Press, 1998), pp. 34–54.
34 John H. Elliott, *Empires of the Atlantic World. Britain and Spain in America, 1492–1830* (New Haven: Yale University Press, 2006), pp. 29–56; Gabriel B. Paquette, *Enlightenment, Governance and Reform in Spain and its Empire, 1759–1808* (Basingstoke: Palgrave Macmillan, 2008).
35 Charles R. Boxer, *The Church Militant and Iberian Expansion, 1440–1770* (Baltimore: The Johns Hopkins University Press, 1978).
36 Paul Spickard, *Almost All Aliens. Race and Colonialism in American History and Identity* (New York: Routledge, 2007).
37 A. J. R. Russell-Wood, "'Acts of Grace': Portuguese Monarchs and their Subjects of African Descent in Eighteenth-Century Brazil", *Journal of Latin American Studies*, 32 (2000): 307–332.
38 Herbert Klein and Vidal Luna, *Slavery in Brazil* (Cambridge: Cambridge University Press, 2010), p. 186.
39 Francisco Bethencourt, "Political Configurations and Local Powers", in *The Portuguese Oceanic Expansion, 1400–1800*, ed. Francisco Bethencourt and Diogo Ramada Curto (Cambridge: Cambridge University Press, 2007), pp. 197–254.
40 *The Cambridge History of South Africa*, vol. 1, *From Early Times to 1885* eds. Carolyn Hamilton, Bernard Mbenga and Robert Ross (Cambridge: Cambridge University Press, 2010).
41 José Vicente Serrão, Bárbara Direito, Eugénia Rodrigues and Susana Münch Miranda, eds, *Property Rights, Land and Territory in the European Overseas Empire* (Lisbon: CEHC-IUC, 2014). This is the best survey available on dispossession of native land in the Portuguese Empire.
42 Linda A. Newson, *Conquest and Pestilence in the Early Spanish Philippines* (Honolulu: University of Hawai'i Press, 2009).
43 Femme S. Gaastra, *The Dutch East India Company: Expansion and Decline* (Zutphen: Walburg Pers, 2003).
44 *The Oxford History of the British Empire*, vols. 2 and 3, ed. Peter J. Marshall and Andrew Porter (Oxford: Oxford University Press, 1998–1999).
45 See the chapters on colonial societies in Francisco Bethencourt, *Racisms: From the Crusades to the Twentieth Century* (Princeton: Princeton University Press, 2013).
46 Lauren Benton, *Law and Colonial Cultures: Legal Regimes in World History, 1400–1900* (Cambridge: Cambridge University Press, 2002); *idem*, *A Search for Sovereignty: Law and Geography in European Empires, 1400–1900* (Cambridge: Cambridge University Press, 2009); Lauren Benton and Richard Ross, eds, *Legal Pluralism and Empires, 1500–1850* (Oxford: Oxford University Press, 2015).

47 Andrew Porter, *Religion Versus Empire? British Protestant Missionaries and Overseas Expansion, 1700–1914* (Manchester: Manchester University Press, 2004).

48 Robert Ricard, *The Spiritual Conquest of Mexico. An Essay on the Apostolate and the Evangelising Methods of the Mendicant Orders in New Spain, 1523–1572*, trans. Leslie Bird Simpson (Berkeley: The University of California Press, 1966); Serge Gruzinski, *La colonisation de l'imaginaire: sociétés indigènes et occidentalisation dans le Mexique espagnole, XVIe–XVIIIe siècles* (Paris: Gallimard, 1988).

49 Aimé Césaire, *Discours sur le colonialisme suivi de Discours sur la négritude* (1955) (Paris: Présence Africaine, 2004).

50 Franz Fanon, *Peaux noirs, masques blancs* (Paris: Seuilk, 1952), *idem*, *Les damnés de la terre* (1961) (Paris: La Découverte, 2002).

51 Du Bois, William, *The Souls of Black Folk* (1903), ed. Dolan Hubbard (Columbia: University of Missouri Press, 2003; *The Frederick Douglass Papers*, ed. John W. Blassingame et al., 9 vols (New Haven: Yale University Press, 1979-); Paulo Freire, *Pedagogia do oprimido* (Rio de Janeiro: Paz e Terra, 1981); Linda Tuhiwai Smith, *Decolonizing Methodologies: Research and Indigenous People* (London: Zed Books, 1999); Ngũgĩ Wa Thiong'o, *Decolonising the Mind: the Politics of Language in African Literature* (London: Currey, 1986).

52 *The Cambridge World History of Slavery*, vols. 3 and 4, ed. David Eltis et al. (Cambridge: Cambridge University Press, 2011–2017).

53 Daron Acemoglu and James A. Robinson, *Why Nations Fail. The Origins of Power, Prosperity and Poverty*, mainly pp. 335–344, 373–377.

54 Michel Cahen, *Les bandits. Un historien au Mozambique, 1994* (Paris: Centre Culturel Calouste Gulbenkian, 2002).

55 John Iliffe, *The African Poor: A History* (Cambridge: Cambridge University Press, 1987).

56 http://povertydata.worldbank.org/poverty/region, accessed 28 June 2017.

Part I

Modern Social Inequality

CHAPTER

2

Race and Inequality in Brazil: A Deep Shadow

LILIA MORITZ SCHWARCZ

One could say that if all histories are polyphonic, there is not a single linguistically pure, unmixed culture on the face of the earth. But Brazil's history, which began before *Brazil* was even called *Brasil* — back when it was still an Amerindian homeland, then Portuguese America, or a Tropical Europe — was always a medley of peoples, cultures and economies. What oficial historiography likes to call and "discover" as America was, before the Europeans' arrival, already a densely populated territory. Historical estimates put the population of the lower South-American land mass at the time at between one and eight and a half million. Today, the Amazon is home to 180 indigenous tribes — 250 throughout Brazil as a whole — and 180 languages. One can only imagine what the figures were back in the sixteenth century, at the time of the "misencounter" with the Europeans.

Though they might squabble about the numbers, if there is one thing all historians agree on, it is the magnitude of the catastrophe. For some, America lost a quarter of its indigenous population between 1492 and 1650. For others, it was as high as 95 or 96 percent. The causes were many: unknown diseases, including the biological weapon of mass destruction known as the common cold, and, unquestionably, the enslavement of the natives.[1]

When Brazil did become Brazil, it was a mix of colours. The name could come from the glowering red of the *brasa*, or embers, from the hell of slave trade, but in fact came from the pigment that leeched from brazilwood and was used to produce red dye and furniture with a rare reddish hue.[2] The mixture of peoples was also a clash. To the European mind, the native tribes were short on F, L and K: they were faithless, lawless and kingless.[3] It was to redress these "lacks", as Pierre Clastres[4] shows, that the Europeans endeavoured to absorb these polygamist, "cannibal" natives wandering around with their "unmentionables" hanging out. Yet these peoples were not cannibals who hunted men for food. Their cannibalism was "anthropophagic", it was an instrument of exchange, an element in the formation of vast communication networks, a weapon of war and a gift of alliance. The important point is that these peoples had long been intermixing, and had their own histories and philosophies.[5] As Oswald de Andrade wrote in his *Manifesto*: "Before the Portuguese discovered Brazil, Brazil had discovered happiness".[6] And though the butchery was wholesale, the Amerindians did not stand passively by while the Western invaders decimated their kind. They expanded their myths and devised whole cosmologies; they conducted their rituals, and put up every imaginable form of resistance to the processes they were being subjected to.

If the language of slavery already existed in these fledgling Brazils, it gained in force and scale with the introduction of the African slave trade in the late sixteenth century, and the "sugar society" that grew up around the recently-discovered delight obtained from the cane. It was a bittersweet civilisation — slave bitter; sugar sweet.[7]

The last Western nation to abolish slavery, Brazil was the destination for 40 percent of all slave stocks shipped out of African ports, its needs fuelling the largest transportations of humans since those of the Roman empire. Brazil also represented the longest-running, most persistent and most deeply-engrained slave society of all, with captive labour operating in every single region of the country. Slave ownership was so widespread that it wasn't even the preserve of the wealthy. Clergy, military men, civil servants, craftsmen, merchants, small miners and even freed slaves owned slaves. For these reasons, and others, slavery was more than just an economic system: it was a language that shaped behaviours, defined social inequalities, turned race and colour into markers of fundamental difference, instilled codes of conduct for masters and their slaves, and created a society that was conditioned by paternalism and a stringent hierarchy.

The real substratum of this society, in the seventeenth century, slaves accounted for as much as 75 percent of the overall population in such places as the Recôncavo in Bahia, where "exhaustion" sometimes appeared on certificates as cause of death. Though the economic mainstay changed from sugar cane in the sixteenth and seventeenth centuries to gold in the eighteenth century, and cattle and coffee in the nineteenth, a growing slave workforce underpinned it all.

The fact is, however, that from the early sixteenth century to Abolition in 1850, the slave population was subject to short lifespans and a low birth rate, which meant that a steady stream of replacements had to be imported from Africa. Enslaved by force, the Africans, like the Amerindians, did not take this lying down. They resisted, broke free, sometimes escaping en masse, formed runaway colonies called *quilombos* (which they staunchly defended), committed suicide, mutinied, and never relinquished their cult of the Orishas. They created cultures and translated traditions. In fact, even in the "tomb ships" that transported them, like hens in a coop, from the African coast to the ports of Salvador, Recife and São Vicente, they formed friendships and exchanged rituals.

The forced removal to Brazil affected countless African nations.[8] If linguistic similarities helped networks of solidarity and friendship to form, diversities produced immense cultural riches. Brazil was fast becoming an Africa away from Africa, or, in the words of Ambrósio Fernandes Brandão, a merchant in Goa and Lisbon before settling as a mill owner in Paraíba, a "New Guinea".[9]

Space constraints prevent me from describing the system as a whole, but let me underscore the escalating violence and, paradoxically, just how slowly the system came apart after the moratorium on the slave trade in 1850. A direct reaction to the disastrous Paraguay War (which drained the national coffers and left a death toll tantamount to a Paraguayan genocide), and a response to mounting pressure on the Empire, the Free Womb Law of 1871 freed slave-born children, but not their mothers. Though the law was an important step in the right direction, Brazil opted to phase slavery out rather than abolish it altogether, and it proceeded timidly. Even so, among a population whose nerves were frayed, the law was received at the time as little more than a gesture to placate the opposition. After all, its only beneficiaries would be children born to slave mothers after the date of the law's promulgation. According to the law, children born to mothers in slavery would be raised by them to the age of eight, whereupon the owner could use the child's services up to the age of 21 or settle for state compensation to the tune of 600,000 reis. The former was far more advantageous to the owner, who could always fudge the slave's birth year for his own benefit. The law gave rise to a whole new vocabulary, much of it from Bantu, used to describe these freeborn children. Terms like moleque, moleca, and freewomber reflected a new hierarchy enshrined in the law, distinguishing those blacks born after its promulgation from those born into slavery.

The law triggered all manner of reactions. The northern provinces signed up to its ordinances in greater number than their southern counterparts, indicating their different concerns. The 1872 census explains the divergence in their respective positions: the north held only 37 percent of the slave population, whilst 59 percent were spread across the four southeastern coffee-growing provinces (including the Court), and a mere 7.3 percent were in the south and midwest.[10] These internal differences meant the coalition in the northeast was able to cause the coffee barons of the south a great deal of trouble, and ultimately destabilise the legitimacy of the regime. As Joaquim Nabuco — by this stage something of a champion of the Abolitionist movement — would say, this discrepancy was the expression of a "dialectic of ambiguity": the State was the embodiment of slavery, but it was also the only power that could topple it".

There was another aspect to the law that caused resentment against the monarchy amongt landowners. In addition to freeing the kin of the last slaves, the measure formally recognised the existence of slave families. Lists that were drawn up for the Emancipation Fund distinguished between individual slaves and indivisible family units.[11]

What is more, the 1871 reforms further stoked the dreaded discussion of political rights. If the "freewombers" were free, then they were also citizens. The imperial constitution only limited the rights of slaves, and these youngsters, though tied to their mothers' owners until the age of 21 by their debt of labour, were, technically speaking, free. The lines were beginning to blur.

In 1884, slavery was officially abolished in the states of Ceará and Amazonas. On September 28 of the following year, the Saraiva Cotegipe Law was passed, which granted freedom to all slaves over the age of 60, though they would still have to work off a three-year period of grace accorded to their owners. The conservative tone of the measure was so obvious that the backlash was immediate. After all, between the passing of the Free Womb Law and the Sexagenarian Law, the slave demographic had changed radically. According to the 1886 Report, 412,468 slaves had been lost to manumission and mortality. As a result, estimated slave stocks for 1886 were 1,133,228. By 1887, this had dropped to 723,419. As slave numbers decreased, distribution became increasingly lopsided: not only were slave stocks concentrated in the south, but manumissions were far more evident in the north.

The conservative tone of the Sexagenarian law remained controversial even after the Golden Law of 1888. Gradualism, tutelage, dependency and control policies ranked high among the State's political concerns, especially when it came to legislating for the freed. There was widespread feeling that the State and society were owed compensation for the loss of their slaves. The prevailing mindset was geared toward prolonging the master's privilege, but the law, which installed the State as mediator, clashed head-on with the interests of the elite.[12] It was also creating a policy of dependence which would keep the slave bound, emotionally at least, to the master. Words like "loyalty" and "protection" became staples of labour-related vocabulary, invoking personal, and therefore more lasting, ties.

With the dismantling of slavery came a slew of racial theories and models that rejected "background" or history as markers of division in favour of biological distinctions. Models based on racial determinism and social evolutionism gained momentum with the demise of the system, and laid down hierarchies that were even more stringent for being grounded in lineage, in the idea that mankind was divided into races and that the differences between them were not cultural, historical or social, but biological. As products of nature, these races were essential and rigid, which meant that miscegenation was a "perversion" that seeded decay. According to this line of thought, Brazil had become a "laboratory", an example of a nation weakened through racial mixing. Instead of freedom and the universal language of rights, the Republic, formed in 1889, immediately set about creating exclusions based on the science of the day and on segregationist inspired eugenics.[13]

Time for establishing a robust society was running out fast, and the concept of "race" inserted itself into the nation's consciousness in many different ways. As Francisco Bethencourt shows, there is nothing universal in this concept, so it is all the more interesting to look at how it was used and repurposed contextually.[14] It was against this backdrop that early twentieth century Brazil became the country of whitening. For an idea of the mindset at work, we need only look at the paper the Brazilian academic João Batista Lacerda, then director of the National Museum, presented at the First Universal Races Congress in London in 1911. Lacerda's paper, entitled "Sur les Mestis", argued that "natural selection" would have all but eradicated the Negro population in Brazil within three generations. Not content with that, he illustrated his paper with a painting by Brocos, produced years earlier, entitled "The Redemption of Ham", in an attempt to rally both science and religion to his claim that white was the colour of Brazil's "future".[15]

Another change came about in the 1930s, when Brazil transformed yet again, this time, apparently, into a racially harmonious democracy. The poison was now the cure, and the nation made peace with its past while rifling through it in search of redoubled relief. Converted into a shining example for a world at war, but mired in professed racial hatreds, Brazil spent the next two decades busily elevating and de-Africanising its symbols. Getúlio Vargas created the national "Race Day" holiday; the Black Mary statue known as Our Lady of Aparacida was fished out of the Parnaíba River; *feijoada* (a black bean stew served with white rice) became the national dish of contrasting components; *capoeira* (a martial arts dance created by African slaves) and *candomblé* (an Afro-Brazilian religion that worships the Orishas of the Yoruba) were decriminalised; the samba was elected the national dance; and Disney's colourful parrot, José Carioca, became the arch symbol of the loveable Brazilian rogue, an inveterate chancer free-and-easy with the law. Depoliticisation was thus a clear attempt at creating a national and emotional project rooted in the notion of "the beneficial legacy of slavery", as if any such aporia were possible.

The 1970s saw a new and tense debate in Brazil concerning civil rights and the defence of difference. This decade gave rise to a positive sea change in our representation of the nation, predicated upon an awareness that if the past, as we have shown, was not "universal", then there was no way of expecting any equality in the present. While race is void as a biological concept on which to base a hierarchy of humanity , there are certainly "social races", ways of reinventing social markers of difference within and among societies. What we are talking about, therefore, are echoes of the past in the present, where they continue to resound. In other words, there is a lot more of the past in the present than "our vain philosophy would have us believe".

Inequality in numbers

We can't blame it all on the past. Brazil is still a formidable exemple of social inequality and a practitioner of silent racism, a phenomenon its citizens have always ascribed to others , but no less perverse for that. While there are no forms of discrimination written into law, the poor, especially the black poor, are far more likely to be condemned in the courts, tend to die younger, have more limited access to public higher education, and are far less likely to hold executive positions.

So let us look at the data and identify the racial discrimination in the numbers.[16] In 2009, Brazil had a population of 191 million, up 26 percent on the census figures for 1995. With regard to the concerns of the current text, it is important to point out that the data revealed life expectancy discrepancies between whites and blacks. This was reflected, for example, in the elderly male category, which was the generational band that showed highest rates of growth. In 1995, white males over 60 years of age accounted for 8.5 percent of the overall white male population. By 2009, this figure had risen to 11.7 percent. The figures for black men in the same age group also increased, but by less than one percentage point, from 9.9 to 10.8 percent.

Another relevant detail, which represents a trend tracked over recent years, is the proportional increase in the black and mulatto population. In 1995, 44.9 percent of the population self-identified as Negro, while this rose to 51.1 percent in 2009. During the same timeframe, the white population dropped from 54.5 to 48.2 percent. However, the data shows that this increase was not caused by a higher birth rate among the Negro population, but by a change in the way people identified themselves in terms of colour.

This rise in the number of people self-identifying as black or mulatto shows how cultural standards have changed in recent years. However, despite these behavioural changes, the data still still suggests racial exclusion in various sectors of society, as we shall see.

According to the Census Bureau, while indicators covering the period 1993 to 2007 showed an overall rise in life expectancy, whites still tended to live longer than blacks. The increase in life expectancy was greater for women than for men, and for whites than for blacks. During the period 1993–2007, the group white men over 60 rose from 8.2 to 11.1 percent, while the same demographic for the Negro population increased from 6.5 to 8.0 percent. The discrepancy between white and black men in this age group therefore moved up from 1.7 percentage points to 3.1. A similar trend was identified among black and white women. In 1993, white women over 60 accounted for 9.4 percent of all white women, while black women in the same age group made up only 7.3 percent of all black women. In 2007, these figures had risen, respectively, to 13.2 and 9.5 percent. The disparity between the two groups thus widened from 2.1 percentage points in 1993 to 3.7 in 2007.

In other words, while there had been a general upturn in life expectancy in the Brazilian population, the increase had not been equal across the board. High mortality rates caused by urban violence among the male population, particularly the young black male population, and precarious access to medical treatment and health care had both taken their toll. In terms of the difference in life expectancy between white and black women, the double-whammy of sexism and racism that black women had to contend with in the jobs market, in the workplace, and in access to public services largely accounted for the gap.

In general, 93 percent of the victims of lethal violence in Brazil were young and/or male. Moreover, if we take the population as a whole, black youths are far more likely to die a violent death. While in 2012 the murder rate among white youths was 29.9 per 100,000 inhabitants — practically the same as for the whole population — the figure for black youths was 82.3. It is not just a matter of comparing per capita death rates. There is a very telling gulf between these two groups when it comes to assessing the risk of murder. Today, a young black man in Brazil is 2.5 times more likely to be killed than a young white man. In the northeast, where murder rates tend to be higher, the difference is doubled: the young black man in the northeast of Brazil is five times more likely to be murdered than a white man of the same age in the same states.[17]

Translated into absolute figures, and taking 2012 as a benchmark, what we see are over 56,000 murders per year in Brazil. Thirty thousand of those killed are youths aged between 15 and 29, and 77 percent of those are black. So, we have a very specific colour and age bias in annual murder rates, and this is, sadly, in-line with the nation's historical inequalities. The data also leaves no doubt as to the vulnerability and limited access to human rights among the black section of the population.

When we look at the municipal level, clear regional differences emerge. In 2014, the Federal Government created a ranking of municipalities with the highest murder rates among black youths.[18] Of the 142 cities and towns listed, 64 were in the northeast, and 52 of these in the states of Bahia, Pernambuco, Alagoas and Paraíba.

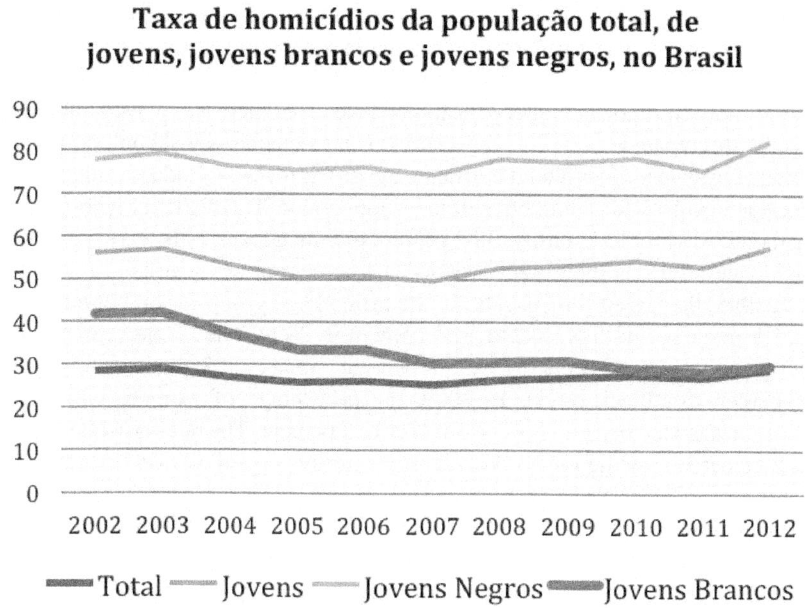

Figure 2.1 Homicide rates for the total population, youths, white youths and black youths in Brazil

So, let us move on to the literacy data. In 1995, 15.5 percent of the population aged 15 or older did not know how to read or write. In 2009, the percentage had fallen to 9.7. However, that same year, it was found that 20.5 percent of the black population in the northeast was illiterate, versus 14.2 percent of whites. In the northeastern hinterlands, the illiteracy rate peaked at 32.6 percent. The data showed that the average number of school years among the population aged 15 or over had increased from 5.5 in 1995 to 7.5 in 2009, representing two extra years of study over a 14-year period. If we look at the black population, however, although we see a 2.4-year increase over the same period, this does not represent a lessening of inequality: in 2009, black people aged 15 or over had, on average, 6.7 years of schooling versus 8.4 for whites.

Over the same period there was a 14.5 percent reduction in the number of people aged 16 or over in gainful employment who had only one to four years of schooling behind them, and an even higher percentage increase among people with between nine and 11 years of formal education. In 2009, 65.5 percent of white women aged 16 or over in gainful employment had completed at least nine years of study, while the percentage was only 48.7 percent for black women. In other words, there is a gulf that needs to be bridged when it comes to gender, colour and formal education.

In general, gross enrolment — which represents the percentage of people attending school or pre-school, regardless of age — increased from 54.7 percent in 1995 to 64.5 percent in 2009. The lower numbers were in the hinterlands, where coverage reached as little as 8.9 percent of school-age children. Considering racial inequalities, in 2009, 20.2 percent of white children aged three and under were enrolled in pre-school, versus 16.7 percent of black children in the same age bracket. The data shows that age-to-grade distortions increased from grade to grade and became more common at higher educational levels, but there was a discernible age-to-grade discrepancy among young black boys. In elementary school, 41 percent of black boys were older than the official age group for their grade, far higher than a 26.9 percent rate for white boys in the same grades. The disparity held for girls too, though slightly less starkly: 38.2 percent of young black girls were outside the official age-group for their grade, versus 24.1 percent of white girls.

In 1995, the net enrolment ratio in the official age group for higher education was 5.8 percent, and this rose to 14.4 percent in 2009. That same year, the rate among white school-goers was 21.3 percent, against 8.3 percent for blacks (6.9 percent for black boys). In 2009, the percentage of women with higher education was 16.6 percent. For men, it was 12.2 percent. The rate for white women was 23.8 percent, while for black women it was 9.9 percent. University education expansion projects, affirmative action and other policies have helped narrow the gap in this area, but the racial inequalities that determine and limit the opportunities available to black youths continue to explain the discrepancies in the data.

In the educational system, the knock-on effect is the reproduction of stereotypes tied in with racial and gender conventions that foster the segmentation by gender of the labour market and social occupations. If, for women, school enrolment and years studied are, on average, higher than those for men, when we look at the racial angle, we see that there are major inequalities in education, with lower rates of enrolment and a lower average number of years studied for blacks in comparison with whites. This is highly significant, since schooling is the bedrock of future opportunities.

In 1993, the illiteracy rate for white men aged 15 or over was 9.2 percent, falling to 5.9 percent by 2007. Among women aged 15 or over, there was a similar decrease: in 1993, the illiteracy rate for white women in this age bracket was 10.8 percent, but 24.9 percent for black women. Fifteen years later, these rates had dropped to 6.3 percent and 13.7 percent, respectively. Whilst the fall in illiteracy rates was solid across the board, black men were still found lagging eight percentage points behind white men, and black women nearly seven and a half points behind their white counterparts.

In terms of years of study, we see that the average for whites is 8.1 years, while for blacks it is a significantly lower, at 6.3. The fact remains that whites have more access to schooling than blacks do, especially in terms of elementary and higher education. For example, fewer white women failed to complete elementary school than do black women (41 percent versus 55.2 percent). The same goes for men, with rates for failure to complete elementary school standing at 42.4 percent for white men and 59 percent for black men. Furthermore, more white women graduat from higher education than black women (17.7 percent versus 6.7 percent). Something similar can be seen among men, with 15.3 percent of the white male population completing tertiary level education and only 4.5 percent of black males.

What we see here is one of many examples of continuity between the slave-owning past and the present. In 1869, the Regulations for Provincial Instruction in São Paulo barred slaves from enrolling in schools. This prohibition was reinforced by another instrument of law in 1887. In the province of Rio de Janeiro, regulations issued in 1847 barred from schools not only slaves but all "black Africans, whether freed or freeborn". Even when schooling did become free for all, teachers tended to label black pupils the "worst students", responsible for holding back the rest of the class. This stigma still holds in any analysis of educational inequality today.

New data shows the differences in access to public and private healthcare. In 2003, the Public Health Service (SUS) was responsible for 63.5% percent of consultations and 69.3% percent of hospital admissions in the country. When this data is broken down by racial group, we see considerable discrepancies. Among the white population, 54 percent of consultations and 59 percent of hospital admissions were on the public health service, while, for blacks and mulattoes, the rates were far higher, standing at 76 percent and 81.3 percent, respectively. The data thus shows how overwhelmingly "SUS-dependent" the Negro population is in Brazil. Even when we compare public health service consultations and hospital admissions by wage bracket, we see that this black-white divide still holds. Among individuals earning more than three times the minimum monthly wage of R$240 in 2003 (+/- US $80: BR3.00 to USD1.00), 21 percent of consultations and 23.8 percent of hospital admissions among blacks and mulattoes were on the public heath system, against 14 percent and 13.5 percent for whites earning an equivalent wage. The reverse is true when we consider private health insurance coverage: 33.2 percent of whites owned and used health insurance, against only 14.7 percent of blacks. Even among those earning more than three times the monthly wage in 2003, whites were the majority of those with health insurance: 75 percent of whites had health insurance, versus 66 percent of blacks.

In 2008, the proportion of the Brazilian population using the health system (public or private) reached 96.2 percent: 97.3 percent of the white population and 95 percent of the black and mulatto population. When cross-referenced with socioeconomic data, the health indicators reveal an important relationship between health, its social determinants and health-system organisation.

Another data set presented in the Census Bureau's "Inequality Panorama" concerns women's health. The Census showed that the percentage of women who had never had a woman's health checkup remained high, and that access to testing was particularly limited among black women. The data revealed that 36.4 percent of women aged 25 or over had never had a mammogram (28.7 percent of white women and 46.3 percent of black women). Even among women with 12 or more years of schooling, the inequality remained: 10.5 percent of white women and 18 percent of black women with this level of education had never had a mammogram.

These figures reveal inequality in the quality of treatment stemming from ingrained discriminatory practices and behaviours. The situation is even graver when the data is distributed geographically. In Brazil, 32 percent of women aged 25 or over living in urban neighbourhoods had never had a mammogram, while 63 percent of those of the same age living in rural environments had never been screened.

In terms of the pension and benefits system, the numbers are even more damning. The Census data for those drawing government benefits on social assistance programmes showed that black households were the vast majority of those receiving this kind of support. Black households accounted for 69 percent of those registered for the Federal Government's Bolsa Família (Family Stipend), 60 percent of those receiving the Prestação Continuada (stipend equivalent to the monthly wage for elderly or disabled people with no other form of support), and 68 percent of those on the Child Labour Eradication Programme. The data is hardly surprising when we consider that poverty and inequality indicators clearly show that blacks have been far more likely to be poor, un- or under-employed, and undereducated.

The positions the different segments of society hold on the jobs market present another fundamental facet of inequality. Men, women, blacks and whites present very different employment profiles when it comes to working life. Employment data paints a persistent and perverse picture: though black men start work earlier, they retire later. In other words, the working life of a black man is considerably longer than his white counterpart's. This can be explained by the fact that black men have less or nothing at all to retire on, which means they have to work longer.

In this sense, while there has been an increase in the percentage of workers in formal employment, if we compare black men and white men, we see that more black males work informally (23.4 percent against 16.3 percent of whites). The position is even worse for black women. A large contingent of black women work in domestic employment (21.4 percent), while a further 15.4 percent engage in growing produce at home or other forms of unpaid labour. Black women are the social segment least likely to be in formal, registered employment (only 23.3 percent) or to be employers themselves (1.2 percent), and so are, by far, the most vulnerable segment of the workforce. Unemployment among black women in 2007 stood at 12.4 percent, against 9.4 percent for white women, 6.7 percent for black men and 5.5 percent for white men.

Still on the issue of employment, another data set that warrants attention is the one for child labour, an indicator that is key to presenting the abiding racial inequalities in the way different social segments are assimilated into the workforce. Though child labour has been decreasing steadily in recent years, the highest rates are still found for black boys aged between five and nine and 10 and 15. The northeast leads the table, followed by the north and the south. However, black boys from the northeast are those who suffer most from the practice: 14 percent of northeastern black boys aged between five and 15 were working in 2007.

Domestic labour is traditionally held in low regard, and is seen as the preserve of poor, largely black, women and girls. It is therefore the form of employment that most symbolically reveals the abiding legacy of slavery and patriarchal exploitation in Brazilian society.

In 2007, of the total number of Brazilians employed in domestic labour, men accounted for only 0.8 percent; and that remains pretty much unchanged a decade later. On the other hand, that same year, of the entire female workforce, 16.4 percent was engaged in this kind of work. In addition, if we compare the total number of white women gainfully employed in domestic labour (13.4 percent in 1996 and 12.1 percent in 2007) with the number of black women in the same line of work (23 percent in 1996 and 21.4 percent in 2007) we see that, at the latter date, despite a dip in the numbers, domestic employment was still firmly and traditionally associated with black women.

The data points to the dual discrimination to which black women have been subjected in many different social spheres, but particularly on the jobs market and in terms of comparative pay. As a result of educational inequality, the corralling of women and blacks into lower-paying jobs, and the social phenomenon of discrimination, men and whites have received better pay than women and blacks. In 2007, while white women earned roughly 62.3 percent of the average salary for white men, black women received 67 percent of the average wage for black men, and only 34 percent of that paid to white men. It is important to note that the wage discrepancies between these groups have been narrowing in recent years. In fact, even between 1996 and 2007, pay differences between whites and blacks and men and women shrank by 13 percent and 10 percent, respectively.

In 2009, 5.2 percent of the population was considered extremely poor. At the beginning of this century, the percentage was 10. However, once again, the inequality is considerable: 7.2 percent of the black population was classified as extremely poor, against only 3 percent of whites. In regional terms, only 2 percent of those in this category were found to live in the south-southeast, while 11 percent were located in the northeast.

Indicators on access to consumer durables and digital exclusion over the last 15 years reveal improvement across the board, but with continued inequality along racial and gender lines. The data was analysed in terms of the gender and colour of the head of households that owned a stove, refrigerator, washing machine, television, freezer and telephone, and, in another data set, those with personal computers, internet access and cellphones.

The period of economic stability that ran from the mid-1990s to the 2010s saw a slow but steady increase in per capita income in Brazil, and this was reflected in higher rates of acquisition of consumer durables. Some items in this category, such as televisions and stoves, can be found in the vast majority of Brazilian homes, while others, such as washing machines, are now much more common but by no means ubiquitous. In general, black and rural households continue to have more limited access to consumer goods, though this has been growing at a steady rate. Digital exclusion now features as one of the main challenges to be addressed in terms of access to information. Though unquestionable progress has been made, there is still considerable inequality in the acquisition of goods and services in this area. The general position reveals far higher digital exclusion among the black population, especially among black women. Access to personal computers and the internet at home or at work remains the preserve of a small section of the population, and only limited growth has been observed if compared with cellphone ownership.

When it comes to racial discrepancies in poverty and indigence, the indicators clearly show rampant disparity in per capita income between whites and blacks. According to data from 2007, 20 percent of the white population was considered below the poverty line, versus 41.7 percent of the black population. The difference was even more marked for indigence: while 6.6 percent of the white population was earning as little as a quarter of the monthly minimum wage, the percentage was 16.9 for blacks; in other words, two and a half times the rate for whites. This meant there were 20 million more black people living below the poverty line than whites, and 9.5 million more black indigents. Income data, for example, shows that average monthly income for households led by a white male was R$ 997 (roughly US$ 500 in 2007), while the average income for a household under a black female breadwinner was R$ 491 (US$ 250). Likewise, 69 percent of families led by black women earned no more than one minimum monthly wage (R$ 380 in 2007, or +/- US$ 190), compared to 41 percent for families led by white men.

Though the rates of extreme poverty and indigence in 2007 were significantly higher among blacks and mulattoes, it is important to note that there has been a considerable reduction in poverty across the board, and that the improvement has been substantially higher for blacks than for whites. Over the last 15 years, federal government policies and programmes geared towards increasing the minimum wage and decreasing inequitable distribution of wealth have rescued some 6.5 million people from poverty, the majority being black and mulatto.

The income disparity between blacks and whites is also clear when we look at per capita incomes. As we move upwards from the poorer percentages of the population to the wealthier ones, the people become decidedly whiter. In 2007, 67.9 percent of the people in the poorest 10 percent of the nation were black or mulatto. If we look at the richest 10 percent, the percentage of blacks in that group was only 21.9. Of the richest one percent, 15.3 percent was black. Even today, despite a very definite improvement in the distribution of wealth in Brazil, social inequality remains a stark reality.

As regards access to basic sanitation, there has been a general improvement nationwide. That said, at 82.3 percent coverage, the sewage system remains the least satisfactory service, despite a nearly 13 percent improvement in the period covered by the Census. In this case, the differences are highly significant. While 88 percent of white households were on the sewage grid in 2007, the same held for only 76 percent of black households.

Another important piece of data concerns excessive urban concentration. While the rates are generally low — the national average was only 5 percent of households in 2007 — and continuously falling (in 1993, for example, the rate was 10 percent), the problem affects black households twice as heavily as whites: 7 percent of all black households were in excessively concentrated areas. Housing conditions have improved considerably over the last 15 years; yet, if we look at the proportion of households located in "subnormal" settlements, we see that the ratios have not really changed over the period. In 1993, 3.2 percent of households were in shantytowns or slums; in 2007, the percentage was 3.6. Though the percentages are low, we cannot forget that they signify some two million homes and roughly eight million people. A quick look at households in subnormal settlements reveals the following: 40.1 percent were led by black men, 26 percent by black women, 21.3 percent by white men and 11.7 percent by white women. While this percentage breakdown reflects the general national reality, it still shows the overwhelming black presence in the country's shantytowns and slums.

Another important indicator in the analysis of how different segments of the population live is how men and women, whites and blacks use their time, and how much of it is spent at work. Brazil is yet to conduct a nationwide survey on this theme, but, since its 1996 edition, the Census has collated statistics on time spent commuting between home and work, and, since 2001, on the average number of hours spent on household chores per week. These factors also reveal some considerable asymmetries within Brazilian society. Most workers spend an average of 30 minutes travelling between their homes and workplaces. If the differences between men and women are not particularly telling, those between blacks and whites are: 70 percent of the white population spends 30 minutes or less commuting between home and work, compared to 65.4 percent of blacks and mulattoes. The 30-minutes to one-hour bracket covers 21.6 percent of whites and 23.8 percent of blacks. Finally, the category that spends over an hour travelling to work each day represents 8.5 percent of whites and 10.8 percent of blacks. This difference can be explained by the fact that there is a greater black population living in the outskirts of the country's major cities. Thus, longer travel time can be understood as a further result of this segment of the population's generally lower quality of life caused by poverty.

The data discussed above underlines the reality of discrimination and racism whilst it can be used convincingly to underpin demands for policies to promote greater racial equality.

A present rife with pasts: or the ghosts amongst us

As we have shown, it was with the end of slavery in 1888 that race and racial theories became rooted in the Brazilian mindset. While racial theories have gone out of vogue, race itself continues to function as an extra factor in the context of data that points toward a model pocked with social gaps.

There is also a lingering guilty conscience about the past that leads not to a critical revision, but to a deep and deafening silence on the issue. When singing the Brazilian National Anthem, composed in 1891, a year and a half after Abolition, patriotic nationals entone (perhaps without noticing it) the following line: "we don't believe that there were once slaves in so noble a land". Can it be that emancipation had only just occurred and already no-one "believed" slavery had ever existed? As Walter Benjamin showed us, history is as much an operation of forgetting as it is of remembering[19], and for a long time slavery was a "non-theme" in Brazil. Another example: in a nationwide survey conducted by the University of São Paulo to mark the centenary of Abolition, in 1988, 97 percent of respondents answered "No" when asked if they were prejudiced about race. Yet when asked if they knew anyone who was, 99 percent said yes, and identified the bigots as close friends and family members. Hence the conclusion drawn from the survey was that each Brazilian considers him/herself an island of racial democracy in a sea full of racists. The problem lies always with the "other", and that relieves the self of guilt and ambivalence.

Since the 1980s, with the consolidation of the Black Movement, affirmative action, and progress in the study of Brazil's slave-owning past and adherence to racial theories, it has become much more difficult to ignore or deny racial prejudice. However, even today, to echo the historian Trouillot, a certain "unspeakableness" continues to hover over the nation's racist past and present. Despite the hard numbers that add up to "inequality" across various segments of our society, these situations continue to dialogue with what Michel Trouillot, writing on the silence surrounding the revolution in Haiti, described as "the unthinkable". For Trouillot; "The unthinkable is that which one cannot conceive within the range of possible alternatives, that which perverts all answers because it defies the terms under which the questions were phrased".[20] Well, Brazilians haven't exactly dealt very well with "those questions", which is why they continue to treat prejudice as an issue that is either absent or "naturalised" and therefore resolved. In an ethnic census conducted by USP, many of the respondents came up with answers like, "I don't have that problem". It is precisely those who "don't have" or see the problem who actually do have it, and refuse to voice the contradiction. It is therefore important that we realise that we continue to produce and re-signify structures of the past in the present.

A deep and obstinate mark, the legacy and echoes of Brazilian slave society shape our culture, with the nation defining itself in a complex language based on social colours. We always classify ourselves in tones and halftones, and we know that the wealthier we become, the whiter we become, and vice-versa. If the border of colour is more permeable to us, and Brazilians really don't recognise themselves according to strict biological criteria; if social inclusion is a reality here, and expressed in so many manifestations that underscore the country's uniqueness — *capoeira*, samba, football; if our music and culture are mestizo in origin and intent; then there is no way we can forget the array of processes of social exclusion. These are processes that are expressed in the still-discrepant access to the advantages of leisure, employment, infrastructure and family planning, to say nothing of the systematic exclusion of blacks from the clubs, theatres and restaurants of the elite (where not even the waiters are black) or in the routine intimidations, shakedowns and pullovers blacks are subjected to by the police, the masters of "colour-coded" discrimination.

In Brazil, colour is language, but also the reiteration of past and present certainty of an inner hierarchy. Here, it is possible to manipulate and even change colours as you would a dress. Until recently, marrying a white person, moving up in the world, graduating with a degree, or winning promotion tended to make you a few shades lighter; and while it is true that this tendency has been somewhat eroded, the colour attributed to someone still largely depends on the light of context: the kind of workplace, the sort of leisure option, or whether the person happens to be standing before the police. In São Paulo's Heliópolis favela, for example, every year's end the community holds a "Whites against blacks" football game. The novelty today is how fluidly people can change sides without anyone noticing. Who is black and who is white is largely determined by external factors.

Even the Brazilian Census is colour-coded. Brazilians can self-identify as white, black, yellow and, up until recently, red (read, indigenous). The most revealing term of all, however, is the fifth option: *pardo* (a sort of dusky brown). Pardo is hard to define, which is what has made it the joker in the pack, an opt-out "none of the above". *Pardo* can also be an accusation, as good as an awkward silence, or a euphemism.

Further echoes can still be heard in Brazilian architecture, where certain "institutions" remain alive and well: take the "service elevator", for example, with its back-door entrance (used for services, but also by servants, the vast majority being black or mulatto), or the "maid's quarters", an isolated bedroom just off the service area or kitchen in most houses and apartments. As we can see, in yet another throwback to its slave past, Brazil has retained something of its historical prejudice toward work, especially manual work, and all forms of "service". Perhaps that was only to be expected from a system in which, as Fr. Antonil once said, "slaves were the hands and feet" of the nation. Perhaps the most "active memory" of slavery in Brazilian society today is violence. Patterns of behaviour coming from the past and repurposed for the present have cemented in Brazil a violent, hierarchized society that straddles both the private and public spheres and makes itself visible in its disrespect for public property and our high crime and murder rates.

The anthropologist Didier Fassin refers to a famous text by Louis Althusser in which the philosopher tackles the concept of "interpellation" (in the dual sense of interrogation and hailing). This pragmatic little theoretical theatre, which consists of forcing the individual to submit freely to the law, is what confers the right to become a subject. Liberty does not, therefore, exclude subjection; in fact, it merely reinforces the legitimacy of the State and the submission itself seems voluntary. The act of interpellation is also addressed by Michel Foucault in his studies on power, when he introduces the idea that this practice leads to a process of "subjectification". Before the police, for example, individuals will often assume a position they would normally reject.[21]

After all, innocence is no guarantee against being considered and made to consider oneself guilty. We learn early how this social construct works, through the gaze of the other, which always reflects back the notion of difference — the black, the foreigner, the poor man, the stoner — but through the prism of stigma. These are heavy social markers of difference, and they are not only external to the individual, but are incorporated into the body too. Worse: the experiences of shame, humiliation and injustice often come accompanied with a sense of guilt in the face of what may be an oft-repeated situation. At that time and in that place — the "wrong time and place", as they do not belong to the subject — they may well be "guilty". This ambivalent response, which implies accepting someone else's blame, shall we say, is what Fassin calls "embodied memory", which the body already remembers before thought can even kick in.

Of course, there is no such thing as a good racism; one racism is just as perverse and laden with suffering as any other. These collective omissions and processes of humiliation represent strong doses of embarrassment, consolidated by the nation. Things proceed as if there were rigid social boxes, never questioned by time and history. These are the "naturalisations" that society prepares or uses to hoodwink nature. The juridical bastardy that proliferated during slavery — when a freed man or woman could be re-consigned to captivity for lack of "usefulness", for "disloyalty" to the former owner, or simply for the lack of emancipation papers — still finds a certain emotional connivance, with the country struggling with the language of civil rights and diversity, with the right to be different.

So having mixed colours, names, religions and customs, we have turned miscegenation into a sort of national representation, and for a long time it has been a consensual one. On the one hand, the mixture was compacted through violence, the kidnapping of peoples and hijacking of cultures and experiences. New figures put the number of imported Africans at 3,800,000;[22] people plucked from their lands to work as slaves on American plantations. Today, with 60 percent of the population either black or mulatto, Brazil can be considered the second most populous African nation, after Nigeria. On the other hand, it is important to remember how that mix, however forced, did generate a society of fused rhythms, arts, sports, aromas, cuisines and literatures. Our many faces, our mixed and varied features, our myriad ways of thinking and feeling the country are proof of the profound blend that has engendered hybrid cultures, spliced together out of disparate strands of experience.

This is, therefore, a country that has conjured a perverse mix of cultural inclusion and social exclusion; which, with each passing moment, flips from one face to the other: faces that are, at the end of the day, basically the same. Diversity expresses one of the great realities of this country, marked and conditioned by separation, but also by the fusions that have resulted from this long process of miscegenation and deep, painful and persistent experience of slavery and its legacy. While Brazil is managing to consolidate itself democratically — with strong institutions and elections won in the ballot box — it is still failing dismally to get a handle on republican values: those that urge respect for what is public and the property of all.

Social inequality is our inheritance from the past; but it is also a challenge to the present that recalls, in some ways, the ghosts in Toni Morrison's *Beloved*. At No. 124, the ghosts that insisted on coming back were the realest things there. Brazil, too, is full of ghosts, and we don't know how to "tame" them.

Notes

1 See Manuela Carneiro Cunha, *História dos Indios* (São Paulo: Companhia das Letras, 2006).

2 Laura de Mello e Souza, *O Diabo na Terra de Santa Cruz* (São Paulo, Companhia das Letras, 1980).

3 Piero Magalhães Gandavo, *História da Província de Santa Cruz* (Lisbon, 1576).

4 Pierre Clastres, *A Sociedade contra o Estado* (Rio de Janeiro: Francisco Alves, 1978).

5 See Cunha, *História dos Indios*; and Eduardo Viveiros de Castro, "Perspectivismo e multinaturalismo na América Indígena" in Eduardo Viveiros de Castro, *A Inconstância da Alma Selvagem* (São Paulo: Cosac e Naify, 2002), chap. 7.

6 Oswald Andrade, see *Pau Brasil* (Rio de Janeiro: Globo, 2010).

7 Sidney Mintz, *Sweetness and Power. The Place of S ugar in Modern History* (New York: Penguin, 1985).

8 Wlamyra R. de Albuquerque and Walter Fraga Filho, *Uma História do Negro no Brasil* (Salvador: Centro de Estudos Afro-Orientais; Brasília: Fundação Cultural Palmares, 2006).

9 Ambrósio Fernandes Brandão, *Diálogo das Grandezas do Brasil*, 1618.

10 José Murilo de Carvalho, *Teatro de Sombras: a Política Imperial* (Rio de Janeiro: Editora Iuperj Vertice, 1988; Editora UFRJ, Relume-Dumará, 1996), p. 290.

11 Hebe Mattos, "Raça e Cidadania no Crepúsculo da Modernidade Escravista no Brasil", in *O Brasil Imperial*, vol.3 1870–1889, ed. Keila Grinberg and Ricardo Salles (Rio de Janeiro: Civilização Brasileira, 2009), pp. 22–3.

12 On the theme of gradualism, see Maria Helena Pereira Toledo Machado, "Teremos Grandes Desastres se Não Houver Providências Enérgicas", in *O Brasil Imperial* vol. 3, pp. 371–373.

13 See, among others, Lilia Moritz Schwarcz, *Espetáculo das Raças* (São Paulo: Companhia das Letras, 1997).

14 Francisco Bethencourt, *Racisms: From the Crusades to the Twentieth Century* (Princeton: Princeton University Press, 2013).

15 See Tatiana H. P. Lotierzo and Lilia K. M. Schwarcz, "Raça, Gênero e Projeto Branqueador: 'a Redenção de Cam', de Modesto Brocos", *Artelogie* 5 (October 2013): http://cral.in2p3.fr/artelogie/spip.php?article254.

16 Data from the Brazilian Census Bureau and the Geography and Statistics Board (IPEA and IBGE). Though we will not analyse gender inequality in this text, as our focus is on race, the data on the theme is just as relevant to any understanding of social differences in Brazil.

17 Amnesty International Report, 2013.

18 The aim of the ranking was to determine on which municipalities the *Juventude Viva* (Live Youth) programme, launched that same year by the President of the Republic, should focus.

19 Walter Benjamin, *The Storyteller*, trans. and ed. Esther Leslie and Sebastian Truskolaski, (London: Verso, 2016).

20 Michel-Rolph Trouillot, *Silencing the Past: Power and the Production of History* (Boston: Beacon Press, 1995), p. 82.

21 Didier Fassin, *When Bodies Remember* (Oakland: University of California Press, 2007).

22 See www.slavevoyages.org.

CHAPTER

3

Inequality and Redistribution: Welfare State Development in Brazil?

CELIA LESSA KERSTENETZKY

Introduction

The news that Brazil was finally coming to terms with its unrivalled level of economic inequality came as a welcome surprise. Over the first decade of the twenty-first century, or, more accurately, between 2004 and 2014, the country went down a path of economic prosperity and social progress that starkly contrasted with the import substitution industrialization (ISI) era of the late 1960s and 1970s, when sizable levels of economic growth and scant social equilibrium cohabited. Justifiably, the recent experience of "redistributive growth" has attracted the attention of international policy-makers, multilateral organizations, and academics, especially in view of the rather ambiguous achievements of other emerging economies, such as China and India, where increasing inequalities have followed spectacular growth rates.

The purpose of this chapter is not so much to delve into the new growth model, tempting as that might be, but to focus on achievements such as the reduction of poverty and inequality, and thus evaluate the advances, and flag the limits, of the Brazilian experience in these areas. A central tenet of the argument is that Brazil was, in the period here considered, building up a welfare state distinctly reliant on regulatory and redistributive policies. However, it is argued that, while moving beyond "social safety nets" (e.g. conditional cash transfers to the poor), the social policies implemented stopped short of delivering truly transformative changes to the very segregated structure of welfare provision — changes which would be needed if advances in public social services and progressive taxation were to be effected. Moreover, the measures undertaken, albeit politically easier to implement in a context of growth, turned out to be particularly susceptible to retrenchment pressures when circumstances changed. In fact, the recession that started in 2015, in combination with recent cost-cutting policies and proposed constitutional change, is set to dismantle the main pillars of the experiment. The argument offered in this chapter is organized in the following way. The first section reviews the recent evolution of poverty and inequality in Brazil; the second looks into the driving forces behind these developments, with an emphasis on factors shaping the dynamics of inequality; the third qualifies the positive achievements with new data from income tax returns which show a resilient concentration at the top of income distribution; the following section draws attention to bets that were not placed, i.e., social investment policies and progressive taxation; and the concluding section evaluates the achievements from the perspective of recent developments that set the context of welfare state retrenchment in the country.

Evolving poverty and inequality

Over the last decade, Brazil has undergone a process of social development, 'catching up' with advanced economies in terms of the incidence of poverty and levels of income inequality.

Reduction of poverty was already substantial in the 1990s, in the period shortly after the 1994 Real Plan — a stabilization plan that reined in hyperinflation and created the new Brazilian currency, the *real*. Between 1993 and 1995, absolute poverty rates plummeted 7.9 percentage points, to 36 percent of the population. There then came a more stable period, up to 2003, before another wave of decline arose, more extensive and consistent than the previous one, leading to a decrease in poverty of 22 percentage points by 2014.[1] In the end, the incidence of poverty shrank to just 13 percent in 2014. Comparing the two good periods, it is now widely accepted that while the Real Plan had the merit of undercutting the confiscatory impact of high inflation on the income of the poorer sections of the population, after 2003 other poverty-reducing factors such as economic growth and (notably) redistribution were at work (see figure 3.1, below).[2]

The reduction of poverty is still shown to be far from negligible when a relative measure — say, the proportion of the population who live on less than 50 percent of the median income — is adopted. The use of this measure, while gauging the percentage of those left behind as the majority prospers, also enables equity comparisons with developed economies in the OECD area, which generally adopt relative rates as their poverty indicator. Thus, Brazil, in 2014, presented a relative poverty rate twice as big as that for the OECD area (22 percent versus 11 percent), down from 2.7 times as big back in 2000 (27 percent versus 10 percent).

To be sure, this Brazilian "catching up" resulted from a double movement, whereby developed economies were increasing their poverty levels whilst Brazil, as well as Latin American (LA) and emerging economies in general, were heading in the opposite direction. Global economic forces were certainly behind this new asymmetry. To mention but one, the rise of "emergent" China, which led the commodity boom, triggered changes that favoured the economic catch-up of

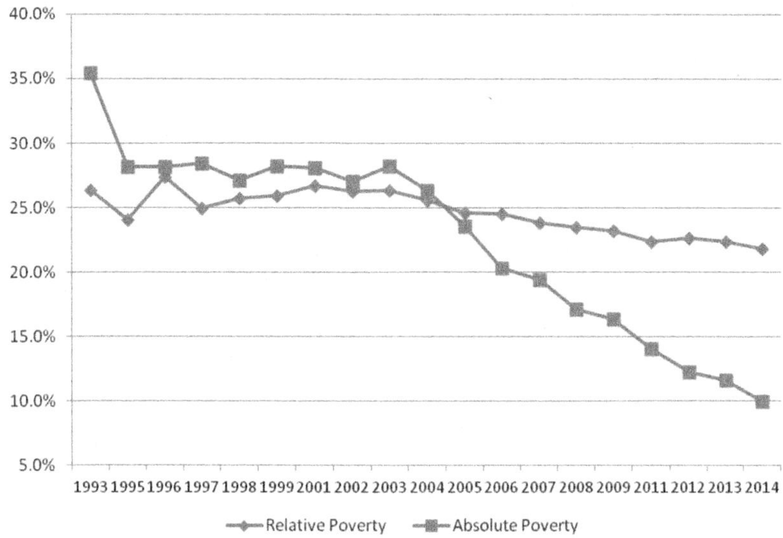

Figure 3.1 Evolution of relative (50% of median income) and absolute poverty in Brazil: 1993–2014

Source: Author's own compilation from IPEADATA and PNAD/IBGE.

commodity exporters in Latin America. The resulting lesser 'between countries' inequality (as the income gap between the developed and the developing countries was diminishing) was in this way aligned with a contraction in 'within countries' poverty in the less developed areas (where incomes were rising). Still, while in emerging economies GDP growth rates were the underlying driving force, in Latin America redistributive policies were just as important.

Processes of economic growth may differ in terms of the changes they bring in income distribution and their impact on poverty. For example, as mentioned above, growth and inequality cohabited during the ISI era in Brazil, which was nevertheless an important period for the decline of poverty. The heyday of the ISI took place under a military dictatorship that stifled the redistributive claims of sectors of the population not encompassed in the new development strategy. Thus, a central component of the export-oriented industrialization model was a policy of devaluation of the minimum wage, which was later shown to have contributed to an increase in inequality in the 1960s and 1970s. Poverty reduction in this period drew instead on spectacular growth rates and high employment levels, with growth offsetting the rise in inequality in much the same way as has been happening in China and India more recently. In recent times in Brazil, the relationship between inequality and growth has changed, with both contributing to a decline in poverty.

In fact, while inequality increased in the three decades between the 1960s and the 1980s, despite the growth regime — high speed, mid speed, and low speed — in the period, things started to change with the re-democratization that took

Table 3.1 Gini indices, growth rates and political regime: Brazil 1960–2010

Year	GINI	Growth rate	Regime
1960	0.50		Limited democracy
1970	0.56	++++ 1960's	Dictatorship
1980	0.60	+++ 1970's	Dictatorship
1991	0.64	+ 1980's	Redemocratization
2000	0.61	+ 1990's	Democracy
2010	0.52	++ "Golden Age"	Democracy and center-left coalition

Source: Author's own compilation. Calculations based on census data in Ribeiro and Scalon, 2001 (Gini 1960–1991); and MDS 2012 (Gini 2000 and 2010).[1]

place in the 1990s, when inequality abated somewhat. Later, in the 2000s, when a centre-left coalition took power, the relationship between growth and inequality became clearly negative, with sizable reductions in the level of income inequality accompanying positive growth rates in the country (see table 3.1). It was in this period that a diminution of poverty started to relate consistently to lower levels of income inequality, as well as to growth. Incidentally, contemporary inequality studies have increasingly drawn attention to the impact of political variables on the dynamics of both inequality and equalization in advanced economies;[3] and the Brazilian experience seems to broaden the geographical reach of the "political turn" in inequality scholarship. We shall explore key aspects of the centre-left policy agenda in the next section.

As regards recent trends in inequality, data from household surveys tracking yearly changes over the 1990s, and the 2000s up to 2014 (figure 3.2, below), shows a consistent fall in income inequality in the final period, the golden years of redistribution policies. Between 2001 and 2014, the Gini index dropped over 13 percent, or 0.07 points, from 0.59 to 0.52.[5] To give an idea of the significance of this achievement, if we compare these figures with the parallel decennial performances of advanced economies transitioning from peak to minimum levels of inequality in the twentieth century,[6] we find that Brazil fared much better than did those countries (with the exception of Spain). Again, the recent sizable decline in inequality happened whilst there was mounting inequality in the OECD area and other members of the BRICS, lending support to the social development catch-up hypothesis.[7] Brazil was on its way to becoming a 'normal' country, coming to terms with its inequality problems.

The shift of millions of families out of poverty fuelled the idea that a robust new middle class was emerging in the country; but this assessment was over-optimistic. More sober analyses would show that conditions such as an occupation at the lower end of the labour market (e.g. an informal or manual job), economic insecurity (lack of property and savings) and consumption patterns similar to those exhibited by the poor placed most of those who escaped material deprivation in

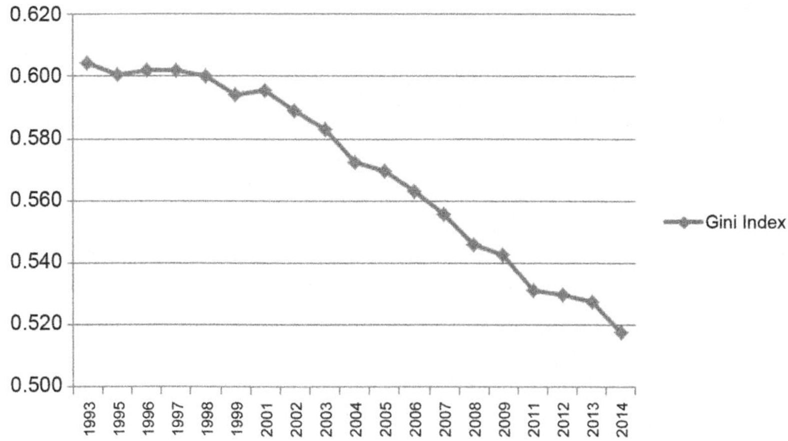

Figure 3.2 Evolution of per capita household income inequality in Brazil: 1993–2014
Source: Author's own compilation. Data from Ipeadata, based on household surveys (the PNADs/IBGE).

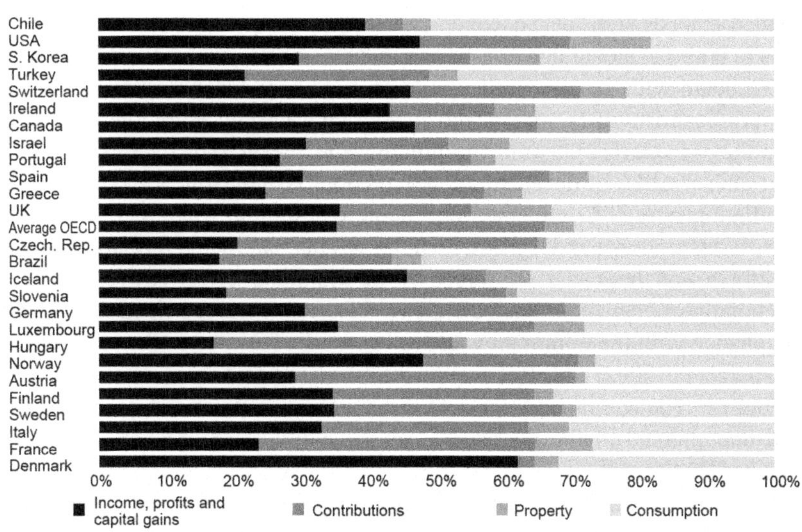

Figure 3.3 Composition of the tax burden: Brazil and OECD countries, 2012
Source: Receita federal, "Carga Tributária no Brasil 2013: Análise por Tributos e Base de Incidência", Brasília, 2013, p. 16.

the category of "strugglers", not yet among the economically secure members of the middle class.[8] Moreover, as consumption taxes weighed heavily in the country's tax burden (51 percent in 2014), their impact on the final income of the poor, who spent their earnings chiefly on consumption items, was far from negligible: a decomposition exercise found that consumption taxes increased the proportion of the poor to levels above those of market income poverty.[9] This is a sign of the country's obstinate "abnormality" as far as taxation goes: in a group of 26 countries, Brazil stands out for its high reliance on regressive consumption taxes and, together with Hungary, its minimal use of progressive income taxes (figure 3.3 above).

Expansion of good quality social services and changes in the tax system are among the missing interventions that might have mitigated this situation — a point we return to in the penultimate section. However, even considering that the depth of the experiment could have been more profound, and its stability more firmly rooted, the golden years in Brazil delivered unequivocal, as well as historically rare, social progress as measured on poverty and income inequality yardsticks.

Driving forces shaping inequality reduction

In trying to disentangle the factors shaping income equalization in Brazil, studies have converged on lower wage inequality as the main driver of the changes and, secondarily, redistributive government transfers to the poor.[10] This result might convey the idea that pure market developments did much of the trick. However, detailed analysis of the data uncovers public policies playing decisive redistributive roles in both the labour and non-labour incomes of Brazilian households.

To begin with, labour market policies, such as the statutory minimum wage and its adjustment rules, were key to countering wage concentration. In particular, the policy of valorization of the minimum wage, meant to recover its living-wage level after decades of devaluation, delivered yearly adjustment indices in excess of inflation rates.[11] Complementing the new minimum wage regulation were a series of institutional and legislative initiatives that facilitated formalization of the workforce, and these were reinforced by the addition of effective oversight of, and functioning of, the labour justice system.[12] These measures helped raise levels of compliance with the minimum wage (20 percent of non-compliance, down from 25.9 percent in 2002) and effective formalization (64 percent, up from 47.3 percent in 2002).[13] The combined impact of these interventions on wage concentration, well documented in the literature, was substantial.[14] Moreover, it was to be expected that contributions to the social security system stemming from this new wave of formalization would translate in the future into lower income inequality, as more and more people gained access to public pensions. Finally, the long-term (however slow) expansion of schooling, most of it publicly provided, paid off. Wage differentials linked to the levels of educational attainment of the labour force, historically among the highest in the world, began to shrink.[15] Taken together, these policies were integral to what became known as pre-distribution intervention, for they potentially affected income distribution even before the actual encounter of employees and employers in the labour market.

Unsurprisingly, classic redistribution interventions such as cash transfers played an inequality-reducing role as well, through the "non-labour income" channel. Both the coverage and the level of benefits expanded markedly in the period. For example, social assistance benefits such as the 2003 *bolsa familia* (a conditional cash transfer targeted at the poor) extended eligibility beyond the early 2001 *bolsa escola* to include poor families without children, practically doubling the latter's coverage; and non-contributory pensions such as the *benefício da prestação continuada* for the elderly and disabled poor soared, on account of more inclusive eligibility rules.

As we explain below, thanks to the 1988 constitution, the influence of the minimum wage valorization policy was felt through the entire process of income equalization, affecting labour and non-labour incomes alike. To begin with, the 1988 constitution set the parameters for a universalist welfare state in the country. It broadened the then-existing social protection system, previously limited to workers who contributed to the social insurance fund, and mandated public provision of universal social services, including health care, previously guaranteed only to insured workers or (via assistance) to the poor. So, following the constitution's enactment, a raft of new social entitlements were established, having as a consequence the doubling of the level of social spending as a proportion of GDP, from 10 percent to 20 percent, within a couple of years.[16] While some of the new spending went on the creation from scratch of a national health service (the SUS), most of it went on social security benefits, notably, pensions and social assistance.

A distinctive feature of the new constitutional parameters in relation to social benefits in cash was their pegging to the minimum wage: none could be established at a nominal level below it. As the constitution also determined that the minimum wage be fixed at an amount compatible with a living wage, the minimum underwent successive adjustments from 1995 on. The reason for these was, as we have seen, that it had been systematically undervalued since the 1960s. These changes impacted strongly on income distribution. In the end, valorization of the minimum wage turned out to be the most important single factor in the decline of income inequality in Brazil — accounting for 72 percent of the decline between 1995 and 2013, and 64 percent, between 1995 and 2014, according to a decomposition exercise.[17]

Various factors combined to produce this favourable outcome. First, the valorization per se was substantial, and has been particularly so over the last decade, when it has become an upfront policy pursued by the incumbent centre-left coalition, and has reached over 72 percent (112 percent if we take the last two decades). Not surprisingly, this has had a bearing on the labour market, directly affecting minimum wage earners (15–20 percent of the employed). However, for reasons previously mentioned, it also affected non-labour incomes such as basic pensions and social assistance benefits. In fact, the strongest redistributive impact came through the latter channel, and basic pensions, which accounted for the majority of pensions in the public system (60 percent) were responsible for most of the effect.[18] Overall, as minimum wage recipients of either labour or non-labour incomes are concentrated in households in the bottom half of the per capita income distribution graph, the income gains distributed through minimum wage adjustments were unambiguously redistributive.

In a comparison with the internationally acclaimed *bolsa familia* programme, a particularly redistributive cash transfer that complements the incomes of eligible poor families and is not included in the constitution (and thus may deliver benefit values that fall well short of the minimum wage), boosting the minimum wage has proved to be much the stronger measure: from 2006 to 2011, the latter had an impact four times as great as the former[19].

It should be noted that many of the achievements of the period took place in the context of a positive growth rate. Yet it is also noteworthy that formal employment (stimulated by public policies) grew at a faster pace than the GDP — a situation Brazil had not experienced either in its fast-growing or its moderate-growing past.[20] It is also remarkable that, through the minimum wage policy, economic growth was able to deliver more balanced distributive results — a rather unfamiliar experience in the country's history. Moreover, redistributive policies taken as a whole increased the disposable income of poor, vulnerable and low middle-class households, and ultimately promoted growth itself.

In this regard, it is estimated that 75 million Brazilians, roughly 40 percent of the population, are directly affected by the value of the MW (because they live in households with at least one recipient of a minimum-wage-indexed income),[21] while 50 million live in households where beneficiaries of the *bolsa família* programme also live. That this massive income (re)distribution stimulated consumption is anything but surprising: in fact, over the last decade, domestic consumption was the component of aggregate demand that led growth rates in the country, well above commodity exports[22]. So, (re)distribution both benefited from and contributed to economic prosperity.

Top incomes (or inequality, according to Piketty)

In the wake of the publication of Thomas Piketty's *Capital in the Twenty-First Century*, new information on, and analyses of, the distributive question in Brazil have emerged, this time drawing on income-tax-returns data.[23] This recent work reveals a quite different picture to the one we have seen earlier, in the section above.

In fact, as well as a huge concentration of income at the top, the data reveals a stabilizing of, or even a slight worsening of, inequality when this is measured in relation to the income share of the one percent richest (from 2006 to 2012)[24] — which starkly contrasts with the declining inequality suggested by various indices based on household-survey data. The diverging perspectives may be explained by the fact that, while tax returns are a good source of information on the incomes of the rich and very rich, household surveys better capture the incomes of lower parts of the income distribution. Considering both databases, the complete picture discloses two "countries": one with intense tectonic movements up to the 90th percentile of the income distribution; the other, practically immobile, starting at that high level and climbing up to the last percentile and even higher (the 0.1 percent or the 0.01 percent richest, and so on).

The figures for the "immovable" landscape, taken on their own, are disturbing. The shares of the five percent, one percent, and 0.1 percent richest inhabitants amount, respectively, to 50 percent, 25 percent and 10 percent of the national income: in other words, they are 10 times, 25 times and 100 times as much as the proportion of the population represented by these people. But an important immediate consequence of this is that income concentration as a whole seems to emanate chiefly from the concentration at the top. For example, according to one study[25] which draws on both household surveys (PNAD) and tax returns, if the incomes of the richest 5 percent of the population were removed from the calculation, the Gini coefficient would shrink by about 40 percent; whereas the removal of lower incomes, those below the 25th percentile, would decrease it by no more than 10 percent.[26] These facts and estimations forcefully indicate the importance of paying attention to top incomes in devising policies aimed at a meaningful degree of income equalization.

Yet, redistributive policies that were implemented in Brazil during the "golden decade" hardly affected the relative position of top incomes. The income shares of those at the top are impervious to modest, albeit successive, minimum wage adjustments and the gradual expansion of educational opportunities. Taking education, for example, a recent study did not find any statistically significant relationship between schooling and the concentration of income at the top: the rich in Brazil are not rich because they have received more education.[27] Top income shares seem instead particularly sensitive to progressive taxation — that much is suggested by the post-war record of distributive achievements in the now advanced economies, a topic extensively discussed in Piketty's 2014 book.[28]

Interestingly enough, post-war Brazil seems to provide additional evidence of this connection, as data revealed by recent research has disclosed.[29] Progressive taxation in the country dates back to 1922–1924, but the period from 1945 to 1964, between the two authoritarian regimes, saw an unusual amount of tinkering with elevated marginal income tax rates. These jumped to 45 percent in 1945 from a low 25 percent in the previous year, and later peaked at 65 percent on the eve of the 1964 military coup. Over these two decades the basic rate incurred by lower incomes never passed 5 percent and even plunged to zero in the beginning of the 1960s. Not surprisingly, by the end of the period, the share of the one percent had plummeted to below 10 percent from well over 30 percent in the previous years. Other contributory factors might have been the unprecedented successive adjustments of the minimum wage, which amounted to a three-fold valorization in the 10 years from 1950 to 1960 (just for comparison, the recent two-decade valorization totaled just over 100 percent). As mentioned, with the military coup, the minimum wage would undergo its strongest contraction, while marginal income taxes would never regain the 65 percent level of the early sixties.

It comes as something of a shock that, with re-democratization, under the José Sarney government in 1989, the marginal tax rate declined from 50 percent (in 1988, the year of the enactment of the current constitution) to 25 percent, and the basic rate increased to 15 percent, implying a thorough paradigm shift in the financing of the state. After that time, the marginal rate would never pass 27.5 percent, even though the basic rate later dropped to 7.5 percent under the second Lula administration, in 2007.

At this point, as we try to connect advances and setbacks, a compelling hypothesis comes to mind: the social pact behind the 1988 "Citizen Constitution" (as the constitution is usually called in the country), while endorsing the expansion of social spending, failed to support this with the necessary redistributive funding. In fact, thereafter, financing of the state as a whole, and social expenditure in particular, would rely either on inflation (up to 1994) or disproportionately on regressive consumption taxes (and regressive public debt), a feature that would distinguish Brazil within the large group of developed and emerging economies in which it would henceforth be included.

Bets that were not placed

Throughout the world, the share of aggregate income accruing to the richest one percent has been growing;[30] Brazil is only leading the way. Worrisome as this seems — if we bear in mind the disproportional influence of the very rich on the political system and thus on decision-making concerning opportunities for wealth hoarding and protection — it also suggests resources for redistribution still untapped. Yet, in Brazil, progressive taxation has been a cause without sponsors in the political system. Not even parties on the political left have pushed for an effective shift in the progressivity of the tax system.

As mentioned above, soon after the enactment of the constitution, marginal income tax rates fell 25 percentage points and the funding of the state turned instead to regressive contributions and consumption taxes. The marginal tax rate now prevailing, 27.5 per cent, is still well below international standards. The regional average in Latin America hovers around 31 percent, while the OECD average reaches over 42 percent. Of course, this limits the decline in inequality that is currently obtained through income tax. The latter reduces the Gini index by 4.9 percent in Uruguay and 6 percent in the OCED area, but only by 2.8 percent in Brazil.[31]

Beyond this minimising of income tax, in 1995, a new law exempted distributed profits and dividends from taxation — a tax advantage that remains to the present day, distinguishing Brazil (and Estonia) as an authentic innovator in tax collection. This huge loophole, the alleged rationale for which is the avoidance of double-taxation (profits would otherwise be taxed at both company and individual levels) and the deterrence of investment, places Brazil among the countries with the lowest total tax rates on profits (28.3 percent against 51 percent in the OECD area, 57.6 percent in the US, 40 percent in Chile and 42 percent in Mexico)[32] and thus the highest retention rate (71.7 percent) in the developed and emerging worlds taken together. And yet, while "double-taxation" is in this case merely a question of allocating total rates among different entities (persons and companies), the preferential treatment given to profits did not lead to additional investment in the country.

Why is taxation on capital income and progressive taxation in general so important? Tentatively, we suggest "equity" reasons, which encompass both "pre-distribution" and "post-distribution" of market income. Reduction of inequality of wealth is one expected effect of taxation on capital income, an effect that comes into operation even before market income is generated (pre-distribution). The very fact that taxes on rents, profits and dividends exist imposes a reduction on the expected net return on wealth invested, and thus on the market value of assets — like real estate, land, financial assets and production capital — that generate these income flows. Moreover, an equalizing effect on labour incomes might also be expected as a result of progressive rates on top-incomes, as these tend to discourage the negotiation of very high salaries. Piketty reports that both rising asset values and the high wages of, say, hedge fund managers and CEOs are contemporary phenomena that underscore the explosion of inequalities the world over, and he compellingly associates these inflated gains with retrenchment of tax progressivity in the OECD area.

Turning to post-distribution reasons, one usual effect of tax progressivity on the distribution of disposable income is that it renders the latter less unequal than the primary distribution of market income. Also, progressive taxation is an important source of funds for financing the provision of public social goods and building up something of a social bequest (a proposal put forth recently by Anthony Atkinson), given the high income concentration at the top of the primary distribution.[33] Moreover, the very financing of the state in a context of fiscal strain, though not only under this circumstance, might benefit from the substitution of progressive taxes for public debt (thus averting increasing interest rates as well as inequalities therefrom) and income taxes for consumption taxes (thus mitigating social problems such as impoverishment).

Testifying to the fruitfulness of increasing tax progressivity in Brazil, simulations show significant positive variation in public revenues and negative variation of the Gini coefficient associated with different scenarios of increased progressivity, none of which is very radical.[34] The stronger scenario considered in the exercise, based on the withdrawal of exemptions for profits and dividends and the imposition of a top income tax rate of just 35 percent (below that prevailing in liberal Chile and the USA), already suggests the collection of an additional amount representing around one third of the current fiscal deficit, and a reduction of the Gini coefficient in excess of 4.3 percent. But the gap is certainly wider than that: property taxes are negligible, especially on rural property; bequests and donations are very undertaxed; and there is no taxation on wealth at all. The Brazilian tax system is a haven for the rich and the very rich.

The other area that did not advance significantly was the provision of public social services. Education and health care spending progressed very slowly — certainly more slowly than social security and the spending that would be required to deliver constitutionally mandated social rights. The SUS (the Brazilian National Health Service) is still an unmet promise, as over 50 percent of Brazilians' health care expenditure comes out of their own pockets. As for education, the country is still failing to cover needs at pre-primary, secondary and tertiary levels. Educational inequities between poorer and richer as well as between blacks and whites are still blatant. Quality of education is a major concern, especially in the public system below college level. In the PISA, a ranking based on an international proficiency exam sponsored by the OECD and applied to 15-year-old students in

60 countries, Brazil, the seventh world economy, has featured in the very lowest positions ever since the exam's inception, without significant improvement in the last decade. Under-funding is a key problem: per capita spending at all schooling levels is markedly substandard. There is, by now, a plethora of academic and non-academic material documenting these sad facts about education in the country.[35]

Universal public provision of quality social services has never been a policy priority in Brazil. And yet the reasons why such services should be prioritised abound. Social needs in these areas are overwhelming — a fact that had already attracted the attention of the representatives drafting the 1988 constitution, who included public provision of these services among social citizenship rights. Insofar as funding was not adequately tackled — the need for progressive financing in particular — the commitment turned out to be more for effect than effective. But services, beyond social needs and rights, are also critical in view of their distributive and productive effects and, of course, their political-economy underpinnings.

To begin with, welfare states that rely heavily on service provision are the most redistributive ones.[36] Education and health services affect people's well-being and agency generally speaking, but also, in more instrumental ways, their productive capacity, helping to sever the often-rigid connection between social origin and social destiny. Also, public provision of these services substantially affects employment and income generation, so much so that, in countries where provision is universal, public sector employment reaches over 30 per cent of the total.[37] In addition, employment in the public sector helps improve the average terms and conditions of employment as a whole, because public sector jobs tend to be regular, pay well and display a rather restrained wage distribution. (There is evidence that this is also the case for Brazil, where public employment is nonetheless meagre, 12 percent of total employment, and less than six percent is the share of jobs in public education and health care proper.[38]) So, the more public employment features in a country's labour market, the smoother the distributive features thereof.

A second tier of social service provision is the so-called care services (elderly care and early childhood education and care, or ECEC) and long-term active labour market policies of training and retraining. These interventions are multifunctional, and are crucial if the country is to respond to new social risks stemming from an ageing of the population, women's economic participation, and rapidly changing labour markets, spurred on by new technologies and the knowledge economy. The whole package of quality external care services and childhood development policies, together with policies for the upskilling of the workforce, has been termed "redistributive-and-efficient" for its contribution both to productivity and equality. These policies integrate the basic tool box of contemporary "social investment" policies.[39]

Again, the well-known potential of public provision of quality services notwithstanding, recent Brazilian experiments in social progress have not broken any new ground in these areas.

Moreover, also from a political-economy perspective, a policy that assigns priority to the expansion of public social services has important consequences, and this signals another missed opportunity in Brazil. To begin with, income gains connected with the redistributive growth experiment, which lifted poor families to the status of lower middle class, might have been reinforced by gains in well-being resulting from access to quality public services. By freeing those families from buying market services, public provision might also have assisted the birth of discretionary (i.e. beyond basic needs) income that might have turned into a source of economic security, if accumulated in savings or property. On the contrary, research has shown that a significant proportion of new entrants into the ranks of the lower middle classes have opted instead to buy health insurance and private education for their children[40] — very likely on the grounds of lack of trust in the extant public provision — from which they have anyway been withdrawing in the current crisis. Expansion of quality services might have reinforced their political defences, this time by creating a broad social coalition of roughly satisfied users including the middle classes. The history of robust welfare states in advanced economies is littered with episodes of cross-class coalitions supporting public provision of social services. As it turned out, the latter were key to the very shaping of a large-scale middle class in those countries.

Concluding remarks

It cannot be denied that Brazil witnessed a substantial process of redistribution over the 2000s, a unique decade in which there was an appreciable evening out of the country's economic inequality. This mainly resulted from the expansion of social protection entitlement and benefits, as well as labour market regulation, where a policy of minimum wage valorization, in tandem with effective enforcement, stood out in a context of win-win economic growth. The resulting decline in inequality basically reflected a rising floor, though the shrinking of education premiums also impacted on somewhat higher sections of the income distribution (but not the top). Of course, the process still has a long way to go, as income distribution remains highly concentrated by international standards, even leaving aside the very rich (if they are taken out of the calculation, Brazil is now the thirteenth most unequal country in the world[41]): further expansion and equalization of educational opportunity and entitlement to public benefits, as well as further labour market policies, are among the missing initiatives.

The action undertaken, it is worth reiterating, was far from trivial and should not be summarized as the mere introduction of residual safety nets to alleviate poverty (e.g. the *bolsa família* programme): the minimum wage policy proved to be the chief redistributive tool, as it cut across a significant section of the Brazilian population. For lack of an accepted category to classify the experiment, we suggest "(re)distributive growth", implying that public action through labour market regulation and transfers were key to the onset of a more socially balanced growth process, steered by domestic consumption. The minimum wage management, due to its affecting both labour and non-labour incomes, did most of the trick — and performed as a sort of guaranteed social wage.

However, in spite of the espousal of expansionist social policy, funding was not tackled in a redistributive way as (non-contributory) social policy continued to be financed by regressive taxation, relying disproportionately on poor and low middle-class tax payers' money. Moreover, as rich people do not pay their fair share in taxes — indeed, far from it — a potentially huge reservoir of resources for redistribution and the financing of badly needed social goods remains unexploited.

Alas, this seems to have been the "political economy" of the changes.

In fact, the "original sin" may be traced back to the 1988 constitution: anecdotal evidence as well as simple inference both indicate that social spending cum regressive financing was the cross-class social pact underscoring the Citizen Constitution. Representatives drafting the law were certainly aware of costs and benefits: on the one hand, indirect taxes are not easily perceived as the foe of equality; on the other, it is easier to build consensus around economic growth than progressive taxation in the search for additional resources for social spending. One should also consider that in Brazil, since the old-days of import substitution industrialization, the favourite strategy for all kinds of top-down "modernization" has been conservatism: an alliance with the incumbent elites that would largely accommodate their interests in exchange for modest social advances. Be that as it may, not even the left has been a champion of directing structural changes in the tax system towards more progressivity and thus international normality. The recent redistributive episode missed that opportunity as the governmental coalition favoured redistribution policies that left unscathed the relative and absolute positions of the wealthiest. More resources for education and other services would of necessity translate into more taxation of those at the top, but this alternative was not on the table.

Compounding the redistribution deadlock are the economic and political crises of recent years. The sad end of the PT era, when policy errors and corruption scandals ended up by contaminating people's perception of what a left agenda was about, and largely discredited it, was succeeded by an even bleaker time of austerity and unfulfilled expectations regarding the consolidation of a welfare state in Brazil.

Thus, in 2014, the international crisis finally reached the country and, in conjunction with what proved to be wrong economic policy wagers, delineated a context of tighter fiscal management. Political circumstances added to the already unpropitious economic scenario, only contributing to plunging the country into the worst recession in a century and also bringing out a thorough reversal of the government agenda. Among these circumstances are popular outrage with the Dilma Rousseff administration's austerity proposals, presented shortly after the president's re-election on a frankly expansionist agenda; large-scale corruption scandals involving the PT's officials and their efforts to buy a supportive parliamentary coalition; and tireless and effective political exploitation of these facts by the political opposition, including systematic blocking of any government legislative initiative to handle the fiscal crisis — all culminating with the impeachment of President Rousseff. The seeming political void was immediately filled by a conservative coalition, led by the former vice-president, which took advantage of the unique opportunity to advance (backed by a perfunctory parliamentary majority) an austerity and "fiscalist" project that would hardly gain the favour of the electorate were the latter to be consulted. Incidentally, the new ruling elite is widely perceived to be corrupt. PMDB, the new incumbent and PT's former senior coalition partner, is enmeshed in the biggest bribery scheme ever to be reported in the country, the very same that damaged the PT's reputation.

As a disturbing sign of the new times, fiscal adjustment, which should be no more than a short-term remedy to address an emergency situation, and in any case one that policy-makers prescribe with heavy hearts, is about to enter the Brazilian constitution in the form of a proposed freezing of fiscal spending in real terms for a 20-year period — another distinctly Brazilian invention.[42] The minimum wage valorization policy, as well as the linking of benefits to the minimum wage, are among the likely victims. Mimicking Ulysses, who ordered that he be tied to a pole whilst hearing the sirens, Brazilian politicians are choosing to tie their own hands: only there will be no sirens to be heard.

The long-term fiscal freeze seems to be the *pièce de resistance* in the development strategy concocted by the current political incumbents. Sadly, inequality is again off the radar in Brazil.

Acknowledgements

The author is grateful to Jaques Kerstenetzky and Antonio Kerstenetzky for comments and suggestions on this chapter, and to Graciele Pereira for assistance with references and figures.

Notes

1 Data from Ipeadata: www.ipeadata.gov.br.

2 Studies have estimated the impact on poverty of redistributive policies in the first decade of the new century to be almost on a par with that of economic growth, over 40 percent of the total reduction. See Nora Lustig, Luis F. Lopez-Calva and Eduardo Ortiz Juarez, "Declining Inequality in Latin America in the 2000s: The Cases of Argentina, Brazil and Mexico", *World Development* 44 (Februaru 2013): 129–141. See also Valeria L. Pero, Gabriela F. Cruz, "A Queda da Pobreza no Brazil: Mudanças no Perfil e Nos Determinantes no Início dos Anos 2000" (ANPEC Proceedings, 2015).

3 See Paul Krugman, *The Conscience of a Liberal* (NYC: W. W. Norton, 2007); See also Thomas Piketty, *Capital in the Twenty-First Century* (Cambridge, MA: Harvard University Press, 2014).

4 Carlos Antonio Costa Ribeiro and Maria Celi Scalon, "Mobilidade de Classe no Brasil em Perspectiva Comparada", *Dados, Rio de Janeiro* 44, 1 (2001); MDS, available at: <mds.gov.br>.

5 The decline in inequality as measured by the Gini index is confirmed when other indices, such as the Theils, and income shares of deciles of the distribution, are used as well. In the latter case, the data shows the rate of annual income growth of the lower deciles to be rising more quickly than that of higher ones, for every paired comparison. Cf. Ipeadata.

6 Branko Milanovic, *Global Inequality: A New Approach for the Age of Globalization* (Massachusetts: Harvard University Press, 2016), p. 320. The countries reported are the USA, the UK, Italy, Japan, Spain and the Netherlands. See also Sergei Suarez Dillon Soares, "O Ritmo na Queda da Desigualdade no Brasil é Aceitável?" *Revista de Economia Política* 30, 3 (July–September 2010): 364–380.

7 Increasing inequality in developed countries has been associated with concentration of market income growing at a faster pace than the increase in governamental redistribution (Organization for Economic Co-operation and Development, *Growing*

Unequal? Income Distribution and Poverty in OECD Countries, Paris: OECD Publishing, 2008). Among the multiple factors pushing market income inequality upward, fundamentally tied to globalization and technological change, are labour market deregulation and reductions in progressive taxation (see OECD, *In It Together: Why Less Inequality Benefits All*, Paris: OECD Publishing, 2015; Piketty, *Capital in the Twenty-First Century*; Milanovic, *Global Inequality*). In the case of emerging economies such as India and China, inequality has seemingly been fueled by market reforms, which have delivered rapid economic growth and urbanization in the context of agrarian economies, à la Kuznets.

8 See Maria Celi Scalon and André Salata, "Uma Nova Classe Média no Brasil da Última Década?: O Debate a Partir da Perspectiva Sociológica", *Revista Sociedade e Estado* 27, 2 (May–August 2012): 387–407; Francisco H. G. Ferreira et al., *Economic Mobility and the Rise of the Latin American Middle Class* (Washington, DC: World Bank, 2013) 203; and Celia Lessa Kerstenetzky, Christiane Uchoa, and Nelson do Valle Silva, "The Elusive New Middle Class in Brazil", *Brazilian Political Science Review* [s.l.] 9, 3 (December 2015): 21–41.

9 See Nora Lustig, Carola Pessino and John Scott, "The Impact of Taxes and Social Spending on Inequality and Poverty in Argentina, Bolivia, Brazil, Mexico, Peru and Uruguay: An Overview", working paper no. 13, Commitment to Equity, 2013.

10 See, for example, Sonia Rocha, "O Declínio Sustentado da Desigualdade de Renda no Brasil (1997–2009)", *Revista Economia, Brasília* 13, 3a (September–December 2012): 629–645; and Sergei Soares, "A Desigualdade de Renda de 1995 a 2009 e Tendências Recentes" (discussion paper no. 51, Center for Studies on Inequality and Development, Niterói , 2011), p. 14.

11 Actually, minimum wage valorization started in 1995, but it was during the Workers Party (PT) era, starting in 2004, that it became a governamental policy. As from 2007, adjustment should amount to the inflation rate for the previous year plus GDP growth rates for the previous two years.

12 A detailed description of these initiatives may be found in Javier Alejo, Guillermo Cruces and Cecilia Parada, "Desigualdad e informalidad en América Latina: el caso del Brasil", in *Desigualdad e Informalidad: un Análisis de Cinco Experiencias Latinoamericanas*, ed. Verónica Amarante and Rodrigo Arim, Libros de la CEPAL, No. 133 (Santiago de Chile: Comisión Económica para América Latina y el Caribe ((CEPAL)), 2015), pp. 129–162.

13 Celia Lessa Kerstenetzky and Danielle Carusi Machado, "Labor Market Development in Brazil: Formalization at last?" in *Oxford Handbook of the Brazilian Economy*, ed. Wener Baer, Edmung Amman and Carlos Azzoni (Oxford: Oxford University Press, forthcoming).

14 For an overview of the literature, see Alessandra Brito, Miguel Foguel & Celia Kerstenetzky (2017): The contribution of minimum wage valorization policy to the decline in household income inequality in Brazil: A decomposition approach, Journal of Post Keynesian Economics, DOI: 10.1080/01603477.2017.1333436. See also Alejo, Cruces and Parada, "Desigualdad e Informalidad en América Latina" for an analysis revealing the outstanding importance of formalization in the decline of wage inequality.

15 Lustig, Lopez Calva and Ortiz Juarez, "Declining Inequality in Latin America in the 2000s".

16 In real terms, spending tripled from 1988 to 2008 — most of the increment occurring in the initial period (1988–1990) and final period (2004–2009). Cf. Celia Lessa Kerstenetzky, *O Estado de Bem-Estar Social na Idade da Razão* (Rio de Janeiro: Elsevier, 2012), p. 295. The rhythm outpaced that of advanced economies when they were constituting

their welfare states in the twentieth century. Note, however, that inequality did not decline in the aftermath of the enactment of the constitution and explosion of social spending as the country was struggling with the debt crisis and hyperinflation. The international context was far from favourable to the Brazilian economy in the 1990s. To this must be added policy choices that generated social problems of their own, such as high levels of unemployment and informality in the labour market.

17 See Alessandra Scalioni Brito, "O Papel do Salário Mínimo na Redução da Desigualdade na Distribuição de Renda no Brasil entre 1995 e 2013" (Ph.D. thesis, Universidade Federal Fluminense, Niterói, 2015), p. 125; and Brito, Foguel and Kerstenetzky, "Minimum Wage Valorization Policy and the Decline in Income Inequality in Brazil between 1995 and 2014".

18 See Brito, "O Papel do Salário Mínimo na Redução da Desigualdade na Distribuição de Renda"; and Brito, Foguel and Kerstenetzky, "Minimum Wage Valorization Policy".

19 Brito, "O Papel do Salário Mínimo na Redução da Desigualdade na Distribuição de Renda ". The number of people involved and the level of benefits — in the case of the minimum wage, many more people, much higher benefit levels — account for the difference.

20 Nor have India or China, which have seen a growth in informal jobs instead.

21 Cf. Miguel Foguel, Gabriel Ulyssea, Carlos Henrique Corseuil, "Salário Mínimo e Mercado de Trabalho no Brasil", in: *Brasil em Desenvolvimento 2014: Estado, Planejamento e Políticas Púbicas*, vol. 1, ed. Leonardo Moneiro Monasterio, Marcelo Cortes Neri and Sergei Suarez Dillon Soares (Brasília: Ipea, 2014), pp. 295–324.

22 And, of course, it is unacceptable to quip that this move stimulated consumerism, as these sections of the population are historically deprived of access to basic consumption items, not to mention durables. See Celia Lessa Kerstenetzky, "Consumo Social e Crescimento Redistributivo: Notas para Se Pensar um Modelo de Crescimento para o Brasil", *Revista de Economia Política* 36, 1 (January-March 2016): 29–45.

23 Piketty's book could not include data on Brazil because the internal revenue service (the Receita Federal do Brasil, RFB) would not disclose it, alleging secrecy concerns. But following publication of Piketty's book, the RFB started to publish special tabulations of tax returns and a plethora of new research followed.

24 Marcelo Medeiros and Pedro H. G. F. Souza, "A Estabilidade da Desigualdade no Brasil entre 2006 e 2012: Resultados Adicionais" (discussion paper no. 2170, IPEA, Rio de Janeiro, 2016).

25 Own calculation based on data in Medeiros and Souza, "A Estabilidade da Desigualdade no Brasil entre 2006 e 2012".

26 Drawing on this combined database, another study, using the J-divergence index (which adds up the Theils T and L), calculated that the participation of the top 10 percent accounted for 67 percent, while that of the one percent accounted for 50 percent of total household inequality. Cf. Marcos Hecksher, Pedro Luis do Nascimento Silva and Carlos Henrique Leite Corseuil, *Preponderância dos Ricos na Desigualdade de Renda no Brasil (1981–2016)*, slides, colour (Rio de Janeiro: Seminário de Metodologia do Instituto Brasileiro de Geografia e Estatística, IBGE, 2016).

27 Marcelo Medeiros and Juliana Castro Galvao, "Educação e o Rendimento dos Ricos no Brasil" (discussion paper no. 2010, IPEA, Rio de Janeiro, 2015).

28 Piketty, *Capital in the Twenty-First Century*; Anthony B. Atkinson, *Inequality: What Can Be Done?* (Cambridge, MA: Harvard University Press, 2015).

29 Pedro H. G. F. Souza, "Top Incomes in Brazil 1933–2012: A Research Note" (unpublished manuscript, UNB, Brasília, 2014).

30 See Piketty, *Capital in the Twenty-First Century*, and Atkinson, *Inequality: What Can Be Done?*

31 Sérgio Wulff Gobetti and Rodrigo Octávio Orair, "Tributação e Distribuição da Renda no Brasil: Novas Evidências a Partir das Declarações Tributárias das Pessoas Físicas" (working paper no. 136, International Policy Centre for Inclusive Growth, Brasilia, 2016).

32 Ibid.

33 Atkinson, *Inequality: What Can Be Done?*

34 Cf. Gobetti and Orair, "Tributação e Distribuição da Renda no Brasil".

35 See, for example, Todos pela Educacao, *Anuário Brasileiro da Educação Básica* (São Paulo: Moderna, 2016), p. 156; OECD, *Education at a Glance 2016: OECD Indicators* (Paris: OECD, 2016), p. 510.

36 Gosta Esping Andersen andJohn Myles, "The Welfare State and Redistribution". 2007. Available at: <https://www.researchgate.net/publication/255583959_The_Welfare_State_and_Redistribution>.

37 Christopher Pierson, *Beyond the Welfare State? The New Political Economy of Welfare* (Cambridge: Policy Press, 2006), p. 273.

38 Kerstenetzky and Machado, "Labour Market Development in Brazil".

39 See Nathalie Morel, Bruno Palier and Joakim Palme, eds, *Towards a Social Investment Welfare State? Ideas, Policies and Challenges* (Bristol: Policy Press, 2012), p. 400; and Anton Hemerijck, *The Uses of Social Investment* (Oxford: Oxford University Press, forthcoming), p. 416.

40 Christiane Uchoa and Celia Lessa Kerstenetzky, "É a 'Nova Classe Média' Classe Média? O Que Diz a Pesquisa de Orçamentos Familiares" (discussion paper no. 66, Center for Studies on Inequality and Development, Niterói, 2012), p. 11.

41 The World Bank, *World Development Report: Risk and opportunity. Managing Risk for Development* (Washington DC: The World Bank, 2014), p. 362.

42 José Roberto Afonso, Felipe Salto and Leonardo Ribeiro, "A PEC do Teto e o Resto do Mundo", *Conjuntura Econômica* 70, 10 (October 2016): 23–24.

CHAPTER

4

Inequality of Income in Portugal

CARLOS FARINHA RODRIGUES

Introduction

High levels of economic inequality and monetary poverty have been a feature of the Portuguese income distribution for decades. However, between the mid-1990s and 2009, significant reductions in inequality and the different dimensions of monetary poverty were achieved: the Gini fell from 0.370 in 1993 to 0.337 in 2009; the poverty rate decreased 4.7 percentage points (hereafter pp) over this period, falling from 22.5 percent to 17.9 percent; poverty intensity, which measures how poor the poor actually are, also decreased. A particular important achievement was the almost halving of the elderly poverty rate in this short 16-year period: it fell from about 40 percent in 1993 to close to 21 percent in 2009. Unfortunately, this result did not extend to the child poverty rate, which remained high throughout (22.4 percent in 2009). These successes still left the Portuguese poverty indicators in 2009 at the high end of the EU member states' poverty tables.

The profound socioeconomic crisis that hit the developed countries from 2008 had deep effects in Portugal from 2010, and clearly reversed the decreasing poverty trends described above. The combined effect of the economic crisis and the austerity policies implemented, particularly following the 2011 Troika agreement, led to an unequivocal deterioration of the living conditions of the Portuguese population, and to increased poverty among large sectors of the population. Between 2009 (last pre-crisis and pre-austerity-measures year) and 2014 (the most recent year for available data), the Gini stopped decreasing; the distance between higher and lower incomes increased significantly, with the S90/S10 ratio rising from 9.2 to 10.6; and the poverty rate rose from 17.9 percent to 19.5 percent, a value close to those observed at the beginning of the century. In fact, it is necessary to go back to 2003 to find higher poverty rates than those estimated for 2013 and 2014. This deterioration in living standards is clearly measured by the increase in the poverty intensity indicator: its value of 30.3 percent in 2013 is the highest ever since publication of this series started in 2004. Finally, one of the most dramatic consequences of the economic crisis and austerity policies was the substantial increase in the proportion of children and young people living in poverty: the child poverty rate rose by more than three pp, from 22.4 percent in 2009 to 25.6 percent in 2013.

The evolution of material deprivation indicators is similar to those for monetary poverty given above, and indicates the worsening material situation of Portuguese households in this period. The Eurostat synthesis indicator for poverty and social exclusion also reflects this deterioration in the living standards and social integration of the Portuguese population: in 2009, 2.6 million were poor or socially excluded, corresponding to 24.9 percent of the population; by 2014 this number had risen by 215,000 to 2.9 million people (and 27.5 percent).

Although the general picture described above is well known and has been extensively discussed in economic literature[1], there remain many doubts in Portuguese society about the meaning and scope of the inequality, poverty and social exclusion indicators, their evolution, and the main determinants of their changes in recent years. The aim of this paper is to try to fill in these gaps by describing, in a simple and intuitive, but rigorous, way, the different indicators, their evolution and, when possible, their changing patterns.

Basic concepts: measuring inequality and poverty

The inequality, poverty and social exclusion indicators are calculated using the data collected by annual surveys which focus on the analysis of the households' monetary income. Since 2004, Portugal has been part of the European Union Statistics on Income and Living Conditions Survey (EU-SILC). It follows specific EU legislation and defines a harmonised system to produce EU-wide statistics on poverty, deprivation and social exclusion.

The starting point for evaluating the resources available to each household is the definition of the household's monetary income. The EU-SILC adopts the concept of net monetary income, which is defined as the monetary income received by the household and each of its members individually from work (wages and self-employed earnings), other private income (capital, property and private transfers), and pensions and other social transfers, all net of taxes and social security payments. The equivalised adult income is obtained from the household net monetary income using the OECD modified equivalence scale. The use of an equivalence scale harmonises the household data in terms of the household's dimension and age structure, and thus makes comparisons based on a single-person household possible. In each household, the OECD modified equivalence scale gives a weight of one to the first adult, 0.5 to all other adults, and 0.3 to each child. Therefore, the equivalised income of single-person households coincides with actual net monetary income, whilst in households with more than one individual, the equivalised adult income is equal to the income that would guarantee to each of its members, if they lived alone, the same benefits as the household provides to all of them living together. In reality, the equivalised income of each household member is calculated by dividing the net total household income by its size expressed in equivalent adult numbers. Thus, the value of the equivalised adult income is the same for each household member, irrespective of whether the individual is an adult or a child. The use of an equivalence scale removes, to some extent, the effects of economies of scale obtained by co-habitation and the extra costs associated with living with children.

The Gini coefficient is the best known and most widely used inequality indicator. Its high sensitivity to asymmetries in the central part of the income distribution is well known, making it especially suited to studying changes in incomes which are close to the average. For analysis of the tails of income distribution, either the highest or the lowest incomes, another type of indicator is used which is specifically designed for this purpose. A group of very simple and intuitive indicators of this type is based on comparison of the income shares of the different income classes along the distribution, and is used in the EU to compare inequality levels across member countries. For example, the S80/S20 ratio compares the income share of the two first deciles (the poorest 20 percent) with that of the highest two (wealthiest 20% percent) and, equivalently, the S95/S05 ratio compares the poorest five percent with the wealthiest five percent.

The main estimated indicator of the poverty of a population, or of any of its sub-groups, is the poverty rate. This is defined as the proportion of the population whose adult equivalised income is below the poverty threshold (or poverty line), which in turn is defined as 60 percent of the median equivalised income. This poverty indicator should be complemented by the poverty intensity indicator, which analyses how far below the poverty line the poor are. Poverty intensity is defined as the difference between the median equivalised income of individuals who are poor and the value of the poverty threshold, expressed as a percentage of the same threshold. The combined use of these indicators clarifies two important poverty dimensions, as the following simple example shows. If an individual has an equivalised income of 300€ and another has one of 100€, and the poverty threshold is defined at 400€, both individuals are classified as poor, although the economic vulnerability of the second is much higher than that of the first. The calculation of poverty intensity reveals this difference through the quantification of the relative distance between both incomes and the poverty line or, equivalently, by calculating the proportion of resources required for either of them to stop being poor (having an equivalised income equal to the poverty threshold).

Lack of monetary resources is a determinant in the evaluation of the living conditions of individuals and households, but is only one of the conditions that can lead to a position of social exclusion. The capacity of a household to satisfy a set of basic needs and purchase essential goods is an indicator of its level of material deprivation, the second dimension of social exclusion in the EU methodology. The EU has defined a group of nine items to measure levels of material deprivation:

1. Inability to face unexpected financial expenses
2. Inability to afford a one-week annual holiday away from home
3. Payment arrears (mortgage or rent, utility bills or hire purchase)
4. Inability to afford a meal with meat, chicken or fish every second day
5. Inability to keep the home adequately warm

6. Enforced lack of a washing machine
7. Enforced lack of a colour TV
8. Enforced lack of a telephone
9. Enforced lack of a personal car.

Individuals or households are materially deprived if they suffer from an enforced lack of at least three (any three) of the nine items, and they are severely materially deprived if the number of items is raised to (any) four or more. As for the poverty indicators, it is possible to complement the analysis of material deprivation with a measure of its intensity. Intensity of material deprivation is defined as the mean of the actual number of items of which individuals or households in privation are deprived. This concept of material deprivation is subject to some criticism, with evident problems connected with the number and choice of items, and also with the fact that all nine selected items[2] are equally weighted in the calculations.

The third dimension of social exclusion in the European statistical system relates to non-participation in the labour market by individuals of working age. A household is said to have of low (per capita) work intensity when its adult members aged 18–59 (but excluding students) work, on average, less than 20 percent of the total possible working time. The aim of this indicator is not to measure unemployment, but rather to investigate the degree of disconnection from, or non-inclusion in, the labour market of adult individuals.

The final concept defined in this section is that of the poverty or social exclusion rate. This is defined as the proportion of the population that is living in (at least) one of the three situations defined above: poverty, a low work intensity household, or severe material deprivation. This is a synthesis indicator for all three dimensions of poverty — monetary poverty, material deprivation, and weak connection to the labour market — and thus emphasises the multidimensional character of social exclusion. The importance of this indicator was enhanced by its adoption, in June 2010, by the European Council as the key indicator to measure the main social target of the Europe 2020 strategy: "to lift at least 20 million people out of poverty and social exclusion".

Although the adoption of a multidimensional poverty indicator represents a substantial conceptual step up from a one-dimensional one (the poverty rate), which is based solely on income distribution, it is subject to some criticism. Ironically, it is its three-dimensional definition that makes it particularly vulnerable to criticism. For example, it is questionable whether an individual who does not participate in the labour market, i.e., is a member of a low work intensity household, but at the same time has an equivalised income above the poverty line and is not materially deprived, is still to be considered as socially excluded.

Portugal: an unequal country

The starting point for this section is an evaluation of, and comparison between, the (average) equivalised income in Portugal and that in other EU countries using the most recently released Eurostat data. Figure 4.1 compares equivalised incomes across the EU in 2014.

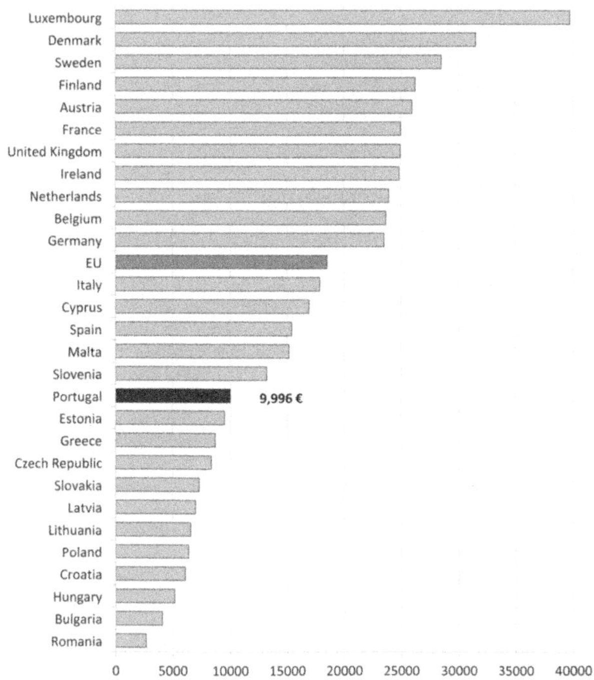

Figure 4.1 Average adult equivalised incomes in the EU, 2014 (€/year)
Source: Eurostat, EU-SILC, 2015.

In Portugal in 2014, the average adult equivalised income, i.e., the net average household income corrected for its dimension and age composition, was just below 10,000€ per year, or about 833€/month. This value was equal to only 54 percent of the EU average equivalised income.

The Portuguese equivalised income distribution shown in figure 4.2 gives the percentage of individuals who fall into each income bracket. The graph reveals a substantial asymmetry in the equivalised income distribution. On the one hand, it shows a concentration of the population in the lower income brackets, with 90 percent receiving an equivalised income of less than 17.6 thousand euros; on the other hand, it shows a wide dispersion of the highest incomes through a lengthy right-hand tail, at the end of which about 0.8% of the population receive more than 40 thousand euros.

Figure 4.3 again shows the (unequal) equivalised income distribution by plotting the proportion of the total equivalised income received by each vintile of the population, ordered by income.

The poorest five percent of individuals (first vintile/column) earned only about 0.9 percent of the total equivalised income, and the poorest 10 per cent (first and second) about 2.5 percent, whereas the wealthiest five percent (twentieth vintile/column) earned 16.2 percent of the total equivalised income generated. This graph also shows the distance between the different vintiles of the population in

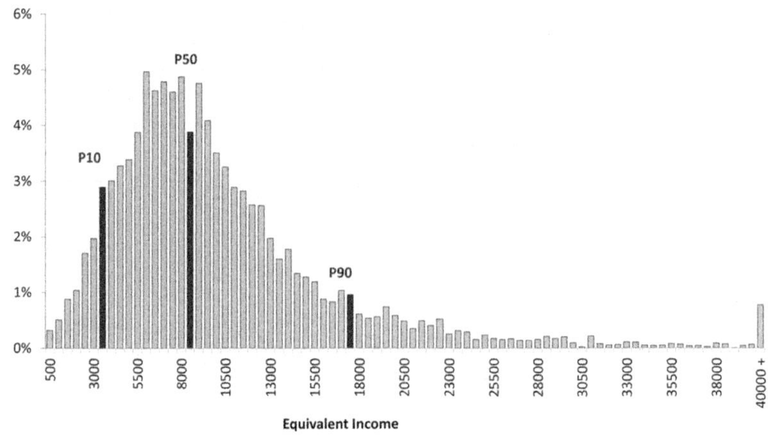

Figure 4.2 Percentage of individuals in equivalised income brackets, Portugal, 2014 (in euros)

Source: Statistics Portugal, EU-SILC, 2015.

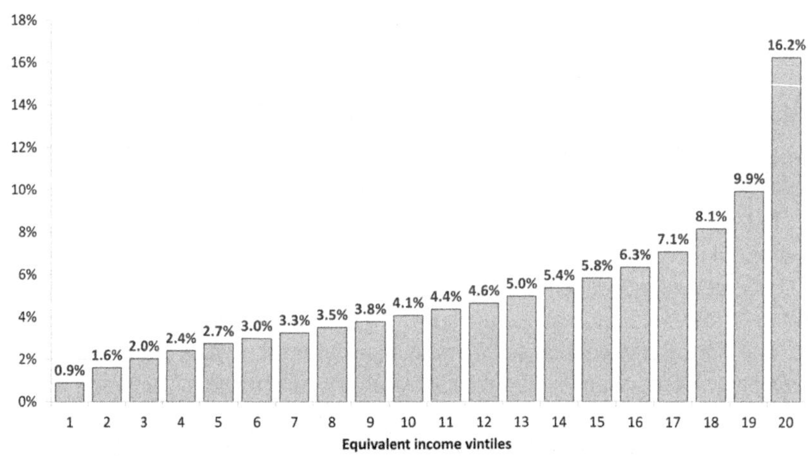

Figure 4.3 Proportion of equivalised income received by each vintile, Portugal, 2014

Source: Statistics Portugal, EU-SILC, 2015.

terms of equivalised income. For example, the wealthiest five percent earned about 18.5 percent more equivalised income than the poorest five percent; and the wealthiest 20 percent about six times more than the poorest 20 percent.

This assessment of Portuguese inequality needs to be put into context by comparing Portuguese inequality with that of countries with similar levels of economic development, particularly with those that are fellow members of the EU. Starting this process with figure 4.4, we use the Gini coefficient to compare income inequality across the countries of the EU in 2014.

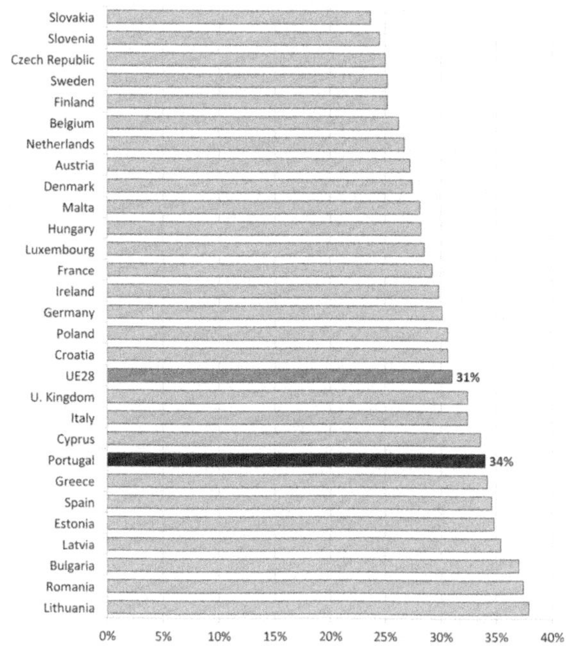

Figure 4.4 Gini coefficient of equivalised disposable income, 2014
Source: Eurostat, EU-SILC, 2015.

The Portuguese Gini coefficient is equal to 34 percent, three pp higher (more unequal) than the EU average of 31 percent. The results produced using the Gini coefficient (with its sensitivity to mid distribution incomes) can be complemented with an analysis of the S80/S20 ratio, which compares the tails of income distribution. Figure 4.5 shows, however, that the relative position of Portugal remains unchanged as the eighth most unequal EU country, with a S80/S20 ratio of 6.0 meaning that the equivalised income share of the 20 per cent wealthiest is six times that of the 20 percent poorest.

Portugal is thus one of the most unequal EU countries, whichever type of inequality indicator, or part of the equivalised income distribution, is used. Further insight can be gained from figure 4.6, where the Gini for market income (defined as what the equivalised household income would be if there were no social transfers) is compared across the EU.

If we ignore all social transfers, Portugal becomes the most unequal EU country, with a Gini 12 pp above the EU average of 52 percent. This is an important result that demonstrates the very significant equalising role of state and social transfers, particularly old age pensions, in Portugal.[3] If they did not exist, the Portuguese Gini would be almost twice as large (62 percent versus 34 percent) and the highest of the EU.

Although multidimensional poverty is a much broader phenomenon than income inequality, the two are closely related. This interaction is emphasised by the EU methodology through the selection, as the basic poverty indicator, of the

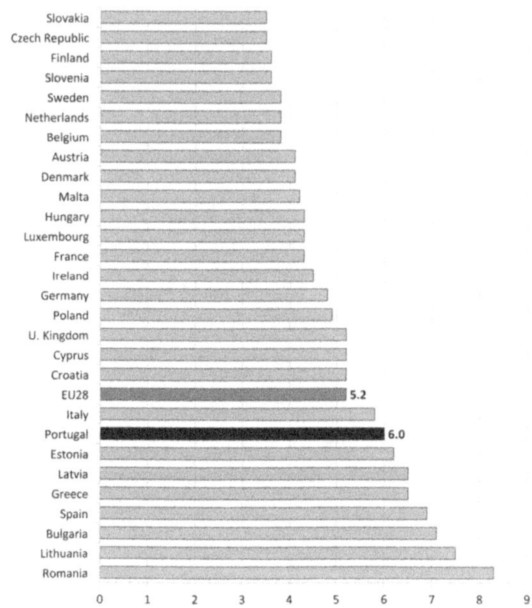

Figure 4.5 S80/S20 income quintile share ratio, 2014
Source: Eurostat, EU-SILC, 2015.

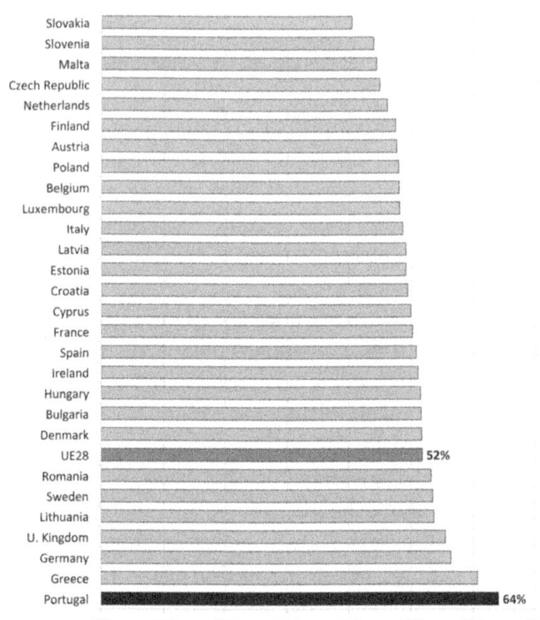

Figure 4.6 Gini coefficient of equivalised disposable income before social transfers, 2014
Source: Eurostat, EU-SILC, 2015.

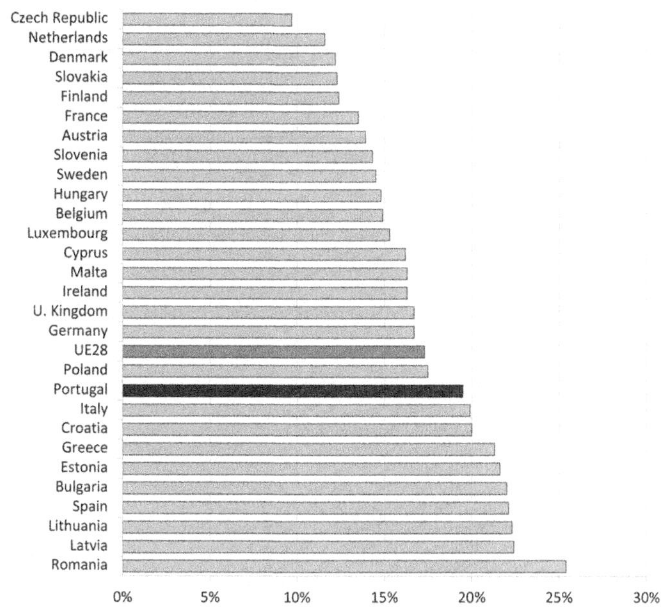

Figure 4.7 Poverty Rate, 2014
Source: Eurostat, EU-SILC, 2015.

monetary income poverty rate. This rate is strongly connected to asymmetries in the lower part of the income distribution because it is defined as the proportion of the population with an equivalised income lower than 60 percent of the median adult equivalised income. Figure 4.7 shows the poverty rate across the EU countries in 2014. The Portuguese rate of 19.5 percent is 2.3 pp above the EU average of 17.2 percent, and is clearly higher than the poverty rate of most of the more developed EU countries.

However, this indicator of poverty incidence offers a limited view of the actual scope of poverty and its effect on individuals and households. Table 4.1 goes further, with its characterisation by gender and age group: in 2014, more than two million Portuguese were poor, of whom more than half were women, 449,000 were children (aged 0–17), and 358,000 were elderly (aged 65+). The child poverty rate (24.8 percent) is much higher than either the national poverty rate (19.5 percent) or the elderly rate (17.1 percent), thus revealing the extraordinary vulnerability of this age group. Finally, poverty intensity was equal to 29 percent.

As discussed above, the poverty rate is calculated using an identical methodology across the countries of the EU, which makes the results easily comparable across borders; but that does not translate into a single definition of what being poor means, i.e., a monetary definition of the poverty line/threshold that is equally applicable to all EU countries. Instead, each country uses the same definition to calculate a country-specific poverty threshold (defined as 60 percent of its median equivalised income) leading to a poverty line that varies with respect to the level and distribution of national equivalised incomes, as figure 4.8 demonstrates for the year 2014.

Table 4.1 Poverty indicators, Portugal, 2014

		Number (thousands)	Poverty rate
Poverty Incidence	Total Population	2019	19.5%
	Male	925	18.8%
	Female	1094	20.1%
	Children (0-17)	449	24.8%
	Elderly (65+)	358	17.1%
Poverty Intensity		29.0%	

Source: Statistics Portugal, EU-SILC, 2015.

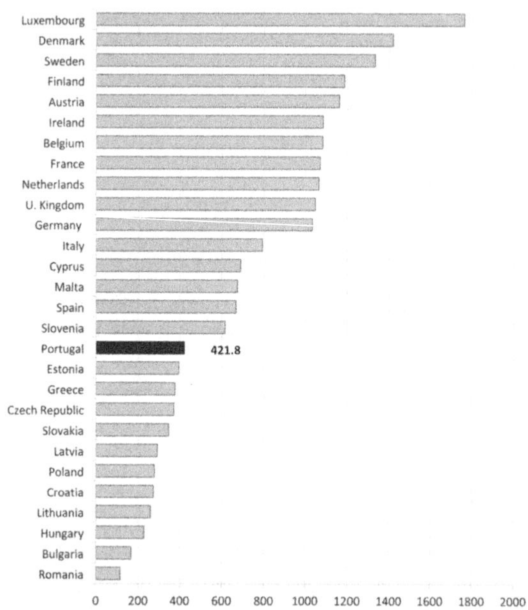

Figure 4.8 Poverty thresholds (€/month), 2014
Source: Eurostat, EU-SILC, 2015.

Comparing Portugal (seventeenth place) with the EU countries with highest and lowest poverty thresholds in 2014, Luxembourg and Romania, respectively, gives a good illustration of the limitations of international poverty comparisons, even in such an integrated statistical context. Being poor in Portugal in 2014 meant earning an equivalised income equal to or below 422€/month, whereas in Luxembourg the threshold was equal to 1,764€, and in Romania to a comparatively paltry 116€. The Romanian threshold represented just over a quarter of the Portuguese one, and only seven percent of that of Luxembourg. Nevertheless, the Portuguese threshold was still just under a quarter of that of Luxembourg.

The EU severe material deprivation indicator, the 2015 results for which are reported in figure 4.9,[4] confirms the relative position of Portugal in the EU, with a rate (9.6 percent) higher than the EU average (8.1 percent) implying a more severely deprived population. This result can be appreciated in table 4.2, which lists in detail the extent in Portugal in 2015 of the nine types of deprivation. The high percentage of the population that cannot deal with unexpected financial expenses (40.7percent of the total population), or keep their home warm (23.8 percent), or that are in arrears with housing bills (10 percent), should be particularly highlighted in a time of economic difficulties such as the one Portugal has been suffering; but the highest deprivation level (51.3 percent) relates to the inability to pay for an annual holiday. This last seems to suggest that the Portuguese are willing to forego an annual holiday in order to be able to afford other expenses or purchases that are be viewed as more essential or pressing.

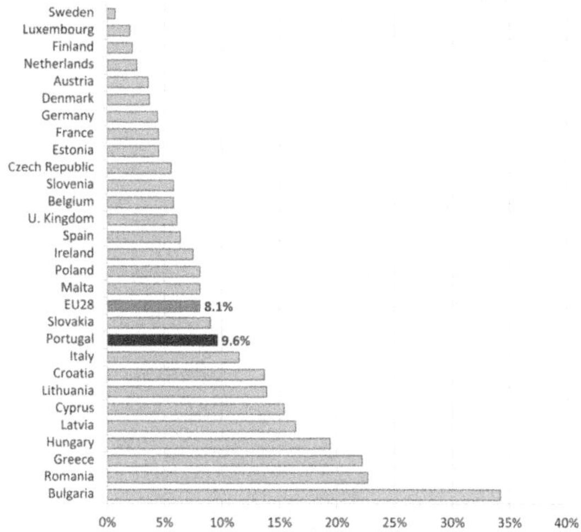

Figure 4.9 Severe material deprivation rate, 2015
Source: Eurostat, EU-SILC, 2015.

Table 4.2 Material deprivation per item, Portugal, 2015

1. Inability to face unexpected financial expenses	40.7%
2. Inability to afford paying for one-week annual holiday away from home.	51.3%
3. Arrears (mortgage or rent payments, utility bills or hire purchase)	10.1%
4. Inability to afford a meal with meat, chicken or fish every second day	3.5%
5. Inability to keep home adequately warm	23.8%
6. Enforced lack of a washing machine	1.2%
7. Enforced lack of a colour TV	0.3%
8. Enforced lack of a telephone	0.9%
9. Enforced lack of a personal car	8.3%

Source: Statistics Portugal, EU-SILC, 2015.

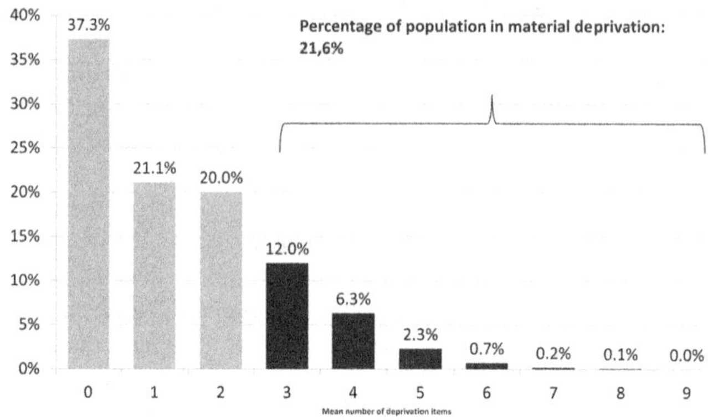

Figure 4.10 Mean number of material deprivation items, Portugal, 2015
Source: Statistics Portugal, EU-SILC, 2015.

Figure 4.10 shows the distribution of the population according to the average number of items they were materially deprived of in 2015. More than one third of the population did not lack any of the nine selected items; 21.6 percent lacked three or more; and 9.6 percent were in severe deprivation (four+ items). This suggests that just over 40 percent of the population could not afford either an annual holiday or unexpected financial expenses — the two items which stand out clearly from the group of nine items as the most frequently lacked. Conversely, only 3.3 percent of the population were materially deprived of five or more items which typically included meals, a car, a washing machine, a phone, and a TV — the five items least frequently lacked.

Finally, table 4.3 summarises the main material deprivation indicators by gender and age group. Again, it is the youngest group, the 0–17-year-olds, that is the most vulnerable, with a material deprivation rate of 22.3 percent that is not that different from the other groups, but with a much higher severe material deprivation rate of 11 percent. Deprivation intensity equals 3.7 items, meaning that those who suffer from material deprivation lack 3.7 items on average, which is close, but still below, the 4+ definition of severe material deprivation.

Being unemployed is usually identified as one of the factors most likely to trigger a poverty situation. However, the connection between the two situations may not always be either significant or relevant. One of the often-suggested reasons is that while unemployment is an "individual" variable, poverty incorporates and reflects the characteristics and resources of the whole household and all its members, and is therefore more a complex "collective" variable. It is not hard to find examples of unemployed individuals who are in opposite or very different poverty situations, depending on their household circumstances. The newer concept of "low per capita work intensity" enables a better connection between individual and household aspects of people's poverty situation by analysing the situation of all household members of working age together. Moreover, by including wider definitions of working practices, such as part-time, short-term contracts, and temporary work, this is a more inclusive and accurate concept than the one previously used and reflects current practices better.

Figure 4.11 lists the proportion of individuals aged less than 60 years who experienced very low per capita work intensity in each country of the EU in 2014. The Portuguese proportion (10.9 percent) is very close to the EU average (10.6 percent), and reflects the current high unemployment rate associated with the present crisis.

Table 4.3 Material deprivation indicators, Portugal, 2015

	Material deprivation	Severe deprivation
Total Population	21.6%	9.6%
Male	21.0%	9.5%
Female	22.1%	9.7%
Children (0-17)	22.3%	11.0%
Elderly (65+)	22.1%	8.2%
Deprivation Intensity	3.7	

Source: Statistics Portugal, EU-SILC, 2015.

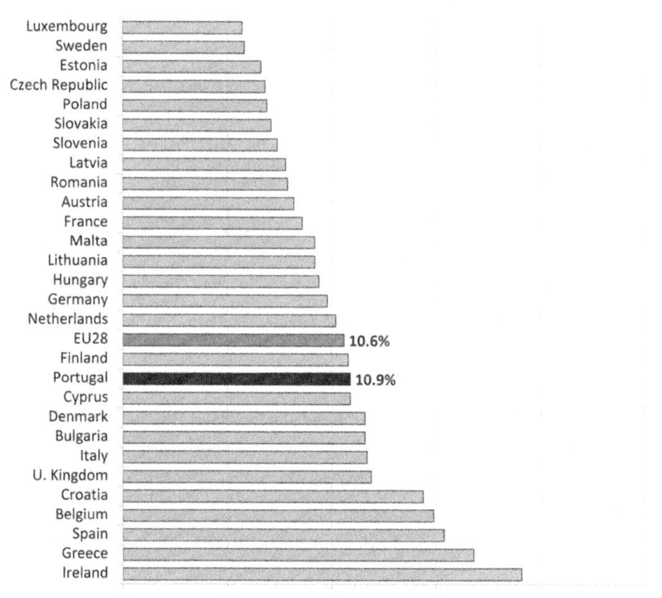

Figure 4.11 People living in households with very low work intensity (population aged 0-59 years), 2014

Source: Eurostat, EU-SILC, 2015.

The combination of all the three dimensions so far studied (monetary poverty, material deprivation, and low work intensity) leads to the poverty or social exclusion rate, the synthesis indicator defined in the first section of this chapter and used in EU methodology.[5] Figure 4.12 shows the value of this synthesis indicator for all EU countries in 2015. The Portuguese rate shows that 26.6 per cent of the population is in a situation of poverty or social exclusion, 2.9 pp above the EU average of 23.7 percent.

As before, table 4.4 analyses the Portuguese data in more detail. Following on from the previous analysis of each dimension that goes to make up the poverty or social exclusion rate, the most pertinent result is that the highest value of the rate is estimated for the youngest age group, the 0–17-year-olds. Its value of 29.6 percent, three pp above the national rate, reflects again the high vulnerability of

Figure 4.12 Poverty or social exclusion rate, 2015
Source: Eurostat, EU-SILC, 2015.

Table 4.4 Poverty or social exclusion, Portugal, 2015

Male	25.9%
Female	27.3%
Children (0-17)	29.6%
Elderly (65+)	21.7%
Total Population	26.6%

Source: Statistics Portugal, EU-SILC, 2015.

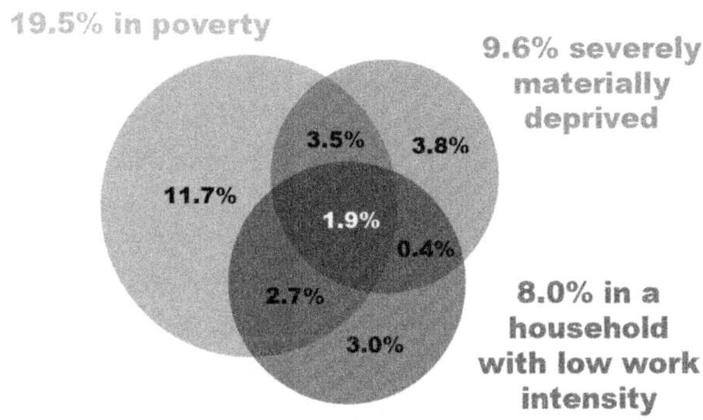

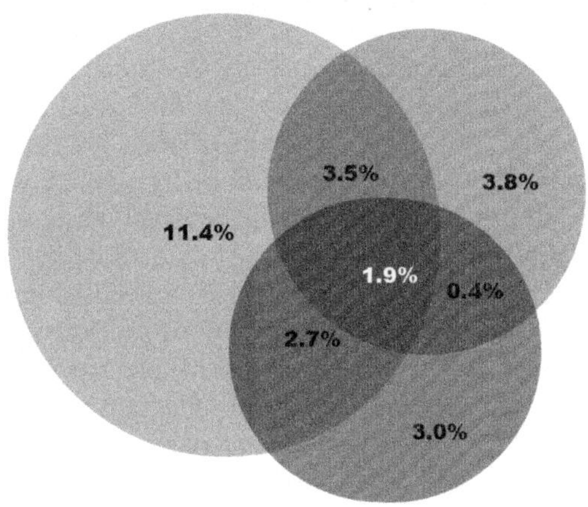

Figure 4.13 Poverty or social exclusion rate, 2015
Source: Statistics Portugal, EU-SILC, 2015.

this age group. A female social exclusion rate of 27.3 percent, 1.4 pp above the male rate, should also be emphasized, and possibly reflects lower work intensity.

Figure 4.13 provides a detailed analysis of the poverty or social exclusion rate in Portugal from a very different angle by identifying the intersection fields of its three dimensions. The biggest "contributor", by far, is the poverty dimension, with the other two dimensions making much smaller, and similar, contributions. Of the 19.5 percent of the population who are living in poverty, 11.7 percent, i.e., more than half, are neither in deprivation nor in low work intensity situations; conversely, 1.9 percent of them are affected by all three dimensions simultaneously. Of all individuals living in situations of either deprivation or low work intensity, less than half (3.8 percent and 3.0 percent, respectively) are affected by that dimension alone. Finally, 6.6 of individuals are affected by two dimensions at the same time: 3.5 percent are poor and severely materially deprived; 2.7 percent are poor and in a situation of low work intensity; but only 0.4 percent are both severely materially deprived and in a situation of low work intensity.

The different indicators analysed in this section create a more detailed portrait of the Portuguese reality in the latest year for which this data is available. Portugal is seen as a country with high levels of poverty and social exclusion in the EU context. Following the Eurostat methodology for assessing poverty and social exclusion, the numbers that define the country and need bearing in mind are:

- 2.8 million individuals (26.6 percent of the population) in poverty or social exclusion
- 2 million (19.5 percent) in poverty
- 1 million (9.6 percent) in severe material deprivation
- About 1.8 million affected by one poverty dimension, 0.7 million by two, and 195 thousand by all three.

The recent past and the effects of the crisis

The previous section was dedicated to an analysis of inequality and poverty in Portugal using the most recent available data, that for 2014/15, and placing it in the EU context. However, the resulting image of our country's inequality and poverty levels as above the EU average would be incomplete without studying their recent evolution. Furthermore, such a further study plays a relevant part in explaining the inequality, poverty and vulnerability situations that were identified.

Figure 4.14 shows the evolution of the average equivalised household income in real terms (2014 prices) in 2003–14, and how two different sub-periods are immediately identifiable. The first corresponds to the pre-crisis years of 2003–09, when the (real) average equivalised income grew at less than one percent per year. This meant a cumulative rise of 5.6 percent, compared to an 11.5 percent rise in the median equivalised income. The second sub-period, that for 2009–14, is a direct consequence of the profound economic crisis and the austerity policies adopted: the (real) average equivalised income fell by 12.2 percent in real terms, whilst its median value dropped by 10.0 percent.

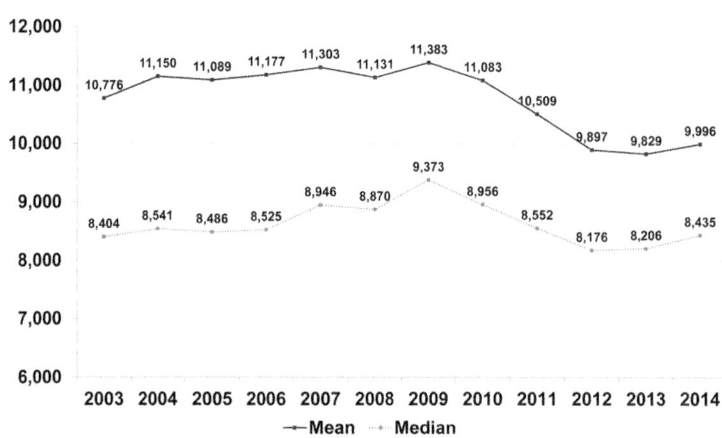

Figure 4.14 Average equivalised household income, Portugal, 2003–14 (in €, 2014 prices)

Source: Statistics Portugal, EU-SILC, 2004–15.

The evolution of the average equivalised income shown in figure 4.14 cannot reveal its redistributive impact in this period or identify the social groups that it benefited or penalised. This is a task that can be addressed by using table 4.5, with its EU-SILC microdata, to calculate the average equivalised adult income of each decile of the income distribution, and comparing their evolution in the two chosen sub-periods, 2003–09 and 2009–14.

The distinctive evolution in the two sub-periods detected in figure 4.14 for the real average equivalised income is confirmed along its distribution, but the key aspect of table 4.5 is how its effect varies across the deciles and sub-periods. In the first, 2003–09, the rise in the first decile (lowest 10 per cent of incomes) average income is almost five times that of the national average. This rise decreases steadily along the distribution, culminating in a fall at the tenth decile (highest 10 percent of incomes). In the second sub-period, all deciles see their average equivalised income fall, but this is more evident in the lower incomes: the decrease in the first decile income is almost double that of the tenth.

Naturally, these changes in the equivalised income and its distribution are reflected in the inequality indicators, such as the Gini coefficient shown in figure 4.15. In the pre-crisis sub-period, the Gini decreases by about four pp, and then changes little in the second. This is a particularly interesting illustration of how the Gini 'picks' the changes along the income distribution. In the first sub-period, there is a pro-equalising increase in average income: higher in the first decile (lower incomes) and progressively decreasing until it becomes negative in the tenth. Given that the Gini is more sensitive to changes in the central part of the distribution, its value decreases significantly in this sub-period. In the second sub-period, the percentage decrease in income is very similar in the central part (third to ninth deciles: between –12 percent and –10 percent), suggesting a certain 'stability' in this part of the distribution that leads to (only) small oscillations in the Gini.

Table 4.5 Average equivalent income by deciles, 2003–2009–2014 (in €, 2014 prices)

	2003	2009	2014	Variation 2003-2009	Variation 2003-2009
1st decile	2572	3292	2469	28%	-25%
2nd decile	4398	5206	4402	18%	-15%
3rd decile	5527	6452	5704	17%	-12%
4th decile	6657	7507	6760	13%	-10%
5th decile	7825	8688	7844	11%	-10%
6th decile	9017	10079	8988	12%	-11%
7th decile	10573	11623	10329	10%	-11%
8th decile	12721	13685	12137	8%	-11%
9th decile	16831	17056	15185	1%	-11%
10th decile	31594	30177	26127	-4%	-13%
Total population	10776	11383	9996	6%	-12%

Source: Statistics Portugal, EU-SILC, 2004, 2010 and 2015.

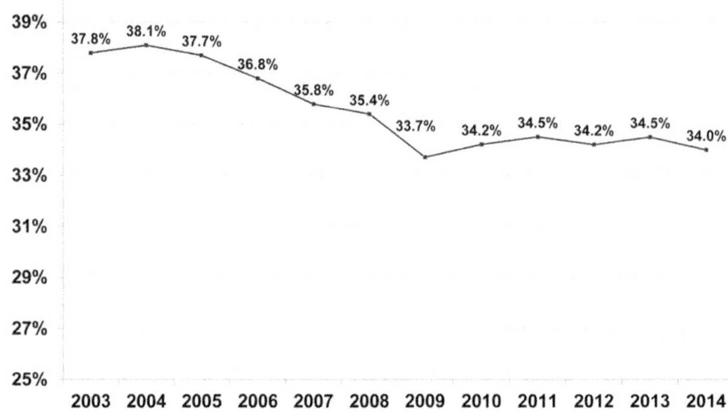

Figure 4.15 Gini Coefficient, Portugal, 2003–2014
Source: Statistics Portugal, EU-SILC, 2004–15.

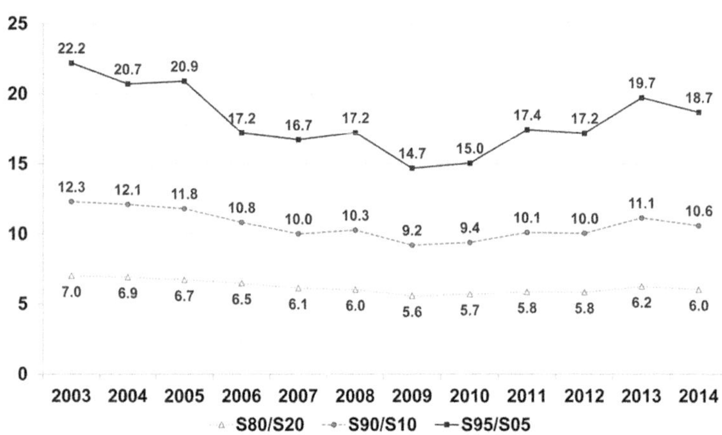

Figure 4.16 S80/S20, S90/S10 and S95/S05 ratios, Portugal, 2003–14
Source: Statistics Portugal, EU-SILC, 2004–15.

Hence, an analysis of the tails of the equivalised income distribution calls for other types of indicators – indicators that are more appropriate to evaluating asymmetries between poorer and wealthier incomes. These indicators, like the S80/S20, are part of the set used by the EU to compare income inequality across member states, and have been defined in the first section above.

As demonstrated in figure 4.16, the information provided by these indicators is rather different from (but complementary to) that provided by the Gini coefficient. They show increased inequality in the crisis sub-period, the more inequality, the larger the difference between deciles compared by each ratio: the S95/S05 ratio rises by 23 percent, from 14.7 in 2009 to 18.7 in 2014, whereas the 'narrower' S90/S10 'only' rises by 15 percent over the same sub-period.

The analysis arrived at by combining the inequality indicators in figures 4.14 and 4.15 suggests a clear decrease in inequality in the pre-crisis sub-period of 2003–09, which stops in the second. Then, in 2009–14 there is a surge in inequality based on the widening of the tails of the distribution, with a rather stable mid distribution. Furthermore, given that average higher incomes also decreased, the increased inequality is linked to a strong contraction in the lowest incomes.

Figure 4.17 shows how the poverty rate and poverty intensity changed between 2003 and 2014. Although the poverty rate decreased from 20.4 percent in 2003 to 19.5 percent in 2014, this reduction is not uniform, and the two sub-periods identified above still hold. During the pre-crisis period, 2003–09, there is an almost continuous fall in the rate, with a minimum of 17.9 percent in 2008–09. During the second, 2009–14, the poverty rate rises to 19.5 percent, its highest value since 2004. An analysis of poverty intensity reinforces this temporal distinction: an irregular drop in intensity until 2009 is followed by a steady rise to a maximum of 30.3 percent in 2013.

A further insight into poverty in Portugal can be gained through an analysis by age group. In figure 4.18, the opposing trends in child and elderly poverty rates in the 2003–14 period are clearly observable. When the national poverty rate falls in 2003–09, the child poverty rate also falls, but by less pp, whilst when the national rate increases in 2009–14, it too increases, by more pp and more quickly. Both situations point to the likely difficulties in designing and implementing specific public policies to reduce child poverty in Portugal, since the young constitute a particularly vulnerable social group, as already repeatedly discussed. It also emphasizes the penalising effect that austerity policies had on the young in the post-2010 years, which led to a maximum poverty rate of 25.6 percent for this age group in 2013.

An analysis of the evolution of the material and severe material deprivation rates shown in figure 4.19 confirms the results already discussed for monetary poverty during this period. Although variations in the material deprivation

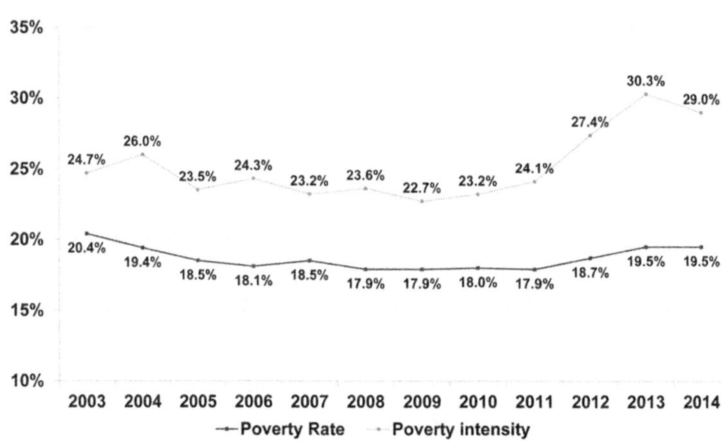

Figure 4.17 Poverty rate and intensity, Portugal, 2003–14
Source: Statistics Portugal, EU-SILC, 2004–15.

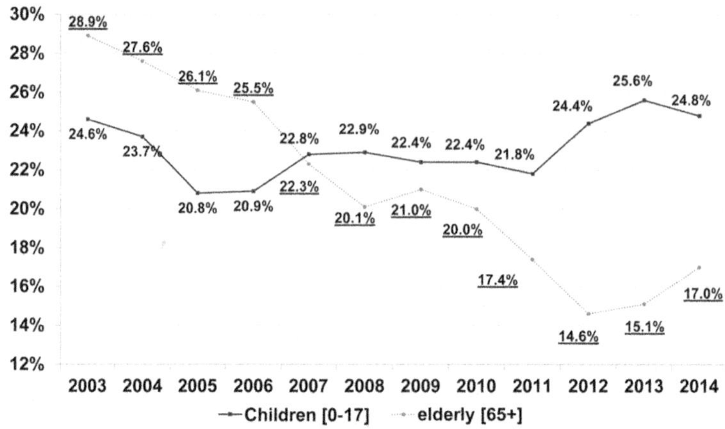

Figure 4.18 Child and elderly poverty rates, Portugal, 2003–14
Source: Statistics Portugal, EU-SILC, 2004–15.

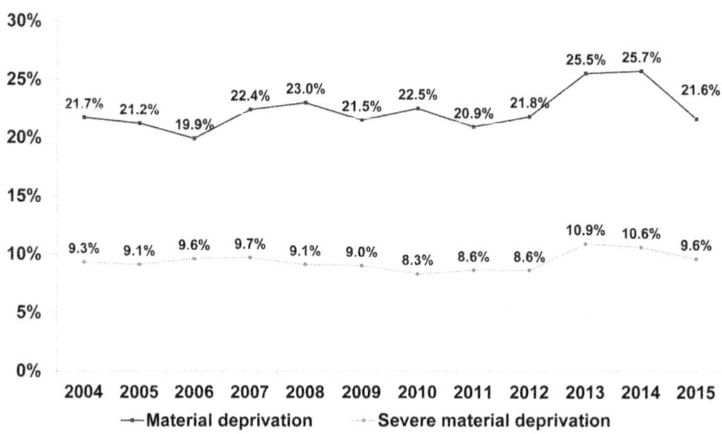

Figure 4.19 Material and severe material deprivation rates, Portugal, 2004–15
Source: Statistics Portugal, EU-SILC, 2004–15.

indicators are much narrower than those in the poverty and inequality indicators, there is still a noticeable increase in material deprivation in the crisis sub-period. This is mostly seen in 2013–14, when both material deprivation and severe material deprivation rates recorded their highest values since these series began in 2003, with a subsequent drop in 2015.

Last, but not least, the indicator that synthesises poverty and social inclusion rates summarises and confirms the trends in all its three dimensions (discussed above). In figure 4.20, it is possible to follow its decrease until 2009 (bar 2008), followed by a strong austerity rise of 2.6 pp in 2009–14 (and a remarkably sharp 3.1 pp increase between 2011 and 2013).

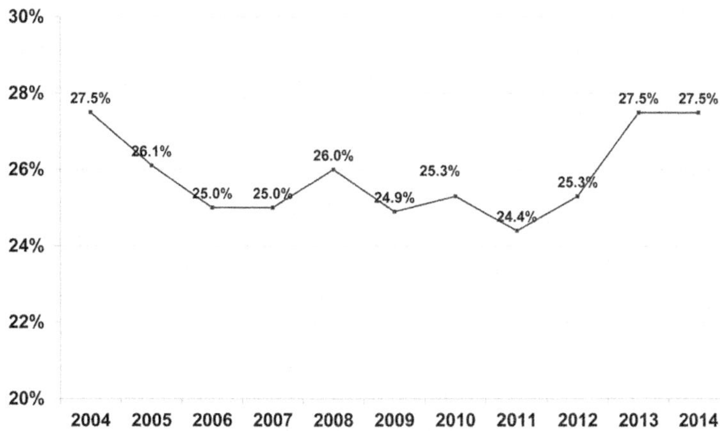

Figure 4.20 Poverty or social exclusion rate, Portugal, 2004–14
Source: Statistics Portugal, EU-SILC, 2004–15.

Which are the most vulnerable population groups?

An analysis of the evolution of poverty and social exclusion over time is not sufficient to get either a full understanding of these issues or to design social policies aimed at their sustainable reduction. It is also necessary to identify the most vulnerable groups, to know who the poor are, and to determine the resources gap that separates them from other groups.

Table 4.6 follows on from figure 4.18 and shows in more detail poverty by age group. It is the youngest group, the 0–17-year-olds, that has the highest poverty rate in 2014, and also suffers high poverty intensity. Conversely, the elderly (65+ years) have the lowest poverty rate and poverty intensity, following the considerable drop in their poverty already discussed. The successful implementation of (largely means-tested) social policies specifically targeting this age group, such as the social pension and the "Solidarity Supplement for the

Table 4.6 Poverty indicators by age group, Portugal, 2014

	Poverty rate	Poverty intensity	Distribution of poor population
0 – 17 years old	24.8%	31.4%	22.2%
18 – 64 years old	18.8%	32.2%	60.0%
65 + years old	17.0%	18.2%	17.8%
Total population	19.5%	29.0%	100.0%

Source: Statistics Portugal, EU-SILC, 2015.

Elderly" (CSI), certainly play a large part in ensuring they experience much lower poverty intensity. A recent study shows that even though the Portuguese population has been ageing quickly, the proportion of poor who are elderly has decreased significantly, and was equal to 17.8 percent in 2014.[6]

Table 4.7 shows the influence of household composition on the incidence and intensity of poverty in 2014, and confirms the vulnerable situation of a significant percentage of Portuguese children. According to the poverty rate, "single parents" (34.6 percent) and "two adults and three or more children" (37.7 percent) are the most vulnerable household types. The category of households with more than one child also has the highest likelihood of poverty intensity (above 30 of these households). In fact, it is households with two or more adults and without children, or with just one child, that have a lower poverty rate (below 17 percent of the national average). Indeed, having children as members of a household leads to a 5.6 pp higher average poverty rate (22.2 percent versus 16.6 percent poverty rate of households without children), and corresponds to 58.4% of the population that are poor.

An analysis of the incidence of adult poverty based on the figures for activity status presented in table 4.8 emphasises two important current characteristics of poverty in Portugal. One is the high poverty rate of adult individuals who are unemployed (42.0 percent), which reflects the high social cost of the increase in unemployment during the crisis period, but also that 25.5 percent of adult poor are

Table 4.7 Poverty indicators by age group, Portugal, 2014

	Poverty rate	Poverty intensity	Distribution of poor population
Single adult	24.4%	24.0%	11.3%
Two adults aged <65	16.8%	34.8%	8.9%
Two adults at least one aged >65	14.3%	18.2%	9.7%
Others with no children	13.7%	28.7%	11.8%
Households without dependent children	**16.6%**	**26.1%**	**41.6%**
Single parent	34.6%	31.4%	7.9%
Two adults + one child	13.7%	26.4%	10.8%
Two adults + two children	20.4%	32.1%	16.0%
Two adults + three or more children	37.7%	33.6%	6.3%
Others with children	26.1%	34.3%	17.3%
Households with dependent children	**22.2%**	**31.4%**	**58.4%**
Total population	19.5%	29.0%	100.0%

Source: Statistics Portugal, EU-SILC, 2015.

Table 4.8 Poverty indicators by age group, Portugal, 2014

	Poverty rate	Poverty intensity	Distribution of poor population
Employed	10.9%	28.9%	28.9%
Unemployed	42.0%	37.5%	25.5%
Retired	14.4%	17.0%	20.6%
Other inactive	31.9%	31.3%	25.0%
Total population aged 18+	19.5%	29.0%	100.0%

Source: Statistics Portugal, EU-SILC, 2015.

NB: This table only includes individuals aged 18 or older.

unemployed and suffer from very high poverty intensity (37.5 percent); the other is that being active in the labour market, having a job, is not enough to avoid a situation of poverty: 10.9 percent of the adults employed in 2014 were poor, or to put it another way, 28.9 percent of the adult poor actually had a job. Again, the lower retired poverty rate (14.4 percent) reflects the lower elderly poverty rate (17.0 percent) discussed in relation to table 4.6.

Conclusion

The figures discussed in this chapter present in some detail the recent evolution of Portuguese inequality, poverty and social exclusion. They also reveal the social impact of the recent economic crisis and of the post-2010 austerity policies, and how the latter contributed to the deterioration of living conditions and increased poverty among large sectors of society, as well as interrupting a cycle in which there was an ongoing reduction in inequality. The significant increase in the main inequality, poverty, and social exclusion indicators noted here shows that Portugal has gone back by about a decade and has widened the gap with respect to EU average levels for these indicators.

This study represents a small part of a wider analysis of the characteristics and causes of poverty and inequality in Portugal, and of what makes the degree of poverty so high and persistent. It excludes some relevant topics, such as the redistributive role of social and tax policies, the importance of the informal economy, and the processes of intergenerational transmission of poverty and inequality. However, it unequivocally underlines the need for a reversal of social polices implemented in recent years, for the adoption of new and more interventionist policies in the fight against poverty and inequality, for social and economic policies that coordinate "corrective" measures against existing poverty and inequality with "preventive" measures against new forms of poverty or generators of inequality.

Economic policies that promote a reduction in inequality are needed to achieve social justice, but also to inspire a model of development that encompasses every citizen, rewards labour, and leads to an economic system that is both fairer and more efficient. They must include measures to correct unequal income distribution, with rules on the sharing of rewards between investors and employees. Hence, it has to be recognised that the processes of wealth creation and distribution are not separate in time, but are instead simultaneous, and define the nature of the economic model itself. They also imply the rejection of development models based on low wages and limited workers' rights, favouring instead fair pay and rights in the work place.

These types of economic policies require active state intervention through the fiscal system, for example by increasing the system's progressive character and combating tax evasion and fraud, to compensate for the inability of the markets to deliver equality. Finally, they demand an active and positive role for social policies to combat poverty and social exclusion and guarantee adequate resources and living conditions for all.

Notes

1 See, for example, N. Alves, "A View on Income redistribution in Portugal and in the EU", *Banco de Portugal Economic Bulletin* (Winter 2012): pp. 41–58; J. Arnold and C. F. Rodrigues, "Reducing Inequality and Poverty in Portugal" (OECD Economics Department Working Paper 1258, Paris, OECD Publishing, 2015); A. B. Costa, *Exclusões Sociais* (Lisbon: Gradiva, 1998); C. F. Rodrigues and I. Andrade, "Portugal — There and Back Again, an Inequality's Tale", in *Changing Inequalities and Societal Impacts in Rich Countries: Thirty Countries' Experiences*, ed. W Salverda et al. (Oxford: Oxford University Press, 1998), pp. 514–540; C. F. Rodrigues, R. Figueiras and V. Junqueira, *Desigualdades Económicas em Portugal* (Lisbon: Fundação Francisco Manuel dos Santos, 2013); . C. F. Rodrigues, R. Figueiras and V. Junqueira, *Desigualdade do Rendimento e Pobreza em Portugal: As Consequências Sociais do Programa de Ajustamento* (Lisbon: Fundação Francisco Manuel dos Santos, 2013).

2 For a critical evaluation of the material deprivation indicators in a Portuguese context see, for example, C. F. Rodrigues and I. Andrade, "Monetary Poverty, Material Deprivation and Consistent Poverty in Portugal", *Notas Economicas* 35 (2012): pp. 20–39.

3 For a detailed discussion of these issues in Portugal see C. F. Rodrigues and I. Andrade, "Robin Hood versus Piggy Bank: Income Redistribution in Portugal 2006–2010", *Panoeconomicus* 5 (Special Issue): pp. 617–30.

4 The material deprivation indicators in the EU-SILC survey refer to the same year as the survey, unlike the monetary indicators, which refer to the income in the previous year. Therefore, the 2015 EU-SILC data reports 2014 income data and 2015 deprivation data, which explains the apparent discrepancy in the tables.

5 As already discussed, the interpretation of this indicator requires some caution. In figure 4.12, all data comes from the 2015 EU-SILC survey; but the income and labour participation data refer to the previous year, 2014, whereas the severe material deprivation data refers to 2015.

6 See C. F. Rodrigues and I. Andrade, "Ageing and Poverty: How Older Portuguese Adults Became Less Poor in the Noughties", *European Journal of Ageing* 11, 4: 285–292.

CHAPTER

5

Organizational Sources of Social Resilience and Progressive Governance: Portugal during and after Austerity (2008–2015)

TIAGO FERNANDES

Introduction

Although an existing body of research has shown that inequality grows during periods of economic recession, there is also much variation between countries in this regard. Portugal during the Great Recession represents quite an interesting — and exceptional — case. In Portugal, not only was the growth of inequality and poverty quite small in comparison with that in the other southern European countries (both those with and those without externally imposed austerity programmes), but also, in the aftermath of the austerity programme, Portugal elected a government which was unique in southern Europe. Constituted by a minority socialist party, but supported in parliament by two radical left parties, the PCP (*Partido Communista Português*, Portuguese Communist Party) and the BE (*Bloco de Esquerda*, Left Bloc), this government has pursued a pro-egalitarian response to the crisis and is committed to a clear ideological rejection of neoliberalism. Since November 2015, it has implemented a pattern of policy-making intent on reversing the effects of austerity and the harsher policies of the previous government. In sum, the case of Portugal is unique and raises two interrelated questions. First, what are the sources of a society's resistance to neoliberalism and austerity programmes? Second, what are the origins of anti-austerity and pro-egalitarian governments during times of austerity and in the aftermath of deep economic crisis?

This paper presents a new argument. Portugal represents a case where the impact of austerity was containd and eventually reversed by a shared committment to wider, progressive coalition-building among disparate social movements and between these and centre-left and radical-left political parties. This committment is an organizational legacy of the long cycle of political protest from the late 1960s to the mid-70s – the phases of liberalization of the previous authoritarian regime and of democratic transition that constituted the Portuguese Carnation Revolution. The years from 1969 to late 1975 were a critical juncture in which were formed the main organizational cultures of civil society (e.g. the unions) and left political parties which together would shape the repertoire of collective action in cycles of protest during the subsequent democratic period. Although before 2015 there had never been a broad-left coalition in the governmental arena like the one that exists today, we argue that such a coalition had always existed as part of a repertoire of possible developments within both the social movement arena and the ideological currents of the Socialist Party. These two strands, under the challenge that austerity posed to the quality of democracy in Portugal, converged politically, and this convergence explains both the smaller impact of the crisis in terms of the welfare of the population and the new path taken in the process of government formation.

This chapter is organized as follows: first, we offer a description of Portugal during the austerity and post-austerity periods in terms of the impact of the crisis on the welfare of the population and the evolution of government formation; second, we discuss and revise existing theories about the impact of austerity and financial crisis on the social welfare of the population, on patterns of inequality, and on government formation; and third, we present our own argument and develop an historical explanation of how organizational legacies created from the late 1960s to the mid-1970s shaped todays' anti-austerity modes of collective action by social movements and left political parties.

Portugal during and after austerity

Almost immediately after the fall of Lehman Brothers, in September 2008, a severe economic and financial crisis hit Portugal. The incumbent Socialist Party (PS) government initially implemented fiscally expansionary and Keynesian policies; but a few months afterwards, in tune with new European Union policy, it resorted to fiscal consolidation and procyclical measures. In order to meet the deficit limits imposed by the EU, a series of austerity plans were enacted between 13 April 2010 and March 2011, and these had the support of the main centre-right opposition party, the PSD (*Partido Social Democrata*, Social Democratic Party). They included upper limits to unemployment benefits; cancellation of temporary social protection and unemployment support programmes; wage cuts and cancellation of promotions for public employees; reductions in pensions and family allowances; the cancellation of all public investment; and the privatizations of the transportation sector.[1]

On 12 March 2011, the government announced another austerity plan and this foresaw further decreases in pensions, the imposition of higher taxes, and cuts to health and welfare services. This plan, which had not been discussed in parliament or with unions and employers' organizations, was tough, provoking not only negative reactions from the opposition on both left and right, but also large popular demonstrations organized especially by the main union confederation, the CGTP. The plan was rejected in parliament by all the opposition political parties, from the radical-left PCP and BE to the right-wing CDS (*Centro Democrático e Social*,

Social and Democratic Center) and centre-right PSD, and under pressure from popular demonstrations, the socialist government resigned.

The fall of the government led to the downgrading of the Portuguese debt and to interest rates above seven percent. In need of urgent financial assistance, the government, on 6 April 2011, requested international financial support. A bailout agreement for 78 billion euros was signed between a troika composed of three lending institutions (the European Community, the European Central Bank, and the International Monetary Fund), the Socialist Party, and the right-wing parties. The two radical-left parties opposed it.[2]

A Memorandum of Understanding (MoU) between the Portuguese government and the Troika included a further package of austerity measures, especially in the labour market, to reduce labour costs: a revision of the unemployment insurance system, the relaxation of laws guaranteeing employment protection, and more flexible working-time arrangements.[3]

However, the resulting austerity policies would prove to be even harsher than the measures foreseen in the Memorandum. The new government, a coalition of the PSD and the CDS, which had won the elections of June 2011 with an absolute majority, set out to radicalize the Troika's programme. Indeed, as early as the electoral campaign, the PSD had declared that its goal was to go beyond the Troika's requirements and to implement even harsher reforms. For the first time in Portuguese democracy, there was a full attack on the basic principles of the 1975 constitution. The PSD and CDS coalition rejected what it saw as the excessive presence of the state in the economy, and proposed abolishing the constitutional principles of free and universal access to health and education and the "fair cause" limitation on the dismissal of workers.[4]

The new government also set out to implement privatizations of the electricity and gas industries, the railways, and the telecommunications and postal sectors; deregulation of the labour market; a reduction in the number of public sector workers; a series of cost-cutting reforms in the pension system; cuts to the amount and duration of unemployment benefits; increases in class size in both primary and secondary education; higher fees for the national health service; and more increases in taxes (VAT, corporate and personal income).

Most of the cuts in salaries, pensions and welfare provision in general went well beyond the agreement with the Troika.[5] Although the MoU gave importance to employment security and flexible working arrangements, alongside active labour market policies and the need for improving human capital, and also emphasized social dialogue, none of these recommendations was taken into consideration by the government.[6]

With the adoption of pro-austerity policies, socio-economic and welfare indicators in Portugal worsened considerably. Unemployment rose from 8.6 percent of the labour force in 2008 to 15.3 in 2013, although in 2014 it declined to 12.2 percent (Eurostat). According to one study, the largest group affected by unemployment were people over 45 (30.4 percent of total unemployment in 2012), and those with low levels of education (60 percent of total unemployment). There was also a fall in the percentage of the unemployed covered by unemployment benefits (from 61 percent in 2008 to 46 percent in 2012).[7] Job insecurity also increased. Jobs offering permanent contracts decreased, while fixed-term contracts grew. In 2010, 37.6 percent of workers between the ages of 15 and 34 were working on fixed-term contracts; in the age group 15–24 years it was close to 50 percent.[8]

From 2011, indicators of inequality, which had been decreasing since the mid-2000s, started to grow. The share of wages in the GDP fell from 58.4 percent in 2010 to 55.6 percent in 2012.[9] In terms of the evolution of income distribution, between 2011 and 2012 the top decile declined. However, the share of the lowest deciles (1 and 2) did not show drastic changes in those years. Deciles 3 to 8, which corresponded to the middle classes and constituted 60 percent of the population, also kept their share of income during austerity. Finally, there was a high risk of poverty or social exclusion among children (aged 17 or below), with 28.6 percent of children falling into this category in 2011, compared with 24.4 percent of the population as a whole.[10]

At the same time, it should be stressed that Portugal performed better than most of its southern European counterparts. The impact of the crisis was less severe than in the other countries of the region, even when compared to countries which did not undergo an austerity program, like Spain and Italy. According to Gutiérrez, Portugal was the best performer in terms of employment rates. In 2013, Greece had a rate of employment of 53 percent, Spain 58 percent, Italy 60 percent and Portugal 66 percent. At the end of 2013, the unemployment rate was 27.2 percent in Greece and 26.1 percent in Spain, while in Portugal it was 16.3 percent and in Italy 11.4 percent. In terms of youth employment rates, Portugal looked better than any other southern European country.[11] The risk of poverty for 2011–13 was 17 percent in Portugal, 18 percent in Italy, 20.5 percent in Spain, and 23 percent in Greece. The severe material deprivation rate for the period 2005–12 rose in Greece from 12 to 20 percent of the population, in Portugal from 8 to 9 percent, in Italy from 6 to 14 percent, and in Spain from 4 to 6 percent.[12]

Other studies offer results congruent with the above patterns. In terms of relative poverty during the period 2009–13, in Greece this went from 20 percent to 45 percent of the population, in Spain from 22 to 25 percent, in Italy from 17.5 to 20 percent, and in Portugal from 16 to 23 percent.[13] The Gini index increased very steeply in Greece (from 0.321 to 0.364), rose slightly in Spain (from 0.314 to 0.318), stayed more or less stable in Italy (0.308 to 0.311), but declined steadily in Portugal, from 0.322 to 0.310. This picture is confirmed if one measures inequality using the income quintile share ratio S80/S20 (measuring the income share of the richest 20 percent relative to that of the poorest 20 percent). In Greece, this ratio rose from 5.27 to 7.77 percent, in Spain from 5.79 to 5.94 percent, in Italy from 5.07 to 5.20 percent, and in Portugal it declined from 4.95 to 4.75 percent.[14]

In terms of Eurostat data for 2014, Portugal also performed reasonably well on most indicators. The country's unemployment was the second lowest (12.2 percent) after Italy's (only slightly lower, at 11.8 percent), and was much lower than Greece's (25 percent) and Spain's (21.6 percent). Youth unemployment (those under 25) was the lowest (31 percent), compared with that of Greece (48.6 percent), Spain (46.7 percent), and Italy (40.5 percent). The same goes for female unemployment (12.6 percent), which was almost as low as Italy's (12.5 percent) and much better than Greece's (29.4 percent) and Spain's (23 percent). In Portugal, the number of people at risk of poverty or social exclusion was also the lowest in southern Europe (27.5 percent), with the figure for Greece being 36 percent, for Spain 29.2 percent, and for Italy 28.1 percent. In terms of inequality, Portugal's quintile share ratio (S80/S20) was the second best in southern Europe (6.2), after Italy's (5.4) but ahead of Greece's (6.5) and Spain's (6.8). Only measured by the Gini coefficient of disposable income was Portugal in the middle of the spread of results (34.5, the same value as Greece), which put it after Italy (32.5), but ahead of Spain (34.7).

But the singular position of Portugal in the southern European context was not seen only in the relatively less severe socioeconomic and inequality indicators. It was demonstrated by the fact that the first general elections held after the implementation of the Troika's austerity program resulted in the formation of a progressive, left-wing government with a clearly pro-equality, anti-neoliberal and anti-austerity program. This new government, supported by a parliamentary agreement between the minority government of the Socialist Party and two radical-left political parties, the PCP and BE, was and still is a unique phenomenon in Western Europe, where most socialist and social-democratic parties are in decay. This is also exceptional in southern Europe, where most socialist parties have moved to the right and espoused austerity and neoliberal policies at one point or another. Finally, it is also the first time in democratic Portuguese history that the radical left has supported a governmental budget and has been integrated into the Council of State.[15]

After more than a year of this government, many pro-austerity policies of the previous government had been reversed: public employees' wages and pensions had been raised and updated; privatization plans for public transportation and water services had been cancelled, the national minimum wage and pensions had been raised, the 35-hour working week for public employees had been instituted, and there were free textbooks in primary schools and tuition fees had been frozen. Although there were no plans for debt restructuring (as defended by radical left parties), and there was a commitment to keep Portugal within the European limits of public deficit, this was still quite a progressive government, running on an egalitarian agenda. In this vein, same-sex marriage was approved; and there were plans for a more progressive fiscal system and an increase in public investment in science and education.[16]

In sum, not only was the impact of austerity less harsh in Portugal during the more dramatic years of the crisis, especially during the implementation of the Troika's program (2011–2014), but the reconstitution of the government and party system after the neoliberal and pro-austerity cycle clearly went in a pro-egalitarian direction. These processes set Portugal apart from the other southern European countries. What explains this?

Competing theories

The literature on the social impact of the economic crisis has stressed the capacity for collective action of popular groups as one of factors in the resistance to, and reversal of, austerity. The more people participate in protests, and the more social movements mobilize citizens to disrupt the policy-making capacity of the state, the less harsh will be the impact of austerity and neo-liberal policies. And, in fact, in Portugal, participation in legal demonstrations almost doubled during the early years of austerity. According to a recent study, it grew from involving 4.2 to involving 7.4 percent of the population.[17] The number of demonstrations also grew, from 298 in 2011 to 579 in 2012 in Lisbon alone.[18] Research based on national surveys shows growth in all forms of social protest. The percentage of Portuguese signing a petition rose from 21 to 32 percent; participating in demonstrations rose from 12 to 24 percent; and participating in strikes rose from 11 to 25 percent.[19]

Comparative data, howeve, has shed doubts on the plausibility of this argument. In Portugal, the amount of protest was the lowest in southern Europe, as measured by the percentage of people participating in protests and by the number of protest events. Protests here were also less disruptive, with only a very a small number of protest events consisting of blockades, occupations or violent incidents.[20]

Institutionalist theories are also not fully supported by the case of Portugal. Ken Roberts, drawing on his work on the political and institutional consequences of austerity programmes in Latin America, argues that it is the position of the centre-left party during a crisis that determines the degree to which there is a subsequent reshaping of the party system. Specifically, if the centre-left party adopts neoliberal policies, thus going against its ideological tradition, and implements austerity, it will provoke a drastic realignment of the electorate which, in conjunction with huge popular waves of protest, will lead to the collapse of the existing party system — in the end to be replaced by populist party governments.[21]

At a first analysis, this argument seems to apply to southern Europe, especially to the Greek case. In Greece, prolonged austerity by centre-right and centre-left governments led to a massive movement among the electorate towards support for the radical left party, *Syriza*; whereas Portugal's socialists never fully supported the troika intervention. The PS abstained from supporting all the government budgets presented up until 2013 and, together with the radical-left parties, even proposed their constitutional review.[22] Still, Roberts' theory fails to account for the origins of these different ideological approaches among the socialist parties when it came to solving the economic crisis. Why did socialists and centre-left parties vary so much in their position regarding austerity policies?

In answering this question, the work of Robert Fishman is particularly relevant. Fishman argues that democratization pathways leave cultural legacies that shape future governments' policies and the degree to which political elites are open to protests from below. Specifically, revolutionary pathways to democracy result, in the long-run, in an open political system (e.g. Portugal); whereas pact- and elite-led transitions result in an elite political culture which is more closed to popular demands, and where measures to curb inequality and to promote the interests of popular groups are given less consideration (e.g. Spain).[23]

In this chapter, we focus on a different set of legacies than the ones identified by Fishman, namely, the organizational capacities and traits of the political parties and social movements representing popular groups.[24] During the troika years (2011–2014), Portugal was a country where protest movements tended to form cohesive organizations, create stable and broad coalitions, to have a national scope, and to establish alliances with unions and centre- and radical-left political parties.

Thus, in spite of the fact that Portugal ranked low for numbers of protest events and citizens participating in demonstrations, this specific form of organization- and alliance-building had a strong impact in terms of reversing neo-liberal policies, mitigating the effects of austerity, and paving the way for a centre-left progressive coalition in the aftermath of the 2015 general elections. This trait sets Portugal apart from the other southern European countries during the Great Recession.

Moreover, the period of austerity represented a break with the tradition of the Portuguese polity to be more open to protesters' demands. Passos Coelho and his ministers were proud of being more neoliberal than the already neoliberal troika programme, and of openly rejecting the legacy, ideology and programme of the revolution of 1974, as exemplified by their plans to revise the constitution of 1975, in which many of the principles of the revolution — in terms of equal rights and social protection — were enshrined. Instead, it was mainly because the disparate social movements were able to forge solid alliances and to draw support from the two main, radical left-wing parties that austerity was less harsh in Portugal. And this, we argue, is an organizational legacy of the revolution.

Finally, we also argue that the propensity of the socialist party to support social movements and to look for political and parliamentary support from the radical left was the result of a cultural and organizational legacy, but one which antedated the revolution. This culture was forged during the last phase of the dictatorship (1968–1974), in which, under the influence of Allende's experience in Chile and the common programme of the French socialists, Portuguese socialists joined left-Catholics and communists in a common oppositional activity. In fact, this culture of common activity lasted only until the end of 1974, and was dissolved by the path the revolution took, with a growing rivalry between the socialist and communist camps. But it continued to exist as the cultural and ideological basis of several factions within the socialist party during the democratic period. The conditions of austerity, and the discrediting of third-way and pro-market currents in the socialist party, offered an opportunity for this current to assert itself.

Progressive coalitions during the period of austerity

In spite of the fact that the only time the two union confederations had united in a general strike was in 1988, during the period of austerity these confederations were able to form an alliance. From 2010 on, five general strikes occurred as a result of in-depth collaboration between the union federations.[25] The general strikes of 24 November 2010, 14 November 2012 and 27 June 2013, as well as the 8 November 2013 public sector strike, were all called jointly by the CGTP and the UGT. And in the general strike of 22 March 2012, although the UGT did not formally take part, 20 of its main unions disobeyed the confederation and supported the CGTP.[26] The main socio-professional organizations of the police and the military were also important in calling for protest, and collaborated with public sector unions, as, for example, in their joint demonstration on 12 November 2011.

Collaboration between protest movements, for example, between workers in insecure jobs, anti-globalization groups, and unions, were also common. Unions and anti-austerity social movements joined and mobilized their constituents for each other's protest events. This was the case with the massive demonstrations of 12 March 2011 (the so-called Desperate Generation protests, initially called by workers in insecure jobs using social media and the internet) and of 15 October 2011 (the Day of Global Action, organized by anti-globalization movements), both of which saw the participation of unions, especially the CGTP. In addition, several demonstrations organized by unions were supported and joined by social movement organizations. The CGTP demonstration on 29 September 2012 had the support of the QSLT Platform (*Que se Lixe a Troika*, Screw the Troika);[27] and the general strike of 14 November 2012 was joined by social movements like *Precários Inflexíveis* (Inflexible Precarious), *Estudantes pela Greve* (Students for Strike action), Platform 15 October (P-15O), and the 12 March Movement (M12M).[28]

As a consequence, organizations of those living in an insecure economic environment, like *Precários Infléxíveis*, developed permanent relationships not only with the CGTP, but also with women's and pensioners' associations.[29] And because of the participation of other social movements in their protest events, unions incorporated marches and demonstrations into their repertoires of protest, in addition to strikes.[30]

Social movements were able to draw support from the radical-left parties, the PCP and the BE. During the crisis, the PCP showed that it had solid organic links with organizations like the CGTP (as of 2013, 60 percent of communist parliament candidates were also members of a trade union), the *Confederação Nacional de Agricultores* (National Farmers' Confederation, the CNA), the National Confederation of Pensioners and Elders (MURPI), and cooperative associations. It also stimulated action through its ancillary youth and women's organizations.[31]

In addition, after the emergence of the "global justice" movements in the early 2000s, the BE created permanent links with these anti-globalization and other social movements[32]. During the first May Day celebration, in 2007, it furnished logistical and material support for the mobilization of movements of those experiencing economic insecurity (FERVE, *Precários Inflexíveis*, and the precarious performing artists' groups). For instance, in early February 2011, it launched a campaign with the slogan "Insecurity is not the future" on small advertising billboards. The BE was also fundamental in the drafting of legislative proposals supporting these groups' demands. Leaders of some of the anti-insecurity movements also became members of the the BE's management.[33]

The availability as allies of these two radical-left parties, which together held almost 20 percent of parliamentary seats, was a valuable resource for the effectiveness of protest, and thus for mitigating the effects of austerity policies. All major demonstrations during the implementation of the troika program had the participation of the BE and the PCP. In the demonstration of 21 September 2012, when thousands of people protested in front of the presidential palace, asking for the dismissal of the government, there was a significant presence of MPs from the BE and the PCP.[34] And at the 2 March 2013 protest march organized nationally by the *Que se Lixe a Troika* platform (its member associations included groups of workers in insecure employment, the CGTP, gay rights organizations, and even military associations), there were also several PCP, BE and even PS members of parliament.[35]

MPs from these parties were also instrumental in securing the partial approval of a law against job insecurity. FERVE and *Precários Inflexíveis* (PI) proposed this law on 19 April 2011. In Portugal, since 2003, citizens had had the right, enshrined in the Portuguese constitution (Article 167), to launch legislative initiatives, as long as they gathered a minimum of 35,000 signatures from individuals. This was used to present the *Lei Contra a Precariedade* (Law against Job Insecurity).[36]

But social movements were also able to find allies in the Socialist Party. In early 2012, MPs from the PS and the BE developed a successful joint petition to the constitutional court seeking to reverse provisions in that year's budget, especially regarding public sector cuts in salaries, pensions and summer and Christmas bonuses for lower paid workers. And after April 2013, the strategic orientation adopted by the PS was to join with the radical left in rejecting all the budgets set before parliament.[37]

Manifestos and public declarations against austerity by prominent socialist politicians appeared at crucial moments, also calling for protest. On 11 November 2011, the *Manifesto em Defesa da Democracia, Igualdade e Serviços Públicos* (Manifesto in Defense of Democracy, Equality and Public Services) was published. This resulted in the presentation of a petition to parliament which was debated during a parliamentary plenary session.[38] In addition, on the eve of the general strike of 24 November 2011, Mário Soares (socialist party founder, ex-prime minister and president of the country) and eight other personalities published a manifesto declaring that "this is the moment to mobilize the citizens of the left, who believe in social justice and in the deepening of democracy as ways to fight the crisis." This position was echoed in the pronouncements of radical-left parties.[39]

Another manifesto was published on 11 March 2014, the Manifesto 3D — *Dignidade, Democracia e Desenvolvimento* (Dignity, Democracy and Development), inspired by the famous expression of the three Ds of the Portuguese revolution (*Descolonizar, Democratizar, Desenvolver* (Decolonize, Democratize, Develop). It was signed by major centre-left figures, who also presented a petition to the Portuguese parliament asking for the restructuring of the public debt, more public investment and protection of employment.[40]

It was also common, during the austerity cycle, for protest events to lead to the formation of platforms for social movements, with the participation of centre- and radical-left political parties, which then organized further protests. These platforms were usually run on the basis of equality among their constituent organizations.

The first major protest event, the Desperate Generation demonstration of 12 March 2011, was the most spontaneous,[41] after a Facebook group called for protest via social media and autonomous groups started to appear in several cities.[42] In the aftermath of this activity, a convention of these groups created a national organization, the *Plataforma Movimento 12 de Março* (Platform M12M),[43] and this platform received support from the BE. Subsequently, the platform organized a national convention to discuss policy solutions to the economic crisis and participated in the national election campaign of 2011, demanding a citizen audit of the public debt.[44]

The most successful platform was the *QSLT*. Created on 27 August 2012 by a group of 29 activists from different movements and political parties, to prepare a demonstration scheduled for 15 September 2012, this was a much broader platform than the previous ones. It included the PI, the M12M platform, representatives of the PCP and the BE, the CGTP, socialist party MPs, civil society organizations like ATTAC, SOS Racism, women's and gay rights groups, workers' commissions and military officers' associations.[45]

The broad span of these platforms probably contributed to making Portugal the site of the biggest anti-austerity demonstrations, some of which comprised between 800,000 and 1.5 million participants (about 8–15 percent of the population) and achieved national recognition. The Desperate Generation demonstration of 12 March 2011, with 2–5,000 protesters, although initially called in Lisbon, spread to several other cities.[46] In the following year, the *Que se Lixe a Troika* demonstrations of 15 September 2012 occurred in all major cities of the country.[47]

It was after the massive *Que se Lixe a Troika* demonstrations that austerity was somehow defeated. Although the centre-right government held onto power until the elections of October 2015, it lost its capacity to implement policy after a major internal crisis in the aftermath of the protest, in which the CDS, the junior partner in the coalition, threatened to resign and bring the government down. The demonstration of 15 September 2012 occurred in part because, on 7 September 2012, the Prime Minister, Pedro Passos Coelho, announced a rise in the contribution of the employed to the social tax. This coincided with new measures of austerity being voted on in parliament and further divisions between government members — the former finance minister criticized the measures on television; and politicians of the ruling CDS party threatened to leave the government.

The effects of the protest cycle in the Socialist Party were also significant. As we have seen, it was common for many personalities from this party to support anti-austerity social movements and to participate in united fronts and protest events. But for a while this was not the official line of the party's leadership, or of its secretary general, António José Seguro, who even participated in talks with the government (with the support of the president) about forming a coalition government. Fearing such a move, a significant section of the party elite asked for Seguro's resignation, and in the aftermath of the 25 May 2014 European elections, demanded a change in leadership. Although the PS had won these elections, the margin of the victory was considered low by most PS elites. After an internal dispute in the primaries, Seguro was defeated by António Costa, the president of Lisbon's city council, and a politician coming from the left wing of the party.[48]

After the change in leadership, the PS made a clear left turn, and in the summer of 2015, during the electoral campaign for the next general elections, it ran on an anti-austerity agenda, declaring also that, should a right-wing government be elected, it would never support any of its budgets.[49] Although the PSD-CDS coalition won the electoral contest (with 36.8 percent of the vote), clearly ahead of the PS (32.3 percent), on 10 November 2015 the right-wing government was brought down in parliament by a vote of no-confidence from all the left parties (PS, PCP and BE). At the same time, these parties presented the president with a common agreement of support for a minority socialist government. This was guaranteed by the fact that, putting all their votes together, the left-wing parties had a majority of the votes and seats in parliament (the BE achieved 10.1 percent and the PCP 8.2 percent).[50]

In sum, it was the fact that the social movements and the centre-left and radical-left political parties were able to cooperate and find common ground for action during the troika years that not only caused austerity to have a smaller impact in Portugal, but also led to a radical shift in the pattern of government coalition formation. This, we argue, was the result of historical legacies which went back to the late 1960s. It is to this topic that we now turn.

Left-tending coalitional and organizational legacies in the making of Portuguese democracy

The radical-left parties in Portugal have, throughout the democratic period, always had a strong mass base, and have helped to organize protest and give voice to activists within state institutions.[51] The PCP emerged in the transition as the most successful mass party, always maintaining a solid organic link with the unions, the cooperative movement, and youth and women's organizations. And the Left Bloc, after its foundation in 1999, also established permanent links with anti-globalization, gay rights, and ethnic social movements and associations. Furthermore, the BE was a clear product of the revolutionary period, stemming from a joint initiative of small, non-communist left parties and revolutionary movements. Students and ecological associations, as well as some unions and workers' commissions, had solid links with the BE. This was reflected in the fact that almost one-third of the founding members had participated in trade unions or workers' commissions (autonomous, company-level workers' committees) during the revolution. Ideologically, the BE is a combination of traditional socialist policies (support for the welfare state, taxation of big capital, and struggle against trade deficits) and libertarian and post-materialist values (environmental protection, gender equality, gay rights, and anti-racism).[52]

The role of these two parties has been to provide a peculiarly Portuguese social forum, which was established between 2003 and 2006 with their active support, not only in terms of organization-building but also in decision-making structures.[53] The forum has also been a site for collaboration between old and new social movements. This collaboration includes new organizations like ATTAC, but its major participants — decisive for its success — have been old movements, such as anti-colonialist organizations, union confederations, and peace and women's rights organizations.[54]

Although the story of Portuguese democracy is usually told as one of exclusion of the radical-left parties, the PCP and the BE, this is only true if seen from the perspective of government formation and the executive. There are at least two other arenas where this pattern is not repeated, and where broad alliances between social movements and radical- and centre-left parties have been the norm. These arenas are: firstly, protest cycles; and secondly, PS intra-party dynamics, where there have always existed relevant factions defending the coalition of the left.

Despite rivalries between the radical- and the centre-left during "normal" times, protest cycles have always shown convergences of the left. A major example of this was the the organization of large, oppositional unitary demonstrations during the revolution of 1974–75, in which the PS, the PCP, the MDP-CDE (a unitary structure comprising communists, socialists and left-Catholics), workers' commissions, unions, and neighbourhood associations joined together in support of decolonization and workers' rights and against right-wing coup attempts (28 September 1974 and 11 March 1975). These demonstrations included the mobilizations of 1 May 1974, in which two million of the country's nine million inhabitants took part), and many other demonstrations through March 1975. As Cerezales has shown, the majority of demonstrations between September 1974 and March 1975 were of the unitary type. These were especially strong between April and May 1974, at the start of the revolution, and in September 1974 and May 1975, as counter-reactions to attempted right-wing coups.[55]

This repertoire of activities became deeply rooted in the Portuguese left parties and in civil society. Other unitary protest events were those of the late 1970s and early 1980s, when it was common for women's organizations to work together with local NGOs, as well as unions and peace movements, in anti-nuclear demonstrations.[56] Major protest cycles, like the demonstrations against nuclear energy in the 1980s, for the independence of East Timor in the 1990s, and against the Iraq war in 2003, are also examples of broad left-wing fuentism.[57]

Throughout the history of democratic Portugal, collaboration between unions and social movements has made the former willing to defend the interests of the non-affiliated. The first moment of this dynamic was the creation, in 1976, of the *Comissões Contra a Carestia de Vida* (Commissions against the High Cost of Living), formed by the CGTP together with local governments, neighbourhood commissions, local party structures, and women's movements.[58] During the democratic period, it has been also common for social movements to participate in strikes and demonstrations called by unions, defending the rights of non-unionized workers and groups like immigrants, women, and workers in insecure jobs.[59]

The participation of unions in local-level environmental protests has also been frequent. Although this type of protest has appeared mainly in small rural localities, unions have joined in 18.5 percent of these events since 1974.[60] There is also a tradition of community-based trade unionism which, since the late 1970s, has worked out grassroots alliances with workers' collectives, and also with other associational and cultural groups. This broad alliance is largely the result of the unions' leadership experiences during the revolutionary period.[61]

There is also in Portugal a strong tradition of creating broad left-of-centre progressive platforms similar to the contemporary QSLT platform. The MDP-CDE (*Movimento Democrático Popular-Comissões Democráticas Eleitorais*, Popular Democratic Movement-Electoral Democratic Comissions), which lasted from the late 1960s to the end of 1975, was such a case. The MDP-CDE was a popular-front party movement composed of communists, socialists, and progressive left-wing Catholics. It had been set up during the dictatorship to run in the elections of 1969 and 1973, and was influenced ideologically by the common programme of the early 1970s between French socialists and communists, as well as by the experience of left unity represented by Salvador Allende's *Unidad Popular*. These influences led it to espouse transition to socialism through a commitment to participatory democracy, nationalization and agrarian reform, a leftist programme that distinguished it right from its inception from its Spanish, Greek and Italian counterparts, which were much more moderate and closer to northern European social democracy. This explains much of this party's recurrent internal pushes to the left throughout the democratic period.[62]

During the revolutionary period of 1974–1975, the MDP-CDE took control of most municipalities, working with the emerging neighbourhood movement to purge old regime officials and develop housing projects. The MDP-CDE introduced consultation between local authorities and neighbourhood movements, and the alliances they made at this particular political juncture were essential in institutionalizing the decisive role associations came to have in future local governance and social welfare delivery .[63] Although socialists and left Catholics left the MDP in late 1974, the memory and example of a united front against the right and in defense democratic progressive values was never abandoned by factions of the Socialist Party, many of which had been active in the CDE structures since the dictatorship. Although many MDP proposals were defeated, they have occasionally become the dominant line of the PS. Several episodes illustrate this, like the conflicts between the leadership of founder Mário Soares and Manuel Serra (who supported an alliance of the PS-PCP and the revolutionary military), in December 1974, and the conflicts with the Trotskyists, in December 1975.[64]

But this line went into the ascendant at two points. The first was during the leadership of Jorge Sampaio, after 1989. A left turn took place in the PS, which allowed for coalitions with the PCP. This was first tested in local elections, especially in Lisbon, under the leadership of Sampaio, with a PS-PCP coalition working for a full mandate. In the local elections of 1993, the alliance was broadened to include two more radical-left parties: the PSR (*Partido Socialista Revolucionário*, Revolutionary Socialist Party) and the UDP (*União Democrática Popular*, Democratic People's Union), two of the founders of the future BE.[65] The second point was during the brief leadership of Ferro Rodrigues, in 2002, when a turn to the left again took place. António Costa, who became the first prime minister to rule with the support of the radical left, had always belonged to the Sampaio faction and worked closely with Sampaio and the communists in the city council during their coalition in the 1980s. Moreover, while he was president of Lisbon's city hall, Costa ruled Lisbon in coalition with the *Bloco de Esquerda*, as well as with a collection of citizens' movements.[66]

Conclusion

The experience of Portugal during the Great Recession represents an exceptional case. Unlike in other southern European countries, both ones the which underwent an adjustment programme (Greece), and ones which did not (Italy and Spain), social resilience in the face of austerity was much more robust in Portugal. The impact of the economic crisis itself, as well as of the neoliberal policies implemented by the PSD-CDS government, was much less severe. Not that the government did not attempt to pursue a radical neoliberal line; but this aim was restrained by two factors: the ability of civil society organizations representing popular sectors to form broad progressive aliances between themselves and to draw support from the radical-left parties, the BE and the PCP; and the willingness of the socialist party (PS) to reject neoliberalism and support for the right, and to look instead for parliamentary support from the radical left. Moreover, this outcome itself was the result of deep historical legacies, particularly the organizational strenght of the radical left forged in the social revolution of 1974, and the memory and experience of the united fronts the left had established after the late 1960s when opposing the dictatorship.

Acknowledgements

The author would like to thank the encouraging comments and criticism of Francisco Bethencourt, as well as of the participants in the conference on Inequality in the Portuguese-Speaking World held at King's College, London, 4–5 December 2015.

Notes

1 Catherine Moury and André Freire, "A Política e as Políticas de Austeridade: O Caso Português", in *Crise Económica, Políticas de Austeridade e Representação Política*, ed. André Freire, José Manuel Leite Viegas and Marco Lisi (Lisbon: Assembleia da República, Coleção Parlamento, 2015), pp. 123–4.

2 Maria da Paz Campos Lima and Antonio Martín Artiles, "Crisis and Trade Union Challenges in Portugal and Spain: Between General Strikes and Social Pacts", *Transfer* 17, 3 (2011): 387–402.

3 Pilar González and António Figueiredo, "The European Social Model in a Context of Crisis and Austerity in Portugal", in *The European Social Model in Times of Economic Crisis and Austerity Policies*, ed. Daniel Vaughan-Whitehead (Geneva: International Labor Organization, 2014), pp. 309–311.

4 Pedro Magalhães, "After the Bailout: Responsibility, Policy, and Valence in the Portuguese Legislative Election of June 2011", *South European Society and Politics* 17, 2 (2014): 20–22.

5 González and Figueiredo, *The European Social Model*, pp. 310–312; Catherine Moury and Adam Standring, "'Não Há Alternativas': Discursive Depoliticization and the Construction of Crisis Meta-Narratives in Portuguese Austerity Policies" (draft paper, FCSH-UNL, 2013), pp. 16–18; Maria de Lurdes Rodriques and Pedro Adão e Silva, eds, *A Execução do Memorando de Entendimento. Governar com a Troika. Políticas Públicas em Tempo de Austeridade* (Lisbon: Almedina, 2015), p.34.

6 González and Figueiredo, *The European Social Model*, pp. 309–10.

7 González and Figueiredo, *The European Social Model*, p. 312.

8 Elision Estanque, Hermes Augusto Costa and José Soeiro, "The New Global Cycle of Protest and the Portuguese Case", *Journal of Social Science Education* 12 (2013): 33.

9 *Ibid.*

10 González and Figueiredo, *The European Social Model*, pp. 311–312.

11 Rodolfo Gutiérrez, *South European Society and Politics* 19, 3 (2014): 386.
12 Gutiérrez, *Southern European Society and Politics*: 377 and 386.
13 Manos Matsaganis and Chrysa Leventi, "The Distributional Impact of Austerity and the Recession in Southern Europe", *South European Society and Politics* 19, 3 (2014): 201.
14 Matsanganis and Leventi, *South European Society and Politics*: 403.
15 Marco Lisi, "U-Turn: The Portuguese Radical Left from Marginality to Government Support", *South European Society and Politics,* DOI: 10.1080/13608746.2016.1225331, pp. 1–20.
16 Lisi, *South European Society and Politics*, DOI: 10.1080/13608746.2016.1225331: 13–15.
17 Lima and Artiles, *Transfer*: 150.
18 Guya Accornero and Pedro Ramos Pinto, "'Mild Mannered'? Protest and Mobilisation in Portugal under Austerity, 2010–2013", *West European Politics* 40 (2014): 1–25.
19 Inês Amador, "Protesto Político nas Democracias da Europa do Sul (Portugal, Espanha e Grécia): Uma Análise Comparada e Longitudinal (2002–2012)" (master's thesis in political science, ISCTE-IUL, 2013), p. 34.
20 D. della Porta, M. Andretta, F. O'Connor, E. Romanos, and M. Vogiatzoglou, *Late Neoliberalism and its Discontents: Comparing Crises and Movements in the European Periphery* (London: Palgrave Macmillan, 2016), pp. 178–180.
21 K. M. Roberts, *Changing Course in Latin America: Party Systems in the Neoliberal Era* (Cambridge: Cambridge University Press, 2014), Chapter 2.
22 Lisi, *South European Society and Politics*, DOI: 10.1080/13608746.2016.1225331: 9.
23 Robert M. Fishman, "Rethinking the Iberian Transformations: How Democratization Scenarios Shaped Labor Market Outcomes", *Studies in Comparative International Development* 45, 3 (2010): 281–310; Robert M. Fishman, 2011, "Democratic Practice after the Revolution: The Case of Portugal and Beyond", *Politics and Society* 39 (2): 233–267.
24 For an earlier statement of this argument see Tiago Fernandes, "Rethinking Pathways to Democracy: Civil Society in Spain and Portugal, 1960s–2000s", *Democratization* 22 (2014): 1074–1104; for organizational factors shaping social resilience see Peter Hall and Michele Lamont, eds, *Social Resilience in the Neoliberal Era* (Cambridge: Cambridge University Press, 2013), Introduction.
25 Accornero and Ramos Pinto, *West European Politics*: 19
26 *Ibid*: 19–20; Lima and Artiles, *Transfer*: 150.
27 *Público*, 30 September 2012.
28 José Soeiro, "Da Geração à Rasca ao Que se Lixe a Troika. Portugal no Novo Ciclo Internacional de Protesto", *Sociologia. Revista da Faculdade de Letras da Universidade do Porto* 28 (2014): 55–79.
29 Fonseca, Dora, "The Crisis in Europe, the Precariat's Movements and Trade Unionism: Differences and Possibilities of Cooperation in Action" (paper presented at the Conference of the Council for European Studies Conference, Amsterdam, 2012).
30 Soeiro, *Sociologia* 28: 71–73.
31 Marco Lisi, "Rediscovering Civil Society? Renewal and Continuity in the Portuguese Radical Left", *South European Society and Politics* 18 (2013): 21–39.
32 *Ibid*.
33 *Ibid*.
34 *Público*, 16 September 2012.
35 *Público*, 2 March 2013.

36 Dora Fonseca, "Precariedade Laboral e a Emergência de Novos Actores Sociolaborais: Os Movimentos de Trabalhadores Precários em Portugal" (paper presented at the Congresso Luso-Afro-Brasileiro de Ciências Sociais No. 11, Salvador, 7–10 August 2011).
37 Elisabetta De Giorgi, Catherine Moury, and João Pedro Ruivo, "Incumbents, Opposition and International Lenders: Governing Portugal in Times of Crisis", *The Journal of Legislative Studies* 21, 1 (2015): 54–74.
38 André Freire, "The Condition of Portuguese Democracy during the Troika's Intervention" (paper delivered at the conference Crisis Politics in Southern Europe: Challenges to Democratic Governance, Cyprus, University of Nicosia, 24 April 2014).
39 *Diário de Notícias*, 20 November 2011, p. 12.
40 *Público*, 11 and 19 March 2014.
41 Britta Baumgarten, "Geração à Rasca and Beyond: Mobilizations in Portugal After 12 March 2011", *Current Sociology* 61, 4 (2013): 457–473.
42 Dora Fonseca, "A Mobilização de 12 de Março em Portugal: Movimento Social ou 'Explosão'? Atores, Processos e Consequências", *Sociologia, Revista da Faculdade de Letras da Universidade do Porto* 24 (2012): 113–131.
43 *Ibid.*
44 Soeiro, *Sociologia* 28: pp. 55–79.
45 Accornero and Ramos Pinto, *West European Politics*: 15–17; Britta Baumgarten, "Why Did So Many People Suddenly Appear? The Success of the Portuguese 15 September 2012 Protests" (paper presented at the Political Science Seminar at FCSH/UNL, 2013); João Camargo. *Que se Lixe a Troika!* (Porto: Deriva, 2013); Soreiro, *Sociologia* 28: 72–23.
46 Soreiro, *Sociologia* 28: 71.
47 Baumgarten, *Current Sociology* 61: 1–3.
48 Filipa Raimundo and António Costa Pinto, "When Parties Succeed: Party System (In)Stability and the 2008 Financial Crisis in Portugal" (paper presented at the 2014 Annual Meeting of the American Political Science Association, Washington DC, 28–31August 2014).
49 Lisi, *South European Society and Politics*, DOI: 10.1080/13608746.2016.1225331: 12.
50 *Ibid.*
51 Baumgarten, n.d.: 13–14.
52 Lisi, *South European Society and Politics* 18 (2013): 21–39.
53 Baumgarten, n.d.: 13–14.
54 Cristina Nunes, "Expressões Alterglobais na Sociedade Portuguesa: Ecos Transnacionais de Novas Formas de Acção Colectiva?", *CIES e-Working Paper*, No. 104/2011.
55 Diego Palacios Cerezales, *O Poder Caiu na Rua. Crise de Estado e Acções Colectivas na Revolução Portuguesa, 1974–1975* (Lisbon: Imprensa de Ciências Sociais, 2003), Chapt. 4.
56 Maria Manuela Tavares, "Movimentos de Mulheres em Portugal Após Abril de 1974" (master's thesis, Universidade Aberta, Lisbon, 1998), pp. 60–70.
57 Interview with Henrique de Souza.
58 Interview with Manuel Carvalho da Silva.
59 Britta Baumgarten, "The Recent Protest Events in Portugal and Spain Compared — Is success only a question of organization?" (manuscript, CIES-ISCTE, 2014).
60 Elisabete Figueiredo and Teresa Fidelis, 2003. "'No Meu Quintal, Não!' Contributos para uma Análise dos Movimentos Ambientais de Raiz Popular em Portugal", *Revista Crítica de Ciências Sociais* 65: 151–173.

61 Elisio Estanque, "The Reinvention of Trade Unionism and the New Challenges of Emancipation", *South European Society and Politics* 9, 2 (2004): 253–283.

62 Vitalino Canas, "O PS: Que Partido é?" in *O Partido Socialista e a Democracia*, ed. Vitalino Canas, (Porto: Celta, 2005), p. 32; Susana Martins, "A Fundação do Partido Socialista em 1973" in *O Partido Socialista e a Democracia*, ed. Vitalino Canas, (Porto: Celta, 2005), pp. 29–50.

63 Tiago Fernandes and Rui Branco, "Social Revolution Outcomes: Civil Society in Portugal, 1974–2000s", in *Civil Society, Inequality and Democracy: Cross-Regional Comparisons, Comparative Politics Series*, ed. Tiago Fernandes, Rui Branco and Michael Bernhard, April 2017.

64 Canas, *O Partido Socialista e a Democracia*, p. 32.

65 Manuel Braga da Cruz, 2005, "O Partido Socialista Português. 20 Anos em Evolução (1973–1993)", in *O Partido Socialista e a Democracia*, ed. Vitalino Canas (Porto: Celta, 2005).

66 Raimundo and Pinto, *Stability and the 2008 Financial Crisis*, p. 12.

CHAPTER

6

The *Estado Novo* and the Making of Portugal's Unequal Modernity

PEDRO RAMOS PINTO

By the time the ailing Republican system was brought to an end by the 1926 military coup, Portugal was undergoing a rapid, but uneven, process of modernisation. Still a predominantly rural nation, poor and largely illiterate, it was however home to a vibrant culture of the modern in its cities, although a range of more negative symptoms of modernity — overcrowding, growing slums packed with rural migrants and unemployment — could also be seen there.

There is still a tendency in some quarters to see the *Estado Novo* from the perspective of "stasis" or of "arrested development". Historians and others speak of the *Estado Novo* as having aimed principally at retarding or avoiding the arrival of "modernity" in Portugal; of preserving a traditional society, and leaving at its downfall a "backward" society. Some authors even talking of an "unfinished modernity".[1] Implicit in this understanding is a view of modernisation as a natural and linear process. When consciously articulated, it is an ideal associated with liberal views of the social and economic spheres. In the context of thinking historically about inequality, these assumptions are problematic to the extent that they help naturalise inequality by embedding it into an inevitable *longue durée* of socio-economic structures, into a narrative of a country repeatedly missing opportunities for modernisation since the "Age of Discoveries", and thus retaining an almost timeless, quasi-feudal, unequal social structure. This comes at the cost of reifying social structures, and failing to see the political and social processes through which inequalities are produced and reproduced.

An alternative approach would be to investigate the *Estado Novo* by asking how it intervened in socio-economic processes, how it conceived of and regulated the social, and whether and how it produced and reproduced inequalities. The authoritarian regime that emerged from the 1926 coup, and which, by the early 1930s, would style itself as the *Estado Novo*, was itself an uneasy and often contradictory mix of modern and traditional ideology, sentiment, aesthetics and governmentality. Much of the emphasis on the nature of the regime headed by

Salazar has been on its underlying conservative ideology, its use and development of a national myth with which to anchor a national regeneration. While not absent, the image of a virile "new man" in the fascist mould was much less present than the ideal of an "obedient, predictable and family man... adapted to the new, harmonious, corporatist political order".[2] But, like Italian Fascism, the fountainhead of authoritarian statecraft in interwar Europe, the *Estado Novo* sought to harness the essence of modernity — the technologies of the modern state, of propaganda and of scientific intervention — for the very modern task of moulding the nation in accordance with its vision.

The paradoxical nature of the *Estado Novo*'s ideology make its role in shaping Portuguese society harder to assess: how transformative was its action? To what extent, or in what dimensions, was it responsible for the reproduction of long-standing social forms, and where did it bring changes? Was it a case of "If we want things to stay as they are, things will have to change" — a recasting of traditional hierarchies in a new era; or can we see patterns of inequality changing over the course of its rule?

These are complex questions, given the difficulty of disentangling the different levels of causation through a period that, particularly after the 1950s, also saw a deep transformation of Portuguese social structures in the wake of the boom brought about by the realignment of the economy in order to access European markets.[3] In addition, the social and economic history of twentieth-century Portugal remains a puzzle with many pieces missing, particularly when it comes to offering a picture of standards of living, wages and other markers of the distribution of opportunity and rewards. Yet much has been done recently, and this chapter synthesises a recent and vibrant historiography the contributions to which, taken together, begin to create a view of the *Estado Novo* that allows us to present a hypothesis about its role in shaping contemporary inequalities in Portugal. It will focus particularly on a range of welfare institutions which arguably contributed to, on one hand, reproducing, or at least not challenging, the inequalities the regime inherited; and on the other hand, helped create and cement new divides as the country changed. Welfare systems — social insurance, healthcare, and other forms of social assistance, including housing and labour legislation — have the power both to equalise life chances and standards and, conversely to shape inequalities.[4] They do so by allocating resources according to values that may reward and privilege some groups or behaviours over others; by reinforcing, or even creating, boundaries of status or category. And, ultimately, the creation of one system means a choice, a set of actions that prevent other paths being followed.

Such inequalities can be expressed in terms of income, but they neither start nor end there. Who was unequal? How was poverty distributed geographically, and how did the experience of it change according to status, gender or age? Many other silences are evident, and there is much that this chapter does not have the space to tackle — not least the great looming inequality upon which the national psyche and myth rests, the oppression of colonial subjects. But the lens of wealth and earnings, understood as a rough proxy for standards and quality of life, is where we begin to chart inequality in twentieth-century Portugal. It gives us a starting point to ask: what was the effect of the implementation of a repressive, controlling and conservative regime?

Economic inequality at the birth of the *Estado Novo*

Today, almost two decades into the twenty first century, Portugal is in the unenviable position of being one of the most economically unequal countries in western Europe. In a recent pioneering work reconstructing income distribution for twentieth-century Portugal, Guilera suggests that incomes followed an "extended Kuznets curve". A pioneer of the measurement of income inequality, Simon Kuznets suggested that, as national economies transitioned from one model to another (say from a primarily agricultural to an industrial model) inequality would increase, driven by higher wages in newly emerging sectors. Over time, as workers moved to new sectors and the relative advantage of these wore out, wage inequality would decrease. Guilera's data, to an extent, bear this out: from the 1950s, a period characterised by rapid sectoral change and Portugal's transition away from a rural economy, changes in distribution seem to be driven primarily by economic factors, namely rising wages in higher skill, emerging sectors of the economy reinforced by high levels of emigration, which put a premium on skilled labour.[5] Inequality would remain high until the transition to democracy in the 1970s — when there was a rapid decline in inequality — only for levels of disparity to return, and perhaps surpass their post-war levels, in the 2010s.[6]

However, Guilera also offers us a striking fact: Portugal experienced a rapid increase in inequality of incomes accompanying the establishment and early decades of the *Estado Novo*. In this period, the end of the Second World War did see a contraction of inequality; but the widening of the gap soon resumed. If we focus on the period between 1926 and the mid-1940s, the growing disparity is striking: the GINI index of inequality rose by a third to 0.36.[7] For the sake of comparison, the distance covered in terms of inequality is the same as that which separates present-day Iceland, one of the most equal nations in Europe (GINI of 0.24), and the United Kingdom (GINI of 0.36), one of the most unequal.[8] This rapid redistribution is the more remarkable if we consider that it happened *before* the Portuguese economy was transformed by urbanisation and industrialisation, that is, before we would have expected a Kuznets effect. Guilera suggests instead that rising disparity in the 1930s was driven by a process of "income redistribution from wage earners to land and capital owners", rather than between wage earners in agricultural and non-agricultural sectors, as Kuznets would have predicted.[9]

There are two sides to this process: one is the degree to which the regime protected the interests of the owners of capital; the other is the very limited nature of any social intervention by the *Estado Novo* that might have mitigated the widening gap. Whilst growing slowly, expenditure in various aspects of welfare remained very low until the 1960s. In a poor, "backward" economy, could things have been different? Arguably they could. Leaving aside the debate as to whether a more Keynesian, demand-led approach would have created a different kind of growth, it is clear that the dictatorship made a conscious choice to opt for a strategy that not only rejected significant elements of redistribution, but that actively privileged elites that were the basis of its political support. The state's overall taxation revenue, from which redistribution could have been effected by investment in social policy, was relatively low. To an extent this is to be expected in one of Europe's poorest countries. In the 1930s and 40s, less than two percent of the population earnt enough to begin paying income tax, and by 1974 it was still only four percent.[10] However, such tax as was levied, particularly on higher incomes and on companies, was very low compared to that in other European countries. Until 1945, the top marginal tax rate (i.e. the tax rate paid by incomes in the top band) was 8.5 percent.[11] After the end of the Second World War, accompanying a trend in western Europe, it rose to 30 percent — but this still left if far below the top marginal income tax rates of nations that saw a significant contraction of inequality in the post-war period: a rate that tended to be at least double that percentage.[12]

These were choices made by the *Estado Novo*, and they had consequences for income distribution. In the first instance, they prevented a broader equalization of incomes as charted for other western countries between the 1940s and 1970s by Thomas Piketty. Portugal started with a high concentration of wealth and, unlike elsewhere, the national income share that went to the top 0.1 per cent remained stable between the 1940s and the late 1960s.[13] The incomes of this elite came primarily from property rents, coincidently (or not) the interests that went unchallenged by the regime in terms of addressing issues of either land reform or housing demand.[14] In short, in Portugal, the "Golden Age" of equality did not take place, or at least not until the 1974 Revolution brought about a sharp reduction in income (and power) inequalities.[15] In addition, the decision to limit taxation also limited the resources that could be allocated to social investment. Even if they were segmented and hierarchical, social insurance, healthcare, education and housing could have made a significant difference to the lives of the population, the large majority of whom remained excluded until the last quarter of the twentieth century. It is to these aspects we turn next.

Risk and welfare in twentieth-century Portugal

A narrow focus on income is insufficient to fully understand the dimensions of inequality. A different way of conceptualising inequality focuses not on resources — material or cognitive — but on differential exposure to risk. The historiography of social policy has paid increasing attention to how the "discovery" and construction of risk(s) was closely tied to the expansion of state regulation and intervention, particularly through social insurance in the late nineteenth and early twentieth-centuries.[16]

In Portugal, until the early twentieth century, public intervention in reducing social risks was constrained, as elsewhere, by the world view of liberalism, which recognised a "right to compassion", but regarded it as distinct from a duty of care by public bodies.[17] Despite the introduction of a right to public assistance in the Republican Constitution of 1911, the extent to which the state was directly involved in its delivery was limited. In this, however, Portugal was not unique: experiments in state provision of social protection were in any case recent, with Bismarckian Germany leading the way. Non-state forms of addressing the risks of poverty, sickness and disability were the norm, often supplied by private charitable institutions. In Portugal this role fell especially to the lay Catholic charitable *Misericóridas*, which ran nearly all the hospitals in the country, or to voluntary associations formed for the purpose of insurance.[18] The boundary between public and private provision was becoming increasingly blurred through the late nineteenth century, and was to do shift further towards state control in the second decade of the Republican regime. In 1866, the state had forced the sale of properties held by *Misericóridias*, and the investment of the proceeds in government bonds.[19] The First World War brought about the combined pressures of a rise in demand (in part driven by the influenza epidemic) and an inflationary surge that eroded *Misericóridia* incomes. By the early post-war period, most were scaling back provision and running increasing deficits.[20] By 1924, driven by the "imperative of the reality of such an enormous crisis", as one of the pieces of legislation drafted for the purpose stated, the Republican Government passed legislation allowing it to cover the deficits of the *Misericóridias* and channel some state revenues to each, in return for further regulatory oversight and an obligation to provide assistance to the "destitute", including mothers-to-be, mothers and infants, as well as pauper funerals.[21] Many *Misericóridias*, including important institutions such as Oporto's (the country's largest) declined to take part, leaving a patchwork of assistance provision, whose gaps that could not be met by under-resourced municipal authorities, as the legislation intended.[22]

Aside from the charitable assistance of the *Misericórdias*, late nineteenth century Portugal had also seen the expansion of voluntary mutualist associations, where members pooled resources to provide insurance against the sudden loss of earning capacity through illness or injury, or against funeral costs. These associations enjoyed a rapid growth in the context of a belated urbanisation and industrialisation from the late nineteenth century to the end of the First World War. The total number of members of mutualist associations offering health, disability and funeral insurance peaked at around 600,000 associates in 1919 — a number that would change little until the 1940s.[23] Multiple memberships mean that establishing a coverage ratio from these figures is fraught with difficulties; but Halpern Pereira estimates that by 1931, gross membership figures stood at 44 percent of the population in Lisbon and 57 percent in Oporto. However, their reach was minimal outside larger cities, in a country that was still primarily rural .[24] A report on mutualism in Lisbon in 1898 also reveals another striking feature: almost a third of mutualist affiliates (a gross figure, once again possibly distorted by multiple memberships) were women, a proportion that was even higher in working class areas of the city.[25] At present, we do not know how effective such forms of assistance and insurance were in protecting their members against the risks they faced. Nor do we have a fine-grained understanding of the socio-economic makeup of those who were assisted, or of mutual society members. However, their existence serves to remind us that welfare, understood more broadly than specifically public welfare, has a longer history than is often recognised.

Like the *Misericórdias*, the mutualist movement was shaken by the post-First-World-War situation, particularly the effects of the influenza pandemic on its liabilities, and in 1918, the state agreed a considerable subsidy to mutualist organisations providing sickness cover.[26] Such developments reinforced a strand of argument for greater state intervention in social insurance, drawing on the models being developed elsewhere in Europe. In 1919, the Socialist Minister for Labour, Augusto Dias da Silva, passed legislation setting up a system of compulsory social insurance, covering sickness and death, through employee contributions; and old age and disability through joint employer-employee contributions. The 1919 legislation was ambitious, but it would be a mistake to read it through the anachronistic lens of the idea of a "welfare state" delivered by public bodies, or as a significant commitment to re-distribution and equality. Instead it built on the existing network of mutualist insurance associations, which, it was hoped, would become the instrument for extending coverage and managing the delivery of compulsory insurance. Equally, the few state funds were committed to the system, which was expected to run solely on the basis of contributions by beneficiaries and employers.[27] There were elements of redistribution through the compulsory contributions envisaged for health insurance, since all men and women between the ages of 15 and 75 were required to contribute, regardless of income; but only those earning under 900 escudos annually would be eligible to receive sickness benefit and medical assistance.[28]

Ultimately, however, the impact of the plan was to be limited. There were political reactions, including early opposition from the mutualist movement, which reacted against its incorporation into a tightly regulated framework, and from employers and the medical profession.[29] But arguably more relevant to the failure of the scheme to meet its aims were organisational obstacles (the institution charged with rolling it out was beset by financial and managerial difficulties) and, principally, the lack of interest on the part of existing mutualist associations from joining the scheme. This hesitance should be understood in the context of the rampant inflation of the 1920s, which rapidly made the scheme's bands and benefits meaningless and rendered a collective savings scheme perilous. By the late 1920s, social insurance administrators were advising that the earnings threshold for entitlement to benefits should be raised to 9,000 escudos, ten times the initial sum.[30]

The Republican welfare system based on compulsory but autonomous social insurance did not go far beyond an aspiration. But it does open up a counterfactual question. Given that inflation was coming under control, had public finances also come under control, could it have been a stepping stone towards greater coverage and social inclusion in Portugal? In many respects, the *Estado Novo* could have created a much more extensive system of social insurance than the Republican regime ever managed; but it opted instead for one built by strangling the mutualist sector, and based on the subjection of labour to the state, and to capital.[31]

The Republican period, characterised by relatively free and plural politics, but also by great political instability, was brought to an end by a military coup in May 1926. Oliveira Salazar, an economics professor from Coimbra active in conservative Catholic politics, was appointed Minister of Finance, with "dictatorial" powers to address the state's near bankruptcy. From that position, Salazar gradually accumulated power, becoming leader of the government in 1932. The following year, he installed the authoritarian *Estado Novo*, a regime that would last until the 1974 Revolution.

The historiography of the Portuguese authoritarian regime's social policy is small, and examinations of the country's welfare trajectory have until recently seen democratisation after the 1974 Revolution as the "year zero" of modern social policy. What literature there is has tended to emphasise the use of social policy as an instrument of political control and repression on the part of the regime. But in Portugal, as in Spain and Italy, there is a growing interest in exploring the authoritarian origins of contemporary welfare systems. As several commentators have noted, the *Estado Novo* was in many respects the antithesis of conservatism, and it is important to take seriously the regime's self-presentation as a "national revolution". That its aims and self-legitimation were dressed in conservative and traditionalist rhetoric, including the use of retrospective utopias of a national golden age, or of an idyllic rural community, should not distract from the modernity of its methods. Like other modern revolutions, the *Estado Novo* had at is core an essentially modern ideology of transformation through state action, of the centralisation of power, and of the creation of a new reality through the deployment of new technologies of state power, including social policy.

The argument presented is, to a degree, speculative, since more in-depth analyses still need to be made; but the synthesis of a decade of recent research points towards a strong hypothesis: that the construction of modern inequality in Portugal (including many inequities that still affect it today) can be attributed to the institutions that were built by the *Estado Novo*, as well as by the alternative paths that the dictatorship strove to make impossible. We cannot yet establish a causal link; but the rapid increase in income inequality in the first two decades of the dictatorship are a symptom of the broader inequalities that were reinforced and even expanded by the actions of the state.

The *Estado Novo*'s programme placed the social question at the heart of the regime's aims. For Salazar, economic struggles and the class interests of capital and labour were to be subordinated to the higher interests of the nation. This meant that workers would be incorporated and educated into this higher calling: "We want only that their work should be honest, orderly and conscious of the common good"; in return "we will look after his [the worker's] employment, his housing, his hygiene, his health, his disability, his salary, his education, his organisation and defence, his social progress and his dignity…".[32] The limits to the extent of the social provision that would eventually be delivered directly by the state should not distract from how significant a departure this was from the tradition inherited from the liberal and republican periods, and also from the nature of a system that, in any case, was meant to be corporatist, rather than statist. The 1933 constitution removed the right to public assistance, replacing it with a vaguer duty of the state to "promote and coordinate" social action with a view to defending motherhood, the family and the improvement of the standards of living of the "less favoured classes".[33]

The regeneration of Portugal and its people was guided by the corporatist ideal. Drawing on models from Italian fascism (as well as Catholic social thought and Portugal's own organicist tradition), the Portuguese corporatist ideal envisaged a model of integrating capital and labour into "natural" corporative sectors that would be hierarchically organised, would regulate production, would prevent unbridled competition, and would provide social services to members, subsuming class conflict into an "organic" structure.[34] The state would have a supervisory and regulatory role, but would not (ideally) intervene directly; nor would it fund social provision, which should emerge from the voluntary collaboration of labour and capital within the context of the corporations. The state's function was primarily suppletive (that is, covering only marginal sectors, or those functions that would require centralisation) and exemplary.[35]

These ideals were put into action by Pedro Teotónio Pereira, Under-Secretary of State for Corporations and Social Insurance, and one of Portuguese corporativism's leading lights.

As far as it ever existed, the blueprint for corporativism in Portugal first saw the light in a swathe of legislative activity between 1933 and 1935. The National Labour Statute, heavily influenced by the Fascist *Carta del Lavoro*, was the showpiece of the regime's corporatist ideal. Whilst recognising a "right to work", the *Estado Novo* prohibited the autonomous organisation of labour by creating single unions organised by economic sector and region.[36] No forms of labour organisation outside this were permitted, and the unions had to obey three fundamental principles: a "hierarchy of interests", where the national interest should stand above sectoral concerns; a renunciation of class struggle and acceptance of a directive to collaborate with the state and employers; and a rejection of internationalism.[37] In theory, unions would have equal representation with employers' organisations in sectoral corporations, even if these only materialised two decades later, and then in watered down form. In practice, it meant the control of the state over labour, since even these unions would have their activity and elected representative vetted by the newly created National Institute for Labour and Social Insurance.[38] Repeatedly, these powers, as well as the broader apparatus of control set up by the regime, were used to thwart attempts by even the recognised unions to demand improvements in wages and working conditions.[39]

In return, the *Estado Novo* promised to regulate child and female labour, and expected the new harmonious relationship between employer and employee to produce a new model of social insurance to replace the Republican 1919 institutions. The new government-approved unions, as well as the rural "People's Funds" and the "Fisherman's Funds", were tasked with creating social insurance funds covering health, old age, disability and death benefits, as well as medical assistance. Employers and employees would jointly contribute; but the exact proportions were left to the discretion of the negotiators. Furthermore, unlike in the 1919 legislation, there was no obligation for unions to set up funds. These were expected to appear gradually through the signing of collective wage agreements within the emerging corporatist sector.

The spread of corporatist welfare was a slow creep, rather than a new dawn. Union social insurance funds struggled to get off the ground: by 1938 only six had been set up, rising to 51 in 1943.[40] The rural "People's Funds" took off relatively quickly, but were concentrated in the southern part of the country, a fact not unconnected to the presence of a restive landless rural proletariat that it was imperative to control. Elsewhere, their establishment lagged behind the regime's hopes and stagnated from the 1940s on.[41] The bulk of welfare expenditure continued to come from the private sector (including the surviving mutualist associations). The corporatist insurance sector only became the largest provider in the late 1940s, and even then, over 80 percent of the population remained uncovered.[42]

Until recently, it was difficult to have a sense of the extent and coverage of expenditure on welfare goods in authoritarian Portugal. Reliable welfare statistics were only collated from 1980 on. Looking solely at expenditure from governmental budgets hides the extent to which the *Estado Novo*'s compulsory system of social insurance succeeded in mobilising employer and employee contributions in this regard. Recent work by Carolo and Pereirinha allows us to look again at the impact of the regime's corporatist social legislation. Their data reveals that, in terms of overall welfare expenditure and coverage, there were significant expansions before 1974, especially following the welfare reforms of 1962. But it also confirms the limited impact of the *Estado Novo*'s corporatist welfare in its first two decades.[43]

The slow development of the welfare side of the corporatist bargain — slower than many within the *Estado Novo*, including Teotónio Pereira, wished for — can be seen as a consequence of an imbalance between the coercion of labour and the unwillingness to pressure employers. Once the autonomous labour movement had been crushed, with political opposition marginalised or driven underground, and existing unions neutered by political control and denial of the right to strike, there was little incentive for employers to rush to develop the welfare institutions the legislative output of the *Estado Novo* required.[44]

In those instances where corporatist welfare was rolled out, it also served to create and reproduce stratification and inequality, as, to an extent, it was designed to do. Where he expressed an opinion, Salazar articulated the idea that inequalities derived from merit were justified, indeed essential: all work was "equally worthy from the human point of view… but not from the economic and social point of view", and thus "there is no limit to the advancement of the living standard of those who work; there is no harm in that it rises ever more, as far as it is bearable by economy of the nation as a whole."[45] As such, "a salary does not have to have an upper limit, although it can have a minimum, so that it does not go below the demands of a sufficient and dignified life."[46] Yet more specifically, Salazar was critical of any hint of egalitarian thinking, arguing that, along with democracy, it brought about a "downward levelling", and stood "against the fact of natural inequalities, against the legitimate and necessary hierarchy of values in a well ordered society."[47] The principle of hierarchisation, of "each in his place" was reflected in the adoption of the contributory principle for almost every aspect of social welfare his government regulated: from insurance to housing, benefits were segmented by class, and expected to be proportional to inputs, instead of to need.

The long life of assistencialism

Mid-century Portuguese debates on welfare made a marked distinction between *previdência* (literally, foresight), or insurance against risks that would have an impact on the individual's ability to work, and *assistência*, (assistance), which encompassed multiple forms of intervention - medical, social, pedagogical — and catered for those who, for the right reasons, could not help themselves. The first was considered a matter of organisation and regulation of labour relations; the second primarily a matter of charity. The *Estado Novo*'s emphasis was on the latter:

the state could create "model" institutions, namely hospitals; but it should principally "guide and supervise" private charitable institutions to deal with this area of need, since replacing them with state action would be to "imperil the poor". Implicit is a critique of the rights discourses increasingly heard in international circles. For the *Estado Novo*, as stated in a key propaganda publication on the topic, the provision of assistance "... must be based on everyone's duty to assist those in need to the extent of their capacity, rather than on the rights of the poor".[48]

Underlying this attitude was an essentially moral view of poverty which, despite occasional critiques of the evils of capitalist exploitation, tended to see it as the result of individual ethical choices. As such the "good" poor, even if exploited or unfortunate, retained their dignity and worthiness; but others were seen as having chosen the path of "vice" and dependence. As such, the provision of assistance, while considered virtuous and necessary, also required constant vigilance so as to distinguish the worthy from the unworthy, and care so as not to encourage parasitism.[49]

In practice, the boundary between *previdência* and *assistência* was as blurred as that between virtue and vice. Corporatist social insurance funds, for instance, were designed to provide medical assistance to members, with the idea that this form of self-help would expand to cover the majority of the population, leaving the private charitable sector responsible only for the destitute, the elderly and other marginal groups. But the limited degree to which the various types of insurance funds were able to provide quality medical care continued to mean that even the minority covered often found it necessary to apply to a very deficient public or charitable medical system.[50] Recognising this, in the mid-1940s the *Estado Novo* encouraged the creation of federations of insurance funds for the purpose of delivering health assistance to their members. Even with these, however, fragmentation and inequalities abounded: the extent and quality of services and entitlements were dependent on which fund individuals belonged to and, more significantly, by the mid-1950s only around 10 per cent of the population were covered by such schemes.[51] The rest of the population continued to rely on the system inherited from the Republican regime: a handful of public hospitals in the two main cities, backed by an incomplete, underfunded and ill-equipped network of *Misericórdia* hospitals and an equally sparse network of municipal doctors.

On occasions when the regime did deal with the question of healthcare and assistance, it simply reiterated its principles of little or no intervention. After a commission had been charged with the task of investigating the issue in 1937, a statute for "Social Assistance" was submitted to the single-party national assembly in 1944. The statute was a restatement of the principle of suppletivity: the role of the state should be that of regulating and supporting voluntary action.[52] That this was a political choice is made clear by the evident disagreements caused by this position even within the regime, and the echoes of transnational debates taking place at the same time. The British Beveridge report was already well-known in the country, having been debated in academic circles, and it was referenced by several MPs who contributed to the debate on the Social Assistance Statute. But in the discussion, the key role of the state in the British plan was elided, and the interventions focused instead on Beveridge's arguments that echoed the regime's views on the family, or simply claimed that the Plan had been pre-empted by Portuguese corporatist legislation.[53] However, there were dissenting voices, perhaps most remarkably the long commentary on the statute drafted for the Corporative Chamber (the Assembly's higher chamber) by Marcelo Caetano, a leading figure in the regime, Salazar's *dauphin* and later successor. The commentary candidly documented the deficiencies of the government's approach and the results of this, noting rising rates of infant mortality since 1929; the severe inequalities in height and weight between well-educated urban children and their rural counterparts; the lack of doctors outside Lisbon and Oporto; and how the majority of the country's 321 hospitals (mostly run by *Misericórdias*) were little better than infirmaries with little in the way of staff or equipment.[54] Caetano argued that the size of the task ahead meant that, even if elsewhere a hands-off approach was viable, in Portugal they required a degree of mobilization only the state could take on directly.[55] The Corporative Chamber's comments were, however, largely ignored and the statute was approved with few changes.

The plain fact was that, in its first two decades, the *Estado Novo* failed to develop a system of healthcare, be it statist or corporatist, that would begin to address the country's significant health problems and inequalities. Instead, the regime focused its assistentialist efforts in highly publicised, but ultimately rather thin maternalistst and pro-natalist policies. The mid-1930s saw the creation of a number of organisations aimed at educating women in their maternal, social and domestic duties — the National Organisation for the Defence of the Family; and the Mothers' Union for National Education (*Obra das Mães pela Educação Nacional*). Both were directed, and often staffed, by elite or upper-middle-class volunteers. The first was limited to providing gifts of food and clothes to poor families, and was never a significant assistential institution. The year 1940, not untypically, saw them give aid to under 4,000 families. The reach of the second was a little wider, establishing some centres in poor neighbourhoods to offer support and education, as well as basic maternal care; but the numbers of families assisted was hardly larger.[56] The Mother's Union also pioneered the training and use of health visitors, an early step towards the professionalization of social service, even if the training emphasized their role in creating, through their intervention, the regime's ideal "new woman": maternal, domesticated and virtuous.[57]

The centrality of the family in the *Estado Novo*'s imaginary was also evident in the introduction, in 1942, of a family allowance. Portugal moved to adopt this allowance relatively early, being only the seventh country in Europe to do so. Italy and Germany had already created subsidies for families, with an explicit pro-natalist (and racial) aim in mind. For the *Estado Novo*, however, the intention was to shore up the institution of the family rather than necessarily to encourage fertility. Unlike in other schemes, ascendant dependents (i.e. older people living with adult children or other relatives) qualified as recipients, as well as people with children, and to an extent this can be considered an incipient form of old age pension. Quantitatively, the family allowance probably had significant reach: while data is only available from the late 1940s onwards, it seems at that point to have significantly increased the (admittedly extremely low) proportion of national income devoted to welfare.[58] However, in keeping with the *Estado Novo*'s corporatist ideology, the family allowance did not involve a direct transfer from the state budget: instead it was to be funded by contributions from employers and all employees, regardless of their family status. This made it, in effect, a minimum or family wage policy, at no cost to the government and, to the extent that it might have been compensated for by a slower growth in wages, benefit-neutral to recipients. Even then, applying only to employees in commerce, industry and services, and excluding rural and domestic workers, it left out a vast proportion of the population.[59] In the end its main distributive elements were most likely to effect a transfer from those without dependents to those with.

One final example illustrates both the degree to which the *Estado Novo* departed from the liberal tradition of limited intervention and how it used aspects of social policy as tools to discipline and arrange society in its image. Despite a long-standing acknowledgement of the desperate poverty of living conditions in Portuguese cities and in the countryside, neither the liberal nor the Republican regime had sought to intervene directly in housing. A solitary attempt to build a state-backed neighbourhood in Lisbon had been attempted under the short-lived Sidónio Pais dictatorship in 1918 (often seen as an ideological precursor to the *Estado Novo*), but the neglect of the project until Salazar's coming to power was testament to the lack of enthusiasm for such solutions. As in other areas of social policy, the *Estado Novo* took what was in effect a fundamentally distinct turn in terms of its intervention, committing the state to backing the building of thousands of new housing units per year.

The hearth (*lar*) had a particular place within the *Estado Novo*'s ideological pantheon, as the focus of the family, seen as the primary building bloc of society. Like much else in the regime's social policy, housing policy was built around the idea of the family. In the words of one of the main architects of the *Estado Novo*'s social policy, Pedro Teotónio Pereira, the aim was to provide "proper homes, around whose hearth familial love is warmed and the bonds of moral life are strengthened".[60] A close connection was made between property-ownership and moral development: "the family that is housed under its own roof is naturally more frugal, more stable and healthier" said Salazar in 1933, rejecting the option of "large *phalanstères*, colossal buildings for workers' housing, with their own restaurants and communal kitchens".[61]

Instead, the ideal home of the *Estado Novo* was presented in the regime's 1933 flagship housing policy, the Affordable Homes programme: detached or semi-detached single-dwelling houses with small gardens modelled on the "garden city" ideal, and which were allocated on a rent-to-buy model. Tenant-buyers would have to be members of a legal trade union, state or state-related employees, or members of the military or police force. Only married couples of "good moral standing" could access Affordable Homes, and selling the property on was conditional on official approval, with lease conditions stipulating that property could not be divided in case of divorce (which in any case was illegal). In short, every effort was made to tie the family to the property, and the property to the family.[62] As in other forms of social provision, the state conceived of these interventions as first and foremost as "exemplary". Financed from state pension funds, they were designed to show other institutions that social housing could provide a steady return on investment.[63] As a result, rents were unaffordable to those in most need, but in any case, the Affordable Homes were not for them.

The first public housing neighbourhoods for shantytown dwellers were built in Lisbon in the late 1930s, resulting from the need to re-house some of the families whose shanties were to be razed to make room for the regime's showpiece, the Portuguese World Exhibition of 1940. Unlike the Affordable Homes these were low-quality, small pre-fabricated bungalows, built with few amenities, on marginal land on the outskirts of the city. A few years later, a scheme for "Houses for Poor Families" was introduced, and the quality of housing improved. In both, the paternalistic, hierarchic and moralistic aspects of the *Estado Novo*'s social policies were clear: houses were banded into classes of quality through which tenants were expected to progress until "ready" to access the middle-class homes of the Affordable Houses scheme. Neighbourhood wardens and social workers had extensive powers to intrude in residents' homes and affairs in order to ensure their "re-education and re-adaptation", and their reports to neighbourhood managers could lead to fines, "demotions" or even expulsion from the neighbourhood. Surviving warden reports for one of these neighbourhoods in Lisbon show an overwhelming concern for women's sexual propriety. The impression overall is one of lives intensely scrutinised and regulated.[64]

The intensity of the state's intervention in the lives of those it housed had a reverse side: such levels of control and management of the everyday required great effort and expenditure within an ideological framework where, in the absence of a right, social housing was mainly to be built on a contributory or charitable basis. Schemes such as Houses for Poor Families were meant primarily to be exemplary, to provide models to be followed by corporations or private charities. But the latter groups were not enthusiastic, preferring to invest in other state-directed housing programmes aimed at the middle classes, where returns were highest. Until the 1960s, the number of homes built that would be accessible even to those willing to tolerate the oversight of authorities was very small: fewer than 5,000 across the country by 1950.[65] The result was the exclusion from the public housing system of those who needed it most. Despite repeated attempts by the Lisbon municipality to remove them, shantytowns continued to proliferate through the city, as did overcrowding and poor living conditions.

From authoritarianism to democracy: changes and continuities

By the 1950s, it was clear that the *Estado Novo*'s ambition to build a working corporative society was still far from bearing real fruit. The growing dominance of planning and state intervention as a model of governance pushed the country in a new direction, as did the need to secure legitimacy at home and abroad in a new international climate. In this context, the regime embarked on a series of reforms that, amongst other things, gradually brought about a much greater degree of direct involvement in the provision of welfare, particularly in terms of assistance. In 1958, a Ministry of Health and Assistance was created that concentrated responsibilities hitherto scattered across different departments. Soon after, in 1962, a major reform challenged the traditional separation between *assistência* and *previdência* by attempting to centralise both social insurance and payments such as family allowances in regional funds, and creating a national fund to aggregate long-term risks, which would allow the expansion of the system to independent workers, including rural workers. Increasingly detached from the employer or even the professional sector, social insurance began to gain universalistic features, while the state increasingly recognised the need to invest directly in provision, moving away from a purely contributory model to allow the expansion of coverage.[66] Between the early 1960s and the fall of the dictatorship, the proportion of the population covered by some kind of welfare element doubled to reach over 40 percent.[67]

These reforms were part of Marcelo Caetano's attempt to give legitimacy to a crumbling regime by transforming the *Estado Novo* into a "Social State": more caring, but no more democratic. Ultimately, they were not enough, and, arguably, the regime's late and patchy expansion of social welfare served only to make its shortcomings more visible. By bringing the state to the forefront of welfare delivery, the regime also helped turn social rights into political issues, which would contribute to its de-legitimation and eventual downfall.[68]

Given the extent to which the dictatorship changed tack, how far can we suggest that Portugal's enduring inequalities are the legacy of the forms of authoritarian welfare established in the 1930s and 1940s, particularly if these affected such narrow sectors of the population? The first part of the answer is a counterfactual. The road not taken was one where an alternative form of welfare would have been created which, if not more generous, would at least have been more equal, and would not have aggravated disparities as the *Estado Novo* clearly did, especially in its first two decades. Even if this might have looked significantly different from the northern European "welfare states", the effects could have been less divisive. The strength of the mutualist movement in the Republican period, choked off by the dictatorship in favour of its corporatist system, might have provided an alternative. Its popularity amongst female urban workers, while no guarantee of actual equality, contrasts with the systematic exclusion and subjugation of women in the *Estado Novo*'s social policies.

The second part of the answer requires us to follow the thread from the beginnings of welfare intervention by the regime through the second half of the twentieth century. Even as it left the great majority of the population outside its reach, the *Estado Novo*'s corporatist welfare nonetheless laid a foundation, to the extent that all reforms that came after it had to build in a landscape shaped by these early institutions. Whether we use the terminology of "path dependence", or Lucena's "continuities within rupture", neither the 1962 reforms nor the reinvention of the welfare landscape that followed the 1974 Revolution started from on a tabula rasa.[69] And these legacies ran deep: the "revolutionary" constitution of 1976, and its extensive list of commitments in terms of social rights, was in many ways a break from, and a reaction against, the dictatorship.[70] Even then, Ferreira et al note how, in many of its essential clauses, the constitution (still largely in effect, despite revisions), continues to see aspects of welfare through a corporatist lens. While a "right to social security" has been declared, this is framed in relation to citizens' capacity to work, as opposed to their status as citizens.[71] In other sections, the onus of redistribution and equalisation is placed on the tax system, rather than on welfare: ultimately, the constitution continues to see work-related benefits as a right of citizenship, but universal, non-work related benefits as discretionary. Even in terms of delivery, the constitution gives pride of place to the third-sector, and *Misericórdias* continue to fulfil extensive welfare functions.[72]

Such legacies are reflected in enduring inequalities within a welfare system that is now nominally universal. Under its umbrella, the old distinction between social insurance and assistance persists in the differences between entitlements due to those who are able to pay regularly into social insurance and payments to those who qualify only for the "non-contributive" sector of social insurance, despite centralisation.[73] Even within the social insurance model, pockets of differentiated rules and entitlements inherited from the multiple social insurance funds created under corporatism, often financed by the state, create their own inequalities and regressive forms of distribution. The Portuguese welfare system, in common with other Southern European regimes with authoritarian origins, remains "fragmented, corporatistic and familistic".[74] This reinforces inequalities between "insiders" with stable careers in long-term employment, and "outsiders engaging in intermittent, underpaid contract work (or with no formal employment at all), and who are entitled to much less generous benefits. With welfare entitlement dependent on one's position in the labour market, these inequalities affect particularly the elderly, less skilled parts of the population; women and the young of both sexes who are unable to achieve job security; and women who continue to bear the brunt of unpaid caring and childrearing functions in the face of limited provision.

Since the 1980s, Portugal has managed to increase welfare coverage and expenditure, and to significantly reduce the incidence and risk of poverty. On the other hand, inequality has remained high, due to the relative inability of the welfare system to effect meaningful redistribution. The introduction of a Guaranteed Minimum Income in 1996 was aimed precisely at lessening some of these disparities, and the evidence suggests a degree of success. However, as long as it is considered a discretionary payment, such transfers are vulnerable to challenges.[75] The *Estado Novo*'s unequal and authoritarian welfare casts a long shadow.

Notes

1 Fernando Luís Lopes Machado and António Manuel Hipólito Firmino da Costa, "Processos de uma Modernidade Inacabada: Mudanças Estruturais e Mobilidade Social", in *Portugal, que Modernidade?,* ed. José Manuel Leite Viegas and António Firmino da Costa (Lisbon: Celta, 1998), pp. 17–44.

2 António Costa Pinto and Rita Almeida de Carvalho, "The 'Everyman' of the Portuguese New State during the Fascist Era: Longing for the Past or Moving towards the Future?" in *The "New Man" in Radical Right Ideology and Practice, 1919–45,* ed. Jorge Dagnino, Matthew Feldman, and Paul Stocker (London: Bloomsbury, 2017).

3 António Barreto, "A Situação Social em Portugal, 1960–1995" (Lisbon: Instituto das Ciências Sociais, 1996).

4 Peter Saunders, "'Inequality and Poverty", in *The Oxford Handbook of the Welfare State,* ed. F. G. Castles, S. Leibfried, J. Lewis, H. Obinger, C. Pierson (Oxford: Oxford University Press, 2012).

5 Pedro Lains, Ester Gomes da Silva, and Jordi Guilera, "Wage Inequality in a Developing Open Economy: Portugal, 1944–1984", *Scandinavian Economic History Review* 61 (2013). The authors also note a contraction in wage inequality between skilled and unskilled workers from the late 1960s onwards, driven principally by the growing openness of the Portuguese economy and the adoption of a model of extensive industrialisation based on low-skill production.

6 Jordi Guilera, "Income Inequality in Historical Perspective: Portugal (1890–2006)", (PhD thesis, University of Barcelona, 2013).

7 Ibid., pp. 128–129.

8 The comparison is, of course, fraught with difficulties, not only because of the challenge of estimating past distribution, but also because inequality is distinct from standards of living, which have changed substantially since the mid-twentieth century: http://www.oecd.org/social/inequality.htm#income

9 Guilera, "Income Inequality in Historical Perspective", p. 135.

10 Ibid., p. 28. table 2.1

11 Facundo Alvaredo, "Top Incomes and Earnings in Portugal 1936–2005'", *Explorations in Economic History* 46 (2009): 408.

12 Facundo Alvaredo et al., "The Top 1 Percent in International and Historical Perspective", *The Journal of Economic Perspectives* 27 (2013): 7, fig.3.

13 Despite their different methodologies, which yield slightly different levels, this reading is common to both Alvaredo and Guilera.

14 Alvaredo, "Top Incomes and Earnings", p. 408.

15 Guilera, "Income Inequality in Historical Perspective", p. 130.

16 See Julia Moses and Eve Rosenhaft, "Introduction: Moving Targets Risk, Security, and the Social in Twentieth-Century Europe", *Social Science History* 39 (2015).

17 Maria Antónia Lopes, "Poor Relief, Social Control and Health Care in 18th and 19th Century Portugal", in *Health Care and Poor Relief in 18th and 19th Century Southern Europe,* ed. Ole Peter Grell, Andrew Cunningham, and Andrew Roeck (Aldershot: Ashgate, 2005), pp. 148–149.

18 Ibid.

19 Isabel dos Guimarães Sá and Maria Antónia Lopes, *História Breve das Misericórdias Portuguesas, 1498–2000*, (Coimbra: Imprensa da Universidade de Coimbra, 2008), pp. 90–92.

20 Ibid.

21 See the summary and regulation in Decree-Law 10.242 of 1 November 1924, reprinted in José Pedro Paiva and Paulo F. de Oliveira Fontes, eds, "Portugaliae Monumenta Misericordiarum", Vol. 9, Tomo 1 of *Misericórdias e Secularização num Século Turbulento: 1910–2000'* (Lisbon: União das Misericórdias Portuguesas, 2010), p.122. The definition of "destitute" created by this legislation hinges on a presumed capacity to do or find sufficient work to survive, and a lack of the family support that was seen as the place where the first responsibility for aid still lay. Certificates of destitution were to be issued by local assistance committees, who could draw on the opinion of local officials, experts or any "trustworthy" individuals. See above cited document, article 45 (pp.134–135).

22 Isabel dos Guimarães Sá and Maria Antónia Lopes, *História Breve das Misericórdias Portuguesas, 1498–2000* (Coimbra: Imprensa da Universidade de Coimbra, 2008), pp. 102–103.

23 Miriam Halpern Pereira, "As Origens do Estado-Providência em Portugal: as Novas Fronteiras entre Público e Privado", in *A Primeira Républica Portuguesa - entre o Liberalismo e o Autoritarismo,* ed. Nuno Severiano Teixeira and António Costa Pinto (Lisbon: Edições Colibri, 2000), pp. 52–57.

24 Ibid., p. 56.

25 Virgínia Baptista, "Participação Feminina no Movimento Mutualista. Do final da Monarquia ao Estado Novo", *Ler História* (2012).

26 Pereira, " As Origens do Estado-Providência em Portugal", p. 62.

27 José Luís Cardoso and Maria Manuela Rocha, "O Seguro Social Obrigatório em Portugal (1919–1928): Aacção e Limites de um Estado Previdente", *Análise Social* 44 (2009): 449.

28 Maria Manuela Rocha, "1ª República e Política Social: Contexto Internacional e Modelo dos Seguros Sociais Obrigatórios em Portugal", in *Economia, Instituições e Império: Estudos em Homenagem a Joaquim Romero Magalhães,* ed. Álvaro Garrido, Leonor Freire Costa, and Luís Miguel Duarte (Coimbra: Almedina), pp. 461–475 (p. 469).

29 Pereira, "As Origens do Estado-Providência em Portugal", pp. 71–72. Cardoso and Rocha argue that the opposition of the mutualist movement was less significant than suggested by Pereira. However, it could also be argued that the reason why the mutualist movement stopped being so vocally opposed to compulsory insurance was the increasing irrelevance of the scheme, rather than a change of position. The mutualist movement would express its opposition again later, when the *Estado Novo* rolled out its own social insurance scheme in 1934 — but by then the possibility of mobilising against the increasingly entrenched authoritarian regime was greatly reduced. On this topic see: Fátima Patriarca, *A Questão Social No Salazarismo*, (Lisbon: Imprensa Nacional Casa da Moeda, 1995).

30 Cardoso and Rocha, "O Seguro Social Obrigatório em Portugal", pp. 462–463. Inflation in the first half of the 1920s stood at over 30 per cent, one of the highest rates in western Europe: Pedro Lains, "Growth in a Protected Environment: Portugal, 1850–1950", *Research in Economic History* 24 (2006): 127–128.

31 Pereira, "As Origens do Estado-Providência em Portugal", p. 75.

32 António de Oliveira Salazar, *Discursos, vol. 1: 1928–1934*, 1st edn (Coimbra: Coimbra Editora, 1935), pp. 181–182.

33 Irene Flunser Pimentel, "A Assistência Social e Familiar do Estado Novo nos Anos 30 e 40", *Análise Social* 34 (2000), 479.

34 Luís Reis Torgal, "Os Corporativismos e as 'Terceiras Vias'", in *Corporativismo, Fascismos, Estado Novo,* ed. Fernando Rosas and Álvaro Garrido (Coimbra: Almedina, 2012).

35 José Luís Cardoso and Maria Manuela Rocha, "Corporativismo e Previdência Social (1933–1962)", *Ler História* (2003): 118–122.

36 Much of the detail, including the extinction of existing union organisations that would not agree to their conversion into national unions, came not in the Statute itself, but in addendums that followed soon after: José Barreto, "Estatuto do Trabalho Nacional (1933)", in *Dicionário de História de Portugal, Suplemento, vol. 7,* ed. António Barreto and Maria Filomena Mónica (Porto: Figueirinhas, 1999), pp. 680–684.

37 Patriarca, *A Questão Social No Salazarismo,* p. 228.

38. Ibid., p. 229.

39 Ibid., pp. 645–647.

40 *Dez Anos de Política Social, 1933–1943*, (Lisbon: Instituto Nacional do Trabalho e Previdência, 1943).

41 Dulce Freire, "Estado Corporativo em Acção: Sociedade Rural e Construção da Rede de Casas do Povo", in *Corporativismo, Fascismos e Estado Novo,* ed. Fernando Rosas and Álvaro Garrido (Coimbra: Almedina, 2012, pp. 273–302 and 278–279. The "Fishermen Funds" (*Casas de Pescadores*) were relatively successful, and by 1946 almost all workers in the fishing industry had joined. But this small, concentrated sector amounted only to 24 funds and under 50,000 members, and was one where the contributory principle was essentially waived and the state financed a greater part of the insurance and assistential schemes: Álvaro Garrido, "Assistência e Previdência no Mar Português. A Ação Social das Casas dos Pescadores (1933–1968)", *Ler História* (2012).

42 Daniel Fernando Carolo and José António Pereirinha, "The Development of the Welfare State in Portugal: Trends in Social Expenditure between 1938 and 2003", *Revista de Historia Económica/Journal of Iberian and Latin American Economic History (Second Series)* 28 (2010): 479–480 and 485–486.

43 Ibid.

44 Patriarca, *A Questão Social No Salazarismo*, pp. 647–651.

45 Salazar, *Discursos*, vol. 1, pp. 198–200.

46 Ibid., p. 200.

47 Ibid., p. 91.

48 *Assistência Social*, (Lisbon: Secretariado Nacional de Informação, 1945), pp. 35–36.

49 Susana Pereira Bastos, *O Estado Novo e os Seus Vadios: Contribuições para o Estudo das Identidades Marginais e da Sua Repressão*, (Lisbon: Dom Quixote, 1997).

50 Ana Campos, "Assistência Médica e Desiguladade Social no Estado Novo", *Revista de Estudos do Século* 20, (2013),: 362.

51 Ibid., pp. 361; 364–5.

52 Ana Campos and Maria Manuela Rocha, "Corporativismo e Assistência Social: Natureza e Produção do 'Estatuto de Assistência Social", *Ler História* (2013): 13.

53 Ibid., pp. 22–23; Paco Ruzzante, "Iberian Welfare Systems and the Beveridge Report, 1942–1950s", (MPhil dissertation, University of Cambridge, 2015).

54 "Parecer Acêrca da Proposta de lei sôbre o Estatuto da Assistência Social", *Diário das Sessões*, 25 February 1944, pp. 84, 89 and 92–95.

55 Campos and Rocha, "Corporativismo e Assistência Social", p. 17.

56 Pimentel, "A Assistência Social e Familiar", pp. 494–497.

57 Francisco Branco, "Itinerário das Profissões Sociais em Portugal, 1910–1962", *Análise Social* (2015).

58 José António Pereirinha, Manuela Arcanjo, and Daniel Fernando Carolo, "Prestações Sociais no Corporativismo Português: a Política de Apoio à Família no Período do Estado Novo", *ISEG/GHES Working Paper Series* 35 (2009): 14.

59 Ibid.The authors note, however, the importance of the scheme in pre-empting some elements of the centralisation and statisation of assistance through the creation of a central clearing institution for family allowance funds which was, in part, funded by a tax on overtime: pp. 21–22.

60 Cited in Marielle Christine Gros, "'Pequena' História do Alojamento Social em Portugal", *Sociedade e Território* (1994).

61 Salazar, *Discursos e Notas Políticas*, vol. 1, 1928–1934, (Coimbro: Coimbra Editora, 1944), Discurso proferido em 16/3/1933. For extensive discussion of the role of the hearth in *Estado Novo* ideology, see: Luís Vicente Baptista, "Casa, Família, Ideologia;

a emergência da política de 'moradias unifamiliares' em Portugal nos anos 30", *Ler História* 34 (1998); João Medina, *Salazar, Hitler e Franco — Estudos Sobre a Ditadura*, (Lisbon: Livros Horizonte, 2000).

62 Pedro Ramos Pinto, *Lisbon Rising: Urban Social Movements in the Portuguese Revolution, 1974–75* (Manchester: Manchester University Press, 2013).

63 Carlos Nunes Silva, "Mercado e Políticas de Habitação em Portugal: a Questão da Habitação na Primeira Metade do Século XX", *Análise Social* 29 (1994): 667.

64 Ramos Pinto, *Lisbon Rising.*

65 Silva, "Mercado e Políticas de Habitação", p. 671.

66 Daniel Fernando Carolo, "A Institucionalização do Estado Providência em Portugal: Da Reforma da Previdência Social de 1962 à actual Reforma da Segurança Social", in *26º Encontro da Associação Portuguesa de História Económica e Social,* (Ponta Delgada, 2006), pp. 8–11.

67 Carolo and Pereirinha, "The development of the Welfare State in Portugal", p. 489.

68 Pedro Ramos Pinto, "Housing and Citizenship: Building Social Rights in 20th Century Portugal", *Contemporary European History* 18 (2009).

69 M. Lucena, "Transformações do Estado Português nas Suas Relações com a Sociedade Civil", *Análise Social* 17 (1982).

70 Filipe Carreira da Silva and Mónica Brito Vieira, "Direitos Sociais na Constituição: uma Análise da Constitucionalização Dos Direitos Sociais em Portugal", *Relações Internacionais* (2016).

71 Ana Rita Ferreira , Daniel Carolo, Mariana Trigo Pereira e Pedro Adão e Silva, 'Fundamentos Constitucionais da Proteção Social: Continuidades e Ruturas', *Sociologia, Problemas e Práticas* (2016): 74–75.

72 Ibid., p. 77.

73 Carolo, "A Institucionalização do Estado Providência em Portugal" , p. 14.

74 Marisol García and Neovi Karakatsanis, "Social Policy, Democracy, and Citizenship in Southern Europe", in *Democracy and the State in the New Southern Europe,* ed. Richard Gunther, P. N. Diamandouros, and D. A. Sotiropoulos (Oxford: Oxford University Press, 2006), pp. 88–89.

75 José Pereirinha, "Poverty and Anti-Poverty Policies in Portugal: The experience of the Guaranteed Minimum Income", in *Poverty and Social Deprivation in the Mediterranean; Trends, Policies and Welfare Prospects in the New Millennium,* ed. Maria Petmesidou and Christos Papatheodorou (New York: Zed Books, 2006). On the vulnerability of discretionary transfers, and for a commentary on the decisions of the constitutional court in the last decade, see: Ferreira et al., "Fundamentos Constitucionais da Proteção Social", pp. 77–79.

Part II

Postcolonial Identities

CHAPTER

7

The *Slow Men*: Daily Rhythms and Social Inequalities in Nineteenth-Century Brazil

LAURENT VIDAL

Slowness: a metaphor for social relegation in the long nineteenth century

As an introduction to this chapter, I offer an observation: the vocabulary usually used to describe social inequality belongs to the spatial field. Social inequality is indicated by words such as segregation, marginalization, exclusion, domination, subordination, outsiders, and so on. Each word was originally a metaphor referring to space: to segregate means to set apart, from the Latin *segregat* (separated from the flock); marginalization comes from margin; exclusion is constructed with the prefix *ex* which means outside; domination is derived from the Latin word *dominatio*, which has the same root as *domus* (home); subordination comes from the Latin *sub* (below) and *ordinare* (to rank or order). Even inequality, etymologically, refers to space, coming from the old French *inéqualité*, which in turn comes from the Latin *inæqualis*, a compound of the prefix *in* (un-) and the word *æqualis*, derived from *æquus* (a flat surface, a flat or level piece of land).[1] This initial definition of inequality works as a substrate, and influences our understanding and reading of inequalities as spatially determined social phenomena.

However, as an historian interested in change over time, I wish to suggest using metaphors that refer to time, in order to analyse the social inequalities of the long nineteenth century: that is, from 1770 to the 1920s.[2] This century, described by Thomas Carlyle as a "mechanical age"[3] is also known as the age of the Industrial Revolution. One of its most important characteristics is the dominance of speed in every part of economic and social life.[4] More than this, Thomas Carlyle, even in 1829, considered that, "Not the external and physical alone is now managed by machinery, but the internal and spiritual also . . . The same habit regulates not our modes of action alone, but our modes of thought and feeling. Men are grown mechanical in head and heart, as well as in hand."[5] For Carlyle, bodies and souls were dependent on this new rhythm. At the beginning of the nineteenth century, the degree to which human beings were able to live and work in accordance with this new rhythm, regulated by the cadence of the machine, became a criterion for social classification. That is why the historian must choose his or her metaphors not only in the spatial but also in the temporal field: the different possibilities for access to speed must be considered when justifying social classification in this century.

But a question remains: if access to speed became, during the long nineteenth century, a criterion for social predominance in industrial Europe and the post-colonial Americas, is it possible to consider that its opposite, "slowness", concomitantly became a criterion for social relegation? Our hypothesis is that the evolution of the social meaning of slowness follows a distinct historical path. If we take the example of the French language, the word *lenteur* meant, when it appeared (in 1355), flexibility, adaptability, viscosity.[6] In the second half of the seventeenth century, another meaning appeared (lack of agility in action and reaction), and replaced the initial meanings. From the middle of the fourteenth century to the middle of the seventeenth century, the word acquired negative connotations. Moreover, in a recent history of rhythms in the Middle Ages, Jean-Claude Schmitt shows how the medieval *rhythmus* was related to harmony. This society in motion sought "to look in human rhythms for an echo of the rhythms of the world".[7] From that perspective, in that period, slowness was more related to devotion and the realm of the intimate. But the switch that took place in modern times, with the extension of the word's signification to every sphere of human activity, carried the semantic universe of slowness from the intimate to the collective sphere.

The author Cervantes clearly identified these changes: "Many grave histories of knights-errant have I read; but never yet have I read, seen, or heard of their carrying off enchanted knights-errant in this fashion, or at the slow pace that these lazy, sluggish animals promise; for they always take them away through the air with marvellous swiftness, enveloped in a dark thick cloud, or on a chariot of fire, or it may be on some hippogriff or other beast of the kind; but to carry me off like this on an ox-cart! By God, it puzzles me! But perhaps the chivalry and enchantments of our day take a different course from that of those in days gone by".[8] Just as Don Quixotte wonders if slowness is a "newly invented . . . mode of carrying off [knights]", my hypothesis is that the discovery of the New World, which put the Europeans in the presence of Amerindian cultures that were organized around other social rhythms, represented a central experience in the discriminatory attitude to slowness.

Since the beginnings of colonization, this notion of slowness has served to characterize the inability of Amerindians to work according to the European criteria of pace. Later, perhaps at the end of the seventeenth century or the beginning of the eighteenth century, slowness also became a way of characterizing the attitude of slaves on plantations (with adjectives such as nonchalant, indolent, lazy, sluggish). Based on these findings, it is possible to formulate the hypothesis that, in the colonial context of the Americas, notions of slowness served cultural discrimination.

From that perspective, an additional assumption must be made. At the beginning of the nineteenth century, perhaps by the 1820s, as the era of acceleration arrived[9], *slowness* became a criterion for social relegation, both in Europe and in the Americas. That is why, in order to describe social inequalities in this age of speed, the use of a category of words belonging to the temporal field is more pertinent. At the top of the hierarchy of these societies, it is possible to place the "conquering bourgeoisie", so well described by the French historian Charles Morazé,[10] with "its new weapon: steam"; and at the bottom — we can summarize here an intuition of the Brazilian geographer, Milton Santos[11] – the *slow men*. Instead of taking Milton Santos's definition, "those who do not have speed"[12], I would prefer the following line of French Caribbean poet Aimé Césaire: "those who never knew how to harness steam or electricity".[13]

The *slowness* of this category of people does not mean that they are not able, when necessary, to accelerate, and to maintain a fast pace, but rather that, like the Little Tramp in *Modern Times*, they are subordinated to this mechanical rhythm. They are considered *slow* because their practices do not correspond to "the temporal architecture of [industrial] societies",[14] which places at the heart of this new civilization the homogeneous and controlling pace of the chronometer. This *slowness*, perceived as a refusal of the constraint of clock time, is often denounced by the new masters of the economy with such words as laziness, idleness and vagrancy. In 1903, Frederick Taylor denounced the "systematic soldiering", or marking time, of working men).[15]

Slow men in nineteenth-century Brazilian port cities

I would like to illustrate these ideas with some examples chosen from Brazilian history. During the nineteenth century, it was no longer on the rural plantations of Brazil, but in the port cities, where the flow of economic life found its most important expression, that a new social discrimination developed, and this was articulated around the possibility of having access to, and control of, speed.

Port districts were the main places where the *slow men* lived and worked.[16] Mainly composed of slaves, or black freedmen, but also of the poorest, unskilled European migrants, the *slow men* represented a displaced population engaged mainly in street trading, construction and port-related activities. My research focuses on the port district of Rio de Janeiro at the end of the nineteenth and the beginning of the twentieth centuries. Here, the population was 60 percent black, and 70 percent of the remaining 40 percent were immigrants. This workforce had no permanent jobs. Recruitment was done daily, according to employers' need. Gathered in front of a wall, the men raised their hands and waited to be called. Those who were not chosen awaited possible new calls during the day. Meanwhile, staying near the calling area, they talked, played or drank.

Those waiting working men were often arrested by the police — who had been tasked with supressing everything that might represent the archaic in that age of industrial modernity. In the first decade of the twentieth century, more than 60 percent of those arrested in the port district were accused of vagrancy, drunkenness, disorder and gambling.[17] While the rationalization of working time should promote greater efficiency in production and trade, this workforce — which was both necessary and troublesome — was controlled, body and soul. By their behaviour during this waiting time, longshoremen and construction workers — who were involved in the entry of Rio into the era of modernity (transforming its port and city centre) — became a negation of this modernity. Their *slowness* came from the impossibility of being included in modern, industrial, society, where speed and acceleration became the new rhythm of reference for labour and trade. In this industrial era, both the masters of the economy and the police denounced and arrested the *slow men*. This reserve of workers, compelled to wait, was condemned for vagrancy — one of the synonyms for *slowness* at the time. From that perspective, *slowness* also referred to their lack of social purpose: these displaced people, considered vagrants, threatened the stability of modern society.

But my research is not restricted to enquiring into historical variations in the lexical use of *slowness* to describe social situations in Brazil; nor even to enquiring into the historical construction of the character of *slow men* during the nineteenth century. It is also necessary to understand the way *slow men*, during this post-colonial century, understood and read the potential of rhythm to access benefits or invent an area of freedom for themselves.

The rhythms of labour: conflict and resistance

Since it was in the area of work that speed became the dominant rhythm, it is not surprising that the social and industrial conflicts of the time can also be understood as conflicts of rhythms. The field of labour was a vital area, where other rhythms could make themselves heard — rhythms that were capable of disrupting the rational march of the bourgeoisie toward progress. Three phenomena could upset this march and introduce a discontinuity: slowing the pace of work, sabotaging it, or launching a strike.

Slowing the flow of work to obtain benefits had been used as a strategy in the plantations and workshops of the Americas since the end of the eighteenth century.[18] Stanley Stein demonstrated, using the case of Vassoura, in the Province of Rio de Janeiro, the various ways in which slaves tried to lower the planters' expectations of the pace of their work. Through these small, daily insubordinations, they provoked "a subtle form of reaction similar to a slowdown in effect", for example, forcing the master "to repeat several times each new detail";[19] or they "responded automatically 'Sim Senhor' to any positive command or opinion", but slowing down the rhythm "if surveillance slackened".[20] When the planter was coming closer, the slaves would sing a refrain ("the red sun is so hot") to warn the others of his arrival, in order that they might increase the rhythm of their work.

We could say the same of sabotage. In the sense of "deliberately and maliciously destroying property",[21] this word of French origin appears, at the beginning of the nineteenth century, to have had two meanings: literally, throwing sabots into a machine to prevent it from functioning; and doing something "quickly and badly".[22] There is evidence that sabotage was tried in some parts of Brazil, for example, by destroying the harvest.

The historiographical position is, however different for the strikes, which bring a total break in the rhythm of work, leading to paralysis. From the north to the south, from the middle of the nineteenth century onwards, each port city experienced strikes of slaves, or movements against the regulation of areas for street trading and the control of what could be sold there. The modernization of cities and societies was supposed to hide as much as possible of these activities, or at least keep them away from city centres. The Brazilian historian João José Reis worked on one such protest, the strike of black workers in 1857 in Salvador.[23] The strike erupted when the municipality proposed controlling slaves' and black freedmen's work in the city — a move which represented a way of disciplining blacks in urban public spaces. With the eventual success of this strike, the traders gained access to space and power in the municipality, thus replacing the planters. One of the objectives of both sides was to control the pace of work in the city. Similar things happened in Rio de Janeiro. In 1857, the slaves who worked in the Ponta d'Areia factory, one of the main manufacturing businesses in the city, which belonged to Viscount Mauá, downed tools. In 1858, the typesetters on the three newspapers of the city also decided to down tools, and circulated a "Typesetters' diary" denouncing their working conditions as similar to those of the slaves.[24]

For the *slow men*, the total shutdown of work was a way of defending their place in an ever more competitive public space.[25] In another example, in May 1872, 50 black *ganhadores* who had done the work of transporting dried meat (*carne seca*) from the port to the market fought with 12 white immigrants recruited by the masters. The *Diário do Rio de Janeiro* explained that these slaves had committed a *parede*, the name given to the first forms of work stoppage in Brazil, resulting in seven of them going to jail.[26]

These few examples illustrate the fact that any attempt to understand the social practices of the *slow men* invites us to develop a history sensitive to "weak intensities"[27] and "silent transformations".[28] Overt resistance is only the most obvious reaction. Other, subtler ones must be considered, since they also constitute a disguised, or veiled, contestation of the dominant rhythm.

Syncopating and swaying: a cunning stratagem to re-state their existence

To be more precise: if, in the domain of work, a protest against the imposition of a new rhythm fits into a logic of resistance, there are other domains where this protest fits into a logic of "re-existence", of restating one's existence.

To understand this path towards re-existence, we should reconsider the definition that French historians Marcel Détienne et Jean-Pierre Vernant gave to the Greek notion of *mêtis*:[29] "There is no doubt that *mêtis* is a type of intelligence and of thought, a way of knowing" (p. 3); "It operates on a shifting terrain, in uncertain and ambiguous situations" (p. 14); "its field of application is the world of movement, of multiplicity and of ambiguity" (p. 20); "*Mêtis* is itself a power of cunning and deceit. It operates through disguise. In order to dupe its victim, it assumes a form which masks, instead of revealing, its true being" (p. 21); "Vigilant and forever on the alert, *mêtis* also appears as multiple, *pantoie*, many-coloured, *poikile* and shifting, *aiole*" (p. 27). Drawing on this work, the sociologist Jean Duvignaud invited social scientists to wonder whether "everyday life is not made up of tricks. Do not these diversions characterize the common life as much as the rite? Tricks mean possibilities, potentialities not yet accomplished. This creates opportunity, or simply a form of freedom in an over-determined world."[30]

As we have already said, it was not in the social field of work that the obvious cunning of the *slow men* unfolded, but more broadly, in the daily routine, where their understanding led them to seize opportunities, to invent another kind of freedom.[31]

As an example, and to return to the case of the port of Rio, many blacks, while waiting for a call for work later in the day, tried to escape from the police by seeking refuge in the *casas de zungu* (black popular housing, hiding places where cheap meals were sold, on which blacks searching for friends, parties, gods, hope… silently converged).[32] To these places we should add the houses of Afro-Brazilian worship. These houses were mainly located in a district adjacent to the port called Little Africa. The court records provide examples of what happened in these places. Antônio Mina, sometimes called Antônio África, was arrested ten times between 1907 and 1910, for vagrancy, and then for sorcery, when his relationship with a house of worship was proved.[33]

In these houses of Afro-Brazilian worship, the black working men, while waiting, gathered at the back of the house so as not to hinder the devotions taking place. While the drum rhythms helped to call the gods, the *slow men* talked and drank, discussing the difficulties of everyday life, such as repression, relations with bosses, and ways to escape from these impositions, or organizing popular celebrations, in order to create an interlude in time. With alcohol, and using everything they had at hand (plate, spoon), it was not uncommon for some to begin to improvise lyrics (Jacques Rancière talks about a "poetry of the humble"[34]) and music.

This music was marked by the use of syncopation — reflecting a singular relationship with time. Syncopation means to value a beat considered weak in a rhythm: for example, beats one and three in a four-four time signature. In a military march, for example, on beats one and three, the soldiers advance a foot (they are symbolizing obedience). Syncopation consists in extending weak beats and thus, symbolically, in bringing the margins to the center. The analogy with the situation of the *slow men* is clear. Excluded, marginalized, they gave themselves, through syncopation, a power they did not have. For the clock-governed time of industrial modernity, they substituted a syncopated — and a "progressive"[35] — time.

This music was often accompanied by dance, marked by the use of small steps (*miudinho*), when the surrounding society required speed and fast walking, and also marked by the use of *ginga* — a way of dancing swaying one's hips. I am aware that these "dissolute movements" of black bodies, and in particular the "artificial rotations and contortions of the hips", had impressed European observers since the beginning of the nineteenth century.[36] But in this particular case, swaying one's hips while dancing could also be interpreted as a "cunning stratagem" to indicate rejection of the search for a correct and speedy way of doing things by the masters of the new economy[37]. For the body disciplined by industrial work, these dances substituted a body liberated by the swaying of the hips. This was another way to occupy space. It was, above all, in the *crioléus* (popular parties of ill repute) that these movements took place. The *maxixe* allowed men and women to move their bodies close together. One of the steps even consisted of putting the buttocks of the woman between the thighs of the man, and shaking vigorously. It is not so much an intention to shock public morality that matters here as a form of reaction to an anthropological transformation inferred by modern culture: the deprecation of the senses of proximity (taste, touch) to the benefit of the senses of distance (sight and hearing). On one hand, the world of the intellect; on the other, the world of the body and the senses. And it is precisely by their intertwined bodies that the *slow men* responded to the injunctions of this modernity.

Most of the time, these gatherings for music and dance took place in the night, often after midnight, when the legitimate face of the city was sleeping. Here was another kind of ability of the *slow men*, which consisted of investing time in activities that others would have considered pointless. In Salvador, a famous regular gathering was the "midnight Mocotó",[38] a diversion for people "who amused themselves without formality".[39] With alcohol, music and dance, they talked, shouted and played, engaging in scenes deliberately shocking to bourgeois morality. In 1901, the poet Leandro Gomes de Barros published a popular poem, "Midnight in the cabaret",[40] which begins with these verses:

> Meia-noite! Repicou
> No sino da catedral
> Um silêncio sepulcral
> Pela cidade passou
> O momento já chegou
> Dos versos da solidão
> A orgia, a corrupção
> Sob o véu da noite escura
> Espalha a negra tortura
> Sob o véu da maldição

Those occasions and those hidden places, such as the houses of worship (like the famous house of Tia Ciata), were the birthplace of a music which was to become known, at the start of the decade beginning in 1910, as the *samba*.[41] However, before being so named, and accepted as a musical form, social practices relating to the situation of waiting for work had already resulted in musical, poetic and material forms. I am aware that there has been a professionalization process affecting some musicians going on since the mid-nineteenth century.[42] But my point is a different one. In this case, the music did not fit into a logical professional development, but broke into a waiting time. For the *slow men*, it was a means of expression,[43] in a society that did not give these men a voice; it was a way of taking their place in time and space. In other words, this music and dance, as a "cunning stratagem", was a way of overcoming exclusion, allowing the *slow men* to insert themselves into the political field.

Conclusion

In conclusion, I should like to point out that the research hypothesis of this paper belongs in what I see as a major research field: "the social history of waiting".[44] From this perspective, for the masters of the new economy of the nineteenth century, *slowness* served to name the attitude of workers who were put in the position of waiting for work.

But if one takes the distinction, proposed by the linguist Kenneth Pike,[45] between a language level used by actors in a given culture (the emic level — that comes from phonemics) and a language level distanced from the observer or investigator (the etic level — created from phonetics), can we say that *slowness*, whilst qualified at the etic level, is lived and felt at the emic level? This question has led me to investigate ways of resistance and "cunning stratagems" related to rhythms — from slowing down to complete strikes, from syncopating to swaying.

The *slow men's* capacity to move from one social universe to another, understanding the negotiating potential of changing rhythms, has transformed them into cultural mediators. Instead of the expression "Atlantic Creoles", proposed by Ira Berlin,[46] João José Reis suggests the notion of "ladinization" (drawn from the Iberian word *ladino*, which means cunning).[47] My purpose in proposing the notion of *slow men* is to insist on their ability to move from one level to another in the social hierarchy of the nineteenth century, when people's relationship to speed put them into different social divisions and became an element of social discrimination.

As Michel Foucault said of "infamous men", we can say that "real lives" were "enacted" in these few sentences,[48] in these few adjectives used by the new masters of the economy and trade to denounce the inability of the *slow men* to fall in with the new rhythms of work. The challenge for the historian is to find, under the mask of the *slow men*, the complexity and singularity of these lives, and under the anomy, unexpected creations. As Kenneth White wrote: "It is in the poor places, where, apparently, nothing takes place, that, from time to time, something of the greatest importance may occur".[49]

Notes

1 Michel Breal and Anatole Bailly, *Dictionnaire étymologique du latin* (Paris: Hachette, 1885), p. 4.

2 For the periodization, I am referring both to Eric Hobsbawm's classic definition of the long nineteenth century (1789–1914), and to its broader interpretation by scholars such as Christopher Bayly in *The Birth of the Modern World (1780–1914): Global Connections* (Oxford, Blackwell, 2004) and Jurgen Osterhammel in *The Transformation of the World: A Global History of the Nineteenth Century* (Princeton: Princeton University Press, 2014).

3 Thomas Carlyle, "Signs of the Time" [1829], in *Critical and Miscellaneous Essays* (New York: Scribner, Welford & Co, 1872), p. 233.

4 Christophe Studeny, *L'invention de la vitesse. France, XVIIIe–XXe siècle* (Paris: Gallimard, 1995).

5 Carlyle, "Signs of the Time".

6 Alain Rey, *Dictionnaire historique de la langue française* (Paris: Dictionnaires Le Robert, 2000).

7 Jean-Claude Schmitt, *Les rythmes au Moyen-Age* (Paris: Gallimard-NRF, 2016).

8 Miguel de Cervantes, *Don Quixote de La Mancha* [1605], trans. John Ormsby (London: Smith Elder, 1885), vol. 1, chapter 47, "Of the strange manner in which Don Quixote of La Mancha was 1764 carried away enchanted, together with other remarkable incidents".

9 Rosa Hartmut, *Social Acceleration. A New Theory of Modernity* (New York: Columbia University Press, 2013).

10 Charles Morazé, *The Nineteenth Century* (London: George Allen and Unwin Ltd, 1976) [*Les bourgeois conquérants, XIXe siècle* (Paris: Armand Colin, 1957)].

11 Milton Santos, "Metrópole. A Força dos Fracos é Seu Tempo Lento", in *Técnica, Espaço e Tempo. Globalização e Meio Técnico-Científico-Informacional* (São Paulo: Hucitec, 1994), pp. 77–82. Milton Santos never returned to this question of *slow men*. The first attempt at an elaboration of his ideas was produced by Ana Clara Torres Ribeiro, "Homens Lentos, Opacidades e Rugosidades", *Redobra* (Salvador) 9 (2012): 58–71. But, like Milton Santos's, her study focuses on contemporary cities.

12 "Se velocidade é força, o pobre, quase imóvel na grande cidade, seria o fraco... Creio porém que na cidade, grande cidade atual, tudo se dá ao contrário. A força é dos 'lentos' e não dos que detém a velocidade... Se pobres, homens comuns, os homens 'lentos' acabam por ser mais velozes na descoberta do mundo... inseridos que estão num processo intelectual contraditório e criativo", *Santos, Técnica, Espaço e Tempo.*

13 Aimé Césaire, "Cahiers d'un retour au pays natal", *Volontés* 20 (1939).

14 Krzysztof Pomian, *L'ordre du temps* (Paris : Gallimard, 1984), p. 232.

15 Frederick Taylor, "Shop Management", in *Transactions of the American Society of Mechanical Engineers,* vol. 24, 1903, pp. 1337–1480 (p. 1349).

16 For more information on *slow men*, see Laurent Vidal, "Les ruses des hommes lents", *L'Histoire* 425–426 (July-August 2016), pp. 94–9.

17 Erika Bastos Arantes, "Negros do Porto. Trabalho, Cultura e Repressão Policial no Rio de Janeiro, 1900–1910", in *Trabalhadores na Cidade*, ed. Elcienne Azevedo, Jefferson Cano, Maria Clementina Perreira Cunha and Sidney Chaloub (Campinas: Unicamp, 2009), pp. 107–156.

18 Lorena S. Walsh, "Work and Resistance in the New Republic. The Case of Chesapeake 1770–1820", in *From Chattel Slaves to Wage Slaves. The Dynamic of Labour Bargaining in the Americas*, ed. Mary Turner (London: James Currey Ltd, 1995), pp. 97–122.

19 Stanley Stein, *Vassouras. A Brazilian Coffee County, 1850–1900. The Roles of Planters and Slaves in a Plantation Society* [1958] (Princeton University Press, 1985), p. 140.

20 Stein, *Vassouras*, p. 168.

21 Douglas Harper, *Online Etymology Dictionary*, http://www.etymonline.com/index.php?term=sabotage, accessed 30 November 2015.

22 Alain Rey, *Dictionnaire culturel en langue française*, vol. 4 (Paris: Dictionnaires Le Robert, 2005), p. 477.

23 João José Reis, "A Greve Negra de 1857 na Bahia", *Revista USP*, 18 (1993): 8–29.

24 Artur José Renda Vitorino, *Máquinas e Operários: Mudança Técnica e Sindicalismo Gráfico (São Paulo e Rio de Janeiro, 1858–1912)* (São Paulo: Annablume/Fapesp, 2000).

25 Maria Cecília Velasco Cruz, "Virando o Jogo: Estivadores e Carregadores no Rio de Janeiro da Primeira República" (Ph.D, dissertation., USP, São Paulo, 1998); Juliana Barreto Farias, "Descobrindo Mapas dos Minas: Alforrias, Frabalho Urbano e Identidades", in *No Labirinto das Nações: Africanos e Identidades no Rio de Janeiro, Século XIX*, ed. J. B. Farias, Flávio dos S. Gomes and Carlos Eugênio Soares (Rio de Janeiro: Arquivo Nacional, 2005).

26 Juliana Barreto Farias, "Mercado em Greve: Protestos e Organização dos Trabalhadores do Pequeno Comércio no Rio de Janeiro — Outubro, 1885", *Anais da Biblioteca Nacional*, 127 (2010): 99–157.

27 See: Paul Veyne, "L'interprétation, l'interprète. A propos des choses de la religion", *Enquête* 3 (1996): 241–272; Arlette Farge, *Le bracelet de parchemin. L'écrit sur soi au XVIIIe siècle* (Paris: Bayard, 2003), pp. 59–61. On the question of weak actors see: Marc Bessin and Laurence Roulleau Berger, "Les armes du faible sont-elles de faibles armes?" *L'homme et la société* 143–144 (2002): 3–11.

28 François Jullien, *The Silent Transformations* [2009] (Chicago: Chicago University Press, 2011).

29 Marcel Detienne and Jean-Pierre Vernant, *Cunning Intelligence in Greek Culture and Society*, trans. Janet Lloyd (Chicago: University of Chicago Press, 1991).

30 Jean Duvignaud, "La ruse", *Cause Commune* 1 (1977): 8–9.

31 Gérard Noiriel has demonstrated this in his book, *Chocolat clown nègre, l'histoire oubliée du premier artiste noir de la scène* (Paris: Bayard, 2012).

32 *Cidades Negras*, p.36.

33 Arantes, "Negros do Porto".

34 Jacques Rancière, *Aisthesis: scènes du régime esthétique de l'art* (Paris: Galilée, 2011).

35 Gilberto Freyre, "On the Iberian Conception of Time", *American Scholar* 41 (1963): 415–30.

36 Johann Baptiste von Spix and Carl Friedrich Philipp von Martius, *Viagem Pelo Brasil, 1817–1820*, vol. 1 (Belo Horizonte: Itatiaia, 1981), p. 180.

37 In the middle of eighteenth century, Laurence Sterne exclaimed: "This *right line* — the path-way for Christians to walk in!" See Laurence Sterne, *The Life and Opinions of Tristram Shandy, Gentleman*, vol. 6 (London: T. Becket and P. Dehont, 1762), p. 155.

38 See Manoel Querino, *A Bahia de Outrora* [1916] (Salvador: Livraria Progresso Editora, 1955).

39 "Na Fonte do Boi", *Jornal de Notícias*, Bahia, 8 February 1905.

40 Leandro Gomes de Barros, *Meia noite no Cabaré* (Fortaleza: Literatura de Cordel, 2001) [1901].

41 Muniz Sodré, *Samba, o Dono do Corpo* [1979] (Rio de Janeiro: Mauad, 1998).

42 For an example see Matthias Röhrig Assunção, "From Slave to Popular Culture: The Formation of Afro-Brazilian Art Forms in Nineteenth-Century Bahia and Rio de Janeiro", *Iberoamericana,* Nueva Época, Año 3 (December 2003): 159–76.

43 Arlette Farge, *Dire et mal dire. L'opinion publique au XVIIIe siècle* (Paris: Seuil, 1992).

44 Laurent Vidal, "Pour une histoire sociale de l'attente", in *Mazagão la ville qui traversa l'Atlantique. Du Maroc à l'Amazonie* (Paris: Aubier, 2005), pp. 251–5.

45 Kenneth Pike, *Language in Relation to a Unified Theory of the Structure of Human Behavior* (Dallas: Summer Institute of Linguistics, 1954).

46 Ira Berlin, "From Creole to African: Atlantic Creoles and the Origins of African-American Society in Mainland North-America", *The William and Mary Quarterly* 53, 2 (1996): 251–88.

47 João José Reis, *Domingos Sodré. Um Sacerdote Africano. Escravidão, Liberdade e Candomblé na Bahia do Século XIX* (São Paulo: Cia das Letras, 2008), pp. 316–17.

48 Michel Foucault, "Lives of Infamous men", in *Essential Works of Foucault*, vol. 3, *Power*, ed. P. Rabinov (New York: The New Press, 1997), p. 160.

49 Kenneth White, *Investigations dans l'espace nomade* (Paris: Isolato, 2014), p. 43.

CHAPTER

8

Inequalities in Brazilian Literature

Muita Saúva e Pouca Saúde, os Males da Literatura Brasileira são

VINICIUS MARIANO DE CARVALHO

To anyone familiar with Brazilian literature, the above title contains a direct reference to the eponymous anti-hero of the novel *Macunaíma*, a man "without any character", who was introduced into the world of Brazilian literature by the writer Mário de Andrade in 1928.[1] Macunaíma, is known, among other things, for his repeated statement that "armies of ants and poor health are the ills of Brazil". The same statement is found in another important Brazilian literary work, Limo Barreto's *Triste Fim de Policarpo Quaresma*[2] (published in 1911 and translated as *The Sad End of Policarpo Quaresma*). The protagonist of Barreto's novel is Major Quaresma, a modern man trapped in a pre-modern Brazil, who must overcome the brutality of nature, represented by the voracious ants destroying his land, and the ineptitude of a state that disregards the health and well-being of its people.

These two factors — a multitude of insects, and poor health — do indeed represent two key paradigms of Brazil: a land of monstrous and exotic creatures capable of destroying a plantation in a few heartbeats; and a society fraught with problems. Each paradigm is still very much alive, and easily identifiable in contemporary Brazilian cultural production. Brazilian literature has always oscillated between these two poles: the demand for magical, fantastic, and exotic storytelling; and the critique of an unjust and problematic social reality. For centuries, authors have gravitated towards one pole or the other; and contemporary Brazilian literature is still engaged in this confrontation between divergent aesthetics and objectives. The international readership of Brazilian literature should, however, be considered co-responsible for the reiteration of these paradigms and the strengthening of a binary that hides the complexity of what Brazilian literature can offer. International readers and film audiences seem to expect Brazilian artists either to reaffirm an exotic image of the country, or to present a social critique in a more-or-less linear and didactic fashion — or both. In expecting these visions, international audiences reinforce their own prejudices and views (sometimes utopian, sometimes politically engaged) about Brazil. The result is that the reception of artistic production coming from Brazil, artistic production which offers important material for critical thinking both generally and globally, has been lacking in nuance, with a failure to fully formulate theoretical questions.

In 2013, Brazil was Guest of Honour at the Frankfurt Book Fair. This event drew attention to contemporary Brazilian cultural production and gave additional visibility to a country whose international prominence had been growing exponentially in recent years. The Brazilian author Luiz Ruffato spoke at the opening ceremony of the Book Fair; and his speech[3] proved to be extremely provocative in several ways. Ruffato's key question was: "What does it mean to live in this region situated on the periphery of the world, to write in Portuguese for readers who are nearly non-existent, to fight every day in the midst of such adversities, to try and construct a sense of life."[4] Avoiding naive generalizations, Ruffato's speech drew attention to the role of literature as a complex transformative device.

For many years, Brazilian literature has found itself on the periphery of the periphery. Situated within the spectrum of Latin American writing, Brazil has traditionally occupied a particularly remote province of world literature. The Portuguese language, already peripheral in the European context, is even more peripheral in the Latin American context. What can the general reader expect from a country which is largely known for carnival, football, beaches and *mulatto* women? The typical response, according to Ruffato, invokes exoticism, i.e., a paradisiac land where people are poor but happy, because they are close to an exuberant nature and embody a spirit free of moral constraints.

But Brazil is also, even as a location on the periphery, a land of social inequalities, a country that needs to break with its cycles of social oppression in order to be able to sit down at the table of developed countries and finally be considered an "adult". What should be expected, therefore, of a country with one of the highest rates of social inequality in the world? Clearly an engagement with reality, especially by denouncing real social ills.

It is no surprise, then, that the novelist Jorge Amado has been universally designated the quintessential Brazilian writer. His poor but happy characters, and colourful scenes with sexy *mulattas* and powerful landowners, have populated the imagination of readers everywhere. In the creation of Brazil's international image, sensuality and exoticism have prevailed, not least due to the global success of TV serials and films based on Amado's novels, including: *Gabriela, Cravo e Canela* (1958, translated as *Gabriela, Clove and Cinnamon*); *Dona Flor e Seus Dois Maridos* (1966, translated as *Dona Flor and Her Two Husbands*); and *Tieta*, (1977). Yet rarely in Amado's fiction do we find evidence of Brazil's complicated past, of its history fraught with violence and subordination. Few questions are raised about the representations of power or the resistance to tyranny.

According to Ruffato, Brazil, a country of enormous social inequalities, must try to "grow" and break its cycles of social oppression. In this coming-of-age process, literature has a very specific role to play. Ruffato's Frankfurt speech repudiates familiar fantasies and illusions about the country and foregrounds the potential that Brazilian literature now holds for Brazil and for the world. Underlining national paradoxes, Ruffato's claim is that the real potential of Brazilian literature to provoke social transformation resides in its pervasive depiction and discussion of "otherness". Indeed, Brazilian literature is able to mirror a multiple, complex, divided, and pluralistic country; to problematize the concepts of self and other, and to demonstrate how, in the words of Ruffato, "we have turned our backs on the other — whether immigrant, poor, black, indigenous, female, homosexual — in an attempt to preserve ourselves, forgetting that in doing so we are imploding our own conditions of existence". I am not referring to pamphleteering works guided by a political agenda, but to a space for reflection in which to counteract indifference towards social issues and consider major ethical and existential questions of global relevance. Ruffato's speech claims, provocatively, that, rather than simply presenting ideas about rightness and wrongness, Brazilian literature today should in fact reflect otherness.

The close of the twentieth and start of the twenty-first centuries saw a number of new and significant literary voices appear in Brazil, able to focus on both formal experimentation and historically neglected issues, such as racism, gender-based exclusion and violence against minorities. Many of these authors address the visibility and empowerment of the subaltern classes directly and are part of an extremely important development in Brazilian literature.

Dilemmas of Brazilian literature: a colonial syndrome

Flora Sussekind, in a highly judicious study, warns that "it is a general rule in Brazilian literary historiography to search for influences and authenticities."[5] This vision tends to perceive literature as reproduction rather than production, and as a consequence, spaces are not opened up for voices that clash with this supposed tradition.

In writings on the history of Brazilian literature, this vision persistently reads Brazilian literary production in the light of the history of European literature, with Brazilian literature always seen as the inferior version. Indeed, the standards of the literary canon privilege those authors whose works divert least from the European model. Again, Sussekind writes:

> The construction of a literary history, like that of a family tree, is done by hiding differences and discontinuities. No emphasis is put on anything that could stain, ridicule or undermine the profile of its great authors. Nothing that could cast doubt over the characterization of this literature as a continuous and evolutionary process of improvement.[6]

Brazil was "discovered" by Portugal in the year 1500. In the context of the great European navigations and the expansion of maritime empires, Portugal and Spain took control of the New World, subjugating lands and peoples and imposing a language, a culture, a religion and consequently a literature.

In the territory that would constitute Brazil, there do not seem to have been indigenous cultures who had mastered writing, and the literature that they had created, like all their forms of culture, was oral, performative and embodied. To borrow a term from Western philosophy, it was phenomenological. In bringing a language and writing to the territory, Portugal also imposed literary models, which started to be cultivated by a local elite of Portuguese descent. Models were adopted with a "delay" in relation to metropolitan Portugal.

It is important to note that during the first years of European presence in the Brazilian territory, two visions populated the European imagination with regards to the New World: that of an earthly paradise, and that of a hell inhabited by absurd beings. The first texts that reported back about Brazil were full of images that were similar to mythological descriptions of the Garden of Eden: exotic, full of colourful plants, trees with succulent fruits, and animals that had never been seen before. Images were of people who were gentle, friendly and fundamentally pure and innocent, indigenous people who walked around naked, unashamed of revealing their bodies. Paradoxically, these same images also served to construct a hellish vision of the New World. This same paradise contained the aggressive brutality of an uncontrollable nature, with wild beasts, monsters, and even worse, cannibals.

With the occupation of the territory by the Portuguese, the latter's "rule" over nature and over the land's native peoples (who were systematically exterminated) led to the imposition of a new exploitative colonial order. Under this new order, another vision was added, that of the Black African, enslaved and subjugated, a phenomenon that during the first 100 years of colonization became another of what I am calling the socio-historical, aesthetic-cultural, ethnic-ethical expressions and realities that have shaped what we call Brazil.

With the imposition of this colonial order, the expression of subaltern and oppressed peoples was mediated through the language and voice of the coloniser, who continued to see them as either exotic or barbaric. They never had their own voice, were never the authors of their own literature.

The process of "taming" the territory, done through the rule of law and an imposed faith, was intended to eliminate its barbaric nature, one of the main justifications for the colonial enterprise. Nonetheless this process of "taming" brought with it a perverse social-economic order, and that violent and barbaric nature was transformed into an oppressive society.

My point is this: in the founding of a colonial Brazil, two visions were forged which pervaded all aesthetic representations of nature and society in the country, namely exoticism and barbarity, or both at the same time. In the founding of a colonial Brazil, an inequality of voices was also forged, a structure of power which used the subaltern as a form of discourse, but which did not allow this subaltern to express by itself. In other words, literary creation was also "tamed".

A national literature

In the year 1808, the then Prince Regent, Dom João VI, fleeing from the Napoleonic troops who were invading Portugal, decided to move the Portuguese court to Rio de Janeiro. For the first time in European history, a colony became the seat of a kingdom. The departure of the Portuguese royal family to Brazil, in addition to elevating this territory to the status of a united kingdom, also led to an intellectual and political awakening for the colony. The drive for independence, which was already strong among elites in the colony, was intensified by King Dom João VI's return to Portugal in 1821, and in the following year, 1822, Dom Pedro, the prince who was heir to the throne of Portugal, proclaimed Brazilian independence and became the country's first monarch.

In the recently-created country, there was a genuine cultural movement to build a national identity which would be anti-Portuguese, and which would emphasize the values of the new country. It was in this context that a group of young Brazilian students in Paris, led by Domingos José Gonçalves de Magalhães (1811–1882) and Manuel de Araújo Porto Alegre (1806–1879), started a movement to reform Brazilian literature. Influenced by French romanticism, they founded the magazine *Niterói: Revista Brasiliense de Ciências, Letras e Artes*. In 1836, Gonçalves de Magalhães published a volume of poetry entitled *Suspiros Poéticos e Saudades*, officially marking the start of romanticism in Brazil. This first wave of romanticism was characterized by an attempt to differentiate itself from the European origins of the movement, adapting itself in a spirit of nationalism to Brazil's exotic natural environment and to its history prior to colonization.

The Brazilian romantics, who were strongly influenced by Montaigne and Rousseau, idealized the indigenous subject as a noble savage living in total harmony with nature; but, in this depiction, they were also reflecting European heroic values. This movement, which was aesthetically broad, and extended to painting and music, was known as "Indianism", and generated what could be called a foundational mythology for Brazil. Works such as *O Guarani* (1857), *Iracema* (1865), and *Ubirajara* (1874), by José de Alencar (1829–1877), became essential reading and inspired the idealization of the Brazilian indigenous people, who had by this stage been practically wiped out by the colonial enterprise. Yet again, the appeal of the exotic became the keystone of this literature. The indigenous subjects themselves remained silent and imagined, figurative and picturesque. On the back of this first movement of the colonial period, realism reinforced the idea of "a literature that is required to be documentary in nature".[7]

The dawn of the Republic in Brazil (1889), and the renewed task of understanding and building a nation, led to an even more intense form of realism in the quest to document the country. This was a quest in which "what mattered what not what was romantic or literary, but rather the possibility that these narratives could portray aspects of the 'Brazilian reality' with 'truth' and 'honesty'".[8] (Authors such as Euclides da Cunha (1866–1909), Monteiro Lobato (1882–1948) and Lima Barreto (1881–1922), who wrote with considerable literary originality and narrative power, have always been read by critics in way that is more socially-minded than literary. Works such as Euclides da Cunha's *Os Sertões* (1902, translated as *Rebellion in the Backlands*) and Lima Barreto's *Triste Fim de Policarpo Quaresma* (translated as *The Sad End of Policarpo Quaresma*) have continued to fall prey to readings that suppress literary ambiguities, connotations and specificities in the name of denotation, transparency and macro-historic concerns.

Brazilian modernism: the dilemma is finally exposed

In 1922 the *Semana de Arte Moderna* (Modern Art Week), a milestone in the development of twentieth-century Brazilian literature, was celebrated in São Paulo. During this event, a group of artists and intellectuals who were heavily influenced by the European avant-garde initiated what they called a reform of national literature. Many expressions and names exploded onto the scene during this first avant-garde moment, which continued the ever more pressing search for a marker of what was genuinely Brazilian, and what could be identified as national literature. Of these exponents, two authors stand out: Oswald de Andrade and Mario de Andrade.

Oswald de Andrade (1890–1954) was the most enthusiastic and articulate member of the modernist movement in Brazil. Although a poet, playwright and novelist, he is better known for his activism and ideological engagement. He launched magazines and manifestos, among them *Manifesto Antropofágico*[9] (1928, translated as *Cannibalist Manifesto*) which, in my view, revolutionized how the construction of Brazilian culture was perceived and became a paradigm for interpreting Brazil as a whole. We will come back to the idea of cultural anthropophagy later. In Oswald's artistic output, what stands out is an iconoclasm in literary form which broke with the established models of "good writing" and freed Brazilian Portuguese of its inferiority complex in relation to the language of Camões.

The erudite Mario de Andrade, who was a great connoisseur of classical art and music, and a musicologist, and who also had a deep understanding of ethnography, always concerned himself with searching for Brazil's roots, which he considered were in danger of vanishing in the face of the rapid modernization, industrialization and urbanization that the country, and in particular São Paulo, were experiencing. A superficial reading of Mario de Andrade's output might suggest that he was an entrenched nationalist; but in fact this was an author who was very much ahead of his time.

Andrade's first work, *Macunaíma – O Herói Sem Nenhum Caráter* (the Portuguese subtitle means "a hero without any character") provoked a revolution in form and narrative style, and called for a re-evaluation of what nationality meant in Brazil. Although his work borders on both exoticism and realism, which, as we have seen, is a constant in Brazilian literature, Andrade does not allow his writing to be dominated by either of these qualities. Rather he combines the two currents anthropophagically, and opens up a unique third way with regards to literary expression.

Throughout his adventures in Brazil, Andrade's protagonist, Macunaíma, repeats the famous phrase that I have adapted as an epithet for this chapter: *Os males do Brasil são: muita saúva e pouca saúde* (Armies of ants and poor health are the poison of Brazil). Obviously, I am mindful of the dangers of analytical reductionism; but I do see in this phrase a synthesis of the author's opposition to the repeated use of either exotic images or those of an extreme critical realism in constructing a national literature. Those excluded from the social and economic order are celebrated by modernism, but nonetheless remain the subjects of literature, rather than its authors or agents. Their voices are still mediated through a covert ethnography.

After the first years of so-called modernism in Brazil, the 1930s saw a second hugely significant movement in Brazilian literature, one which once again relied on the paradigms of an exotic or realist criticism of society, and which came to be known as regionalism. Originating in Recife, Pernambuco, and influenced by the sociologist Gilberto Freyre, this movement aimed to preserve the traditions of this region which, according to Freyre, were in danger of vanishing in the face of advancing social and economic modernization. In 1926, Freyre convened the Primeiro Congresso Regionalista do Nordeste (First Regionalist Conference of the Northeast) in Recife, and this laid the foundations of a movement which extended beyond literature. Many writers immediately identified with its aesthetic and produced a fantastic body of material comprising the best known and most frequently translated texts of all Brazilian literature.

The first of the so-called regionalist novels was *A Bagaceira* (1928, translated as *Trash*) by José Américo de Almeida. This was followed by *O Quinze* (1930, translated as *The Fifteen*, meaning the year 1915), a literary debut by Raquel de Queiróz (1910–2003), and the "sugar cane" cycle of novels by José Lins do Rego: *Menino de Engenho* (1932), *Doidinho* (1933), *Bangüê* (1934), *Moleque Ricardo* (1935), and *Usina* (1936). These authors set their works in the sugar-producing Northeast of the country, and constructed whole sagas whose subject matter appeared exotic even to readers in other parts of Brazil. In these sagas, social problems were caused by continuous and hard droughts, and by a patriarchal society that had been moulded by slavery. The generation the novels depict, usually called the *geração de 30* (generation of 1930), was deeply influenced by communism and by intellectual attempts to encourage social change. Once more, literary subject matter was addressed with the logic of extreme realism, which had become almost a political obligation for the author, with the "primitive" backlands providing an exotic setting, the other constant of Brazilian literature. It should be noted that this was not (and still is not) simply a writers' concern, but also a concern for readers and critics, particularly foreigners, and all of these people have together been responsible for shaping the model of Brazilian literature.

This is the point where we return to Jorge Amado, whom I mentioned earlier. This regionalist author constructed a series of novels overflowing with exoticism but also, simultaneously, with social critique. In his work, we find the two currents which, I argue, shape the way in which literature produced in Brazil is read. This encounter in the work of Jorge Amado is not simply a matter of literary theory by critics, but represents readers' acceptance and assimilation of these drivers as productive stimuli. It comes as no surprise that Jorge Amado is the most frequently translated Brazilian author — translated into many languages — in the history of Brazilian literature. His works have also been adapted for cinema and serialized for television, making him the most popular Brazilian author worldwide.

Another author who is considered a regionalist, but who, in my view, surpasses this label to create something unique, is Graciliano Ramos (1892–1953), who, like Mario de Andrade, manages to navigate the troubled waters of exoticism and realism without drowning in either of these currents. The author of masterpieces such as *São Bernardo* (1934), *Caetés* (1933), *Angústia* (1936) and *Vidas Secas* (1938), Graciliano deals with real political action without giving it the leading role.

At the same time, his work is profoundly Northeastern, without descending into caricature or a picturesque style. His novels have philosophical depth and unrivalled aesthetic rigour: the language is stripped-back and precise in a manner unmatched in Brazilian literature.

This literature may, with Graciliano Ramos, have developed beyond the original traits of the regionalist label; but the poor, black people, the backlands dwellers remain its subjects and have no space to express themselves. Again, objects. There is still no opportunity for them to be the speaking subject.

After modernism: contemporary currents

The last quarter of the twentieth century witnessed the arrival on the scene of a number of authors who, for various reasons, defined their generation. The harsh and cruel existential experience of AIDS was tackled by authors such as Caio Fernando Abreu (1948–1996) with a stripped-back narrative voice, full of both anguish and hope. The short story and the *feuilleton* grew in popularity during this period, and humour was used as a successful antidote to political repression. Authors such as Luis Fernando Veríssimo, Carlos Scliar, and Carlos Heitor Cony succeeded in writing short narratives full of social critique disguised with subtle forms of humour. What was clear was that literature had regained its prominent position as a form of social critique, and that authorial political engagement had become increasingly relevant in the historical context in which these writers lived.

On the other hand, exotic representations were now being blended with social critique in brutalist urban narratives by authors such as Rubem Fonseca (1925–), who uses urban violence as a major theme in his short stories. His most famous work, *Feliz Ano Novo* (1975), is a collection of short stories whose style became influential due to its handling of brutality and violence in an almost iconic manner. This brutalist style gained disciples and developed into a trend we see today, in which the representation of urban violence, particularly that of the favelas, is the hallmark of a series of authors such as Patrícia Melo, Nelson Faria, Ferrez, Paulo Lins, and others. Paulo Lins, famous the world over for his best-seller *Cidade de Deus* (1997, translated as *City of God*), succeeds in combining the exotic element of excessive violence with a text whose realist-naturalist currents emphasize social critique, reinforcing the paradigm of "armies of ants and poor health".

The beginning of the twenty-first century brought with it a number of interesting innovations, with a wave of young writers experimenting with new forms of language and new perspectives. These writers brought to the literary scene issues that had historically been neglected in the field of literature and in Brazilian society, issues such as race, gender, minorities: essentially, the empowerment of the subaltern classes. Conceição Evaristo, in *Um Defeito de Cor* (2009), brings us the unique voice of a black woman, taking us back to the year 1960; recalling Carolina Maria de Jesus, a black woman from the favelas, in her novel *Quarto de Despejo*[10] (1960, translated as *Beyond All Pity*), who was a pioneer in a narrative of the periphery which calls for the empowerment of the subaltern classes in Brazil .

In a movement that calls for a non-revolutionary uprising, many authors from geographical and social locations on the periphery are now making their voices heard and, in contrast to the clichéd representation of the periphery as a locus of violence, they narrate their own visions of the world, lending a poetic voice to this marginalized space. Marcos Vinicius Faustini is a good example, with his *Guia Afetivo da Periferia* (2009). In this same area of subaltern empowerment, Brazil has also witnessed the birth of a literature written by its indigenous people.

There are clear signs of change in the paradigms of Brazilian literature, with works and authors that challenge the established images and representations of Brazil. At the same time, there is a perception that the historical inequalities have shifted from the field of thematic representation to that of challenging who has the power of expression. Regina Dalcastagnè, critic and Professor of Brazilian Literature at the University of Brasilia, provides a good definition of the panorama of Brazilian literature in a recent work, calling it a "contested territory". What stands out in her study is that the road is long, and that in this literature the inequalities are still striking. Dalcastagè writes:

> To cite just some of the figures, of all the major Brazilian literary prizes (Portugal Telecom, Jabuti, Machado de Assis, São Paulo de Literatura, Passo Fundo Zaffari and Bourbon) awarded between the years 2006 and 2011, 29 were awarded to men and only one to a woman (in the "new writers" award category of the *Prêmio São Paulo de Literatura*). Another, more extensive, piece of research, which I myself coordinated at the University of Brasilia, shows that of all the novels published by the main Brazilian publishing houses over a period of 15 years (1990 to 2004), 120 of the 165 authors, or 72.7 percent, are men. More shocking still is the racial homogeneity: 93.9 percent of the authors are white. More than 60 percent of them live in Rio de Janeiro and São Paulo. Almost all of them are in the professions, operating in spaces that are privileged for the production of discourse: journalistic and academic environments.[11]

In contrast, the characters, as subjects, continue to be subaltern: the drug dealer, the criminal, the poor. What Dalcastagnè's study shows clearly is that this is without doubt a literature which reflects the dilemmas of a society that is changing radically, a county that has moved beyond being an exotic, colourful, utopian paradise, a nation with a multiplicity of creative forces which produce a literature that does not necessarily need to confine itself to the task of providing descriptions of the world rooted in realism. Finally, contemporary Brazilian literature, although still fulfilling the demand for realist social critique or portrayals of a picturesque Brazil — whether this demand comes from readers or critics — demonstrates a vitality which challenges the aesthetic parameters that are applied to it. In conclusion, and this is to pick up on the issues Luiz Ruffato raised in his speech at the Frankfurt Book Fair in 2013, contemporary Brazilian literature, in dealing with issues that are deeply Brazilian, becomes a literature that is universal in nature, since ultimately it is dealing with ethical and philosophical questions which are of importance for the whole world.

One thing is certain: Brazilian literature is no longer a literature that refracts imposed aesthetics, but one which stands on its own two feet aesthetically, and challenges any critical criteria that fail to consider the socio-historical-cultural reality in which it was produced. In a country which has historically sought to challenge forms of power, and in which socially subaltern groups have revealed a critical and creative voice, contemporary Brazilian literature is able to reflect this reality, and transform it.

Further reading

Afrânio Coutinho, *Introdução à Literatura no Brasil* (Rio de Janeiro: Civilização Brasileira, 1968).

Antonio Candido, *Formação da Literatura Brasileira*, vols 1 and 2, 6th edn, (Belo Horizonte: Editora Itatiaia LTDA, 2000).

Haroldo de Campos, *Metalinguagem e outras linguagens* (São Paulo: Perspectiva, 2010[a]), pp. 231–255.

Roberto Schwarz, *Que horas são?* (São Paulo: Companhia das Letras, 1987), pp. 29–48.

S. Santiago, "Apesar de independente, universal", in *Antologia de textos fundadores do comparatismo literário interamericano*, ed. Zilá Bernd, disponível em< http://www.ufrgs.br/cdrom/>, accessed 10 June 2013. [2001].

Notes

1 Mário Andrade, *Macunaima* (Aarhus: Husets Forlag, 1989).

2 Limo Barreto, *Triste Fim de Policarpo Quaresma*, Edição Crítica de Antonio Houaiss e Carmen Lucia Negreiros de Figueiredo (São Paulo: ALLCA XX, 1997).

3 Luiz Ruffato, "Discurso na Abertura da Feira do Livro de Frankfurt", *Estadão. Caderno Cultura* 8 (October 2013), http://cultura.estadao.com.br/noticias/geral, leia-a-integra-do-discurso-de-luiz-ruffato-na-abertura-da-feira-do-livro-de-frankfurt, 1083463, accessed 28 August 2015.

4 All excerpts from Luiz Ruffato's speech have been translated by Rex P. Nielson.

5 Flora Süssekind, *Tal Brasil, qual Romance? Uma Ideologia Estética e Sua História: O Naturalismo* (Rio de Janeiro: Achiamé, 1984), p. 54. This and subsequent quotations have been translated from the Portuguese by Juliet Gryspeerdt.

6 Süssekind, *Tal Brasil,* p. 33

7 Süssekind, *Tal Brasil*, p. 32.

8 Süssekind, *Tal Brasil*, p. 38.

9 Oswaldo de Andrade, *A Utopia Antropofágica* (São Paulo: Globo, 2011).

10 Carolina Maria Jesus, *Quarto de Despejo* (Rio de Janeiro: Livraria Franciso Alves, 1960).

11 Regina Dalcastagnè, *Literatura brasileira contemporânea: um território contestado* (Vinhedo: Editora Horizonte, 2012), p. 2.

CHAPTER

9

The Garden of So Many Men? Women, Equality and Liberation in Mozambican Cinema

HILARY OWEN

> I found an amazing river, the Mussapa Pequeno, which I chose because I needed a river free of crocodiles where two hundred women could bathe. I was totally amazed, I had never seen so many beautiful women bathing together before.[1]

> It is worth investing in women because they guarantee continuity, they guarantee the sustainability of the very system of development itself. I think it is worth struggling on their behalf.[2]

In both of the above quotations, the figure of woman marks a crossing point. For Paulina Chiziane, as a writer, women are transcultural guarantors of the future, the source of stability and continuity in the rapid transition processes propelled by development and change. For Licínio de Azevedo, directing a film, the exposed bodies of women transform the boundary zone of the river into a utopian vision of amazement or, in the original Portuguese, *maravilha*, replacing the threat of a crocodile-infested river with a reassuringly pleasurable prospect, readily mastered by the man behind the lens. The aim of the present paper is to explore how, and to what end, these constructions of woman as social "crossing points" or figures of mediation between times and places of transition, are developed by two male film directors in Mozambique, both of whom have set out in the past decade to depict in cinematic form some of the country's historical gender demons, and to explore the legacies of inequality faced by women in relation to the patriarchal politics of Frelimo at different points in the nation's history. The first film I consider is *Virgem Margarida* (The Virgin Margarida), made in 2012 by Licínio de Azevedo, Mozambique's best-known and most prolific director; and the second is *O Jardim do Outro Homem* (Another Man's Garden) (2007), directed by João Luís Sol de Carvalho, whose construction of strong female protagonists in twenty-first-century Mozambique has led to his being compared to the novelist Paulina Chiziane.[3]

Both directors, in different ways, set out to expose hidden and unacknowledged forms of sexual discrimination that have been historically disavowed by official Frelimo policies of non-sexism, the former in the immediate post-revolutionary context of the Frelimo re-education campaigns against prostitution; and the latter in the post-democracy context of the struggle for women's rights to educational and professional development and the battle against HIV.[4] In so doing, both films also effectively index the emergence of an appropriate cinematic and representational lexicon for voicing these issues through visual media.

Virgem Margarida is the second fiction feature film by the Brazilian-born Mozambican director, Licínio de Azevedo, who has a series of successful documentaries to his credit, and it retains various elements of his documentary style. It is set in the immediate post-independence period of 1975, and it takes on the controversial topic of the re-education camps in Niassa to which hundreds of women, some prostitutes and some, as it turns out innocent, were driven from the capital city in order to be re-educated and transformed into the tutelary *mulher nova* (new woman) and model citizen of the new Frelimo Marxist-Leninist state. The main focus of this film is the much-proclaimed sexual innocence of the 16–year-old Virgin Margarida of the title, a young woman who has recently undergone a *lobolo*, an official, traditional engagement ceremony, involving payment of appropriate goods to her family, and is simply caught up in the randomised purges sweeping the capital city, as she is caught without papers.[5] As Azevedo himself notes in an interview with Ana Dias Cordeiro:

> "This is a dark page of our history, which no-one talks about, no-one criticizes themselves about it, it has simply been wiped clean," adds Licínio Azevedo, who nonetheless feels that *Virgem Margarida* is not a political film.[6]

Licínio de Azevedo, with Isabel de Noronha, had already co-directed a documentary on this theme in 1999, *A Última Prostituta* (The Last Prostitute). The five women interviewed for that film had told Azevedo the tragic story of Margarida and he had eventually decided to make a feature film about this story, in fictional format although based on historical fact, in *Virgem Margarida*. As the director explains in an interview with Marta Lança published in *Buala*:

> My film, *A Última Prostituta* [is] a classic documentary consisting of interviews, and inspired by a photograph taken by Ricardo Rangel of two soldiers escorting a prostitute. What caught my attention at the time was the story of a young peasant woman who had gone to the city to buy her wedding trousseau and because she had no documents with her she got taken off to the camps by mistake. I made the film *Virgem Margarida* based on that story which two other women in the reeducation camps told me: the story of one virgin in the middle of 700 prostitutes.[7]

The second of my two films, O *Jardim do Outro Homem*, draws its title from a Ronga proverb: *mandar uma filha para a escola é o mesmo que regar o jardim de outro homem* (sending a girl to school is like watering another man's garden).

The story here concerns a young woman, Sofia whose family works in a quarry but who dreams of becoming a medical doctor following in the footsteps of Inés, the older sister of her best friend Jéssica, the more beautiful but less academically gifted of the two classmates. However, Sofia is pressured into giving unprotected sexual favours to a biology teacher at her school, who is also financially bribing pupils, in return for obtaining good grades in her biology exam, which she has to pass to get into medical school. Her dilemma is thus represented in extreme terms: she risks losing her life in order to have any chance of her own life and improving the living conditions of her family. In a somewhat melodramatic narrative, she finally escapes the clutches of her teacher through a woman-centred team effort that involves help from her grandmother, and from Jéssica and Inés, when they are alerted to her clandestine tryst with the rogue biology teacher, Sr Mangueira. Pursuing Sofia to Mangueira's borrowed apartment, where the grandmother breaks a window to force entry, the three women catch the teacher *in flagrante,* while Sofia is hiding terrified in the bathroom having fought off the teacher's attempt at unprotected rape. Changing school in order to retake her biology exam, Sofia finally does realise her professional ambitions, and at the end of the film, she dreams about saving a woman's life. The ending thus reconnects with the dream sequences at the beginning of the film, which projected Sofia's desire to work as a woman doctor dedicated to furthering national progress through better, safer maternity services and eradication of HIV.

Sponsored by Portuguese, French, Swiss, Swedish, EU and US funding entities, as well as the *Conselho Nacional do Combate à Sida de Moçambique* (The National Committee to Fight HIV/AIDS in Mozambique), the film received the prize for best feature at the 2008 African Film Festival. On one level its mission — to educate society as a whole about HIV — is clearly the significant overarching theme; and yet at the same time, the social realist narrative framework in which this message is conveyed, necessarily foregrounds the lives and experiences of women.[8] As the sociologist Ana Maria Loforte notes:

> The quality of health services and public services in general, communications and transport, the defence of human rights, the quality of education systems, the concept of sexuality and the feminization of poverty, among other things, are factors directly linked to the probability of contracting AIDS as well as being able to access treatment for it.[9]

Taking this theme a step further through its focus not only on women's sexual identities, but also on the gendering of access to all of the above services, Carvalho's film makes a notable move to feminize the risk of, and resistance to, AIDS, as a function of vestigial but still predominant patriarchal power abuse cutting across every level of social, cultural, economic and educational relations in urban society. As a result, the most significant innovation to be observed in this heavily didactic, public-education-style film lies in its clear attempt to de-articulate female experience from the symbolic burden of national iconography in which "the feminine" can conventionally only figure the land, the *jardim*, the *machamba*. Thus, whilst the theme of AIDS education is clearly one of national-scale significance, it effectively affords a broader contemporary matrix of meaning beyond the gendered straight-jacketing of compulsory national symbolism. In this sense, *O Jardim do Outro Homem* marks a notable move towards analysing the ongoing process of gender struggle itself within the context of Frelimo state education and medical projects as a necessary underpinning of the national future, but no longer as the privileged narrative terms on which "nation" and "futurity" themselves must be articulated.

Both films posit national unity as a project defined by its impossibility. For Azevedo, this is evident already at the inception of the new nation in the 1970s as the unacknowledged but intersecting regional, ethnic, linguistic and gender fault-lines of national integration are brought sharply into focus by the situation of the Niassa re-education camp in *Virgem Margarida*. As Maria Tavares observes:

> By going back to this very particular moment of Mozambican history, Azevedo... examines the utopian ideal of the Mozambican nation under construction, revealing its tendency to exile rather than integrate.[10]

Tavares goes on to note, as does Cordeiro in her interview with Azevedo, that *Virgem Margarida* also affords a very contemporary perspective on how national unity remained a self-deconstructing project, in the early twenty-first-century climate of renewed Frelimo and Renamo hostilities under the premiership of President Armando Guebuza (2005 to 2015), the original Frelimo architect of the women's education camps in the 1970s.[11] The Guebuza Presidency is also the implicit, though never stated, historical backdrop for Carvalho's film of 2007, in which he picks up and expands upon the nation's ongoing "tendency to exile rather than integrate", this time making woman the subject, rather than the symbol, of the nation's internal displacement and self-exile.[12]

Hamid Nacify has written iconically and productively about the advent of what he terms "accented cinema", positioning it in relation to the breakdown of the classic Jamesonian national allegory. I draw on Naficy, somewhat unconventionally here, to read his foregrounding of displacement, exile and deterritorialization in terms of a post-national sexual identity that is freed from its obligations to figure ethnicity, region or race. According to Naficy:

> As a cinema of displacement, however, the accented cinema is much more situated than the Third Cinema, for it is necessarily made by (and often for) specific displaced subjects and diasporized communities. [Its] engagement is less with 'the people' and 'the masses,' as was the case with the Third Cinema, than with specific individual, ethnicities, nationalities, and identities, and with the experience of reterritorialization itself. In accented cinema, therefore, every story is both a private story of an individual and a social and public story of exile and diaspora. These engagements with collectivities and with deterritorialization turn accented films into allegories of exile and diaspora – not the totalizing 'national allegories' that Jameson once categorized Third World literature and cinema to be.[13]

Although gender is not central to Nacify's considerations here, the implications of this are nonetheless profound for the cinematic figuration of women, given her historic burden of national symbolization in the business of literary and cinematic allegory. Where the totalizing national allegories of the independence movements and Third Cinema break down, do women necessarily remain constrained nonetheless to symptomatize its disintegration, its fault-lines of displacement or self-exile, as arguably happens in *Virgem Margarida*? The literary critic Florence Stratton, in her now classic study of African women's writing in English, affords a valuable framework for analysing the specific gendered epistemologies that have historically structured women's allegorical function. For Stratton, unpicking the national allegory in literature and criticism, woman has been historically condemned to represent either the "sweep of history", meaning the "index of the state of the nation" or the "pot of culture" which analogizes woman to the heritage of African values, an unchanging Africa essence.[14]

As we see, the cinematic framing of the women in *Virgem Margarida,* for all the script's narrativization of their personal backstories, still largely serves to index the state of the nation, albeit by metonymically collapsing the sweep of history and symbolising the arrested progress of a revolution, reduced to decadence and impossibility. Azevedo's film ends with the (narratively necessary?) sacrifice of the virgin Margarida, who implicitly takes her own life after her virginity has been taken by the Frelimo officer who rapes her, thus also foreclosing her planned future marriage. This brutal loss of primary innocence is directly paralleled with the loss of belief in a unifying revolutionary cause, undifferentiated by the regional, tribal, ethnic and linguistic differences, as well as the cruel sexual hypocrisies that are explored in the film through the women's experiences in the camps. As Rosa remarks in response to her constant harassment by Comandante Felisberto, he is "worse than our colonial masters".

Well-intentioned though *Virgem Margarida* undoubtedly is in its exposure of largely taboo, and purportedly true, episodes in Frelimo history, it over-relies on this construction of woman as the 'sweep of history' and index of the state of the nation, falling back on the unquestioned polarization of virginity versus prostitution to construct its main axes of meaning. It can only signify at all through this defining virginal limit. Its narrative tension depends completely on the premise that those women who are rounded up as prostitutes, or at least sexual "marginals" accept and even defend a fundamental difference between themselves as *mulheres de má vida* (low-life women), and Margarida, the virgin of the title, engaged to be married, captured in error, and deserving of special treatment. Their lives in the camp are a misfortune, but hers is a tragedy. If the "virgin" remains the gold standard of social value in this powerful critique of the Frelimo sexual economy, then the coinage hasn't actually changed. This story of the flawed and fractured Mozambican revolution, retold for the twenty-first century, effectively counter-narrates classic Frelimo national maternalism through its opposite, the dream of a Frelimo utopia figured through the death of a virgin, made sacrificial.

The women prisoners that we meet, Rosa, Susana and Luisa, are certainly given individual biographies at the level of narrative and the extent of their association with prostitution is also thrown into doubt. However, they are nonetheless cast as sexually active, vocal and independent, and therefore comparatively culpable, a status they seem to accept, in relation to Margarida.

As figures of internal exile and displacement, the bodies of these "low life women" are correspondingly made very available in the film, fetishized, physically exposed and lingered upon as in the mass naked bathing scene in the river. Margarida, in contrast, is never actually *seen* naked or being physically harmed as such. Her body is thus, in a sense, kept enticingly "virgin to the lens". In both the internal examination of her virginity by the old woman, and her brutal gang rape by the Frelimo soldiers, we hear, but do not explicitly see on screen, the effects of her ordeal. The bodies of the so-called "prostitutes", in contrast, particularly Rosa, become hyper-visible sites of dispersal, metonyms of internal exile and displacement, too openly and readily available to the eroticizing gaze for their sad personal stories to maintain any lasting impact.

When Margarida finally accepts her release, engineered by a well-meaning Rosa who has struck a deal with Comandante Felisberto, she believes she will be safe and leaves the re-education camp in his company, only for him to promptly exact payment for his generosity by violently raping her and ordering his comrade to do the same. The ending of the film implies that Margarida will use her previously indicated knowledge of local plants to poison herself. The women ultimately leave the camp, liberated on the orders of their previously brutal Frelimo woman commander, Maria João, who has turned against her male comrades, on realising what Felisberto has done to Margarida.

As Margarida leaves too, ironically surrounded by the other rejoicing women, the film's ending is left deliberately unclear. After her rape, Margarida does not want to leave the camp at all. Feeling unable now to return to her old life as a future bride, she gives to Luísa, the handkerchief on which she had, at the beginning of the film, embroidered the name of the place they were taken to, so that fiancé would know what had happened to her. She refuses to leave unless Luísa accepts the handkerchief, saying that if anything should happen to her, and her fiancé sees this memento of their former life, he will know, "I did no wrong, that I was taken". This embroidered handkerchief from her wedding trousseau effectively metonymizes the hymen, spiritually and symbolically preserved for her fiancé alone, in a way that her virginity has not been. Margarida then covertly plucks and hides some wild berries that she knows to be poisonous. Significantly, however, we do not actually see her eat them. Casting a backward glance at the marching column to check she is not being watched, she appears simply to walk on in a closing gesture of open-ended ambiguity. Viewed in the context of her embroidery, however, affording a final proleptic meaning to her story, the suicidal death of Margarida seems already, and inevitably, prepared for and pre-ordained, potentially internalising the poison much as she has internalised the rape. By sparing the viewer the screening of her actual death however, her physical integrity continues to be as it has been throughout the film, "virgin to the lens", never the object of on-screen violence. Her symbolic, and therefore sacrificial, function is thus preserved as the invisible, disembodied obverse of the hyper-visible, over-embodied and physically brutalized "prostitutes". As Stratton notes, the aesthetics of female embodiment is instrumental in this process of female exclusion from the authorship of national narrative.

> The trope [woman as "pot of culture" or "sweep of history"] elaborates a gendered theory of nationhood and of writing, one that excludes women from the creative production of the national polity or identity and of literary texts. Instead, woman herself is produced or constructed by the male writers as an embodiment of his literary/political vision.[15]

Although *Virgem Margarida* is certainly a courageous and controversial film, denouncing the previously taboo abuses of sexual power in Frelimo itself, committed in the name of re-education and post-independence national reconstruction, the figure of the feminine rarely goes beyond playing the role of a national abjection zone or defining limit. As Naficy has noted, in determining the possible subcategories of "accented cinema" through reading protoexilic films in which "the key chronotope of homeland is that of prison", the experience of prison is also powerfully connected to exile.[16]

> The nation is not always imagined as a timeless, boundless, and primordial home, synonymous with nature and associated with the rural or the monumental. Sometimes, it is imagined in an opposite space-time configuration, particularly by film-makers who have escaped authoritarian regimes and societies… Even those who manage to escape to exile are haunted by the prison-house of their homelands.[17]

Given that Margarida has effectively been imprisoned for nothing more than the fact of being a woman, and this finds its ultimate expression in her violent rape, the boundaries of her own body configure the limits of a homeland from which she has now been exiled for good, to which there is no self-return. Consequently, her ironic refusal to leave the prison camp is mitigated only by her determination to leave her body's metonymic narrative trace, through the handkerchief, as a testimony to her history. In this conventionally gendered nationalist syntax, Margarida has no logical narrative option but to die at the end of the film, thus maintaining the image of woman as precisely the telluric, natural essence of nationhood, which had been the utopian "opposite space-time configuration" of the prison, for Frelimo's male nationalists in 1975.[18] For this reason, we are repeatedly shown instances of Margarida's superior rural and farming knowledge as she ironically exemplifies the very agricultural nation-building skills that the camp is trying to inculcate, only for her rape and probable death to connote the Frelimo nation's ultimate self-violation.

Given the film's important testimonial grounding in historical reality, initially retrieved from documentary interviews and then deployed as a base for a partly fictionalised feature, this begs a further significant question, as to whether Margarida ever actually existed. And if she had not, would the other women have had to invent her in order to validate their own testimonies to cruel and unreasonable treatment? As Azevedo notes, Margarida's story was not narrated to him directly by her, but by two other women in *A Última Prostituta*. Constructed from the multiple experiences of these survivors, she seems, in this sense, to operate as a kind of composite entity, a necessary fiction of authorization.

The interesting innovation to this gendered repertoire that Sol Carvalho's film brings us relates both to his inversion of the "woman as index of the nation" topos and to what he correspondingly chooses to do with the concept of internal exile and displacement in relation to a didactic evolution of sex and gender roles. Here too, one could argue, we witness the heroine Sofia, exiled not to the remote rural regions, but progressively from all the conventions of sociality pertaining to the urban communities around her. A form of cognitive alienation and self-exile marks the risk, threat and failure of the modern, urbanised dream offered to poor women, not unlike that experienced by the hero Víctor in Zezé Gamboa's famous Angolan feature film of 2004, *O Herói*, but here given a strong gender slant. As we will see, the grandmother is not here cast as the unproblematically redemptive figure for Sofia that she is in Gamboa's film. Indeed, the traditional saying of the title, repeated by the mother, sister and grandmother in Carvalho's film, *mandar uma filha para a escola é o mesmo que regar o jardim de outro homem* (sending a girl to school is like watering another man's garden) is overturned by Sofia's proleptic vision of professional success, rather than her belonging, through patrilinear marriage convention, to her future husband's "garden" or kin. In this sense, Carvalho chooses rather to make the current state of the nation's modernity, its ongoing vision of medical scientific progress and its commitment to education, serve as the index for the living conditions of women and their options for survival. For this reason, the film covers a broad panorama of almost all the familiar political, economic and social problems of post-democracy Mozambique that militate against Sofia's survival.

High level corruption dictates the allocation of the best teaching jobs. Professor Mangueira is bitter and exploits Sofia because he has been denied a post in a private school offered instead to the nephew of a minister. Sofia's father will never return to give moral guidance to his daughters as he has grown sick in the mines of Johannesburg and taken a South African mistress. Sofia's aging grandmother is trying, with disastrous consequences, to treat her great grandson's illness with herbal medicines. The various solutions and interventions attempted by white teachers and NGOs have no long-term effect and the French teacher who tries to help, fails to gain Sofia's trust. Sofia's educational efforts are also thwarted by the indifference and machismo of her footballer boyfriend, Salvador; and her other male classmates get her into trouble by copying her tests, leaving her even more vulnerable to the sexual blackmail of her teacher.

As Oliveira, Avelar and Miranda note, dialogue is often brief and the framing of Sofia's problems in the broader framework of AIDs education militates against her individualization.[19] However, much of Sofia's emotional development does not depend on dialogue or character interaction as such. Rather, Sofia interacts negatively with space, with her crowded and stressful Maputo environment, which is constantly evoked through an alternating play of panning and travelling shots, capturing well-known city streets and landmarks. Against this background, the film deploys a series of long takes depicting Sofia herself travelling by bus, train or scooter, walking through the city, or standing alone in contemplation as if mentally detached from her physical surroundings, and constantly between spaces, against a backing sound track consisting solely of heterodiegetic Mozambican dance music while Sofia weighs her different options. The sociability of this dance music works here ironically to emphasize her solitary nature isolated from participation in the community by her will to overcome convention and think "beyond". The film's various cuts to the fleeing impala at moments of key decision-making emphasize her entrapment in a series of lethal situations, despite the apparently open spaces around her. This series of visual leitmotifs culminates in the teacher ripping her clothes, as Sofia conjures up the image of a colonial-style white hunter lining up the sights of a rifle to shoot the impala, the film's only reference to the pre-independence era, as well as to the macho safari-style game hunts that emulate it. This alignment of the sexual harasser with a white colonial predator makes an obviously counter-national statement since the impala is also, as observed by Oliveira, Avelar and Miranda, the national symbol of Mozambique.[20] As we are told at the beginning of the film in a subtitle, "if the conditions of possible survival for the future offspring are not good enough, the impala may delay their birth or even deliberately abort them . . .". By the same token, the image of Mangueira himself, drinking beer and waiting for his sordid assignation with Sofia, while sitting in front of a heroically backlit statue of Eduardo Mondlane, the founder of Frelimo and architect of the Liberation Struggle, ironically highlights Mangueira's betrayal of the idealised masculinities enshrined in the Mozambican Revolution.

As Sofia tries to find safe spaces, her constant, repeated journeyings across the city, function in the manner of what Naficy terms "journeys of identity", internal journeys which are "composite and serial, since most exilic conditions involve multiple motivations and evolutions".[21] This process of evolutionary journeying is further reflected in Sofia's constant linguistic switching between Portuguese, Changaan and English depending on her interlocutor and situation. Her most distant journey, physically and linguistically is her visit to her estranged father, taking her across a national border to South Africa as she travels by train to Johannesburg. There she finds that her father has accepted his fate as an ex-miner to die of emphysema, a kind of industrial hazard which she sees as parallel to her own decision to accept the risk of AIDS, to get her biology mark. Her ultimate rescue from this scenario along with her own future vision of remaining in Mozambique as a doctor, equates her reterritorialization of Maputo as "home", with generational progress in relation to her father's abject and, very typical, fate for southern Mozambican men.

While the episodic cinematic style and sudden reversals of fortune certainly on one level, recall *telenovelas*, the film still manages to avoid descent into a series of clichés by allowing Sofia such a high level of self-reflective consciousness. We witness her responding to events by becoming a conscious, politicised, figure who appropriates and reformulates the idealised image of Mozambican womanhood at a crossroads, (rather than succumbing to its contradictions as Margarida had done) in order to ground it in her own, pedagogically exemplary story of self-affirmation. As she gradually asserts her determination to secure a well-paid and valuable profession so as to escape the trap of poverty and/as sexual vulnerability, the scenes depicting her solitude chart a progressive transformation until her body becomes demonstrably her own, to be made available to others on her terms. This is underlined by her successful resistance of rape, her break-up with her unfaithful boyfriend and rejection of his material goods offered as a *lobolo*, her decision to change schools, and her self-recognition in the birth scene, not as a future mother but as a future doctor.

By the same token, Sofia thinks conspicuously beyond her grandmother's ineffectual traditional remedies. Avoiding a simplistic validation of pre-rational female knowledge transmitted through maternal genealogy, she secures her own family's economic future precisely through her grasp of modernity not tradition. In contrast to her migrant worker father who has left his Mozambican home and family, Sofia finally becomes a counter-diasporic pole of stability for her family, resisting exile and displacement not through any essentialist link to the land as a *jardim do outro homem* (another man's garden) but rather through a reterritorialization of women's right to live, learn and work in an urban environment without being traded as whores. In so doing, she effectively reverses the patriarchally-determined dispersal of female bodies witnessed in *Virgem Margarida,* staging a form of composite "homecoming" for women.[22]

O Jardim do Outro Homem marks an important step towards integrating the cinematic image of woman into a Mozambican historiography that would also be aware of sexual relations and gender power dynamics as themselves having a material history and a specificity of their own beyond the limited stock signifiers of the nationalist lexicon. While Carvalho certainly highlights the power of female community across four generations, the need for the younger generation to transform the older is also emphasized by the counter-balancing of the grandmother with the figure of Sofia's young medical mentor Inés. The transversal female solidarity and community this creates offers a glimpse of a female subjectivity that takes gender equality far beyond Stratton's "sweep of history" or "pot of culture" effectively sketching the cinematic conditions of representational adequacy for women's material history in the multiple contact zones of Maputo.

Notes

1 Licínio de Azevedo, "Entrevista com Marta Lança sobre o Filme *Virgem Margarida*", *Buala* (13 September 2012), www.buala.org/pt/afroscreen/reeducacao-de-mulheres-entrevista-a-licinio-azevedo-sobre-o-filme-virgem-margarida, accessed 6 May 2016. All translations into English are the author's own unless otherwise stated.

2 Paulina Chiziane, "Entrevista com Lúcia Maria Marques Seia Borrego", *Faces de Eva. Estudos Sobre a Mulher* 10 (2003): 55–163, p. 163.

3 Alberto Gomes de Oliveira, Kátia Avelar, and Maria Geralda de Miranda, "O Pedagógico em *O Jardim do Outro Homen*, de Sol de Carvalho", *Mulemba* 1, 9 (July/December 2013): 9–21, 19 http://www.setorlitafrica.letras.ufrj.br /mulemba/download/artigo_9_2.pdf., accessed 4 May 2016.

4 Maria Tavares, "'Mulheres Novas com Cabeças Limpas': Pitfalls of the Revolution in Licínio de Azevedo's *Virgem Margarida*", *Journal of Lusophone Studies* 1, 1 (Spring 2016): 153–76. See also, Hilary Owen, *Mother Africa, Father Marx. Women's Writing of Mozambique 1948–2002* (Lewisburg: Bucknell University Press, 2007).

5 For a detailed analysis of the ways in which this film also speaks to the fragmentation of national unity and the re-emergence of the Renamo and Frelimo conflict in the 2000s, see Owen, *Mother Africa, Father Marx*, esp. pp. 167–74.

6 Ana Dias Cordeiro, "O Inimigo de Dentro da Revolução", *Público* (22 November 2013). http://www.publico.pt/temas/jornal/o-inimigo-de-dentro-da-revolucao-27421613, accessed 7 May 2016.
7 Licínio de Azevedo, "Entrevista com Marta Lança", *Buala*. See also Jorge Pereira, "Entrevista com Licínio de Azevedo. O Realizador de *Virgem Margarida*", *C7nema* (21 November 2013), http://www.c7nema.net/entrevista/item/40529-entrevista-a-licinio-azevedo-o-realizador-de-virgem-margarida.html#sthash.4KwyX4nb.dpuf, accessed 4 May 2016.
8 See Oliveira, Avelar and Miranda, "O Pedagógico", p. 20.
9 Ana Maria Loforte, "Mulher, Ida e o Acesso a Saúde na África Subsahariana, sob a Perspectiva das Ciências Sociais", VITA, p. 5, http://www.sidafrica.net/publicaciones/VITA_port_WEB.pdf, accessed 25 February 2017.
10 Tavares, "Mulheres Novas com Cabeças Limpas": 154.
11 As Cordeiro, notes, in response to Azevedo's denial of a political reading for his film: "There is no way not to see protest (or politics) even in Margarida's final, clandestine gesture, or in her progressive transformation. . . . *Virgem Margarida* is not a political film according to Licínio Azevedo. But there is no way not to see politics in the very similar excesses that are being committed in other parts of the world in other revolutions today, or even just in the irony of fate: the person who set up those camps is now [2012] President of the Republic of Mozambique, Armando Guebuza, the same Frelimo leader who launched Operation Production in 1983, another dark chapter in Mozambican history." Cordeiro, "O Inimigo de Dentro da Revolução."
12 Tavares, "Mulheres Novas com Cabeças Limpas": 154.
13 Hamid Naficy, *Accented Cinema. Exilic and Diasporic Filmmaking* (Princeton: Princeton University Press, 2001), p. 31.
14 Florence Stratton, *Contemporary African Literature and the Politics of Gender* (London: Routledge 1994), p. 41.
15 Ibid., p. 51.
16 Naficy, *Accented Cinema*, p. 181.
17 Ibid., p. 181.
18 Ibid., p. 181.
19 Oliveira, Avelar and Miranda, "O Pedagógico", p. 15.
20 Oliveira, Avelar and Miranda, "O Pedagógico", p. 17.
21 Naficy, *Accented Cinema*, p. 237.
22 The ending of *O Jardim do Outro Homem* makes for interesting comparison with Lília Momplé's novella, *Neighbours*, in which the heroine's decision to betray to the police a domestically violent husband, who has himself betrayed Mozambique by colluding with South African destabilisation, makes national stability and futurity effectively coterminous with women's bodily rights to be free of domestic violence. Furthermore, a young Muslim woman's decision, in this novella, to remain in Mozambique and study medicine in defiance of her traditional mother's marriage plans, affords a significant correlation of gender equality with the health of the future nation. See Lília Momplé, *Neighbours* (Maputo: Associação dos Escritores, 1995).

CHAPTER

10

Inequalities, in Other Words: Literary Portrayals of the Cities of Luanda and Maputo

MARGARIDA CALAFATE RIBEIRO

Foreword

Every city contains its history. Luanda and Maputo are no different. Luanda, with its Atlantic coastline, reveals Western influence in its Luso-Brazilian architecture. Maputo, facing the Indian Ocean, boasts other influences in its mix of Africa, Portugal, India, and South Africa. These cities sediment the temporal, the spatial and the political. Past experiences overlay and underpin the urban experience. The archaic occurs with the modern; progress with backwardness. Political moments crash into one another. Geography becomes fluid. Skewed temporalities contribute to multiple layers. The precolonial era, coastal settlement, modern colonialism, then independence and postcolonialism, all stake claims to historical attention. This mix impacts on, and is influenced by, many subjectivities, both collective and individual. The result of a European arrival either for commerce or to colonize, the mix had a political impact on the ordering of space, and in the power relations seen in each city.

The cities contain divergent signs that never cancelled each other out. The erasing flow of history seems suspended there. In Luanda, the Fort of San Miguel, the churches of the Alta, as well as the streets in the Baixa connected to commerce, all provide a historical link to Portuguese colonialism, the slave trade and commerce with Brazil. On the other hand, any reflection on Luanda's *musseques* (slums) or the shantytowns of Maputo indexes local cultures and the disadvantaged populations, once the organizational backbone of resistance to the Portuguese, harbouring a commitment to the struggle for independence. We see this social-political landscape reflected in the literary work of José Luandino Vieira, António Cardoso, Costa Andrade, Rui Noronha, José Craveirinha and Noémia de Sousa among so many others. In contrast, a contemporary view of South Luanda highlights an elite whose pockets have been lined by oil, diamonds and clientelism.

The research project, "From S. Paulo de Luanda to *Luuanda*, from Lourenço Marques to Maputo: colonial capitals in postcolonial times", was developed by a team of architects and literary studies researchers from different continents working at the University of Coimbra's Centre for Social Studies, and was coordinated by me (cultural studies) and Walter Rossa (architecture and urbanism). The project's approach was remarkably comparative — between spaces and narratives — and interdisciplinary, drawing on literary criticism, history, cultural studies, architecture and urban studies. It took an interdisciplinary look at the colonial project and how literature reflected urban planning, capturing discursively the city architecture that fashioned it. We analysed the continuities and ruptures, either in reality or in the construction of the cities' imaginaries, having in mind the concept of "the city as a text", (Lévi-Strauss) or as a palimpsest of texts, constructed of imagined, triumphant, and defeated spaces. The analysis focused on the city/capital as a colonial space; as a place of resistance; and as a force forging the new nation; as the centre of the post-colonial state. Engaging with the city as a text requires a methodology able to draw on both literary studies and architecture. We collected and analysed representations of spaces and social life in the Angolan and Mozambican capitals in literary and historical writing, photographs, images and maps. As colonial spaces, a double perspective on these cities was identified. On the one hand, we examined how the colonial Portuguese state and settlers had secured, organised, built and used both capitals, and to what extent they had reproduced a metropolitan political and cultural imaginary through architectonic and literary narratives. On the other hand, we looked at the way colonized people had interpreted European intervention and lifestyle, and had started rehearsing political independence through their literature: writing about the "unseen" city, "beyond the tarmac". We analysed colonial literature and texts by colonized writers and, from the point of view of architecture and urbanism, the same assumptions were followed to investigate differentiated presentation. This is the investigative route we pursued to produce the research that led to the following reflections.

The cities of Luanda and Lourenço Marques/Maputo and the literature

In this chapter, I will draw on the literary images and descriptions of the cities of Luanda and Maputo to demonstrate a design that used political and social inequality to determine their urbanism. A struggle for terrain and citizenship — in the conquest of spaces by the colonizers and the reconquest of lost spaces by the colonized — draws the lines of that inequality as they existed in the time of colonialism.

The authors of the emerging national literatures of Portuguese-speaking Africa, particularly in Angola and Mozambique, generally grew up in the colonial capitals. The literatures they produced foretelling liberation were thus essentially a phenomenon of urbanism.[1] They were concerned with city life, and with fostering an urban culture focused on newspapers, clubs and social activities. The *polis* was the stage they chose to expose inequality. They portrayed inequality first hand by drawing on their observations of the planning and functioning of the cities of their youth.

Given the historical and geographical context in which these authors wrote, the concept of literary formation rather than foundational literature seems a more appropriate tool on which to draw in order to read their work, born of a self-interrogating colonial heritage fused with African roots. Expounded by Antonio Candido in relation to Brazilian literature, with a variant offered by Mário António referencing Angolan literature, simply put: "formation is something which is formed."[2] Why do I prefer the concept of formation over the more classical vision of foundational literatures closely associated with the emergence of nationhood in nineteenth-century Latin America? It comes down to colonial and postcolonial connotations. Foundation, a term applied in relation to cities and cultures in previously colonized spaces, was a colonial act that disciplined literature and cities into binary hierarchies: there was colonial literature and the Other's literature, the colonial city and the Other's space. The use of the term foundational, as Antonio Candido points out, perpetuates a narrative that implies that, prior to the arrival of Europeans, there was nothing there. It creates the impression of a ground zero on which history started at a foundational moment. Published in 1989, *"Vilas e Cidades": Bourgs et Villes en Afrique Lusophone*, edited by Michel Cahen,[3] was the first study of urban space in Portuguese-speaking Africa. At the time, the issue of the foundation of cities as such, and its interpretation, was not the object of much analysis. There was a greater emphasis on description. Recently, *Cidades e Império: dinâmicas coloniais e reconfigurações pós-coloniais*, edited by Nuno Domingos and Elsa Peralta, shows how research of an essentially ethnocentric hue has been conducted in colonized spaces since the arrival of Europeans.[4] Certainly, there were no cities in the Western sense of the word. As Walter Rossa affirms, the city was "*uma criação da civilização ocidental, e pelo menos no Ocidente, a civilização continua a ser impensável sem elas e sem as redes que elas formam*",[5] as far as Southern Saharan Africa was concerned. In these parts of Africa, there was a different ordering of spaces where people lived together in communities, as can be seen on early maps and in early descriptions of colonization, an ordering that underwent tremendous change as Europeans began their processes of conquest.[6] Rossa asserts that, "*inevitavelmente as cidades foram um dos principais instrumentos usados pelos europeus no estabelecimento dos seus sistemas coloniais, começando logo com os primeiros, o português e o espanhol, no início da primeira modernidade.*[7] Consequently, studies produced about African cities are overwhelmingly part of a grand European narrative defining these locations. By analysing the voices of African literatures about Luanda and Maputo, I aim to show the other side of a seemingly common history, one with very different memories.

The colonial era

The imposition of cities in the European sense on colonized spaces introduced the dynamic of a struggle for territory which gained weight and took various forms. One domain in which the struggle became obvious was literature that described urban life. From within the variegated contours of the cities, local elites and cultures emerged, which in the case of Luanda became apparent from 1576, passing through various historical stages; though in Lourenço Marques, the urban settlement only began to show some size and importance in the last quarter of the 1900s. Initially, portrayal of the city was steeped in the political affirmation of colonial power, as early descriptions highlighted strategic places and architectural marvels so that readers could grasp what they looked like, judge their importance and understand their nature as a capital. Like every Portuguese colonial capital, and the metropolis itself, Luanda and Maputo were founded on the coast, with the result that the maritime districts played a fundamental role in city life and were correspondingly prevalent in literature. They rivalled Lisbon with monuments on their skylines and buildings that affirmed power — their port, forts, squares, churches and administrative offices, filled with elites and colonial bureaucrats who exercised that power either locally or through their connections with Lisbon.

António Oliveira Cadornega, in his *História Geral das Guerras Angolanas*, published in 1680, describes the strategic impressiveness of a city that functions as a center of commercial and military power, and with which he identifies as both a resident and citizen of São Paulo de Assunção de Luanda and as a native of Vila Viçosa, Portugal. His *História* includes poems, among which are unattributed verses that allow Cardonega to broach from an urban perspective the city's insularity, its streets, its colors, its speech and its people, linked to slaves and every type of legal and not-so-legal trade.

That trade gave Luanda an architecture echoed in Salvador da Baía, since both cities operated in similar ways for the centuries of the slave trade. Both were also colonial capitals on the South Atlantic, exporting raw materials and agricultural

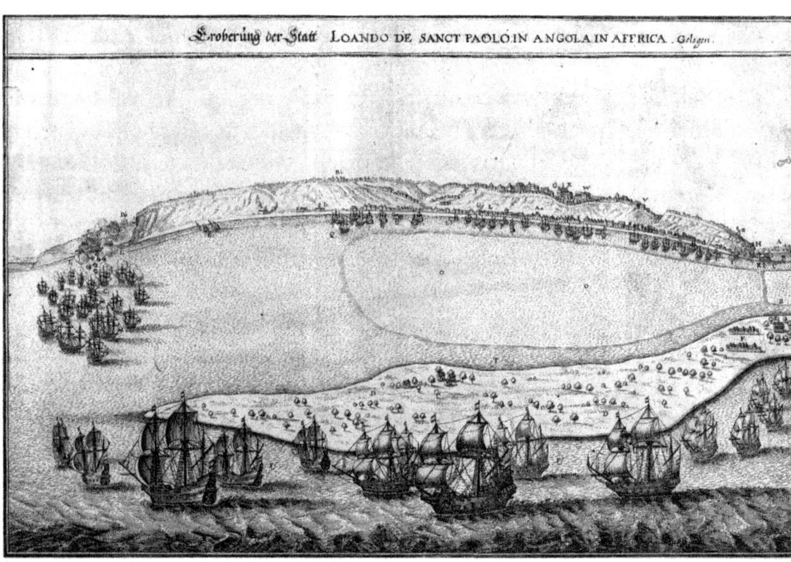

Picture 10.1 *Eroberung der Statt Loando de Sanct Paolo in Angola in Affrica Gelegen*. Engraving of a sea battle in the harbour of Luanda, Angola. Matthäus Merian, published in Frankfurt, 1646.

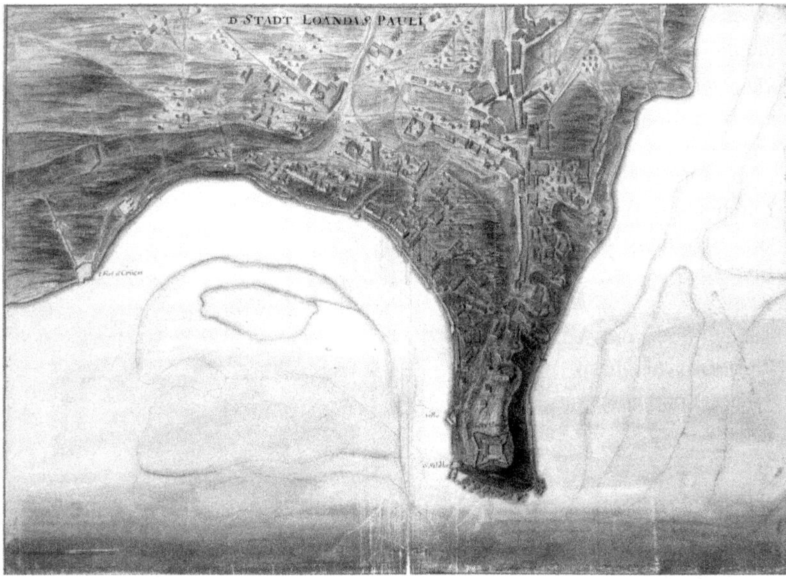

Picture 10.2 *D Stadt Loandas Pauli.* Plan of Luanda during the Dutch occupation. Johannes Vingboons, published in 1665.

products. They were centers of cultural, financial and social circulation, bound up with trade, as shown in Luís Félix da Cruz's poem, "*Descrição da Cidade de Loanda e Reyno de Angola*":[8]

Nesta turbulenta terra
almazem de pena e dor,
confuza mais de temor.
Inferno em vida.

Terra de gente oprimida,
Monturo de Portugal,
por onde purga seu mal,
e sua escoria

Onde se tem por vãa gloria,
a mentira e falsidade,
o roubo, a malinidade,
o interesse

Donde a justiça perece
por falta de quem a entenda,
donde para haver emenda,
uza Deos

do que uzava com os Judeos,
quando era Deos de vingança,
que com todas as três lanças
de sua ira[9]

In this turbulent land
warehouse of pain and sorrow,
confusion more than fear.
Living hell.

Land of the oppressed,
Portugal's dungheap,
Where it purges its sin
And its slag

Where glory means
lies and falsehood,
Theft, malice,
Profit

Where justice dies
Of loneliness
Where to make amends,
They turn to god
The same god the Jews prayed to

When he was the God of vengeance,
With his three spears
Of anger[10]

In the modern colonial era, an era in which Maputo came to imperial prominence and which changed the feel of Luanda, the colonial city was characterized by cement and tarmac, a place where whites were concentrated and power structures solidified. Further out, on the peripheries, there was the "other" city, constituted by an amalgam of mixed races: blacks and poor whites who lived in Luanda's *musseques* and Maputo's *caniços*. As a result of this social apartheid, the colonial city became a spatial expression of the inequality instated by the colonial order, but also a locus of opportunities. It gave access to work, education and culture. It provided living conditions of sorts. In effect, this urbanism of inequality transformed the city's peripheries, where people from throughout the colonial territory lived, into the cultural backdrop for a new political awareness and the cradle of nationalist movements and a literature of nationhood.

The cities of Luanda and Maputo are interrelated through the long Portuguese colonial presence that, in unequal combination with other influences, progressively defined the cities as a textual polyphony.[11] However, their very diverse geographies, with Luanda on the South Atlantic and Maputo facing the Indian

Picture 10.3 Panorama of Lourenço Marques, from the harbour. Postcard, 1910.

Ocean, their different temporalities, and their distinct historical pasts, separate them, as is reflected in the literature representing and presenting the cities. While a large part of Angolan literary imagery centred on the city of Luanda, textually represented ever since its creation, and from the 1950s abundantly portrayed, the same cannot be said of Maputo, which never occupied a similarly central place in Mozambican literature. From the perspective of the imagery of centrality and power, Portuguese colonial and Mozambican literature celebrated the Ilha de Moçambique far more than Lourenço Marques (as Maputo used to be known). In fact, Maputo is a relatively recent administrative and political capital. Its colonial writers had very little time to describe their city-as-capital. The Other's city, on the capital's periphery in districts like Mafalala, and neighbourhoods like Chamanculo and Xipamanine, became the fundamental references of colonial subalternity abundantly portrayed in Mozambican literature. As Nuno Simão Gonçalves points out:

> *As medidas segregacionistas para com as comunidades africanas, em particular, e não europeias, em geral, seguiam não só a narrativa colonial da missão civilizadora como também incorporavam o discurso higienista desenvolvido ao longo do século XIX nos países do Norte.*[12]
>
> Segregationist measures towards African communities in particular and non-Europeans in general were informed not only by colonial 'civilizing mission' narratives, but also by the hygienist discourse that developed throughout the nineteenth century in Northern countries.

José Craveirinha and Noémia de Sousa were early poetic giants to emerge from, and celebrate, these peripheral districts. Later, Calane da Silva, Luis Carlos Patraquim and Nelson Saúte contributed to the establishment of Mafalala as a byword for poetry, the struggle against colonialism and a free nation.

The history of Luanda and Maputo, recorded in the various forms of literature arising from their midst, is the history of a struggle for territory, whether from a perspective of conquest and appropriation in Portuguese colonial literature, or with a view to the recovery of that territory in Angolan and Mozambican literature from the 1940s and 1950s onwards. Poetry marks the territory, emphasising it, and conjuring images of people who parade under our gaze as if they were in a photo album. Narratives describe the cities as places in motion through their denizens, with their customs, their work, their houses, their talk, their cosmogonies and their stories.

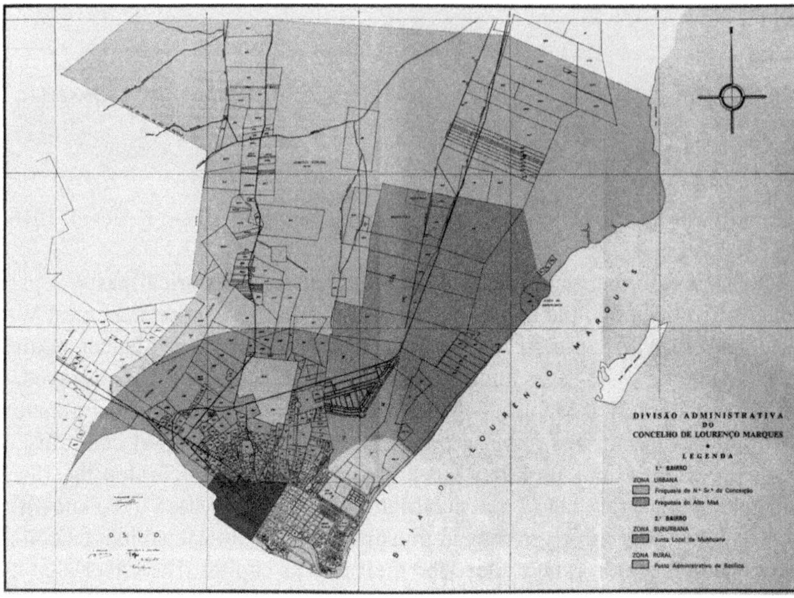

Picture 10.4 Plan of the administrative division of Lourenço Marques district (1969).

Any analysis of the city implies various forms of recording, appropriation and description. The two cities under analysis share a common feature: they were designed and very often described by those who did not live in them, but merely imagined them as aspects of a formal city, particularly a colonial city. Yet they were effectively formed by those who gave them life and resided in them. This group often came from outside the urban boundaries, as was the case of those from mainland Portugal (e. g. the *metropolitanos*) in the colonial era, portrayed in Portuguese colonial literature, or the case of migrants from the hinterland, attracted by the development inherent to a capital, in a general movement from the countryside to the town both before and after independence. The majority of the latter were the men and women who lived in the *musseques* of Luanda and the *caniços* of Maputo. They embody and shape Angolan and Mozambican literatures. In their numerous literary expressions of belonging to, and conquest of, the territory there is an interplay of the concepts of foundation and formation. Through that interplay, the city unveils its ethnic, social and political multiplicity, delineating the various layers of inequality generated within its terrain in the very place that, in principle, should welcome and foster the equality of those who live in it.

The literature of the 1940s and 1950s can be put into at least two categories: colonial literature and local literature. Local literature, produced by those who lived in the cities, gave birth to the national literatures of Mozambique and Angola. Local literature affirmed feelings generated around urban models, flourishing among a mixed-race elite in the early twentieth century, gaining momentum especially through newspapers and the first cultural and sports associations. It was marked by an experience of the colonial-oriented and segregated city. In a different form, but with the same content, in the post-independence era, city models were also discussed by focusing either on the alienation of a city occupied by those who had never lived there before; or by talking of a city bursting at its seams that did not welcome those in search of a better life or fleeing lengthy civil wars.

In 1943, Júlio de Castro Lopo wrote at the beginning of his book *Alguns Aspetos dos Musseques*:

> *Os europeus que vivem na cidade-baixa e na cidade-alta - nos lugares enfim civilizados de Luanda - estão longe de fazer ideia exata do que sejam os musseques, os lendários arredores da capital de Angola. (...) Todos estes musseques (além dos não citados) constituem subúrbios da capital de Angola: a sul, leste e nordeste da cidade, ou seja: desde o bairro da Maianga (parte alta) até Sambizanga.*[13]

> The Europeans who live in the downtown and uptown parts of the city — in short, the civilized places of Luanda — know very little about the *musseques*, the notorious outskirts of the Angolan capital (...) In truth these *musseques* (as well as those I haven't mentioned) make up the the city's suburbs, to the south, east and northeast, from the uptown Maianga neighbourhood to Sambizanga.

It is not difficult to find an equivalent observation about the city of Lourenço Marques/ Maputo. Literary texts, more than any other genre, present us with the subtle differences inherent in the histories of both cities highlighted by Castro Lopo. He outlines various ideas. First, and most obviously, there is a line dividing

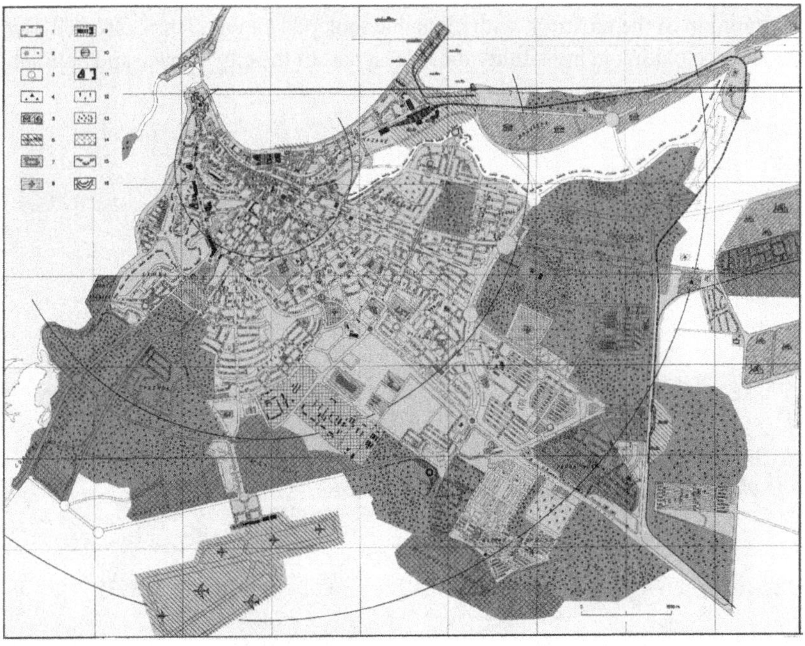

Picture 10.5 Plan of Luanda (1965). Grey indicates the *cidade de asfalto*. Dark grey the *musseques*.

the city, and, beyond that line, a varied and heterogeneous city emerges that is totally unknown to the colonial population. Second, the reverse is not the case, because blacks and mixed-race people work in the heart of the colonial city, coming to know the habits, culture and language of those who live there. Third, the line divides the populations not only according to their economic condition, but also by race. And, finally, the geography of the *musseques* announces other forms of struggle for the territory that will take place. The *musseques* encircle the white, colonial city. From the 1940s onwards, they will be the place for the enunciation of the struggle, and for Angolan and Mozambican literatures.

Clear lines thus divide the colonial city, essentially white, from the rest, whose cartographic portrayal ranges from pure non-representation — emptiness — to lines marking the beginning of the indigenous neighbourhoods, in the colonial formulation. In the middle are transition neighbourhoods, normally with indigenous names or linked to the profession of their residents — Alto Maé or Chamanculo in Maputo, and Bairro Operário in Luanda — usually inhabited by poorer whites and low-ranked administration employees and traders.

Colonial literature replicates that erasure or ignorance of anything beyond the white city. According to Francisco Noa, from the 1930s onwards, due to the policy of the Estado Novo, colonial literature began to take on a decidedly ideological tone.[15] By the late 1950s and early 1960s, it had become aesthetically more sophisticated and cosmopolitan, coinciding with the city's replication of districts similar to those found in Lisbon, like Alvalade and Benfica. It even copied their names, as well as major social infrastructures such as schools and leisure facilities. At different stages, colonial literature reaffirmed the conquest and urban acculturation of the territory, with plots that took place in the white city, with white characters, cloaking in invisibility the largest part of the city's space and population.

Picture 10.6 Photo of the musseque and the Bairro do Prenda, Luanda (1965).[14]

Hipólito Raposo, António Pires, Maria Archer, Henrique Galvão, Maria da Graça Azambuja among many wrote about Angola in this way. Brito Camacho, Julião Quintinha, Guilhermina Azeredo, Manuel Rodrigues Júnior, Eduardo Paixão did the same about Mozambique. The titles produced included works that revealed the ambiguity of the colonial situation by showing the borderline spaces in which many people moved. These narratives of colonialism contained a version of history that numerous individuals, mainly white, would later invoke to justify a relationship of "belonging" to that colonized land. Distancing themselves politically from their context, a series of voices stood on both sides of the fence, recalling the old city through the metaphor of a childhood in which white, black and mixed-raced children played together peacefully, against the modernization ushered in by progress, but also segregation as mixed-raced elites were pushed to the city's peripheries. Examples of this can be found in the poetic voices of the magazine *Cultura*, in the autobiography *Era o Tempo das Acácias*, by Carlos Ervedosa, and in the poems of Mário António, Cochat Osório, Tomás Vieira da Cruz and António Jacinto. Jacinto's "*O Grande Desafio*" talks of children of all races playing in the street until adult restrictions meant that games had to be played in different ways.

Naquele tempo
a gente punha despreocupadamente os livros no chão
ali mesmo naquele largo - areal batido de caminhos passados
os mesmos trilhos de escravidões
onde hoje passa a avenida luminosamente grande

e com uma bola de meia
bem forrada de rede
bem dura de borracha roubada às borracheiras do Neves
em alegre folguedo, entremeando caçambulas
... a gente fazia um desfio...

(...)

Mas talvez um dia
quando as buganvílias alegremente florirem
quando as bimbas entoarem hinos de madrugada nos capinzais
quando a sombra das mulembeiras for mais boa
quando todos os que isoladamente padecemos
nos encontrarmos iguais como antigamente
talvez a gente ponha
as dores, as humilhações, os medos
desesperadamente no chão
no largo - areal batido de caminhos passados
os mesmos trilhos de escravidões
—
onde passa a avenida que ao sol ardente alcatroámos
e unidos nas ânsias, nas aventuras, nas esperanças
vamos então fazer um grande desafio...[16]

In those days
We tossed our books to the ground
Right there at the dusty crossroads — beaten from old journeys
The same slave tracks
Where now the gleaming avenue runs
And with a ball of rags
Wrapped up in mesh
Gummed up in rubber we nicked from the rubber men in town
We tore around, laughing, playing catch,
... We took on the world

(...)

But maybe one day
When the bougainvilleas are flowering happily
When the birds are whistling dawn hymns in the long grass
When the shade of the sacred fig is deeper
When all who suffer alone
Find ourselves as we were before
Maybe we can fling
Our pain, our shame, our fear
Desperately to the ground
Right there at the dusty crossroads — beaten from old journeys
The same slave tracks
—
Where the avenue runs that we tarred under the burning sun
And united in longing, in adventure, in hope
Take on the world again ...

António Jacinto, Viriato da Cruz and Agostinho Neto wrote poetry denouncing the colonial situation, portraying the *musseque,* with its workers, their poverty, their hunger, and their uneducated children. Yet this was also a place of alternative wisdoms, other orders, other ideas, other languages and cultures, as shown in the short stories of *Luuanda*, by José Luandino Vieira. Later, prose by Boaventura Cardoso, Jofre Rocha, and António Cardoso, among others, presented the *musseque* as a political space by converting it into a metaphor for the shackled and struggling nation and so, literarily speaking, this was the place of the enunciation of pre-Independence Angolan literature, indelibly shaping practically all its novels and many poems.

In Mozambique, Rui Noronha or Orlando Mendes configured the divided city by contrasting the cement city with the reed city. As in Angola, the borderline sites were spaces privileged by literature in order to illustrate the porosity of those divisions, a situation that persists to this day, as portrayed by Helder Faife in his 2010 novel, *Contos de Fuga*:

Dobrei a esquina que fronteira os bairros. Não cai, habituado ao súbito contraste do chão que carateriza o litoral urbano. Ali, o casal pavimento e asfalto divorcia-se bruscamente e deixa a amante, a areia, orientar os caminhos.[18]

Picture 10.7 *"Luuanda"*, drawn by José Luandino Vieira, with the *musseques* and the cement city.[17]

> I turned the corner along the border of the neighbourhoods. I didn't slip, used to the way the city floor suddenly changes underfoot at the seafront. There, the marriage of pavement and tarmac abruptly breaks down and the lover, the sand, shapes the paths.

As today, neither in Luanda nor in Lourenço Marques/Maputo were the colonial city or its peripheries homogenous. Within these two stark divisions, marking the inequality that characterized colonialism and was reflected in the design of the city, a series of other inequalities scarred the landscape, divided by professional, ethnic and economic conditions that defined the social status of each neighbourhood and its inhabitants.[20] Colonial society was itself stratified, like the

Picture 10.8 Photo of the *caniço* and the Bairro COOP, Lourenço Marques (1965).[19]

suburbs, with a range of divisions based on religion, ethnicity and origin, as well as cultural differences. There were *assimilados, mestizos*, blacks, Muslims, Christians, political leaders, poets and musicians. In fact, in the city of Lourenço Marques an Indian, Chinese or white, low-income worker who was resident of Maxaquene or Alto Maé, with their dirt tracks, poor lighting and humble houses, was as unlikely to cross paths with someone from Polana as with an inhabitant of Mafalala or Xipamanine. However, these frontier spaces were fundamental to the struggle for independence which developed as their denizens crossed between one place and the other. This was not merely a physical transit, to go to a club or to visit prostitutes, but also a cultural and political transit, and involved an awareness of subalternity, inequality and injustice. While these frontier spaces were of crucial importance, the reed neighbourhoods of Xipamanine and Mafalala were most significant as culturally affirmed metaphors for the shackled and struggling nation, expressed through the voices of their great poets. The workplaces, the deportations to São Tomé in the dead of night in the silent city, the port, the *caniço* and its appalling conditions, its hungry and uneducated children, the cosmopolitan movement of its bars, clubs and sports associations were spaces of affirmation and conviviality gathering various social layers around the cinema, jazz, cabarets and prostitution. The places enjoined poets to denounce injustice and proclaim the struggle. Noémia de Sousa and José Craveirinha were the first to set the tone in their poems. Noémia de Sousa was particularly attentive to the double subalternity experienced by women, in verses such as "*Cais*" and "*Moças das Docas*". José Craveirinha's extensive work included poems dealing with urban divisions, poems like "*Nossa Cidade*", "*Afinal a Bala do Homem Mau*", and "Mamanô".

As in Angola, inequality was not just defined by evoking poverty, exploitation and inadequate conditions, but also by the affirmation of cultural differences unknown to the white city, or else considered "savage". José Craveirinha epitomizes that difference in his poem, "Quero ser tambor", through images of drums and the black city's dances, the noise of which the colonial city would rather not hear. Rui Knopfli is an example of a poet who came from Polana, one of the most elegant zones of Lourenço Marques. Even so, he became involved in the active denunciation of the colonial situation in Mozambique, capturing the anaesthetic climate of the cement city in his poem, "Winds of Change":

Ninguém se apercebe de nada. (...)
como é boa e mansa a Polana
nas suas ruas, túneis de frescura
atapetados de veludo vermelho
Tudo joga tão certo, tudo está tão bem
como num filme tecnicolorido
Passam. Passam
e tornam a passar
Ninguém se apercebe de nada.[21]

No one notices a thing. (...)
How pleasant Polana is, how peaceful,
The streets are breezy passageways
With red velvet carpets.
Here, life is technicolour, and like a film
everything will turn out alright.
They stroll. They stroll
Up and down.
No one notices a thing.

Rui Knopfli, like several other poets from the colonial city, crossed the city's divisions and became one of the most visual poets of Lourenço Marques. Colonial Mozambique's capital remained forever in his memory when he went into exile after independence. While he lived in colonial Mozambique, he saw and gave voice to the "invisible people", the "transparent people" — those labourers who worked in the white city and lived in the *caniço* — as we can read in his poem "*Ao Cair da Noite*", which recounts crossing the spaces in the "*Cantinela de Subúrbio*":

Do Jardim Vasco da Gama chega o percutir
seco das bolas de ténis, para lá da sombra
(...) Do caniço, o soluço entrecortado da cantiga:
"Eu vou morrer na cantina
com um copo de vinho na mão.
A cantina será cemitério
e o barril o meu caixão.
(...)
Principia, lento, o agonizar dos dias."[22]

From Vasco da Gama Garden comes the dull thud
of tennis balls from the shadows
(...) From the caniço, sobbing snippets of song:
"I will die in the kitchen
with a drink in my hand.
The canteen shall be my cemetery
and the barrel my coffin.

(...) So begins, slowly, the misery of days

The sense of struggle heralding a confrontation to come that was embodied in the texts of that time expressed the tension of different groups living in close proximity, a situation characteristic of colonial society, and of the colonial city in particular. It was not a linear opposition between whites and blacks or mixed-race people, but between freedom and submission, social justice and inequality. These were the very same values that would underpin the struggle for independence, activating mechanisms of belonging and identity which, in a post-Second-World-War context, were reflected in being Portuguese, Angolan or Mozambican, while never neglecting class and racial differences. In Noémia de Sousa's poem "Godido", which echoes a character from João Dias's 1952 collection of short stories, *Godido e Outros Contos,* we hear of a black child wandering uncomfortably in the city's centre, which does not belong to him and where he feels like a foreigner, searching for his own place in the world. The poem describes the violence of assimilation, a process based on sacrifice and the annulment of difference. At the same time, through formal education, racialized subjects became aware of the possibilities inherent in critical thought. The very education they received as part of their assimilation in the colonial city lead many blacks to rethink their own position and situation, as de Sousa's poem implicitly contends:

Dos longes do meu sertão natal,
eu desci à cidade da civilização.
Embriaguei-me de pasmo entre os astros
suspensos dos postes das ruas
e atração das montras nuas
tomou-me a respiração
Todo esse brilho de névoa, ténue e superficial
que envolve a capital,
me cegou e fez de mim coisa sua.
(...)
Mas a cidade, a cidade, a cidade, a cidade!
Esmagou-me com os pneus do seu luxo,
sem caridade,
meus pés cortados nos trilhos duros do sertão,
Encarcerou-me numa neblina quase palpável de ódio e desprezo,
e ignorando a luz verde do meu olhar,
a maravilhosa oferta

(essa estrela, esse tesouro) de cada minha mão aberta,
exigiu-me impiedosamente a abdicação
da minha qualidade intangível de ser humano!
(...)
Ah, mas eu não me deixei adormecer!
Levantei-me e gritei contra a noite sem lua,
sem batuque, sem nada que me falasse da minha África,
da sua beleza majestosa e natural,
sem uma única gota da sua magia!
A luz verde incendiou-se no meu olhar
e foi fogueira vermelha na noite fria
dos revoltados.[23]

From the backlands where I was born
I went down to the city of civilisation.
I lost myself in wonder between the stars
That hung from street posts
And the tug of the bare shop windows
took my breath away.
All that delicate shimmering mist that
wraps the surface of the capital
Blinded me and made me its own.
(...)
But the city, the city, the city, the city!
It crushed me cruelly with the tyres of its luxury,
My feet hardened by the backland tracks,
It prisoned me in a haze of hatred and disgust that I could almost touch
And ignoring the green light in my eyes,
The marvellous gifts
(This star, this treasure) from each of my open hands,
It demanded mercilessly that I abdicate
My intangible humanity!
(...)
Oh, but I did not let myself sleep!
I got up and screamed at the moonless night,
Without the music of the drums, without anything that spoke of my Africa,
Of its majesty and natural beauty,
Without a single drop of its magic!
The green light caught fire in my eye
and became the red bonfire in the cold night
of rebellion

From this overview, two crucial aspects of understanding the city and its literature are revealed. The first is the observation of the contrasts of the dual city during colonial times, where the dichotomy between the formal urban area (inhabited by a predominantly European colonizer minority) known as the

Picture 10.9 Photo of the *caniço*, Lourenço Marques in the sixties.[24]

"cement city", and the suburb (where the predominantly African colonized population lived), either in the *musseque*, in Angola, or in the *caniço*, in Mozambique. The second is the discovery of urban continuities and discontinuities after independence in 1975.

After independence

By the time the Colonial or Liberation Wars began, Portuguese literature written from an experience of the Colonial Wars provided mainland Portuguese with impressions of the cities of Luanda and Lourenço Marques in an approach that perpetuated colonial literature, to the extent that it looked merely at the "cement city" and the social and power relations inherent in it. In contrast, in the literatures of the Angolan and Mozambican armed struggles, the liberated site is not the city, but rather the bush — the sacred space of freedom fighters, as depicted in several Portuguese novels about the Colonial Wars. In African novels and poems from that time, the capitals are places that symbolize colonial power, and therefore the real and symbolic spaces of a territory that must be won back.[25] Thus the capital city is converted into a symbol of the need for conquest of the entire territory, and for independence. As such, it also the space from which, and on top of which, the new nation will be constructed, as signalled in Agostinho Neto's poem "*Havemos de voltar*".

After independence, in 1975, various trends took root in the urban fabric, modifying the landscape, effectively constituting a different city with a different use of space, different symbols of power and different concepts of functionality. These changes were reflected in many novels and poems born of the new nation. A first stage imposed change on the city's toponyms, embodying a strong image of the end of colonialism by the re-appropriation of the city's territory, excluding some and including others in the public space. A number of colonial symbols disappeared, especially through the pulling down of emblematic statues, as Mia Couto captures in a text about the toppling of the equestrian statue of Mouzinho da Silveira – "*A derradeira morte da estátua de Mouzinho*". Simultaneously, socialist-style statues

Picture 10.10 Toppling of the Portuguese Mouzinho de Albuquerque statue in Maputo, photographed by António Costa Pinto in 1975.[26]

began to appear, designating where power and sovereignty resided in the new capitals through the erasure of the symbols of the old order and the erection of a new order. Companies and services were nationalized, significantly transforming their presentation in the context of the city. Formal trade and the canteens decayed and, in their stead, "people's shops" and duty-free shops appeared, with a parallel growth in informal trade in huge open-air markets. There was an influx of suburban residents coming into the cement city, filling the massive gaps left by the departure of settlers, a process portrayed in novels such as *Crónica da Rua 513.2*, by João Paulo Borges Coelho, and *A Canção de Zefanías Sforza,* by Luís Carlos Patraquim. Carlos Cardoso succinctly describes it in his poem "Primeiro Aniversário":

Hoje
aromas chamanculos
politizam os fogões
da polana.[27]

Today
Suburban scents
petition stoves
in polana.

Later, the Angolan Civil War's encroachment on significant parts of the country, and the subsequent arrival of displaced people from rural areas with an urgent need for accommodation in a city where their presence had never been countenanced, offers the historical context for the plot of Manuel Rui's epic tale, *Rio Seco*.

Regarding Luanda, as Silvia Leiria Viegas underlines, although "inequalities derived from the period of Portuguese colonial rule (1576–1975)", they "persisted throughout the civil war (1975–2002) that followed independence. In 2010, official projections suggested that Luanda had a population of 4,772 million within an area of approximately 350 square kilometres, with nearly 80 per cent of its inhabitants residing in self-produced peri-urban areas known locally as *musseques*."[28]

The flow into the city of people from the hinterland who, replaying the colonial pairing of civilized-uncivilized, saw in the city a space for progress and civilization, is a dynamic portrayed in the Mozambican Suleiman Cassamo's *Palestra para um Morto*. The arrival of foreign aid workers from the most diverse parts of the former socialist block and their participation in the education and life of the city is portrayed in novels by a generation born after independence, including Ondjaki, and by the photographic works of Kiluanji Kia Henda, and other young African artists, as shown on the recent exhibition *Things Fall Apart — Red Africa,* where the socialist inheritance is beginning to be questioned. As stated in the exhibition booklet, "the civil war that began in 1975 following Angola´s independence from Portugal saw the involvement of the Soviet Union, Cuba and the United States, amongst others, who supported rival political factions in an attempt to gain influence over the newly independent country."[29] At the time of the socialist revolution, their presence was celebrated by the introduction of words into daily life that indicated what these countries were contributing to the Angolan and Mozambican urban space. For example, "Hungary," which appears in *O Cronista* by Areosa Pena, refers to the buses Hungary donated to Mozambique as part of an aid and development package provided by the former Eastern bloc. In a similar vein, but involving post-revolutionary Portuguese assistance, the "*Ramalho Eanes*" in *Quem me Dera ser Onda* by Manuel Rui, refers to the wine the former colonial power sent during an era of great economic and social upheaval, when there was a political rapprochement with Angola and Mozambique under Ramalho Eanes's presidency. In fact, the shortage of many basic items brought about changes in the urban population's habits and even in their vocabulary, with words like "bichar" designating the long queues at the rationing shops, or the sarcastic "peixe-fritismo" which in Mozambique originally referred to the fish Agostinho Neto, the Angolan president, sent in ideological solidarity at a time the Mozambican population had next to nothing in their shops. Fried fish was one of the few foods available. The term was transformed in daily and literary language into a metaphor expressing a commitment to an independent revolutionary Mozambique, resisting the onslaughts of global capitalism.

Post-independence fiction reflects the dawn of a new day, and is full of the great hopes of a new nation, constantly undermined by the spectre of war and the difficulties of subsistence. In Lilía Momplé 's *Neighbours,* the hostile actions of Apartheid-era South Africa are depicted with the appalling impact they had on urban Mozambique. Similarly, Nelson Saúte's poem, "*Ruth First,*" pays homage to the famous South African anti-Apartheid activist killed by a parcel bomb addressed to her at the Universidade Mondlane in Maputo, where she worked in exile. Carlos Cardoso's "*Cidade 1985*" expresses the heroic survival of Maputo's citizens, portraying the violence of daily life, its power cuts and its water shortages, in a way replicated in short stories and poems, such as "*Anos 80*", by Nelson Saúte. In *Quem me dera ser onda,* Manuel Rui captures the difficulty people had in adjusting to their new residential space through the combination of a series of absurd daily routines, and simultaneously anticipates the tragic end of the farce. The rural culture of the people propelled by the independence process into old colonial parts of the cities, and the presence of the war and its consequences, also affected the city with immediately visible impacts, like the disabled war veterans representing a stain on the city's fabric who are evoked by Luís Carlos Patraquim in the poem "*Formulação da Avenida*":

Sentam-se, sob as acácias, no asfalto roto,
os mutilados com cigarros de embalar.
Nenhum som os recorta
E todos os sentidos foram amputados.[30]

Under the acacias, on the pot-holed tarmac,
The maimed ones sit with roll-up cigarettes.
No sound disturbs them
or their amputated senses.

Ana Paula Tavares, in "November without water" depicts people displaced by the war, such as the street urchins in Luanda:

Olha-me p'ra estas crianças de vidro
cheias de água até às lágrimas
enchendo a cidade de estilhaços
procurando a vida
nos caixotes do lixo.[31]

Just look at these glass children
so full of water that their eyes spill tears
filling up the splintered city
searching for life
in rubbish bins.

Today, with the peace, a growth in wealth and the embrace of neo-liberalism, these countries and cities have undergone numerous transformations, which their literature is actively recording, thus continuing their path of political engagement. In cities with a temporarily resident foreign population and an enriched local bourgeoisie, the changes are evident. While there has been a recovery of these cities, mainly in their former colonial zones, there has also been a radical transformation of their spaces, documented by contemporary poets with an intense nostalgia for the Luanda that is disappearing, and an indignation against the conditions under which the transformation has taken place. An example of this occurs in Ana Paula Tavares's poem, "*As portas de Luuanda*", where machines devour the city, or in simultaneously outraged and nostalgic poems by Carlos Ferreira, who takes us through the streets of Luanda, through its names, its poets, and the people who fought for freedom, only to find nothing.[32]

Another crucial element in these modern cities is the metamorphosis of their outskirts, some into luxury neighbourhoods, others into new shantytowns, the destination of the population expelled from former shantytowns that are now in the middle of the city, occupying terrain coveted for new neighbourhoods based on an urban model of major social segregation. These new neighbourhoods are materialising in gated communities, isolated in all senses from the rest of the city, so well illustrated by Pepetela in *O Desejo de Kianda* and in some poems by João Melo, Aires de Almeida Santos and José Luis Mendonça. As Silvia Leiria Viegas points out,

> In the current century, after the end of civil war (2002), most of the socio-spatial restrictions, which had emerged during the colonial, socialist and early neoliberal periods, grew worse. In addition, the conflict between the urbanised centre and the self-produced peri-urban areas became critical, and a new wave of self-produced housing occurred. In response, the government adopted the strategy of seeking to control urban society, particularly in Luanda, by eradicating the *musseques*. So, the government created new instruments of socio-spatial production and/or transformation — for example, new laws, programmes and urban plans.[34]

Picture 10.11 Photo of the old Bairro Operário, 2015.[33]

Like the dividing line between the colonial city and the shantytown drawn by Luandino Vieira in the earlier imaginary of these literatures, demarcating the European space from the African space, the new dividing line of the current cities is still based on the same stamp of power and inequality, albeit expressed in an alternative form. And perhaps, in another hangover from the colonial past, the most effective place from which to denounce this inequality remains literature, depicting the interplay between the archaic and the modern, between poverty and the extravagance of the *nouveau riche*, between exploitation and the easy display of wealth portrayed by Pepetela in *Os Predadores*, Luandino Vieira in *O Livro dos Guerrilheiros* and Ondjaki in *Os Transparentes*, as well as in Carlos Ferreira´s poetry. In contemporary fiction, there are still many invisible cities which form and reform the historic and textually polyphonic cities under permanent mutation.

The cities' most culturally decolonising and politically revolutionary moment is probably in the literary projects of the Angolans Pepetela and Luandino Vieira, when they go back to the historic texts of António Oliveira Cadornega. As we have seen, the *História Geral das Guerras Angolanas* contains one of the first descriptions of Luanda, as well as poems about the city. In *A Gloriosa Família*, set during the seventeenth-century Dutch occupation of Luanda, Pepetela reproduces Cadornega's text, rewriting it in order to identify a city and a territory, as well as a people fighting for these. Luandino Vieira does something similar when he purposefully paraphrases Cardonega in his *O Livro dos Rios* in order to identify a territory and a people suffering but valiantly struggling, from that early moment, to be Angolans, thus assuming a common written literary heritage with the then-colonizer, but one that will become wholly Angolan. The process of taking on this inheritance implies selection, re-arrangement, a writing of difference. Through

Picture 10.12 Photo of the "vertical *musseque*", Largo do Kinaxixi, Luanda (2015).[35]

intertextuality, the new writing re-interrogates the original text with which it dialogues, bringing it up to date in a different context and through a different hue of Portuguese. Moreover, *A Gloriosa Família*'s narrator is a slave, bringing into focus the Other side of history through the voice of those who experienced it. Ironically, this slave, who is the property of Baltazar van Dum, the novel's protagonist, is mute and illiterate. As such, he does not have at his disposal the instruments required to tell his story. Yet precisely through this ontological silence, the subaltern's history emerges. In other words, the Other does have a story to tell, and s/he is quite capable of telling it. It is just that the conditions of production and expression they have long endured have led them to an apparent silence. Through his novel, Pepetela writes about Luanda drawing on a different spatial and human geography, pronounced in the language of an Other, a person hitherto excluded from History's grand narrative. Through an "unfaithful copy", the multiple legacies that define Angola and, more specifically, Luanda come into play, and the inherent hierarchy between copy and original, between origin and influence, fade away[36].The action of rewriting constitutes a political movement to conquer the territory and its history by narrating versions of history previously told by other voices and in other places, making the history of the city from its beginning textually more polyphonic. This is a movement against the inequality of power in the narration of history, a movement of Angolanness, or Mozambicanness. These are forms of re-foundation and re-formation of citizenship, and therefore of struggle against inequality. They also reflect cities as spaces wide open to life and full of the possibilities of citizenship-in-difference.

Acknowledgements

This chapter results from work developed in "Memoirs — Children of Empires and European Postmemories", financed by the European Research Council (ERC) under the European Union's Horizon 2020 Research and Innovation Programme (nº 648624), and partly from the project "De S. Paulo de Luanda a *Luuanda*, de Lourenço Marques a Maputo: capitais coloniais em tempos pós-coloniais" (PTDC/CLE-LLI/122229/2010 - FCOMP-01- 0124-FEDER- 019830), financed by Fundos FEDER, Programa Operacional Factores de Competitividade and Fundação para a Ciência e a Tecnologia; both carried out at the Social Studies Centre, University of Coimbra. The author wishes to thank Walter Rossa for his reading and suggestions, and Nuno Simão Gonçalves for his choice of the photographs that complement the text. An earlier version of some parts of this text was published in the *Journal of Lusophone Studies* 1.1 (Spring 2016): 88–106.

Notes

1 See Salvato Trigo, "Literaturas Africanas de Expressão Portuguesa — um Fenómeno de Urbanismo", in *Ensaios de Literatura Comparada Afro-Luso-brasileira*, ed. Salvato Trigo (Lisbon: Vega, 1986).

2 The classic definition of formation as "the history of Brazilians in their desire to have a literature" fits the idea of literature that is formed. See Antonio Candido, *Formação*

da Literatura Brasileira: Momentos Decisivos vol. 1 (Belo Horizonte: Itatiaia, 1981), p. 25. For the variant offered by Mário António see Mario António Fernandes de Oliveira, *A Formação da Literatura Angolana: 1851–1950* (Lisbon: Imprensa Nacional — Casa da Moeda, 1997).

3 See Cahen, ed., *"Vilas et Cidades"*.

4 See Nuno Domingos and Elsa Peralta, eds, *Cidades e Império: Dinâmicas Coloniais e Reconfigurações Pós-Coloniais* (Lisbon: Edições 70, 2013), p. xii.

5 Walter Rossa, "Stone Raft: Allegory on the Spread of European Urbanistics in Early Modern Times" *Joelho* 6 (2015): 78.

6 See Isabel Castro Henriques and Miguel Pais Vieira, "Cidades em Angola: Construções Coloniais e Reinvenções Africanas", in *Cidade e Império*, ed. Domingos and Peralta, p. xiii, footnote no. 2.

7 Rossa, "Stone raft", p. 78.

8 Francisco Topa proves Cruz's authorship of this poem initially published by Cadornega. See Francisco Topa, "Entre a Terra de Gente Oprimida e a Terra de Gente Tostada: Luís Félix da Cruz e o Primeiro Poema Angolano", *Literatura em Debate* (programa de pós-graduação em letras da U. Regional Integrada do Alto Uruguai e das Missões, Rio Grande do Sul, 7, 13, 2013), pp. 122–47.

9 Irene Guerra Marques and Carlos M. Ferreira, eds, *Entre a Lua, o Caos e o Silêncio: A Flor (antologia da poesia angolana)* (Luanda: Mayamba Editora, 2011), p. 466.

10 All translations of texts in Portuguese are by Alexandra Reza (University of Oxford).

11 See Massimo Canevacci, *A Cidade Polifónica: Ensaio sobre a Antropologia da Comunicação Urbana*, trans. Cecília Prata (São Paulo: Nobel, 2004).

12 Nuno Simão Gonçalves, "O Urbanismo da Mafalala: Origem, Evolução e Caracterização", in *Mafalala — Memórias e Espaços de um Lugar* , ed. Margarida Calafate Ribeiro and Walter Rossa (Coimbra: Imprensa da Universidade de Coimbra, 2015), p. 112.

13 Júlio de Castro Lopo, *Alguns Aspetos dos Musseques* (Luanda: Editorial Angola, 1943), p. 5.

14 Ilídio do Amaral, "Luanda: Estudo de Geografia Urbana", *Memórias da Junta de Investigações do Ultramar* 53 (Lisbon: Junta de Investigações do Ultramar, 1968): 128.

15 See Francisco Noa, *Império, Mito e Miopia — Moçambique como uma Invenção Literária* (Lisbon: Caminho, 2003).

16 António Jacinto, *Poesia (1961–1975)* (Vila Nova de Cerveira: NósSomos, 2011), pp. 36 and 39.

17 José Luandino Vieira, *Papéis da Prisão: Apontamentos, Diário, Correspondência (1962–1971),* (Alfragide: Caminho, 2015), p. 45.

18 Hélder Faife, *Contos de Fuga* (Maputo: A2 Design, 2010), p. 9.

19 António Rita-Ferreira, "Os Africanos de Lourenço Marques", *Memórias do Instituto de Investigação Científica de Moçambique* 9, 95–491 (1967–8), p. 174.

20 In "Ronda dos Leques ou Terapêutica da Ocupação Laurentina a partir do Litoral", the poet Grabato Dias offers a description of the socioeconomic status of the residents of the city of Lourenço Marques based on car brands and the women associated with places in the city. See João Pedro Grabato Dias, *Uma Meditação 21 Laurentinas e Dois Fabulírios Falhados* (Lourenço Marques: Dias, 1971), pp. 48–49.

21 Rui Knopfli, *Memória Consentida: 20 Anos de Poesia: 1959–1979* (Lisbon: Imprensa Nacional-Casa da Moeda, 1982), p. 152.

22 Rui Knopfli, *O Monhé das Cobras* (Lisbon: Caminho, 1997), p. 37.

23 Noémia de Sousa, *Sangue Negro* (Maputo: Associação dos Escritores Moçambicanos, 2001), p. 130.

24 "Pancho" Guedes and Amancio d'Alpoim Miranda, "The Caniços of Mozambique", in *Shelter in Africa*, ed. Paul Olivier (London: Barrie & Jenkins, 1961), p. 204.
25 See Margarida Calafate Ribeiro, *Uma História de Regressos, Império, Guerra Colonial e Pós-Colonialismo.* (Porto: Edições Afrontamento, 2004). See also Noa, *Império, Mito e Miopia.*
26 Private collection. *Cedida pelo fotógrafo à autora.*
27 See the poem by Carlos Cardoso in Fátima Mendonça and Nelson Saúte, eds, *Antologia da Nova Poesia Moçambicana* (Maputo: Associação Escritores Moçambicanos, 1988), p. 57.
28 Sílvia Leiria Viegas, "Urbanisation and Peri-Urbanisation in Luanda: A Geopolitical and Socio Spatial Perspective from the Late Colonial Period to the Present", *Journal of Southern African Studies* 42, 4 (2016): 595.
29 See booklet for the exhibition, *Things Fall Apart - Red Africa,* EGEAC, from 7/12/2016 to 12/03/2017, Galeria da Avenida da Índia, Lisbon.
30 See the poem by Luís Carlos Patraquim in *Antologia da Nova Poesia Moçambicana*, ed. Saúte Mendonça (Maputo: Associação de Escritores Moçambicanos, 1993), p. 300.
31 Ana Paula Tavares, *O lago da lua* (Lisbon: Caminho, 1999), p. 36.
32 I am referring to poems such as "Ao Mário António", "Na curva do Bairro Operário", "Eu do Makuluso me confesso", "Ao Viriato da Cruz" among others from Carlos M. Ferreira. See Carlos M. Ferreira and Irene Guerra Marques, eds, *Causas Perdidas (Trinta Anos de Poesia) 1979–2009* (Luanda: União dos Escritores Angolanos, 2011).
33 Unknown photographer.
34 Viegas, "Urbanisation and Peri-Urbanisation in Luanda: A Geopolitical and Socio Spatial Perspective from the Late Colonial Period to the Present", *Journal of Southern African Studies* 42, 4 (2016): pp. 606–607.
35 Unknown photographer.
36 See Walter Rossa and Margarida Calafate Ribeiro, "Modos de Olhar", in *Patrimónios de Influência Portuguesa: Modos de Olhar*, ed. Walter Rossa and Margarida Calafate Ribeiro (Coimbra: Imprensa Universidade de Coimbra, 2015), p. 29.

Part III

The Colonial Period

CHAPTER

11

Inequality, Difference, and Violence: The Brazilian Case in Historical Perspective

LAURA DE MELLO E SOUZA

Point of departure

A number of societies have had slavery without necessarily being slaveholding societies; that is, without their social and economic organization being based on a slave system. This was true of many European societies, Portugal being a prime example in the early modern period. Foreign travelers disembarking in Lisbon during the golden age of Dom Manuel and Dom João III were shocked by the size of the city's dark-skinned population. In the eighteenth century, one Frenchman even referred to the Portuguese as "*des genz basanés*" — literally, swarthy people — who spoke a Spanish dialect. In a climate where the literate classes of northern Europe generally dismissed southern Europeans, this statement demonstrates an absolute ignorance of the language of Camões and Vieira.[1] But the quintessential element of exclusion here is the insinuation that this is a nation with black blood: "*genz basanés*".

Portugal had black slaves in the countryside and in its cities as well; but this was not all. From the sixteenth to the eighteenth centuries, the Portuguese in the Orient took part in the intense trading of Chinese slaves to Goa, notwithstanding the protests of Jesuits, administrative authorities, and even monarchs. These Chinese slaves were also brought to the metropolis, and in the Lisbon of the 1580s, many became cooks, as attested by Filipe Sassetti of Florence.[2] However, even though slavery was adopted across much of the Empire, the only Portuguese society that constituted a slave system existed in Brazil, where slaves comprised the majority of the labour force and social relations were slave-based. Portugal could have existed without slaves; without slaves, Brazil would have withered away.

The slave system is a necessary point of departure when contemplating the violence and inequality that are distinctive features of Brazilian society even today. More than this, it is a requisite explanatory element for these features. But does this make it a sufficient, or a sufficiently thoroughgoing explanatory element?

Inside slavery

In Portugal, there was near unanimity about the need for slavery throughout the colonial period. The attitude of eminent Jesuits like Antonio Vieira and Andreoni (also known as Antonil), as well as those of other, less illustrious, Jesuits, like Jorge Benci, are well known and have been widely studied. "Without Negroes, there is no Pernambuco and, without Angola, there are no Negroes," wrote Vieira in one of his famous letters, incisively synthesizing the elements of the South Atlantic slave system.[3] There was consensus on the topic among colonizing Europeans, and in 1640 the decision-making hub of the West India Company (WIC), Heeren XIX (the Lords Nineteen), voiced a similar opinion: "Without Negroes and oxen, nothing could be expected of Pernambuco."[4] More than a necessary evil, slavery was a constituent part of the system.

Right from its earliest days, the nineteenth century witnessed pressure to abolish the slave trade and slavery. There were good reasons for this, such as the spread of the Enlightenment in all its aspects — notably, in this case, its reflections on different customs and its belief in the progress of humankind. There were also some less good reasons, like Great Britain's growing interest in consolidating markets for wage earners. Claiming its independence in 1822, Brazil was the scene of discussions about the problem of securing a labour force, and even those who, in their hearts, favored abolitionist ideas acquiesced to the continuance of the slave system from this standpoint. Notable political representatives in the early days of the nation, like José Bonifácio de Andrada e Silva and Nicolau Pereira de Campos Vergueiro, worked to see the slave labour force replaced by free labour, which might not only "whiten" the country but also "create the [Brazilian] people"; for the idea was spreading that Brazil did not have people, but rather masters and slaves, an idea enshrined through the pens of various authors, including the Frenchman Louis Couty.[5]

The complexity of nineteenth-century Brazil's historical circumstances can encourage hasty conclusions. It has been suspected for some time that Vergueiro, the brain behind the so-called partnership system with European immigrants which began in the early 1840s, and the man who introduced the system to the province of São Paulo in 1847, was active in slave trading. No empirical evidence has proven this; but today we know very well how that era's ideas and practices concerning slave and free labour could appear contradictory. Take the case of other individuals who, like Vergueiro, were members of the Sociedade Auxiliadora da Indústria Nacional (Society to Aid National Industry), founded in 1827, and who gradually shifted to defending free labour. If we compare the Society's membership list for 1838 with a list of the main slave traders in Rio de Janeiro from 1811 to 1830, presented by Manolo Florentino in his book, *Em Costas Negras*, we will see that a considerable number of names appear on both, always identified as "merchant" (*comerciante*) or "owner" (*proprietário*).[6] Commerce and property ownership in general were hard to separate out from the slave trade, at least until 1850, when Brazil banned it. According to recent research, some of these men, for example José Botelho de Siqueira Matos e Araujo, had owned slave ships between 1824 and 1827, and had had them seized by the British off the African coast; but by 1838, whether in response to English pressure or because they were satisfied with the fortune they had amassed, they were no longer engaging in this activity.[7] We also find the names of some the era's biggest slave owners on the Society's membership list, like José de Sousa Breves — the famous Commander Breves — and Lucas Antonio Monteiro de Barros. Even if unwished for, abolition was considered inevitable, and the elites believed the transition from a system based on slave labour to one based on free wage labour was up to them.

We know that the fight to defeat slavery was primarily a matter for slaves themselves, who rebelled countless times during the Empire.[8] But we also know that even the slaves who resisted slavery — and this resistance took manifold forms — might themselves at times own slaves.

Certain previous studies have shown numerous cases of freedmen who owned slaves.[9] In *Domingos Sodré, um sacerdote africano* — published in English in 2015 under the title *Divining Slavery and Freedom: The Story of Domingos Sodré* — João José Reis evokes the many-faceted, surprising universe of freedmen in mid-nineteenth-century Salvador, when slaves had slaves and brought them from the African coast.[10] This was a world where slaves could participate in the trafficking of other slaves, and where the mightiest traders — always protected by euphemisms like "businessman" or "merchant" — gradually moved toward the defence of free labour.

In recent years, the historiography of slavery in Brazil has grown more sophisticated. However, it has also become increasingly fragmented and focused on empirical cases, steering away from attempts to arrive at a more general understanding. The latter endeavor was inaugurated by *Casa Grande e Senzala* (*The Masters and the Slaves*), with its generalizing, atemporal idealization of a mestizo Brazil; but unless I am mistaken, since Jacob Gorender produced *O escravismo colonial*, published in 1978, nothing more has been accomplished along these lines.[11] Empirically focused documentation has unveiled the complex dynamics of the religious practices exercised by Brazil's African and Afro-Brazilian populations in their brotherhoods, and in rural and urban Afro-Brazilian religious rites like *calundus* and *candomblés*. Inspired by the micro-historical approach, it has revealed some extreme stories, such as that of Rosa Maria Egipcíaca, whom Luiz Mott described as an "African saint of Colonial Brazil"; or that of Manoel Joaquim Ricardo, a slave who was Domingos Sodré's friend, and whom João Reis considered a transatlantic slave trader; or that of Domingos Álvares, an African slave who traveled three continents, supporting himself as a soothsayer and healer in eighteenth-century Rio de Janeiro, and who, at the end of his life, found himself banished to one of Portugal's isolated *coutos de homiziados*.[12] The current state of research, characterized by the investigation of specific cases and an abandonment of overall syntheses, seems to manifest a certain perplexity, or at least indecision, about the possibility of arriving at valid general explanations. A significant proportion of professional historians would seem to feel that the wealth and multiplicity of concrete situations defies the application of theoretical frameworks and hampers the development of syntheses.

Outside slavery

Perhaps it would be worthwhile to return to some major syntheses and overviews of the whole, in an effort to see the question differently.

If we take up some of the key facets of Sérgio Buarque de Holanda's thought in *Raízes do Brasil*, published in 1936,[13] and of Caio Prado Júnior's ideas in *Formação do Brasil Contemporâneo*, published in 1942, we can bring new elements into the discussion. From the beginning, colonization was characterized by its focus on immediate gains, easy wealth, and the idea that overseas conquest provided lands from which entrepreneurs could extract the maximum value and then return to Portugal as fast as possible.[14] This was the meaning behind the refrain cited by Frei Vicente do Salvador in 1627: "*Papagaio real para Portugal!*" — royal parrot, back to Portugal. This was the crux of the Weberian ideal type of the adventurer constructed by Holanda. And, in the looser interpretation of Prado Júnior, this was the purpose of colonization: to produce whatever yielded quick and substantial returns.[15] The vastness of the territory and the open frontier, of course, facilitated extensive, cruel exploitation.

It seems to me that it is within this vast, complex picture that we must try to understand the problem of the labour force, and of a population in the process of formation. It was a population composed of slave masters, merchants, functionaries, and other elements of the colonial elites; of more easily classifiable social layers, like artisans, paid soldiers, sailors, and retailers; of a mass of slaves, whom recent historiography has shown to have displayed diverse features; and of vast contingents of the dispossessed, whose precarious, uncertain situation left them particularly vulnerable to the vicissitudes of the economic, political, and social circumstances of the day. In *Formação do Brasil Contemporâneo*, Caio Prado Júnior referred to the latter as *desclassificados* — loosely translated, the outcasts, or those who have been denied even a classification — and he believed they abounded as never before in Brazil's eighteenth-century gold mines. Earlier, in passages of *Populações Meridionais do Brasil*, published in 1920, Oliveira Viana had called attention to this social group and especially to the role they had played in the world of major rural landholdings, serving as a private militia for powerful landowners. There is a yawning chasm between Prado Júnior's Marxist perspective and Oliveira Viana's conservative, authoritarian, and racist outlook; but both help us to contemplate the permanent discomfort that the elite felt before the poor free men who constituted the Brazilian people.

While these poor free men were often mestizos, it was not merely their mixed blood that rendered them "disqualified" but rather their itinerancy, their fluidity, and, although this was not verbalized, their very status as free, a quality deemed incompatible with the condition of poor, dispossessed men in a slaveholding society. Oliveira Viana, who in a fit of oversimplification qualified these men as "the historical product of great landed estates", detected their troubling rootlessness: "[He] is rootless, displaced, unsettled. From a nomadic hunter, he is thus readily transformed into a nomadic warrior of the *sertão*," while the rural master shows "the utmost interest in keeping him at his side, thusly unsettled and idle". It was Viana's view that the large landholding system transformed the idle and the good-for-nothings, the outlaws and the brigands, into its defenders; the colonial aristocracy made them the foundation of its power.[16]

Yet the role of these poor free men went well beyond that of protagonists in the entrenchment of seigniorial power. The disparaging judgments pronounced about these men helped concretize a negative vision of the Brazilian people, and this justifies a thoughtful examination of another historical context: eighteenth-century Minas Gerais, where these same protagonists appear with a different label: vagrants.

Free men and vagrancy

The vagrants I would like to focus on here are those who, more than 50 years after the outset of the Portuguese colonization of Minas Gerais, vexed colonial rulers and jeopardized the region's already precarious political and social stability. They were emblematic of a situation of economic unbalance and social injustice that sought constantly to reproduce them.

Around 1750, Minas Gerais was still the most important piece of the Portuguese Colonial Empire. But the region's gold mining activities, which had always relied on panning or open-cast methods, were entering a dramatic decline, while *quilombos* — colonies of runaway slaves — were spreading across more remote areas. About 75 percent of the population consisted of blacks and mestizos, and the white minority, nearly all of Portuguese birth, lived in constant fear of a slave uprising.

When gold mining entered its decline, local authorities, like governors, sought to devise a distinct colonization policy. As men of their times, and servants of a colonial Eempire, they had to cope with the constraints inherent in their circumstances. In any case, the texts they bequeathed us on the economic reorganization of the captaincy of Minas Gerais, and on the use of idle labour — a crucial point — are of vital importance in understanding the political imagery of the eighteenth-century Portuguese colonial bureaucrat. These texts also shed light on the way of life of the poorer, socially outcast, layers of what was the Empire's richest region.

Vagrants constituted a transgressive group characterized first and foremost by their very way of life. It was the fact that they did nothing, or did nothing systematically, that made them suspicious in the eyes of the better-organized sectors of society. Since they had no ties — no families, no fixed homes, no jobs — they formed an ill-defined, fluid group, hard to control or even to classify. Once the early days of the gold rush were past, itinerancy merited less and less tolerance. It would appear that Minas took its first official action against vagrants in 1766: on July 22, Governor-General Luís Diogo Lobo da Silva received from the King an incisive *carta régia* condemning the itinerancy of vagrants and their chosen way of life. Such men, said the document, lived outside the bounds of civil society, stuck away in Brazil's barren *sertões*, in *volant domiciles*, that is, with no fixed residence. This could not be tolerated, and these vagrants should start living in settlements of more than 50 houses, with the standard administrative apparatus of colonial towns. Once established, the settlers would be granted adjacent arable land to farm. Those who failed to comply with this procedure would be arrested and dealt with as highwaymen and "common enemies".[17]

Three years later, the Count of Valladares, as governor-general, sent to all *capitães-mores*[18] and all district commanders within the captaincy a list of 11 instructions determining what procedure to adopt in relation to vagrants, who had become increasingly bothersome, and more visibly so. These instructions reveal the fluidity of eighteenth-century Minas society. Extreme care is taken to warn commanders to arrest only *true* vagrants, to give no heed to false accusations by enemies, and to make certain that any persons deemed vagrants are made to perform some type of worthwhile activity. Deviant behavior by those having a defined trade was regarded as irrelevant; for the object of this rule, according to the text, was not to regulate private conduct, "so long as it did not offend the public". Furthermore, any crimes should be judged carefully: idlers who stole or ambushed, who challenged third parties, who caused serious bodily harm — or even slight injury if at night — should be arrested. But "upright, peaceable" men who "for some reason of chance transgress" — even if their transgression resulted in death — were not punishable under the provisions of these instructions, the major purpose of which was to root out vagrants and felons.

The instructions show that it was often hard, in a newly settled and highly miscegenated society, to tell a malefactor from a worthy subject: how could servants and slaves be distinguished from outlaws and felons? Furthermore, the instructions underscore official concern with the need to fix rootless, itinerant elements in one place, in this case to be achieved by a return to, and development of, formulations contained in the Philippine Ordinances. Up until the 1770s, the authorities were more concerned with vagrants' marginalized lifestyle, and with possible ways of controlling this, than with possibilities for putting them to work. However, the worsening situation in gold mining meant that this "worthless burden of the Earth" would have to be transformed into a useful element within society. Starting with the administration of the Count of Valladares, the governors-general of Minas searched for economic alternatives to mining. To this end, they insisted on the advantages of establishing settlement outposts, drove out groups of Brazilian natives from these areas, and widened the borders of the region effectively controlled by the Portuguese Crown.

The story of Inácio Correia Pamplona's expedition is especially enlightening when it comes to understanding the gap that separated daily practice in eighteenth-century Minas Gerais from the colonizers' ideas on using social outcasts to open up frontier lands. The enterprise in question was a 1769–70 campaign to conquer Campo Grande, Piauí, and Bambuí, and to open up trails into Goiás, along the border region between the captaincies of Goiás, São Paulo, and Minas Gerais. The purpose was to capture and rout so-called savages, as well as blacks installed in *quilombos*, and to then set up ranches and settlements in these "sanitized" *sertão* lands.[19]

Finding people willing to live in those parts was not easy, however, and it became necessary to resort to violence, that is to say, to arrest vagrants and force them to settle in those frontier lands. Pamplona believed this procedure should be applied to vagrant prostitutes, those guilty of misdemeanors, and even concubines. These people's unbridled sensuality would be subdued by work at cotton and linen looms and on wheat plantations:

> In Minas Gerais, idleness, especially on the part of women, is the cause of their poverty and of the perversity of their habits. I cannot accept that a white woman in Portugal — I refer to peasant women — should be caring for her household, rearing her children, fetching water for her kitchen, preparing and taking food to her husband in the fields, spinning until midnight, always joyfully, while here a freed slave woman is hard put to wash a plate, indulging in the most excessive slothfulness.[20]

If mild medicine had no effect, the commander of the expedition suggested turning to violent means; he needed people but, in his opinion, these sluggards preferred "living destitute in idleness to wealthy in work". Pamplona propagandized the colonization of frontier areas, painting a pretty picture of the possibilities open to settlers in those new regions and enticing potential homesteaders with land deeds and with the earnings they supposedly stood to make on grain crops. The unemployed responded with indifference, alleging that the distant location of those places made the shipment of produce infeasible, and, further, that their lack of personal resources would hinder settlement, for they possessed nothing of their own, not even clothing.

In the end, Pamplona himself seemed to grow discouraged and lose faith in the outcasts' homesteading potential, perhaps realizing they were not Portuguese peasants: "As concerns the vagrants, I believe such settlement to be most difficult. They are all a caste of people governed by idleness, swept up by vices, and, lastly, exceedingly poor, which presents the greatest hindrance. Sending them is easy; making them stay is what is difficult. Of what use is it to distribute land to them if they lack all means of planting? Without money, how are they to purchase weapons, gunpowder, lead shot and bullets, hoes, scythes, axes, lard, salt, and the other things needed for raising crops, and for sustenance?"[21]

Despite Pamplona's discouraging conclusion, the following years saw a reinforcement of the idea that vagrants could be useful. Their principal defender was Governor-General Dom Antonio de Noronha, who, in a letter to the Marquis of Lavradio, the Portuguese Viceroy, expressed disapproval of the idea of recruiting these idlers for the wars against the Spanish then being fought in southern Brazil, and advocated their employment in a series of activities unsuitable for slave labour or better-skilled white workers.[22] Dom Antonio's ideas gained prominence, thanks to Desembargador Teixeira Coelho, circuit magistrate of Vila Rica. Teixeira Coelho worked in close collaboration with the governor-general and wrote one of the most notable texts of eighteenth-century Brazil: the *Instrução para o governo da Capitania de Minas Gerais*, or Instruction for the Government of the Captaincy of Minas Gerais, thought to date from 1780. To quote the magistrate: "Vagrants are objects of loathing for all civilized nations, and many times have laws been passed against them; however, common rules on this point cannot be applicable throughout the whole of the territory of Minas, because these vagrants, who elsewhere would be a nuisance, may here be of use."[23] Thus took shape the idea that the dead weight of vagrants could be metamorphosed into something useful.

But who, after all, were these vagrants, and when might they be useful?

Except for a small number of whites, according to Dom Antonio and Teixeira Coelho, these vagrants were all mulattoes, mixed-race Indians, or freed slaves. They made up the forces that ventured into the woodlands in pursuit of runaway slaves and to destroy *quilombos*. They joined the armed groups that waged war against so-called savages, driving the latter into uninhabited regions. They populated remote areas, establishing settlement outposts, or *presídios*. Finally, they worked to open the trails that led to these frontier lands. They were not exactly "idlers" but individuals living off odd jobs and who, for a variety of reasons, were not suitable for systematic work.

Governor Dom Rodrigo José Menezes continued to defend the policy of utilizing the unemployed to counteract the potential burden they represented. He ordered that all vagrants throughout his captaincy be arrested and put to work building the *presidio* (fortifications) of Cuieté, "in this way undertaking that important work at little expense, and also purging civil society of its disrupters".[24]

Such recruitment was not, however, accomplished peacefully. Under the rule of Governor Luís da Cunha Menezes, vagrants worked to build the *Casa de Câmara e Cadeia* (municipal chambers and jail). Recruited by force, held under constant guard, shackled one to another, with nothing but bread and water to eat, these men were immortalized in the verses of Tomás Antonio Gonzaga, in letters 3 and 4 of the *Cartas Chilenas*.[25] Inside the walls they had helped to raise, other wretches would moan and suffer as they had. Momentarily useful to civil society, the idlers thus purged themselves of their sin of indolence and their disdain for productive work.

In eighteenth-century Minas, concern over vagrants was one facet of the intense fear that those who wielded power felt when they identified disruptive forces capable of undermining their control over the Brazilian colony. Along with blacks in *quilombos*, who on official documents were denominated "Enemies," with a capital "E" — as if representing the devil himself — vagrants were "Enemies within," agents of disorder and adherents of a counter-society that disdained fixed residences, the "nuclear" family, systematic labour, and private property — in short, those values that the healthy portion of the social body revered as essential.

Around the 1750s, the potentially explosive situation in the captaincy grew apparent to the colonial rulers. Runaway slaves and idle poor men abounded, finding no space in an economy that rewarded the richer and discarded the "lowly". The continuance of colonial domination depended on urgently finding solutions. If blacks were to rise up in revolt, or if vagrants gained awareness of their potential power, the restricted world of white men might be blown apart.

In bureaucratic texts, instructions, and reports, such as that by Correia Pamplona, what stands out is a desire to create something new out of what was then available. The vagrant portrayed here was not always a vagabond: in certain passages, this classifier was a label serving to designate a poor free man, the very fruit of colonial living conditions.

It is precisely the contradictions of "*o viver em colônias*" — living in the colonies — that are reflected in concerns over the utilization of vagrants. Both the representatives of the metropolis and the more aware colonists attempted to address the question: Unless vagrants were part of society, were they not a threat to it? Efforts to make use of them, however, inevitably relied on violence, since such people could not adjust to the systematic activities then typical of the European tradition.

Vagrants indeed proved useful in cases where slave labour was infeasible, that is, in clearing woodlands and in paramilitary expeditions against *quilombos* and belligerent Indians. As members of a slaveholding society — one with a mixture of characteristics from the Ancien Régime and class-based societies — the impossible was always asked of them: from an Ancien Régime perspective, they should fix their residence; from a capitalist class perspective, they should apply themselves to hard work.

The enemy within

In concluding, I would like to reiterate the value of using the slave system as a point of departure when contemplating the violence and inequality found in Brazilian society down through time. Virtually all social, political, and economic relations were linked to the system, and the examples cited above have been indicative of this. Former slave traders drifted over to the field of abolitionist discussions and mingled with the Empire's most illustrious political figures, as was the case with the Society to Aid National Industry. Slaves purchased slaves and, once freed, engaged in the transatlantic trading of black Africans. Poor free men were left without a raison d'être in a world where African slaves furnished most of the labour; and thus rendered useless, they were soon transformed into members of private wealth's militia and into forced labourers who opened up public roadways and built prisons. Forged from inequality, while also its victim, epitomizing fluidity and inchoateness, the poor free stratum also displayed internal stratification that overlapped with the stratification of slaves, reflecting the complexity of the problem. Here was complex inequality, and a complexity of concrete situations.

This extreme complexity, this plurality that makes Brazil such a unique case, has drawn comfort from explanations that rest on the slave system as the root of all evil. While it is legitimate to take this system as a prime point of departure for these discussions, over time this approach has come to paint in strokes that are too broad, obscuring both complex inequality as well as the heterogeneity of situations. Brazilian memory has gradually learned to cope better with the slave system than with inequality. When endeavoring to construct a synthesis, invoking the slave system as the supreme evil ultimately harmonizes that which is incompatible with any harmonization.[26]

The importance of the slave system as an explanatory element should not, in my opinion, preclude a search outside the system for elements that cannot always be reduced to it. The disqualification of physical labour, and the perpetuation of inequality, continued to present themselves in places where their agents were no longer slaves. Expressing biases comparable to those directed decades earlier against the black and mestizo population, the medical discourse of the elites in major urban centres systematically denigrated the European immigrants who came to Brazil between the end of the monarchy and beginning of the republic, and the example I would like to cite here is the city of São Paulo. In the first quarter of the twentieth century, when one-third of the population comprised people from other places, and the population contained 66 nationalities, it was believed that the city lived under the sign of danger, a Babel of tongues and a den of myriad diseases, beleaguered by endemic and epidemic enemies: madness, typhus, dysentery, scarlet fever, diphtheria, leprosy, the bubonic plague, and so many others. Disheartened by the harsh labour system in force on coffee plantations, the new arrivals crowded chaotically into São Paulo, descending into mendicancy, vagabondage, and crime. In 1912, this situation prompted the physician Pereira Barreto to give callous voice to what most of the elites thought: "What good does it do us to have an elegant mansion if a consumptive has a coughing fit while passing by our door and spits onto the ground phlegm that is heavy with Koch's bacillus?"[27] In 1919, another doctor, José de Toledo Piza, declared that diphtheria had been introduced to the town by an Italian child; ergo, immigration was spreading disease. In 1922, Dr Bruno Rangel Pestana blamed immigrants for the dissemination of typhoid fever, freely venting his xenophobia: "To these *trabalhadores estranhos* (foreign workers, outsiders) falls the responsibility for the propagation of the Eberth bacillus among *our people*" (emphasis added).[28]

How could barriers be erected to impede contact between this "us" and these "outsiders" if they were employed as workers in factories, as maids in homes, and as traveling vendors in the streets? If rich ladies hired them as wet nurses, and thus infected the comfortably situated portion of the social body, of "our people"?[29] The eugenicist arguments that, around the same time, proclaimed the need for white immigrants to dilute black blood and attenuate the miscegenation of the Brazilian people further demonstrated the complexity of the situation: like the vagrants of colonial times, the immigrants were necessary and unwanted, pernicious and useful.[30]

In insisting that the lower classes propagated death, the physicians of Brazil's young republic provided a powerful image of the country's social formation. By marginalizing popular elements and invoking the constant menace represented by a people as yet unformed and, in this historical context, diseased as well, these doctors fell into line with an age-old tradition previously represented by colonial governors, men of letters, magistrates, and all those keen to cover up the real problem: the perpetuation of social inequality.[31]

For all these reasons, and to avoid the risk of historicist simplism, it would be wise not to view the inequality that reigns in Brazilian society as deriving solely from the slave system. Once slavery had been abolished and the system itself undermined, the expansion of a form of life grounded in the exploitation of free men — already embedded in the heart of the slave system — grew stronger and more entrenched and once again served the elites' goal of self-preservation and self-reproduction. In closing, I quote the words of the physician Renato Kehl, a well-known eugenicist activist who was especially active in the Old Republic (1889–1930): "Let us then forge our elite, for all else we have in abundance! The masses can remain formless, with or without their abcs, in the role of those who are ruled."[32]

Notes

1 "Le voyage au Portugal d'Etienne de Silhouette (1729–1730)", in Daniel Henri-Pageaux, *Images du Portugal dans les lettres françaises (1700–1755)* (Paris: Fundação Calouste Gulbenkian, 1971), pp. 82–94, quotations pp. 90–93.

2 Charles R. Boxer, "Muitsai em Macau", in *Fidalgos no Extremo Oriente* (Lisbon: Fundação Oriente/Museu e Centro de Estudos Marítimos de Macau, 1990), pp. 227–45.

3 Cited in Charles Boxer, *Os Holandeses no Brasil — 1624–1654* (São Paulo: Companhia Editora Nacional, 1961), pp. 192 and 193. On the south Atlantic system, see Luiz Felipe de Alencastro, *O Trato dos Viventes* (São Paulo: Companhia das Letras, 2000).

4 Among others, see Ronaldo Vainfas, *Ideologia e Escravidão — Os letrados e a sociedade escravista no Brasil colonial* (Petropolis: Editora Vozes, 1982).

5 Louis Couty, *L'esclavage au Brésil* (Paris: Librairie de Guillaumin et Cie Editeurs, 1881).

6 André Luís Alípio de Andrade, *Variações sobre um tema: a Sociedade Auxiliadora da Indústria Nacional e o Debate Sobre o Fim do Tráfico de Escravos (1845–1850)*, (master's thesis, UNICAMP, 2002), pp. 163–171. On the partnership system, see Davatz, *Memórias de um Colono no Brasil* (1850), foreword by Sérgio Buarque de Holanda (São Paulo: Livraria Martins Fontes/EDUSP, 1972); Emilia Viotti da Costa, *Da Senzala à Colônia* (São Paulo: DIFEL, 1966); Maria Lucia Lamounier, *Da Escravidão ao TrabalhoLi vre (A lei de locação de serviços de 1879)* (Campinas: Papirus, 1988); Manolo Florentino, *Em Costas Negras — Uma História do Tráfico de Escravos entre a Africa e o Rio de Janeiro (séculos XVIII–XIX)*, 2nd edn (São Paulo: Companhia das Letras, 1997), list on pp. 254–6.

7 I refer to research Geraldo Dutra de Andrade and I are now conducting, which has not yet been published.

8 Among others, see Maria Helena Machado, *O Plano e o Pânico — os Movimentos Sociais na Década da Abolição* (Rio de Janeiro/São Paulo: Editora UFRJ/EDUSP, 1994).

9 See, for example, Pierre Verger, *Os Libertos: Sete Caminhos na Liberdade de Escravos da Bahia no Século XIX* (Salvador: Editora Corrupio, 1992), and Maria Inês Côrtes de Oliveira, "Viver e morrer no meio dos seus: nações e comunidades africanas na Bahia do Século XIX", *Revista USP* 28: 174–93.

10 João José Reis, *Domingos Sodré, um Sacerdote Africano. Escravidão, Liberdade e Candomblé na Bahia do Século XIX* (São Paulo: Companhia das Letras, 2008). One notable case is that of Manoel Joaquim Ricardo, a friend of Domingos Sodré, see pp. 226 on. An English language version of *Domingos Sodré*, trans. H. Sabrina Gledhill, was released by Cambridge University Press (New York) in 2015, under the title *Divining Slavery and Freedom: The Story of Domingos Sodré, an African Priest in Nineteenth-Century Brazil.*

11 Gilberto Freyre, *Casa Grande e Senzala — Formação da Família Brasileira sob Regime de Economia Patriarcal*, 9th edn, 2 vols (Rio de Janeiro: José Olympio, 1958). Jacob Gorender, *O Escravismo Colonial* (São Paulo: Editora Atica, 1978).

12 Luiz Mott, *Rosa Egipcíaca — Uma Santa Africana no Brasil* (Rio de Janeiro: Bertrand Brasil, 1993); Reis, *Domingos Sodré*; Sweet, *Domingos Alvares — African Healing and the Intellectual History of the Atlantic World* (Chapel Hill: The University of North Carolina Press, 2011).

13 An English-language version of Sérgio Buarque de Holanda's *Raízes do Brasil*, translated by G. Harvey Summ, was released by the University of Notre Dame Press (Indiana) in 2012, under the title *Roots of Brazil.*

14 Sérgio Buarque de Holanda, "Trabalho e Aventura", in *Raízes do Brasil* (1936), 9th edn (São Paulo: José Olympio Editora, 1976), pp. 12–40.
15 Caio Prado Júnior, *Formação do Brasil Contemporâneo* (1942), reprint (São Paulo: Companhia das Letras, 2011).
16 Oliveira Viana, *Populações Meridionais do Brail — Populações Rurais do Centro-Sul* (1920), reprint with introductory text by José Murilo de Carvalho (Rio de Janeiro: Editora Nova Aguilar, 2000), pp. 977–9.
17 "Coleção sumária das próprias leis, cartas régioas, avisos e ordens . . .", *Revista do Arquivo Público Mineiro* 16: 451–2.
18 *Capitães-mores* were local militia commanders.
19 "Do mestre de Campo Ignácio Correia Pamplona sobre a Expedição do Campo Grande, Cuieté, e Abaeté termo de Paracatu — De todos os sujeitos, que escreveram sobre esta material." Biblioteca Nacional do Rio de Janeiro, Seção de Manuscritos, 18, 2: 6.
20 *Ibid.*, pp. 271–2.
21 *Ibid.*, p. 336.
22 Biblioteca Nacional do Rio de Janeiro, Seção de Manuscritos, 2, 2, 24, fls. 52–53, carta de 19 novembro 1776.
23 J. J. Teixeira Coelho, "Instrução para o Governo da Capitania de Minas Gerais", *Revista do Arquivo Público Mineiro*, 8: 479.
24 "Exposição do Governador D. Rodrigo José de Menezes sobre o Estado de Decadência da Capitania de Minas Gerais e Meios de Remediá-lo", *Revista do Arquivo Público Mineiro* 2: 314–5.
25 Tomás Antonio Gonzaga, *Poesias: Cartas Chilenas*, ed. Manoel Rodrigues Lapa (Rio de Janeiro: Instituto Nacional do Livro, 1957).
26 I would like to thank Renato Lessa for his suggestions concerning "complex inequality," which helped me to set out my arguments better.
27 Cited by Mariza Romero, "Construção da Nação e Exclusão Social. Medicalização da Saúde em São Paulo (1889–1930)", *Revista do Arquivo Municipal* 1 (2014): 79–100.
28 *Ibid.*, p. 85.
29 *Ibid.*, p. 85. On wet nurses, see also Mariza Romero, *Do Bom Cidadão: As Normas Médicas em São Paulo (1889–1930)* (PhD dissertation, Universidade de São Paulo, 1995).
30 Here I am citing Romero, "Construção da Nação", p. 88.
31 *Ibid.*, p. 84.
32 Once again, I am making use of both the suggestions of Renato Lessa, who read the first version of this text, as well as the excellent article by Marisa Romero, broadly cited. I am, however, wholly responsible for my conclusions.

CHAPTER

12

Social Inequality in the Portuguese Empire

FRANCISCO BETHENCOURT

The Portuguese empire has been discussed in political and economic terms, but strangely enough it has not been analysed in a systematic way in relation to social inequality, a feature which nearly all historians would agree was at the core of the system. My argument is that social inequality drove the imperial system from beginning to end, contributing to its shaping and reshaping, inspiring policies, and explaining divergences from region to region and from the periphery to the centre. However, the imperial system cannot be conceived of exclusively as a top-down enterprise driven by the interests of central, regional and local elites. Negotiation and compromise between ethnic and social groups of different origins and with different agencies must be introduced into the picture if we are to understand how such a loose set of territories managed to hold together for several centuries through spontaneous and forced migration, the regular circulation of people for administration and trade, and the constant need for adaptation to local conditions. Gaps between policies and outcomes need to be taken into consideration, while the unintended consequences of the Portuguese presence should lead us to think deeply about the unexpected patterns of constant social improvisation that define human history. What I intend to write here is an essay resulting from extensive historical research and reflection on the available bibliography, most of it local and concentrated on short periods of time.

First of all, we need questions to guide us on this brief and necessarily condensed approach. Why did Portugal pursue a policy of overseas expansion for five and a half centuries? What were the driving forces behind this endeavour? What were the main benefits and losses resulting from overseas expansion? Who were the main beneficiaries from the Portuguese expansion? What was the social impact back in Portugal? What was the social impact of the empire on native populations? Were there major differences in the social impact over time and space? In what ways can we assess the relationship between the empire and social inequality?

Recent research has shown that the economic output generated by the empire increased Portugal's income per capita by at least one fifth in the early modern period. When compared with recent data collected for other European empires, this estimate shows that the exceptional benefits of empire for English and Dutch economic growth were followed closely by those for Portugal, and all three were way ahead of France and Spain, although the Portuguese capacity for extraction was not translated into economic convergence with the country's rivals.[1] The debate over the real economic benefits of the empire will not be settled by this new finding; the social distribution of the benefits or disadvantages of the empire is still to be fully understood. Here, I will try to provide a framework for further research, divided in two parts, the first based on Portuguese emigration, the second on the impact of the empire on native populations.

Portuguese emigration: possibilities opened up by the empire to different groups

Data on European emigration from the early sixteenth to the early nineteenth century show a persistent flow of Portuguese people overseas, beating that of people from all other European countries, both in absolute and relative terms: more than 1.5 million people, the vast majority heading to the Americas (Brazil), from a population that grew from one to three million in this period.[2] Structural emigration, which increased even further in the nineteenth and twentieth century, and has reached new heights in the past six years, due to the latest economic recession, means that the country has hardly ever managed to support its own population (or, to turn things around, the population has not sufficiently developed its own country). However, significant immigration has occurred since the 1980s, reaching its highest level in the 2000s, and now the number of legal immigrants resident in the country is under 400,000 in a population of 10.4 million.[3]

The reason for structural emigration during the *ancien regime* has mainly been attributed to the seigneurial system, which was based on the nobility's practice of entailing property, complemented by the accumulation of mortmain property by the Church. The two superior orders of society thus excluded from the market the best land, more than one third of the available (arguably the best) rural properties.[4] Exclusion and dependency were thus the main reasons for emigration. However, research in the 1980s threw new light on demographic regimes and stem family structures based on small properties in the north, particularly the northwest of the country, which privileged inheritance by one single child, condemning to celibacy the other male siblings, who were thus tempted by migration.[5] Research on migration confirmed that this had been the trend since at least the seventeenth century: emigration came overwhelmingly from the fertile rural areas; it did not result from starvation but from unequal family structures.[6]

However, the constraints of seigneurial structures cannot be dismissed, for two reasons: they supported the model of one single inheritor, determining the exclusion of other siblings; and they kept the standard of rural life at a low level, not only for tenants but also for landowners, by making capital scarce and thus delaying the introduction of innovations. The Portuguese nobility was permanently in debt, and this was one of the main reasons for this social group to search overseas for rewards under royal patronage.[7] Finally, the property available to support the clergy, even complemented by entitlement to the tithe, could not cover the increase in the first order, which probably grew from 15,000 ordained men and women at the end of the fifteenth century to 60,000 by the 1730s, that is from 1.5 percent to 3 three percent of the total population, with the major increase recorded during the sixteenth century, when the number of convents increased from 203 to 396, reaching 450 by the mid-seventeenth century and 477 in the first third of the eighteenth century, after which there was a decline.[8]

Peasants

Long-term overseas expansion was therefore the outcome not of royal policies but of convergent interests among different groups of the population. The rural population, which up to the 1960s traditionally constituted the vast majority of Portuguese emigrants, tended to migrate in two steps, moving first to coastal cities, or to the Atlantic Islands, where they learned new trades and accumulated money beyond the initial (meagre) resources provided by their family of origin as payment for their exclusion from inheritance.[9] They could then pay for the trip to Brazil with their accumulated financial resources, managing to avoid the status of indentured labour. We know what an important role indentured labour played amongst most English and Dutch migrants to the New World, who were dependent on loans and forced to work for a considerable period of time for their creditors.[10]

This also explains the possibilities available to the Portuguese emigrants, who established themselves as shop keepers in the coastal cities of Brazil, or invested in sugar or tobacco plantations in the northeast. The same family structures that had ejected them would respond to their need for replacement from generation to generation, with new arrivals of nephews helping, and in many cases succeeding, their uncles in business.[11] The empire opened up new possibilities for these people, not only in the rural areas, in which many managed to acquire land, but also in the urban areas, since the Iberian empires were defined by strong urban investment and urban structures from the very beginning, contrasting with the predominantly rural British Empire in the Americas.[12] In any case, social mobility was a feature of emigrated rural populations, with many emigrants becoming land owners. They moved between areas of activity, responding to the need for soldiers, sailors and artillery men, but also acting as shop-keepers, cooks, and artisans. They became priests, members of religious orders, clerks, and even agents of the king.

Brazil was by far the main destination for Portuguese emigrants, since it meant an average of two months at sea, compared to six months to India, implying a low mortality rate . However, in the sixteenth century, most migrants went to India, where major opportunities in trade and war (booty) existed, whereas in Brazil the main sugar plantations that would provide the economic backbone of the colony were only created from the 1550s onwards.[13] In India, the social mobility of this vast layer of rural emigrants was even more striking, since scattered colonial territories were structured around towns and fortresses, with the exception of the 'Northern Province' (a stretch of coastal land between Bombay and Daman) and Sri Lanka (virtually controlled by Portugal, with the exception of the mountainous kingdom of Kandy, between the 1590s and the 1620s).

Wars drove the social mobility of this vast group, with some of the migrants offering their services to local and regional Asian powers, while keeping a connection with the *Estado da Índia*.[14] This was naturally the migrant occupation with the highest mortality rate. Many migrants were involved sooner or later with trade, which was the main means of earning a living, affecting all Portuguese social groups operating on the continent, from governors and captains to clergymen and artisans. The well-known author Fernão Mendes Pinto had had a rural background in Portugal, before acting as a trader, the captain of a ship and (briefly) a Jesuit in Asia. His book *Peregrinação* reveals a prodigious imagination. It contains elements of an autobiography, a travel account, and a picaresque novel, as well as giving voice to the indignation of local rulers with its revelations about the plunder and atrocities perpetrated by Portuguese navigators.[15]

In Sri Lanka and the Northern Province, some of these emigrants took possession of rural properties that were redistributed to religious orders or Portuguese noblemen; but the vast majority changed their occupation and engaged with an urban environment.[16] The same occurred with the prazos (African chieftaincies leased as Crown estates for three generations in Zambesia, Mozambique), where properties transmitted through the female line became controlled by mixed-race families.[17] In Angola, there were no serious plantations until the late nineteenth century. During the early modern period, the main activity among the small number of Portuguese migrants established there was the slave trade.[18] The same trend occurred in Mozambique, at a late stage in the Transatlantic slave trade, between the late-eighteenth and mid-nineteenth centuries.[19] This was also the main activity of the similarly sparse Portuguese populations who lived in Cape Verde, between the Rivers of Guinea, and on the Gulf of Guinea, up to the early nineteenth century.[20]

The discovery of gold in Brazil in the last decade of the seventeenth century increased the previous flow of emigration from Portugal, which had been concentrated on that destination since the early seventeenth century.[21] What is interesting is that this flow did not diminish with independence, but rather recorded new heights after the abolition of slavery in 1888. This was probably a period in which Portuguese emigrants were more involved with agriculture. Emigration from Portugal maintained extraordinarily high levels throughout the nineteenth century, and this was repeated during most of the twentieth century, as the emigrants searched for new final destinations. Emigrants to the Azores re-emigrated to New England, first due to their expertise in whale hunting, then attracted by the textile factories established there in the second half of the nineteenth century, and finally adapting their skills to providing services in the area. California became another favourite destiny for emigrants from the Azores, this time attracted by the opportunities opening up in rural areas. [22] Venezuela and some Caribbean islands (such as Trinidad and Tobacco or Barbados) became the destinations for the emigrants from Madeira, some of whom also searched for an alternative in South Africa during the twentieth century.

The major destinations for rural emigrants from continental Portugal became France and Germany in the late 1950s, the 1960s and the early 1970s, despite the efforts by the Salazar regime to direct that flow towards the African colonies.

The presence of Portuguese immigrants in the colonies, first fostered by the conference of Berlin in 1884–5, then encouraged during the occupation wars that took place from the 1890s to the 1920s, only dramatically increased during the 1950s and 1960s.[23] Late occupation of the territory followed an internationally imposed disruption of the slave trade and then of slavery. Expropriation of what had traditionally been native communal land, a written register of privatised property, and geological surveys of the territory were the main mechanisms for imposing a new colonial reality, with the extraction of minerals and extensive rural production now driven by the colonists.[24] These procedures followed similar steps taken by the other colonial powers, mainly the British and the French.

Portuguese migrants came from rural Brazil after independence to implement the first plantation projects – sugar, then coffee – in Angola; but it was only after the military campaigns of occupation, which really started in the mid-nineteenth century and the concession of large areas to international companies, such as the *Companhia de Mozambique* and the *Companhia do Niassa* in Mozambique, or the CADA in Angola, or national companies such as the *Companhia União Fabril* in Guinea, Angola and Mozambique, that rural activity for export really took off.[25] In the meantime, initiatives in Portugal, in which privatised communal land in the north was re-distributed to dislocated populations from the south, managed by *Junta de Colonização Interna*, were replicated in Angola and Mozambique. These initiatives did not achieve major success, however. Entrepreneurial rural activity needed to involve the native population, which was resistant, while the Portuguese acted as technicians and supervisors. The exploitation of minerals became extremely important in Angola with the creation in 1917, based on international capital, of Diamang , which controlled an average of 10,000 employees for the extraction of diamonds for several decades.[26] The discovery of offshore oil fields in Angola occurred in the late colonial years, and played a major role in the new political regime established after independence, reinforced after the final defeat of UNITA.[27]

Urban workers

Artisans and specialist workers, by contrast, did not play an important role among Portuguese emigrants until the nineteenth century. It is true that foundry workers who could make cannons, and other specialists in artillery, were in high demand in the early sixteenth century, when the Casa da Índia hired German specialists; but by the early seventeenth century the decline in the quality of Portuguese artillery was lamented as meaning that the Portuguese were no match for Dutch and English naval competition in Asia.[28] There were certainly Portuguese artisans in Goa, Macau and Salvador; but the only city with sustained privileges for this social group, and only for a while, was Salvador.[29] Highly specialised workers, such as shipbuilders, were crucial in the main shipyards of Salvador, Rio, Cochim and Goa; but the involvement of competent local workers in India allowed the Portuguese to restrict their functions to supervisory ones.[30] This is one of the areas in which native workers played a major role. In Africa and Brazil, a specialist artisan labour force could also be built on the competence of Africans, who knew about mining and metallurgy; whilst in India, native jewellers played an important role in diffusing innovation. For example, Rauluchantin, from Goa, who was invited to Lisbon by King Manuel in the early sixteenth century, introduced the technique of filigree to Europe.[31]

The competences of Portuguese workers were developed to the full in the new colonial societies that emerged in the 1950s and 1960s, due to the diversification of urban functions that accompanied the building of new roads, the diffusion of cars and trucks, the production of beverages, the development of the fishing industry, and the growth of tailoring, printing and education, to name just some of the sectors of economic activity. The idea of social mobility among Portuguese migrants, who are generally seen as relatively detached from native populations, has to be nuanced. The case of Luandino Vieira (born José Mateus Vieira da Graça in Lagoa de Furadouro, Ourém, Portugal), who spent 11 years in jail for political activities in favour of the independence of Angola, is exceptional, but can still help us here. He emigrated to Angola in 1938, when he was three years old, with parents who had a rural background, the father as a shoemaker and the mother from peasant stock. The family lived in the African quarter of Luanda, and Luandino left school at the age of fifteen; but later he completed high school and quickly became the director and deputy director of important enterprises. It was in school that he discovered his talent as a writer. After being arrested for political activity in support of independence for Angola, Luandino developed his literary skills in prison; his novel *Luuanda*, published in 1964, is one of the best examples of anti-colonial literature written in Portuguese.[32] For now, we need to leave aside two important issues: how a man with Luandino's background could acquire the enormous culture he shows in his novels, short stories and the notebooks he wrote in prison; and the political scandal of the literary prize he received in 1965, while in prison. What matters here is that white people from humble backgrounds could be close to the native population.

Noblemen

Portuguese noblemen were, from the beginning, deeply involved in overseas exploration. They benefited from territorial expansion in North Africa, where they built a network of fortresses on the coast and for long periods kept a permanent fleet controlling the Strait of Gibraltar. They ruled the Portuguese enclaves as captains, and used the area as a military training field for further promotion in India.[33] They extended their influence to Cape Verde, the Gulf of Guinea and Angola, then to India and East Africa, and finally to Brazil. Initially the Military Order of Christ had spiritual jurisdiction over the nascent empire; but soon dioceses were structured, and royal patronage directly controlled tithes and licensed religious orders. Nonetheless, military religious orders, particularly the Order of Christ and the Order of Santiago, became major ladders for access to the nobility by overseas elites.[34]

The institution of captains donatary in the Atlantic islands, Brazil and Angola meant that the king delegated his jurisdiction overseas to these noblemen and courtiers, who had to guarantee to promote colonisation and provide military service.[35] In time, this model declined: the king had to repossess most of the captaincies, and direct royal rule through the nomination of governors and captains became the norm. In India, the model of the captaincy donatary was not implemented, although the Northern Province, Sri Lanka and the Valley of the Zambezi in Mozambique functioned through seigneurial systems of land possession, which covered both Portuguese and local legal systems of inheritance.[36]

Research on Portuguese overseas nobility has been focused on the high-status jobs of viceroy or governor in India and Brazil, which were monopolised by the titled nobility until the liberal revolution, except during the government of Pombal.[37] In the seventeenth and eighteenth centuries, it became standard procedure to negotiate nomination for a job considered dangerous (mainly in India, due to the hazards of a long trip and a lethal climate) against a higher noble title. Titled nobility thus depended on overseas rewards to complement the rents from their land. And in addition to the significant salary related to their overseas job, they were entitled to use the maritime trips for a certain amount of trade.[38]

The vast number of captaincies (of fortresses in India or provinces in Brazil, but also of vessels in the significant royal fleet) were filled by noblemen of various ranks, including members of titled noble houses excluded from inheritance, but also by members of the middle and lower aristocracy. Overseas expansion was very much in the interest of this diversified social group, which benefited not only from significant salaries but also from other forms of remuneration, including pervasive corruption. The few cases of sales of office in the Portuguese Empire reveal the hierarchy of the most coveted places, which was not related to differences in salary but to the possibility of trade, legal and illegal, to which we have to add the permanent opportunity for corruption. This is why Ormuz and Diu were at the top of the bids during the rare auctions for the office of captain. [39]

To live like a nobleman implied huge debts, the push factor for the whole imperial system, whether top down or bottom up.[40] Jobs meant, purely and simply, access to money that could not be obtained through traditional methods of land management. The pursuit of trade was widespread among noblemen. Magalhães Godinho coined the social type of the knight-merchant who exemplified the early modern period of overseas expansion, calling attention to the completely blurred boundaries between traders and noblemen in the Portuguese case, which included the king, known internationally in a contemptuous way as the king of pepper.[41] The liberal revolution in 1820, and then the republican revolution in 1910, prompted the decline and then the virtual extinction of the Portuguese nobility.

Merchants

Merchants were thus entangled with noblemen, but also with people from different social backgrounds, including former peasants and artisans. If we look at the royal court, it is striking how the king, the queen, the princes and the princesses, not to mention the main secretaries and ministers of finance, needed bankers with access to international capital: initially Genoese, Florentines and other Italians, who rushed to Iberia in the late fifteenth and sixteenth century to take advantage of the opportunities offered by the overseas expansion; but also New Christians of Jewish origin, who created a formidable network across continents, based on hubs in Rome, Seville, Antwerp, Amsterdam, Lisbon, Goa, West Africa, Salvador, Rio, Mexico and Lima. The centrality and importance of the latter group shifted over time under new economic trends or inquisitorial repression. From the 1520s to the 1630s, the most powerful New Christian bankers won contracts with both the Portuguese and the Spanish kings, particularly contracts related to the slave trade. Some of these New Christians became members of the Order of Christ. Moreover, a tiny number were ennobled by the king or married into noble families.[42] Thus they contributed to a further blurring of the boundaries between manual work and "clean" noble hands.

However, New Christians were always under surveillance by the Inquisition, not only in Portugal but also in the Portuguese colonies in America, Africa and Asia. They could at any point be sent for trial which in many cases led to confiscation of the accused's property and exclusion of his descendants from the universities and liberal professions. Persecution came on top of the statutes of purity of blood imposed on confraternities, colleges, religious and military orders. The New Christians were also forbidden to migrate overseas.[43] All this meant that they simultaneously benefited and suffered from overseas expansion: their commercial success made them a target, and the Inquisition was used by their rivals to exclude them from trade, particularly in Spanish America, where they reached extraordinary positions of power from the 1590s to the 1630s;[44] but until the 1670s, they managed to buy periods of pardon, licences for migration, exceptional access to military orders and even the suspension of the Inquisition between 1674 and 1681.[45]

Trade was thus important throughout the Portuguese empire, involving noblemen and former peasants, artisans and clerks, agents of the king, and clergymen. Debt was the main push factor for all this enterprise, in which reward for royal service represented only a fraction of the motivation, since salaries were systematically in arrears and many were never paid. The implicit assumption of the system, until at least the mid-eighteenth century, was that royal jobs gave access to opportunities for trade and for extortion, since temporary associations with traders were imposed by governors, captains and clerks on merchants already operating on the field. The notion of corruption certainly existed, and was lamented by upright officials, since it would put an unjustifiable burden on the system, making all operations more costly. However, prosecution was only activated in cases where the official went beyond the limits or failed to comply with his obligations to collect the minimum revenue from customs houses or support the king when the latter was in need, for example by buying royal bonds or making a contribution during financial emergencies.[46] Political allegiance was thus at the core of the system at its different levels, with a clear impact on the mechanisms of trade. In any case, the opportunities opened up by the empire in different continents increased the number of traders dramatically, offered social mobility to many former peasants and urban workers, and guaranteed liquidity for indebted noblemen.

The contrast between the opportunities for trade created by the empire and the reduced market back in Portugal was staggering. However, the stakes were high and the life of the trader was precarious: if certain routes in the Far East, mainly for trade between Japan and China, could mean 1000 percent profit on a successful trip, the risks of shipwreck or piracy would involve bankruptcy.[47] Insurance could alleviate the risk but never exclude it. The pattern of trade was based on temporary associations for specific trips. Insurance was not a specialised trade in the Portuguese empire until the late sixteenth century; it depended on temporary agreement among merchants and centres of world economy, such as Amsterdam and London. Among all the possibilities, perhaps the most stable and profitable trade in the long run was the transatlantic slave trade.[48] The number of people involved, directly or indirectly, in the slave trade explains why abolition was imposed from outside, and never represented any internal movement of public opinion. It also explains why slave traders were involved in politics even in the nineteenth century, opting to join the *Setembristas*, the liberal radical party which advocated abolition but only implemented it as a result of constant pressure from the British.[49]

The patterns of trade started to change with the government of Pombal, who finally managed to create chartered companies for operating in Brazil and in Africa, a move which had been tried but failed in the previous century, mainly with a company formed to pursue trade with India, in 1629, and one formed to pursue trade with Brazil, in 1649 (although here the results were mixed for fifteen years).[50] The idea was to create monopolies that could face competition from other European powers. However, in creating an effective dynamic of capitalisation among a reduced number of hands, the policy undermined for a while the typical characteristic of the Atlantic as an open space for private traders. A favourable balance of trade occurred from the 1790s to the 1800s, due to the production of cotton in Brazil, fuelled by the new textile industry in England, and the implosion of St. Domingue as the main producer of sugar in the world following the slave revolt. This favourable period was interrupted by the French invasions of Portugal in 1807–12.[51] The nineteenth century saw the disruption of the colonial pact between Portugal and Brazil immediately after the arrival of the royal family in Rio in 1808, fleeing the French, and the termination of the highly prosperous trade in African slaves in 1850, when it was imposed by the British.[52] The impact of these two events on Portuguese traders was quite important, especially the latter one.

It took the wars of occupation, from the 1890s to the 1920s, to attract major investment in the African colonies, and this focused on plantations and the exploitation of mineral resources. Meanwhile, native political entities, such as Kasanje and Lunda in Angola, lost their previous autonomy and capacity for defining the rules of trade with Europeans.[53] Again, chartered companies with international capital and sovereign rights over vast territories were introduced, which meant that accumulation of capital was concentrated in a few hands. Small local, regional and inter-regional trade certainly thrived, involving many merchants; but the twentieth century would register another process of concentration of capital around the companies already mentioned, to which we could add the enterprise Cassequel, created in Angola for the production of sugar and sisal, and with links to the Espírito Santo Bank, which was then the beneficiary of political support from the *Estado Novo*; or the Entreposto Group, created in Mozambique, which operated in agriculture, industry and the import of vehicles.[54] In the modern period, having the protection of the state became crucial in colonial trade, while the scattered activity of small traders revealed a much more hierarchical business with few possibilities of significant investment without the support of banks, which frequently invested in shares. Concentration of capital and the financial upper hand are among the main features of modern colonial history.

Clergymen

Finally, we need to look at clergymen. Royal patronage meant that religious orders needed to obtain the authorisation of the King to operate overseas, where the tithe would be collected by royal agents. Although the Portuguese empire had an important network of dioceses, established between the sixteenth and the eighteenth centuries (18 with territorial ecclesiastical jurisdiction), the most important clergymen were regular, not secular.[55] Religious orders were autonomous, and followed their own religious policies; but they were supposed to respect political allegiance. This was why several religious orders, such as the Jesuits, had prominent Italian and Spanish members in the Portuguese Empire (for example, José de Anchieta, Francisco Xavier and Alessandro Valignano, among many others) who never expressed alternative allegiances until the mid-eighteenth century and the implementation of state jurisdictionalism, which undermined the coexistence of plural jurisdictions, including the jurisdiction of the Catholic Church.[56]

Religious orders had schools and colleges which compensated for the absence of universities in the colonies until the transfer of the Portuguese royal court to Brazil in 1807–8. Although several religious orders coexisted in the big urban centres such as Goa, they generally tried to divide the different territories among them. Religious orders, like bishops and archbishops, always had the possibility of making a political intervention. For example, the archbishop of Goa stepped in as temporary governor during periods of vacancy; and the Dominicans in Timor acted as representatives of the Portuguese King in the absence of a regularly appointed captain, which occurred until the eighteenth century.[57]

The creation of the Sacred Congregation for the Diffusion of Faith (*Sacra Congregatio de Propaganda Fide*) by the Pope in 1622 in Rome meant a new dynamic within the centralised organisms of the Catholic Church, and this clashed with the interests of royal patronage. The activities of Portuguese missionaries began to be scrutinised by the *Propaganda Fide*, since they claimed jurisdiction over the regions of Asia and Africa beyond the territories controlled by the Portuguese Empire. Ensuring an effective presence in these regions became a real issue, since the claims of Portuguese royal patronage meant blocking access to missionaries from other countries, particularly France. The report by Francesco Ingoli, secretary of the *Propaganda Fide*, written between 1629 and 1631, is remarkable in its accusation that the Portuguese missionaries were avoiding regions, like Madagascar, in which there was no profit to be made. Moreover, Ingoli denounces the exclusion of natives from religious orders as a self-interested policy of Portuguese regular clergymen, who did not want to share rents.[58]

Ingoli's extremely sharp report brings to our attention the economic side of the missions, which was generally hidden, either because the mendicant orders were not supposed to accumulate wealth, and their members were expected to live in poverty, giving all their property to the Church, or because their accumulation of wealth, as with the Jesuits, was supposed to support their activities, which included charity and distinctive gifts to the authorities. But we now know that religious orders also used to smuggle inheritance or accumulate money for purposes other than missionary work.[59] The involvement of the Jesuits in trade is well known. This was considered necessary to sustain large missionary operations that included bribery of foreign powers.[60] The problem was that many priests and regular clergymen were involved in trade as individuals, using their private wealth to profit from their political positions and favour their relatives and clients. There is no doubt that in the early modern period royal patronage offered enormous possibilities (spiritual, cultural, economic and political) to clergymen who migrated overseas. However, the modern period registered a sharp decline in the economic activities of religious orders, while a new ethical code became widespread among a much-reduced number of clergymen.

Conclusion: opportunities as a whole

Up to now, we have been reflecting on the possibilities opened up by the Portuguese empire to the metropolitan population. It is undeniable that the empire offered access to jobs, trades, finance and social promotion that would have been unthinkable in Europe. Emigrant populations benefited from this situation, but not many returned to assume a better social position in their society of origin. The vast majority stayed on other continents; many died (the mortality rate in West Africa was staggeringly high, and in Asia was not much better); and others generated families with new roots, mainly in Brazil. The impact of the empire seems to have been to maintain inequality back in Portugal, where economic and social structures did not change radically until the liberal revolution, but to reduced it among the emigrant metropolitan population overseas.

There is also a gender effect of emigration that we need to acknowledge. As emigration was overwhelmingly male, the females who were left behind were empowered at all social levels, since they were in charge of properties, shops, business, entailed land, and small properties. Even if male supremacy was not disrupted, gender inequality was reduced in Portugal, due to new opportunities for abandoned women and widows.[61] We will also see how native women related to Portuguese traders, and in certain regions of Africa, in special economic environments, registered an even stronger dynamic than of women's empowerment in Portugal.

It is striking how Portuguese from humble origins, when overseas, sometimes engaged in fierce discussions of a fictitious noble pedigree they created for themselves, even involving in physical conflict about the matter in one occasion while detained in China, and thus confirming local visions of a barbarian Portuguese background.[62] This story reveals that it was certainly easier to change profession and social group overseas, with emigrants reconstituting their social background to conform to the noble model of the *ancien regime*. Positions on municipal councils, which were supposed to be composed of people from the non-manual professions, were in many cases filled by mixed-race people and people with a peasant or working class background.[63] In Brazil, landlords of sugar plantations, major traders and military officers managed to obtain, in certain cases, membership of a military order with the status of familiars (*familiares*) of the Inquisition, which supposed an enquiry into purity of blood, and this offered an ideal ground from which to project an image of nobility.[64] In the modern world, the distinctive image of the successful entrepreneur, the liberal professional or the high administrator of the colonies replaced the image of the nobleman, while clergymen lost some of their social prestige.

The impact of the empire on native populations

Now we need to consider colonial societies built up overseas by the constant emigration of metropolitan Portuguese, and address the impact of the empire on social inequality between the Portuguese and native populations. First, we need to understand what colonial societies were. The Greek example shows the creation of new cities by communities of emigrants who kept a close tie with the former motherland.[65] This model of a relocated community is to be found in Brazil. There, since the Portuguese were dealing with nomadic and semi-nomadic native communities, colonial societies were built up almost from scratch.[66] But we have to avoid the anachronistic mistake of conceiving of colonial society in Brazil bounded by modern frontiers. In the early modern period, colonial reality was restricted to pockets on the coastal side of the country, with the exception of São Paulo, and there was a loose connection between these. Although connections with the interior were fostered through the prodigious system of rivers, which helped long-distance expeditions in search of native slaves, it was only with the discovery of gold in Minas Gerais in the late seventeenth century that the occupation of the territory started to be taken seriously. In Africa, colonisation according to the Greek concept of emigrant communities relocated from the motherland took a long time to become established, and the complex African societies which surrounded the Portuguese presence had a major role until the nineteenth century. Occupation of the territory created an entirely different dynamic between the Portuguese and the Africans. In Asia, the Portuguese lived a relationship even more dependent upon the surrounding society, which had been much more structured before their arrival on the Asian coast than society in Africa, with long-established traditions of maritime trade. Occupation of the type that occurred in Africa never really occurred in Asia, except in Sri Lanka, for a short period of time, and East Timor, in the twentieth century.

Native Americans

From the earliest days of overseas exploration, the Portuguese mixed with local populations, in some cases creating significant lineages. They also enslaved natives and involved them in the plantation system. After the mid-seventeenth century, colonial society was largely based on the work of African slaves.[67] Individual integration was always a possibility, but it did not lead to a significant and continuous integration of native communities under the colonial system. In the meantime, native communities in Brazil were decimated by disease, as was the case in other parts of the Americas. Natives were displaced from the coastal areas, and from São Paulo, where they lost control of their lands. Religious orders created villages for converted natives, where the work of these people contributed to public and private enterprise; but natives declined as forced labour, except in the Amazon basin.[68] The Portuguese King exercised jurisdiction, and delegated jurisdiction, over lands he claimed as his; and where local populations did not have a settled lifestyle, rights to land were considered non-existent.[69]

Thus, the first victims of the Portuguese expansion were clearly Native Americans, who lost their ancestral rights to land. They were forced into successive migrations, and suffered waves of epidemics that dramatically reduced their numbers. Trade in the Brazil wood which gave its name to the land created a framework of exchange between the semi-nomadic natives and the Europeans; but in the long run native integration into plantations and skilled labour did not involve massive numbers. It was the villages of converted natives run by religious orders that provided public and private labour for the colonial society, under fixed conditions set by clergy. In any case, the natives lost their land, they struggled to keep their way of life, they were forced to migrate from place to place, their numbers were decimated; and in the long run, they became marginal to the new colonial society built by Europeans and African slaves.[70] However, those who integrated, or who lived on the colonial peripheries, negotiated their position, resisted, engaged in revolts and claimed their rights within a hybrid cultural framework.[71]

Colonial Brazil was largely created by around 1.4 million Portuguese, who emigrated from the early sixteenth to the late eighteenth century, plus around four million slaves brought from Africa.[72] African slaves performed the main agricultural tasks in the countryside, from the planting to the production of sugar and tobacco. Later, they were involved in mining, and also in urban labour and public works. They were initially supervised by white people, but miscegenation, mainly between white and black but also between white and native, reached very high levels, with mixed race people favoured among emancipated slaves, as they contributed to the creation of a social buffer between slaves and white owners.[73] Freed African and mixed-race slaves were not only important supervisors of plantations, but they also filled skilled jobs both in the countryside and in urban areas. Moreover, they moved into trade and were involved in the slave trade themselves.[74] Over time, boundaries between white people and mixed-race people became blurred.

Inequality was structured around the division between free people and slaves, meaning white people and black people. This is perhaps the most profound area of inequality, mixing social and racial prejudices, and founded on the stigma of slavery and prejudices concerning descent, even though mixed-race people were very much part of the system. In colonial Brazil, African slaves had been uprooted to the point where they could no longer rely on their original society: they had to adapt to a society where they were pushed to the bottom. In some cases, they certainly managed to negotiate their position, and a significant number were manumitted, far more than in British, Dutch or French colonial societies, partly due to the fact that they were forced to convert, which made them vassals of the King, while having access to confraternities which supported, including financially, their process of emancipation.[75] But the fact of their inferior social position had long-term consequences, and is felt even nowadays, almost two centuries after independence and one and a half centuries after the abolition of slavery.[76]

Africans

In North Africa, the fortresses built by the Portuguese following the conquest of Ceuta in 1415 became in time like stranded ships, since the surrounded areas of "peaceful Muslims" tended to shrink dramatically, due to the constant raids for booty and enslavement.[77] This typical operation of knights dedicated to plunder and traffic in human lives eroded the alliances patiently built by the first generations of Christians after the conquest, who had taken advantage of divisions among the Muslim powers in the area. When the new power of the Sharifs of Souss (southern Marocco) emerged in the first decades of the sixteenth century, leading to the conquest of Fez in 1549 and the establishment of a new Saadi dynasty, the Portuguese were not in any condition to face the new threat. They were defeated at Santa Cruz do Cabo de Gué (nowadays Agadir) and between 1541 and 1550 they withdrew from most of the forts.[78] They had become progressively detached from local populations, which proved that when they lacked the means of political negotiation, colonial powers could be expelled, especially in areas where complex societies had technological and military capacities equal to their own. The Portuguese forts in North Africa were ethnically relatively homogeneous, although Jewish communities were allowed, temporarily, to keep their distinctive presence after forced conversion was imposed in Portugal in 1497. Inequality between the Portuguese in the forts and the surrounding native populations was profound, as the former plundered and enslaved the latter.[79] The military model of a Portuguese presence in a Muslim area proved to be unsustainable in the long run, due to the tradition of war and the pervasive practices of extreme abuse. However, it has to be said that the movement of contraband goods between the Portuguese forts and the main Moroccan cities was maintained at a high level both before and after the 1540s.[80]

The Portuguese presence in West Africa followed an entirely different pattern, with overt military control largely confined to the Cape Verde islands, which were populated after discovery by Portugal.[81] The forts created in the rivers of Guinea had, until the nineteenth century, the purpose of protecting trade, rather than signifying jurisdiction over significant territory. Portuguese based in and around the forts lived side by side with local and regional African powers, with whom they had daily dealings. The same pattern occurred in the Gulf of Guinea, where the military presence was limited to the islands of São Tomé and Príncipe and the fort of Mina. In this latter case, there was no intention of territorial conquest, but rather of protection for the gold trade and provision of a base from which to negotiate with local powers.[82] This model, certainly imposed by local conditions, was shaped by the requirement to offer trade in a way African rulers would consider fit for their needs. Mixed-race society in the Cape Verde islands was based on miscegenation between Portuguese and uprooted Africans; while in the rivers of Guinea, the same mixture created distinctive lineages of Luso-African descent with strong links with local societies.[83] Some of these lineages lived outside the Portuguese reach from Cape Verde; but many kept a position in between, which suited the interests of both parties: the local rulers and the Portuguese authorities.

Inequality here was again defined by the divide between free people and slaves, since the slave trade was the main source of profit in the area. However, this was one of the areas in which the Portuguese systematically mixed with local populations. This practice eroded gender inequality, since the high mortality rate among Europeans meant that African or Luso-African women would survive their European husbands or partners and take over the businesses as heads of large families. The *sinhá* (*senhoras*, ladies) of the rivers of Guinea, who could be found in other parts of the Western Coast of Africa with a Portuguese presence, such as Luanda and Benguela, maintained a high profile until the early nineteenth century.[84] At this time, in the Gulf of Guinea, the Portuguese and Luso-African presence had only recently started to have a higher profile, since competition from the Dutch, the French and the English had made the Portuguese less visible. However, they were resilient, keeping links with São Tomé and performing an important role as regional authorities (*caboceers*) under different African powers on the coastal side of the country.[85] In these two cases (the rivers of Guinea and the Gulf of Guinea), the relationship maintained by the Portuguese and their mixed-race descendants with local African societies was extremely close: they acted as brokers, were recognised as distinctive by local and regional powers, but were sufficiently African to have the trust of those rulers. In certain areas, like the areas controlled by the kingdom of Dahomey in the eighteenth and early nineteenth century, the Portuguese (like the other European powers) had to pay tribute.[86] Inequality was thus present here at the lowest level, although increased flows in the slave trade reinforced the divide between free and enslaved people.

In Angola, there was one colonial project, resulting from the concession of a captaincy donatary to António Dias de Novais in 1570, that fast reverted to the king, due to the captain's failure to conquer a significant amount of territory. The Portuguese managed to build two strongholds in Luanda and Benguela, complemented by several forts along the Cuanza river; and though they never controlled much of the hinterland, they maintained a crucial presence, due to their military power. An alliance with the Congolese kings was based on a successful project of religious conversion, which worked until the early eighteenth century, due to the interest of the local political elite.[87] This alliance was strained by the Dutch conquest of Luanda and São Tomé in 1641 (both areas re-conquered by the Portuguese in 1648), and disrupted by the battle of Ambuila in 1665, in which Portuguese fought on both sides, but the troops from Luanda defeated the Congolese.[88]

The Portuguese presence was defined, until the mid-nineteenth century, by the slave trade, which was controlled by African powers with whom the Portuguese had to negotiate. The relationship between the Portuguese and local rulers was more hierarchical than in West Africa, since Portuguese military power on the coast had an impact on the hinterland. However, to maintain this power, the Portuguese had to negotiate with African political entities and depended on them for regular access to slaves.[89] There were a significant number of Africans and people of mixed race in the Portuguese forts, some of them free, some slaves. Inequality was significantly more pronounced here than in West Africa, although the Portuguese presence in the hinterland had undergone a degree of Africanisation, adapting to Bantu political symbols and practices.[90]

The phenomenon of Africanisation in the early modern period was even more visible in Mozambique, where the Portuguese presence was established on the island that provided the future name of the territory, and in the Zambezi valley, as well as in other small strongholds on the coast. The *prazos* of the Zambezi consisted of large domains transmitted through the matrilineal line for three generations, controlled since the sixteenth century by descendants of the Portuguese who had mixed with African women.[91] They were recognised both by the African rulers, mainly the Monomotapa, and the Portuguese authorities. The slave trade became important by the end of the eighteenth century, having the same impact as in other parts of Africa, such as Angola.[92]

In the African enclaves controlled by the Portuguese, the ruling councils, which expressed the political power of the local elite, accommodated the reality of mixed-race descent, due to high mortality rate among Europeans. The fiction of pure Portuguese descent, which was perpetuated in India and Brazil, could not be staged in the African case, where the mixed origin of the elites was much more visible.[93] This underlined the different realities of colonial projects, which adapted to local circumstances. Although racist prejudices and behaviour were part of the picture, racial inequality showed different degrees along the western and eastern coasts of Africa that had a Portuguese presence. The disruption came with the long-term reorganisation of economic activity to encompass agriculture and industry after the abolition of the slave trade and slavery.

Inequality arguably grew in the modern period: colonial society spread with the occupation of territories in Africa, breaking local and regional powers, as well as previous ties between Portuguese and natives. Integration into colonial society, meaning adhering to Christianity, assuming European dress, eating habits and style of housing, learning to read and write, and behaving in a "civilised" manner, became paramount.[94] Modernity also brought with it new, educated, people from Europe, who occupied the higher levels of colonial administration, while the middle levels were increasingly controlled by Portuguese emigrants, who also competed at the lower levels with native elites, mainly of Cape Verdean origin.[95] Classification of native people according to European criteria of civilisation became obsessive: the notion of *assimilado* (or civilised) was introduced by the Salazar regime to measure the degree of success of religious missions and secular education.[96]

The census of 1950 classified natives from Cape Verde, India and Macau as all being "civilised", while among the natives of São Tomé and Príncipe only 69 percent were put in that category. The problems of this classifications became clear in other colonies, such as Angola, Guiné and Timor, where only one percent were considered civilised, while in Mozambique, the percentage went down to 0.1 percent. These percentages went slightly up during the 1950s, until the census of

1960 wiped out the distinction between civilised and uncivilised.[97] It was unsustainable to claim that four centuries of colonisation had achieved such weak results in the Europeans' supposed "civilising mission". There is no comprehensive study on the status of *assimilados*, who were discriminated against by the colonial Portuguese population, while at the same time being seen as separate from, and thus being uprooted from, traditional African society. However, it is recorded that they played an important role in the liberation movements of various African countries before and after independence, a role that has not been sufficiently acknowledged.

Asians

In India, the scattered nature of the Portuguese settlements and the limited emigration, most of which took place in the sixteenth century, favoured a high degree of miscegenation. The Portuguese were initially treated favourably by Hindu natives, who saw in them the possibility of ousting Muslim rulers, as happened in Goa. However, the policy of conversion and the destruction of Hindu temples implemented in the 1550s, although it was limited to Goa, created a disruption in relations. Religious homogeneity was established in the area, and only in the long run – mainly after the mid-eighteenth century – did religious tolerance become the rule. In the other enclaves and territories (the Northern Province and Sri Lanka), religious pluralism was the rule, although non-Christians were subordinate to the Portuguese authorities and colonial social elite. This colonial elite was the result of mixed marriage, since Portuguese emigration was almost exclusively male. The female orphans sent to India in a move sponsored by the King never reached significant numbers.

In the classification "married people", in two registers kept in Portuguese settlements in Asia before 1630, "white married" were in fact mixed-race people of Portuguese descent, while "black married" were converted natives and their descendants. There was thus a hierarchy defined by racial prejudices, but also religious ones, since non-Christians would not have had access to structures of power. The system of castes permeated the social arrangements of Hindus, and those of the (few) Muslims families that converted to Christianity. However, the Portuguese depended on non-Christian merchants and bankers for their operations in India, particularly the famed Parsis, who also served Dutch and English companies.

Naturally the Portuguese were much less assertive in territories they did not really control, such as communities established with a certain degree of autonomy in ports around the Bay of Bengal, since these communities depended on the good will of local powers. In Timor too, the Portuguese presence was quite limited until the nineteenth century, being focused on the sandalwood trade; so, their impact on local societies, in this as in other peripheral cases, was not important. In Macau, where the Portuguese presence was tacitly authorised by the Chinese authorities, a colonial society based on trade was established, with limited miscegenation between Portuguese and Chinese. In all these places, racial and religious prejudices were visible, although mediated by the regular practice of political negotiation with different powers. But evangelisation in Japan, where the Portuguese had no political power, reached a significant dimension by the end of the sixteenth century, while evangelisation in China also became relatively significant in time.

Trade competition, final expulsion from Japan in 1639, and military defeat by the English and Dutch in the seventeenth century all reduced the Portuguese network in Asia, a loss slightly compensated by territorial gain around Goa in the mid-eighteenth century. Scarce manpower justified the promotion of a mixed-race Christian elite in those enclaves and territories, although discrimination against, and segregation of, native populations, even those converted to Christianity, were visible. In Goa, where there existed a strong tradition of native initiative, local recruits were soon excluded from religious orders, and could only aspire to becoming secular priests. Although some went directly to Rome and obtained full membership of the priesthood – one example was Mateus de Castro, who became bishop of Chrisopolis *in partibus infidelium* – they had to face discrimination on their return to Goa, even in the face of papal nomination.

Many inhabitants of Goa migrated to Bombay after the ceding of the territory by the Portuguese to the British in 1662 as part of the dowry for Catherine of Braganza's marriage to Charles II, and thus showed their disaffection towards a system of religious intolerance. The recruitment of natives into the military, which was practiced by the Portuguese very early, never propelled these recruits very high in the system, and they were limited to the lower ranks. It was the exclusion of natives from the distinctive artillery arm of the military that motivated the conspiracy of the Pintos, in 1789. It is true that the government of Pombal imposed the access of Christian natives to religious orders on the latter, recognised freedom of movement for the Chinese in Macao, so that they started to have access to public offices, and allowed women from Timor to migrate to Macau; but these measures probably came too late.

The liberal revolution of 1820 tried to re-establish connections with Christian natives in India, with some well-known liberals from the territories passing through the *Assembleia Constituinte* in Lisbon, followed by the establishment of links with liberal native politicians in British India. This apparent openness did not last: regular protests and riots were recorded in the Portuguese colonies in India, particularly by the end of the nineteenth century. In 1956, when the geographer Orlando Ribeiro went on a mission to those colonies in India, he wrote, perplexed, that after four and a half centuries of colonisation very few people could speak Portuguese. The forced integration of those territories into the Indian Union in 1961 put an end to the colonial era there, representing the first anti-colonial blow against the Salazar regime's refusal to accept new historical realities.

Conclusion: the overall impact on native populations

To sum up, the main impact of inequality in the Portuguese empire occurred in colonial Brazil, where native communities were devastated by disease and war, and were forced to migrate from the coast. There was a significant level of miscegenation between Portuguese and natives, but colonial society was mostly constituted by Portuguese and African slaves after the mid-seventeenth century. In time, manumission became significant, particularly among mixed-race people, who created a social buffer between the Portuguese and the slaves. Forced conversion led to an unintended margin of protection for the slaves: they became vassals of the King, and participation in confraternities contributed to support for their projects of emancipation. However, violence, abuse, prejudice and discrimination were engrained in a society based on slavery, and the consequences of this can still be seen today. In North Africa, the Portuguese started to created areas of "peaceful Muslims", though these relationships were eroded by constant activities of plunder and enslavement, and the Portuguese were defeated and forced to withdraw between 1541 and 1550. The impact was thus temporary, but it certainly deepened religious prejudices. In West Africa, the Portuguese were deeply involved in the slave trade; but their rootedness in local African society, represented by Luso-African lineages, indicates a low level of prejudice and inequality.

Even as regarded inequality between the genders – always extreme, due to predominantly male emigration – West Africa represented a low point, due to the high mortality rate for Europeans, which led to the empowerment of African women whom they married and left widows. This feature would also become visible across the Portuguese enclaves in Western Africa. In Angola, the military impact of the Portuguese presence was significant, although penetration into the hinterland for the slave trade required a certain degree of Africanisation, alongside the usual racial hierarchy and racism. This degree of Africanisation was also visible in the valley of the Zambezi in Mozambique, where property was transmitted through the female line, with mixed-race people recognised by both the Monomotapa and the Portuguese King. From the 1890s to the 1920s, the military campaigns for the occupation of territory in Guinea, Angola and Mozambique opened the way for chartered companies with sovereign status, giving them rights over large territories, along with other big companies involved in agricultural development and industry. The transition from slave to forced, and finally to free, labour was a difficult one, in which taxation was an important tool. Inequality deepened in this process of modernisation, since the European criteria of civilisation were paramount, excluding the vast majority of the native population from that category. The irony of history is that the policy of creating *assimilados*, which bore so little fruit until the 1950s, was promoted by the colonial war and the extraordinary, paradoxical, economic development of those years. It was the *assimilados*, initially discriminated against by the Portuguese, and enduring difficult relations with their original communities, who would contribute to the new social elites created after independence.

Notes

1 Leonor Freire Costa, Nuno Palma and Jaimes Reis, "The Great Escape? The Contribution of the Empire to Portugal's Economic Growth", *European Review of Economic History* 19 (2014): 1–22.

2 Vitorino Magalhães Godinho, 'Portuguese Emigration from the Fifteenth to the Twentieth Century: Constants and Changes', in P. C. Emmer and M. Mörner (eds.), *European Expansion and Migration. Essays in the Intercontinental Migration from Africa, Asia and Europe* (New York: Berg, 1992), pp. 13–48.

3 *Estatísticas demográficas 2015* (Lisbon: INE, 2016), table 5.3.2.1.

4 Vitorino Magalhães Godinho, *A estrutura da antiga sociedade portuguesa* (Lisbon: Arcadia, 1971)

5 João Pina Cabral, *Sons of Adam, Daughters of Eve: the Peasant Worldview of Alto Minho* (Oxford: Clarendon, 1986).

6 Robert Rowland, *População, família e sociedade. Portugal, séculos XIX e XX* (Oeiras: Celta, 1999); *dem*, 'Velhos e novos Brasis', in *História da Expansão Portuiguesa*, eds. Francisco Bethencourt and Kirti Chaudhuri, vol. 4 (Lisbon: Círculo de Leitores, 1998), pp. 303–373.

7 Nuno Gonçalo Monteiro, *O crepúsculo dos grandes: a casa e o património da aristocracia em Portugal, 1750–1832* (Lisbon: Imprensa Nacional, 1998); Mafalda Soares da Cunha e Nuno Gonçalo Monteiro , 'Vice-Reis, governadores e Vice-Reis de governo do Estado da Índia, 1506–1834: recrutam,ento e caracterizaçao social', *Penélope*, 15 (1995): 91–120.

8 Francisco Bethencourt, *O imaginário da magia. Feiticeiras, adivinhos e curandeiros em Portugal no século XVI*, revised edition (São Paulo: Companhia das Letras, 2004), pp. 245–6.

9 João Pina Cabral, *Sons of Adam, Daughters of Eve.*

10 Pieter C. Emmer (ed.), *Colonialism and Migration: Indentured Labour Before and After Slavery* (Dordrecht: Nijhoff, 1986).

11 Robert Rowland, 'Velhos e novos Brasis'.

12 John H. Elliott, *Empires of the Atlantic World. Britain and Spain in America, 1492–1830* (New Haven: Yale University Press, 2006), pp. 181, 262.

13 Stuart Schwartz, *Sugar Plantations in the Formation of Brazilian Society: Bahia, 1550–1835* (Canbridge: Cambridge University Press, 1985).

14 Sanjay Subrahmanyam, *Improvising Empire. Portuguese Trade and Settlement in the Bay of Bengal, 1500–1700* (Delhi: Oxford University Press, 1990).

15 Fernão Mendes Pinto, *The Travels*, ed. and translated by Rebecca D. Catz (Chicago: University of Chicago Press, 1989); see the restored Portuguese text, notes and studies in Jorge Santos Alves (ed.), *Fernão Mendes Pinto and the Peregrinação*, 4 vols. (Lisbon: Fundação Oriente, 2010).

16 Jorge Flores (ed.), *Re-exploring the Links. History and Constructed Histories between Portugal and Sri Lanka* (Wiesbaden: Harassowitz Verlag, 2007); Zoltan Biedermann and Alan Strathern (eds.), *Sri Lanka at the Crossroads of History* (London: UCL Press, 2017).

17 Giuseppe Papagno, *Colonialismo e feodalesimo. La questione dei Prazos da Coroa alla finme del secolo XIX* (Turin: Einaudi, 1972); Allen F. Isaacman, *Colonialism and the Africanisation of a European Structure, the Zambesi Prazos, 1750–1902* (Madison: The University of Wisconsin Prtess, 1972); Malyn Newitt, *A HIstory of Mozambique* (Bloomington: Indiana University Press, 1995), pp. 217–242.

18 Adriano Parreira, *Economia e soiciedade em Angola na época da rainha Jinga (século XVII)* (Lisbon: Estampa, 1997); José Carlos Venâncio, *A economia de Luanda e hinterland no século XVII. Um estudo de sociologia histórica* (Lisbon: Estampa, 1996), Luiz Felipe de Alencastro, *O trato dos viventes. Formação do Brasil no Atlântico Sul. Séculos XVI e XVII* (São Paulo: Companhia das Letras, 2000).

19 José Capela, *O tráfico de escravos nos portos de Moçambique, 1733–1904* (Porto: Afrontamento, 2002).

20 Philip Havik, *Silences and Soundbytes. The Gendered Dynamic of Trade and Brokerage in the Pre-Colonial Guinea-Bissau Region* (Münster: Lit, 2004); António Carreira, *Cabo Verde: formação e extinção de uma sociedade escravocrata (1460–1878)* (Bissau: Centro de Estudos da Guiné Portuguesa, 1972).

21 Vitorino Magalhães Godinho, 'Portuguese Emigration'; for the new estimates on the importance of gold see Leonor Freire Costa, Maria Manuela Rocha, Rita Martins de Sousa, *O ouro do Brasil* (Lisbon: Imprensa Nacional, 2013).
22 Maria Ioannis Baganha, *Portuguese Emigration to the United States, 1820–1930* (New York: Garland, 1990).
23 *Anuário Estatístico do Ultramar* (vols. related to the years 1943–1973) (Lisbon: INE/Centro de Estudos Demográficos, 1945–1975).
24 José Vicente Serrão, Bárbara Direito, Eugénia Rodrigues, Susana Münch Miranda (eds.), *Property Rights, Land and Territory in the European Overseas Empires* (Lisbon: CEHC-IUL, 2015).
25 Mário Murteira, 'A economia colonial', in *História da Expansão* Portuguesa, vol. 5, pp. 103–150; Manuel Ennes Ferreira,*Angola-Portugal: do espaço económico português às relações pós-coloniais* (Lisbon: Escher, 1990).
26 Mário Murteira, 'A economia colonial'.
27 Ricardo Soares de Oliveira, *Oil and Politics in the Gulf of Guinea* (London: Hurst, 2007).
28 Francesco Carletti, *Raggionamenti del mio viaggio intorno al mondo*, ed. Paolo Collo (Turin: Einaudi, 1989; Diogo do Couto, *O primeiro soldado prático*, ed. and introduction António Coimbra Martins (Lisbon: CNCDP, 2001).
29 Charles Ralph Boxer, *Portuguese Society in the Tropics. The Municipal Councils of Goa, Macao, Bahia and Luanda, 1510–1800* (Madison: The University of Wisconsin Press, 1965).
30 Leonor Freire Costa, *Naus e galeões na Ribeira de Lisboa: a construção naval no século XVI para a rota do Cabo* (Cascais: Patrimonia, 1997).
31 *The Heritage of Rauluchantim*, ed. Nuno Vassalo e Silva (Lisbon: Museu de São Roque, 1996).
32 Luandino Vieira, *Papéis da prisão. Apontamentos, diário, correspondência*, eds Margarida Calafate Ribeiro, Mónica V. Silva, Roberto Vecchio (Lisbon: Caminho, 2016), pp. 1011–1036 (biography).
33 Francisco Bethencourt, 'Political Configurations and Local Powers', in Francisco Bethencourt and Diogo Ramada Curto (eds.) *The Portuguese Oceanic Expansion, 1400–1800* (Cambridge: Cambridge University Press, 2007), pp. 197–254.
34 Ana Isabel Lopez Salazar, Fernanda Olival, João Figueiroa Rego (eds.), *Honra e sociedade noi mundo ibérico e ultramarino. Inquisição e ordens militares, séculos XVI–XIX* (Casal de Cambra: Caliedoscópio , 2013); Evaldo Cabral de Mello, *O nome e o sangue* (Rio de Janeiro: Topbooks, 2000).
35 António Vasconcelos Saldanha, *As capitanias do Brasil: antecedentes, desenvolvimento e extinção de um fenómeno atlântico* (Lisbon: CNCDP, 2001).
36 Malyn Newitt, *History of Mozambique.*
37 Laura de Mello e Souza, *O Sol e a Sombra. Política e administração na América Portuguesa do século XVIII* (São Paulo: Companhia das Letras, 2006).
38 Francisco Bethencourt, 'Political configuration'.
39 Francisco Bethencourt, 'O Estado da India', in *História da Expansão Portuguesa*, vol. 2, pp. 284–314.
40 The crucial book by David Graeber, *Debt. The First Five Thousand Years* (New York: Melville House, 2011) still needs to be absorbed by the historians.
41 Vitorino Magalhães Godinho, *A expansão quatrocentista portuguesa* (1962) 2nd ed. (Lisbon: Dom Quixote, 2007)
42 Fernanda Olival, *As ordens militares e o estado moderno: honra, mercê e venalidade em Portugal (1641–1789)* (Lisbon: Estar, 2001); Francisco Bethencourt,

The Inquisition: a Global History, 1478–1834 (Cambridge: Cambridge University Press, 2009), pp. 327–329.

43 José Pedro Paiva, 'The New Christian Divide in the Portuguese-Speaking World (Sixteenth to Eighteenth Centuries)', in Francisco Bethencourt and Adrian Pearce (eds.), *Racism and Ethnic Relations in the Portuguese-Speaking World* (London/Oxford: British Academy/Oxford University Press, 2012), pp. 269–280.

44 Daviken Studnicki-Gizbert, *A Nation Upon the Ocean Sea. Portugal's Atlantic Diaspora and the Crisis of the Spanish Empire, 1492–1640* (Oxford: Oxford University Press, 2007); Nathan Wachtel, *La foi du souvenir: labyrinthes marranes* (Paris: Seuil, 2001).

45 Claude B. Stuczinsky, *New Christian Political Leadership in Time of Crisis: the pardon negotiations of 1605*, offprint of *Bar-Ilan Studies in History* (Ramat-Gan, 2007); Claude B. Stuczynski (ed.), *Political Dimensions of the Converso Phenomenon in Portugal and Beyond*, special issue, *Journal of Levantine Studies*, 6, 2016; Giuseppe Marcocci and José Pedro Paiva, *História da Inquisição Portuguesa (1536–1821)* (Lisbon: Esfera dos Livros, 2013), pp. 202–209.

46 Fernando Dores Costa, *A Guerra da Restauração, 1641–1668* (Lisbon: Livros Horizonte, 2004); *idem*, *Crise financeira, dívida pública e capitalistas, 1796–1807* (MA dissertation, Universidade Nova de Lisboa, 1992); Jorge Pedreira, *Os homens de negócios da praça de Lisboa de Poimbal ao Vintismo, 1755–1820* (PhD dissertation, Universidade Nova de Lisboa, 1995).

47 George Bryan Souza, 'Commerce and Capital: Portuguese Maritime Losses in the South China SEa, 1600–1754', in *As Relações entre a Índia Portuguesa, a Ásia do Sueste e o Extremo Oriente*, eds. Artur Teodoro de Matos and Luís Filipe Thomaz (Lisbon, 1993), pp. 321–48.

48 Luiz Felipe de Alencastro, *O trato dos viventes*.

49 João Pedro Marques, *The Sounds of Silence: Nineteenth Century Portugal and the Abolition of Slave Trade*, trans. Richard Wall (Oxford: Berghahn, 2006).

50 Leonor Freire Costa, *O transporte no Atlântico e a Companhia Geral do Comércio do Brasil, 1580–1663* (Lisbon: CNCDP, 2002).

51 Jorge Pedreira, *Estrutura industrial e mercado colonial: Portugal e Brasil, 1780–1830* (Linda-a-Velha: Difel, 1994); Valentim Alexandre, *Os sentidos do império: questão nacional e questão colonial na crise do Antigo Regime português* (Porto: Afrontamento, 1993).

52 Leslie Bethell, *The Abolition of the Brazilian Slave Trade* (Cambridge: Cambridge University Press, 1970).

53 Isabel Castro Henriques, *Percursos da modernidade em Angola. Dinâmicas comerciais e transformações sociais no século XIX* (Lisbon: IICT, 1997).

54 Mário Murteira, 'A economia colonial'.

55 See the chapters by Francisco Bethencourt, Isabel Sá and Caio Boschi on Church and Empire in *História da Expansão Portuguesa*, vols. 1, 2 and 3.

56 Kenneth Maxwell, *Pombal, Paradox of the Enlightenment* (Cambridge: Cambridge University Press, 1997).

57 Artur Teodoro de Matos, *Timor português, 1515–1729* (Lisbon: Instituto Histórico Infante D. Henrique, 1974).

58 Francesco Ingoli, *Relazione delle Quattro Parti del Mondo*, ed. Fabio Tosi with an essay by Josef Metzler (Città del Vaticano: Urbiana University Press, 1999), pp. 163–169 and 225.

59 Work in progress by Benjamin James, who is preparing a PhD on this subject.

60 Dauril Alden, *The Making of an Enterprise. The Society of Jesus in Portugal, its Empire, and Beyond, 1540–1750* (Stanford: Stanford University Press, 1996).
61 Darlene Abreu Ferreira, 'A status of her own: women and family identities in seventeenth century Aveiro, Portugal', *Journal of Family Studies* 34, 1 (2009) 3–24; Margarida Durães, 'Providing well-being to women through inheritance and succession: Portugal in the 18th and 19th centuries', in *The Transmission of Well-Being: Gendered Strategies and Inheritance Systems in Europe (17th–20th Centuries)*, ed. Margarida Durães et alii (New York: Peter Lang, 2009).
62 *Enformação das cousas da China. Textos do século XVI*, ed. Rafaella d'Intino (Lisbon: Imprensa Nacional, 1989).
63 Charles Ralph Boxer, *Portuguese Society in the Tropics*.
64 Evaldo Cabral de Mello, *O nome e o sangue*.
65 A. J. Graham, *Colony and Mother City in Ancient Greecew* (Manchester: Manchester University Press, 1964); Gocha R. Tsetskhladze (ed.), *Greek Colonisation: an Account of Greek colonies and other Settlements Overseas* (Leiden: Brill, 2006); Guy Bradley and John-Paul Wilson (eds.), *Greek and Roman Colonisation: Origins, Ideologies, and Interactions* (Swansea: Classical Press of Wales, 2006).
66 Jorge Couto, *A construção do Brasil: ameríndios, portugueses e africanos do início do povoamentpo a finais de quinhentos* (Lisbon: Cosmos, 1995).
67 John Russell-Wood, *The Black Man in Slavery and Freedom in Colonial Brazil* (London: MacMillan, 1982).
68 John M. Monteiro, *Negros da terra: índios e bandeirantes nas origens de São Paulo* (Sao Paulo: Companhia das Letras, 1994).
69 A. Vasconcelos Saldanha, *As capitanias*.
70 Manuela Carneiro da Cunha (ed.), *História dos índios no Brasil* (São Paulo: Companhia das Letras, 1998).
71 Ronaldo Vainfas, *A heresia dos índios. Catolicismo e rebeldia no Brasil colonial* (São Paulo: Companhia das Letras, 1995).
72 Vitorino Magalhães Godinho, 'Portuguese Emigration'.
73 Herbert Klein and Francisco Vidal Luna, *Slavery in Brazil* (Cambridge: Cambridge University Press, 2010).
74 João José Reis and Elciene Azevedo (eds.), *Escravidão e suas sombras* (Salvador: Edufba, 2012); Bruce Chatwin, *The Viceroy of Ouidah* (London: Cape, 1980).
75 Caio Boschi, *Os leigos e o poder: irmandades leigos e política colonizadora em Minas Gerais* (São Paulo: Ática, 1986).
76 André Cicalo, 'From Racial Mixture to Black Nation: Racialising Discourses in Brazil's African Affairs', *Bulletin of Latin American Research*, 33, 1 (2014): 16–30.
77 António Dias Farinha, 'Norte de África', in *HIstória da Expansão Portuguesa*, vol. 1, pp. 118–136.
78 Robert Ricard, *Études sur l'histoire des portugais au Maroc* (Coimbra: Imprensa da Universidade de Coimbra, 1955).
79 Ahmed Boucharb, *Os pseudo-mouriscos de Portugal no século XVI*, trans. Maria Filomena Barros (Lisbon: Hugin, 2004); José Alberto Tavim, *Os judeus na expansão portuguesa em Marrocos durante o século XVI* (Braga: APPACDM, 1996).
80 Francisco Bethencourt, 'Contrabando: um estudo de caso', in *Historia da Expansão Portuguesa*, vol. 1, pp. 387–392.
81 Luís de Albuquerque and Maria Emília Madeira Santos (eds.), *História Geral de Cabo Verde*, 3 vols. (Lisbon/Praia: IICT/DGPCCV, 1991–2002).

82 Isabel Castro Henriques, *São Tomé e Príncipe. A invenção de uma sociedade* (Lisbon: Vega, 2000); J. Bato'ora Ballong-Wen-Mewuda, *São Jorge da Mina, 1482–1637*, 2 vols. (Paris: Fondation Calouste Gulbenkian, 1993).

83 George E. Brooks, *Eurafricans in Wesat Africa: Commerce, Social Status, Gendr and Religious Observance from the Sixteenth to the Eighteenth Century* (Oxford: James Currey, 2003); Jean Boulègue, *Les Luso-Africains de Sénégambie XVI*[e]*–XVIII*[e] *siècles* (Lisbon: IICT, 1989); Peter Mark and José da Silva Horta, *The Forgotten Diaspora: Jewish Communities in West Africa and the Making of the Atlantic World* (Cambridge: Cambridge University Press, 2011); Toby Green, *The Rise of the Trans-Atlantic Slave Trade in Western Africa, 1300–1589* (Cambridge: Cambridge University Press, 2012).

84 Philip Havik, *Silences and Soundbytes.*

85 Inês Guarda, *Slave Trade Brokers in the Gold Coast, Slave Coast and Angola, 1680–1720* (PhD dissertation, King's College London).

86 José Joaquim Lopes de Lima, *Ensaio sobre a estatística das possessões portuguesas na África Ocidental e Oriental, na Ásia Ocidental e na Oceania*, 5 vols. (Lisboa, Imprensa Nacional: 1844–1862).

87 Francisco Bethencourt, 'Creolization of the Atlantic World: The Portuguese and the Kongolese', *Portuguese Studies*, 27, 1 (2011): 56–69

88 John K. Thornton, *The Kingdom of Kongo. Civil War and Transition, 1641–1718* (Madison: The University of Wisconsin Press, 1983).

89 Joseph C. Miller, *Way of Death. Merchant Capitalism and the Angolan Slave Trade, 1730–1830* (Madison: The University of Wisconsin Press, 1988); David Birmingham, *Trade and Conflict in Angola: the Mbundu and their Neighbours under the Influence of the Portuguese, 1483–1790* (Oxford: Clarendon Press, 1966).

90 Inês Guarda, *Slave Trade Brokers.*

91 Malyn Newitt, *History of Mozambique.*

92 José Capela, *O tráfico de escravos nos portos de Moçambique.*

93 Charles Ralph Boxer, *Portuguese Society in the Tropics*; *idem*, *Race Relations in the Portuguese Colonial Empire, 1415–1825* (Oxford: Clarendon Press, 1963).

94 Miguel Bandeira Jerónimo, *The "Civilising Mission" of Portuguese Colonialism (1870–1930)*, trans. Stewart Lloyd-Jones (Basingstoke: Palgrave, 2015).

95 João Carlos Paulo, 'Da "educação colonial portuguesa" ao ensino no Ultramar', in *História da Expansão Portuguesa*, vol. 5 pp. 303–333.

96 Isabel Castro Henriques, 'A assimilação como método de recusa da criação de cidadania' in *História da Expansão Portuguesa*, vol. 5 pp. 225–230; Washington Santos Nascimento, *Gentes do mato: os novos assimilados em Luanda, 1926–1961* (PhD dissertation, São Paulo: USP, 2013).

97 *Anuário estatístico do Ultramar* (vols. related to 1943–1973) (Lisbon: INE, 1945–1975).

CHAPTER

13

Inequalities on Trial: Conflict, Violence and Dissent in the Making of Colonial Angola (1907–1920)

FILIPA LOWNDES VICENTE AND INÊS VIEIRA GOMES

In 1919, Captain José Veloso de Castro, Administrator of Luanda and the country's Police Commander, was the subject of a judicial prosecution by military tribunal. Only one side of the process can still be found, and this offers us the twelve accusations Veloso de Castro was charged with, though these accusations are no longer available as part of a complete documentation for the trial. Rather, they are to be found in Veloso de Castro's own defence, available in the Lisbon Military Archive, to which part of the colonial documentation was sent after 1975 to provide examples of texts related to decolonisation and Angola's independence. Each of Veloso de Castro's twelve answers represents a mirror of the accusation itself, even if a broken mirror, where some charges become clearer than others. Sometimes, the defendant quotes specific selected passages of the allegations, giving us a glimpse into the text we do not possess.

The Archive itself is an unequal place, a place of deliberate selection, resulting from the classification and safeguarding of some documents and the dismissal of others. In this case, there is the added factor of national and colonial transformations interfering in the history of the Archive itself. Political and governmental upheavals, added to the relocation of material, resulted in documents getting lost. The movement of documents and objects from one place to another, in this case from one continent to another, meant that the records that were sent off were not necessarily the same as those that arrived. The only complete judicial documentation available for Veloso de Castro concerns a previous trial in which he was involved, arising from a disagreement between him and another officer that took place in Angola in 1915. Another possible factor — one that should not be dismissed — is the intentional removal of documents. The fact that there are missing parts in the 1919 judicial process may be due to someone's decision to remove items from their filing place.

An analysis of the different layers of inequality implicit in the judicial process applied to Veloso de Castro will form the core of this article. However, in order to better understand what happened in 1919, we will also examine the public, military, and institutional itinerary of a man whose life embodies so many dimensions of the inequality possible in this period and in these locations. The times and places of Veloso de Castro's biography had an important influence on the hierarchies, differences, and power struggles in which he was involved. The places were Portugal and Angola: the former a metropolitan centre trying to consolidate its control over, and exploration of the West African territories of Angola; the latter a country whose frontiers were an embattled ground fought over by the Portuguese, local tribes, and other colonizing European nations. Veloso de Castro's adulthood was lived through three very different Portuguese political contexts, which had enduring repercussions for Portugal's colonial territories and for the position and voice he could aspire to. When he went to Angola in 1902, Portugal was a monarchy, as it had been since the twelfth century; whilst he was in Angola, the monarchy was replaced by a republic, following a coup d'état in 1910; and a few years after his return to Lisbon, in 1920, a right-wing military dictatorship replaced the First Republic. This last context, one in which public perception of republican upheaval and instability was replaced by the heavy hand of military dictatorship, was clearly the one in which Veloso de Castro could play his most public role.

Picture 13.1 Tenente José Veloso de Castro, Angola, 1910
Photograph, 9x12cm, José Veloso de Castro, PT/AHM-FE-CAVE-VC-A10-1404.

Writing, mapping and photographing military expeditions

Veloso de Castro was born in 1869, in Braga, in the north of Portugal, and enlisted for military service in 1887. In 1902, in his early thirties, he left for Angola, where he participated in several military campaigns before becoming Administrator of Luanda. In 1906, he returned to Vila Real for a few months, but by the time his daughter was born, in November 1907, he had already returned to Angola, the previous June, to take part in the Military Campaign of Cuamato. From 1901 to 1920, he climbed the military hierarchy, starting as an *alferes*, and ending up as captain, a rank that he continued to occupy when he became Administrator of Luanda. The permanent Portuguese military campaign of "pacification" in the region — that is, occupying and controlling it, and killing any indigenous warriors who opposed the enterprise — lasted through the last decades of the nineteenth century and the first of the twentieth century, and involved a militarisation of the public functions of the colony. Most of the administrative positions were occupied by military officers, many of whom had taken an active role in "pacifying" the terrain, something that gave them the political legitimacy of men who had risked their lives in expeditions and combats.

It is in this context of a militarised colony that Veloso de Castro's career trajectory should be understood. A military career offered a way of making a living, and an opportunity to have a professional occupation, to men from different social backgrounds and education. It was based on the idea of inequality, in the form of hierarchy, but contained within itself the possibility of moving up the social ladder and thus subverting the original assignation of a low position. The military provided training in various specialised types of knowledge, which benefited men who would otherwise never have had an equivalent opportunity. Moving into colonial territories might even widen these possibilities. Colonial societies, not yet consolidated, could provide more flexible environments, where the imperatives and determinants of social class could be more easily subverted.

In the case of British India, social mobility was a major subject in the nineteenth century, one characterised by its conflicting premises, positive for some, negative for many others. For some, moving from Great Britain to British India meant the possibility of assuming a higher-class identity, of moving up the ladder in a way that would have been impossible at home. However, for those whose birth already gave them an elite status, to witness the social ascension of those who, at home, would have been ascribed a lower position, often meant a threatening reminder of how colonial spaces subverted the social stratification that many — mostly those who occupied the highest ranks — would have preferred to see remain unchanged. A major context for this subversion lay in the military careers the empire provided for thousands of men. Castro's case is certainly an example of how the army could be a source of education, and how moving overseas, where social inequality was overshadowed by more obvious racial and political inequalities, enhanced the possibilities of poorer white men.

In the late nineteenth century and the beginning of the twentieth, science was part of these territorial expeditions in Angola led by the Portuguese military, not as an end in itself, but as way of controlling, possessing and exploring. Mapping was a crucial skill, but so was photography. At first sight, the case we are analysing here seems to fit perfectly with the idea of photography as an instrument of knowledge and power, not only as a witness to inequalities — social, political, gender and ethnic — but also as an active agent in their creation. For many, the reproductions of colonial imagery that appeared in Portuguese newspapers constituted the main knowledge of the national overseas territories, as they came to be called. Photography had been a discipline within Portuguese military education since 1864, but only in 1917 did a ministerial decree create a photographic and cinematographic section with the aim of "recording subjects related to the education and preparation of the Army, in peace and in war", and of "building an historical archive".[1] José Veloso de Castro illustrates well a tradition of officers who also became photographers: 2,374 photographs, glass negatives some of them, were made by him in Angola; and, in addition, 27 images of Vila Real, dated 1907, were taken when he was home for a few months.[2] The Lisbon Military Historical Archive (Arquivo Histórico Militar), where this rich corpus of images is kept, places them in the period between 1904 and 1914, even though Castro did not leave Luanda until 1920.

The list of materials and persons involved in a 1905 expedition to survey the navigability of some Angolan rivers was published in a report. In a total weight of ca. 500 kilos, 30 kilos were weapons, 60 kilos topographical instruments, and 20 kilos photographic materials.[3] The material of the photographic process became part of these expeditions, where travellers were colonisers, and weapons and cameras were put at the service of surveillance and control. Many comparisons have already been established between the eye of the camera and the eye of the gun, and Susan Sontag's words on the predatory violence of photography, written in the late 1970s, still sound particularly poignant when we reflect on the practice of photography by European military expeditions within an imperial frame. "Aggression is implicit in every use of the camera," Sontag wrote. "It turns people into objects that can be symbolically possessed."[4]

Veloso de Castro was photographing precisely at the moment when technological progress made it easier and cheaper for photography to be published in books. This meant a revolution in the format of books and newspapers, and Veloso de Castro's only book as an author became an early, and relatively rare, example of this combination. What had already become a regular practice of military expeditions — the inclusion of writing, maps and photographs within the format of a report — could now produce a book available to a wider audience: a metropolitan audience that could feel empowered by the progress of military expeditions in Africa and the assertion of Portuguese power in the region.[5]

Veloso de Castro transformed his experience of an "expedition" or "campaign", the words used to designate territorial wars imposed on local populations by Portuguese troops, into published narratives where he also used the photographs he had taken along the journey.[6] The same event was recorded by others within the narrative tradition of officials writing as witnesses and participants, and where photography contributed to the "we have been here" effect.[7] In one of these books, General Roçadas, then Governor of the district of Huíla, described how his aid, Veloso de Castro, had been wounded.[8]

Picture 13.2 'Passagem do rio Lucala', Angola, 1905
Negative, 6x6cm, José Veloso de Castro, PT/AHM-FE-CAVE-VC-A10-0078.

When, in 1919, Veloso de Castro had to defend himself against a number of accusations — different accusations from different people — one of the arguments he used to legitimate his service to the "good name and prestige of the military", was that he had aimed to "publish books of military techniques and colonial military history" and to "contribute to the progress of this colony with frequent works of geographical and hydrographical record, some of which were published by the government itself and honoured with flattering references by the most eminent men who have governed here."[9]

In his introduction to a book published in 1908 on what the Portuguese called the Campaign of the Cuamato, the *alferes*, a low rank position within the military hierarchy, dedicated the book to Henrique Paiva Couceiro, a high rank military officer who had been the Governor of Angola since 1907, precisely the year of the Cuamato Campaign.[10] As Patricia Hayes writes, the "expedition's purpose was to avenge the 1904 slaughter of a large Portuguese expedition that had sought to occupy Owambo", which, in the opinion of Veloso de Castro, as Hayes also notes, "was 'the most disastrous reverse to figure in the annals of our colonial military history'."[11]

Paiva Couceiro had already lived in Angola and in Mozambique in an earlier period, around the time of the British Ultimatum to Portugal of 1890, which marked the culmination of many tensions between the two nations in relation to their colonial control over African territories. He had been a protagonist in many military campaigns and expeditions to assert and consolidate Portuguese control of different regions of Angola and Mozambique, and he had also contributed, on his African travels, to the military tradition of expeditionary writing in which Veloso de Castro's work should be placed.[12] After a few years back in Portugal, his name was suggested by the King of Portugal, an acknowledged supporter both of him personally and of his public political positions, to occupy the prestigious position of Colonial Governor.[13] Despite the approval of his government by the local elites, he only stayed for two years, and it was during this period that Veloso de Castro dedicated his book to Paiva Couceiro, as mentioned before, thanking him for authorizing its publication by the National Press of Angola, the Angolan printing press which, since its creation in 1845, had published daily government publication as well as many other books.[14] This also explains the existence, in the Arquivo Histórico Ultramarino, of two photographic albums of Angola dedicated to Paiva Couceiro.[15] The albums were compiled by Veloso de Castro from his own photographs and offered to the highest ranking member of the Portuguese colonial state in Angola, the Governor General, also a military man, and therefore his hierarchical superior.

In 1908, and then in 1913, Veloso de Castro also published two reports, both of them written with Eugénio Torre do Valle, another military man who was, like him, a low ranking official, an *alferes de infantaria*. The first report, published in 1908, presented the maps and descriptions of the River Cambo that they had done in September and October of 1905.[16] To investigate the possibility of navigating the rivers was an important task in the occupation of a territory, as it meant controlling a major means of transport when no alternative routes were in place, and when railway lines were still under construction and only covering very specific areas of the territory. The book is much more than that, however. More than 100 photographs, all with a short descriptive caption, in a small format, and the result of poor techniques of reproduction, occupy the end section of the booklet. Many are of the river itself, almost always to show the tree trunks and branches that had fallen into the river, complicating the passage of their boat. But many of them also show the Africans who were working for them in various roles, for example their African boatman or their guide, as well as the many populations they met along the river shores. The second booklet, published in 1913, was also a study on river navigability.[17] Photography was also widely used on this occasion, with 94 images, while the visual dimension of map drawing became more relevant here, with 20 drawings illustrating the course of the river.

Photography was one more instrument of military expeditions and scientific inquiry mastered by the colonial authorities - a device utilized for a multitude of ends by agents in colonial contexts.[18] However, beyond the photographs that are kept in the Archive of Military History in Lisbon because they were taken by a military man in the context of his service in Angola, it is clear that Veloso de Castro was commercializing his images, and possibly making a profit out of what was a thriving business, while still in Angola (his self-portrait is displayed on postcards on the wall).

This was a period in which photography was booming globally. There was a democratization of its possibilities, as it became easier and cheaper, and responded to a growth in image consumerism. Veloso de Castro was taking part in that global process, where the colonial as subject became a major thread. He had acquired the technological and scientific knowledge of handling the camera and developing the photographs within the context of his military life and very probably it was this institutional realm that provided him with the laboratory-like conditions that enabled the practice of photography far beyond his military obligations. Examples of Veloso de Castro's participation in the commercial world of photographic postcard circulation were the series of postcards booklets he published. A series called "Province of Angola" was issued in a thematic series where each of the atleast 17 booklets opened like a fan displaying 10 postcards, most with one image, some with multiple images in a single frame, which were meant to fit into the category announced on the cover.[19] "Customs from the interior of Portuguese Western Africa: Malange, Population" was one of the titles on a cover where the photographer's name was clearly visible.

In this great quantity of photographs of colonial scenes, situations of inequality are present in multiple ways. Hayes analyses a photographic album entitled "Auto de vassalagem"[20] from the Portuguese expedition to Cuamato Pequeno (Ombandja) in 1907, considering it a pioneering example of war photography.[21] When looking at the images Veloso de Castro took of the African carriers who transported all kinds of heavy materials, one can relate these to the rich critical bibliography that has reflected on the intersection of observation with pain, violence, war, atrocity — elements that were an inevitable part of colonial imposition.[22] We could even argue that, at a moment when the "colonial" as a frame of analysis for photography has been questioned, this analytical frame could be an alternative. Susan Sontag's *Regarding the Pain of Others* called attention to the ethical failure of photography in stopping what it was witnessing.[23] Whatever the black African workers were carrying, they continued to do so. The richness of

Picture 13.3 Rio Lucala. Junto às quedas de Riansundo, Angola, 1905
Negative, 6x6cm, José Veloso de Castro, PT/AHM-FE-CAVE-VC-A10-0080.

the photographic archive of Veloso de Castro goes beyond the scope of this text.[24] It is relevant, however, to understand how photography empowered him: even when he occupied a lower rank in the military hierarchy, the lens extended his vision and grasp of the experiences he was undergoing, somehow subverting the minimal power he had as an *alferes* in his first Angolan years. Being a soldier in a colonial location, no matter how low in the military hierarchy, was very different from being one in a national location. The colonial situation itself presumed the intrinsic inequality of the colonizer vis-a-vis the colonized. Any soldier, in the context of colonial Angola at the beginning of the twentieth century, no matter how low his rank, occupied a superior position in relation to the black population. Veloso de Castro's photographic camera added an extra layer of inequality to already existing ones.

Some of these campaigns could be placed in the category of survey expeditions, aimed at producing all kinds of knowledge on territories that were not previously known — or not well enough known — by the people requesting the surveys. Other military campaigns in which he participated were aimed at controlling, negotiating, and subjugating specific territories and peoples. This was a period for the "mapping and remapping of power between the colonisers and the African societies undergoing colonisation", and Veloso de Castro was actively participating in such mapping, literally.[25] Very often no frontiers could be established between the two military tasks - war and knowledge were entangled in the same experience - and Veloso de Castro illustrates well the case of colonial agents who assumed different identities and roles. In a period when occupying a position in a colonial location was only possible through the use of arms and force, it was within the military orbit that many areas of knowledge intersected with the colonial. The scientific instruments could only be used because there were weapons, instruments of military imposition and power, even if not always used.

Veloso de Castro, himself, in his judicial response to the accusations levelled against him, mentions his "most important collaboration, for the international exhibition of London in 1917, on the documentation of the Portuguese military campaigns".[26] It is not clear which exhibition he is referring to, and the only possible exhibition we could identify in London was the Allied War Photography Exhibition. Such photography exhibitions were quite common during the First World War, as they were seen as a valuable medium of propaganda, co-opting visitors into the war effort and showing the united efforts of different countries.[27] The 1914–18 war coincided with a great democratisation of photographic technology. Its practice was available to a growing number of people, soldiers included, and the possibilities for reproducing images, much easier with the development of lithographic techniques, meant that newspapers could keep a visual track of the development of the war.[28] It also meant that photographs were easily reproduced and exhibited under a propaganda banner, which showed an understanding of the possibilities of images. Having done research in archive of the Victoria and Albert Museum, a major site for photographic exhibitions in London during the First Word War, we could not find any reference to Veloso de Castro's participation in the Allied Exhibition, as the Portuguese Commissioner.[29] A military document states that he was the photographer of all or some of the images sent to represent Portugal's participation during the War;[30] and Portugal appears in the poster[31] of the exhibition alongside the other participating countries; but there is no mention in the album-catalogue[32] that was published to accompany the exhibition.

The 1919 judicial prosecution

In twelve entries, Veloso de Castro responds to the twelve accusations against him, while sometimes quoting directly from the accusation, and thus giving us a glance into the document we do not have access to. In 25 typed pages, dated 19 October 1919, and addressed to Major Pedro Augusto de Souza e Silva, Veloso de Castro gives his version of each of the accusations — his motives, justifications, and decisions.[33] By doing so, he enables us to access many different layers of inequality, not only the more obvious ones inherent in a colonial presence which had inequality at its core, but also heterogeneous layers of inequality. Here we will focus especially on the rich insights into gender inequality which emerge, frequently and strongly, from the document: insights which the historiography of military subjects tends to overlook as belonging to a non-political and non-military sphere.

Very often these inequalities saw their threads entangled in further inequalities, where other identities were at stake. The same person could experience subordination in one context, while holding the power to subdue others in another context. This document, therefore, works as a case-study to explore how the experience of inequality can be a malleable one, being continuously challenged by the different spaces a specific person or group of people occupies and the interpersonal relationships these establish. Taking place in a colonial location gives the process an added challenge at different levels. In contexts where inequality was a necessary condition for the existence of colonial, external, governments, we have to search beyond that obvious inequality to look for other dimensions of inequity.

One immediate conclusion to be drawn from reading about the trial is how the political and the intimate, the public and the personal, the state and the private, are intertwined, not necessarily in hierarchical ways. While here we will give more attention to the intimate, sexual and personal layers of violence that encroach on the judicial process — those where women appear — it is also pertinent to briefly refer to the wider context within which this should be placed. First, we focus on the militarisation of the colonial state and its conflicts with the political parties that emerged from the 1910 Republic. One of the accusations against Veloso de Castro was that he was an enemy of the Republic, and that this motivated his actions and personal pursuits. His self-representation was that of an agent of military order. He exemplified the many military men who occupied administrative colonial positions, while revealing the constant tensions with those political party members who, he believed, brought disorder and turmoil to the desired stability of the colonial state. "In those occult spaces, or in political associations, your Excellency can be sure not to find me", he responds to one of the accusations, in a double reference to freemasonry and the republican parties.[34]

Veloso de Castro's angry words sometimes hint at the path to a totalitarian political trend which would be consolidated by 1926 with, precisely, the intervention of a military coup-d'état. The fact that he emerged as an active contributor to the 1930s colonial project may help us to understand the political conflicts he was going through in 1919. Implicit in his words is also the military right to the exercise of colonial power. The military were the ones risking their lives in the expeditions and campaigns that enabled the subjugation of colonised people and colonised territories. Beyond the widespread political conflicts, his prosecution gives us an indication of, and also reveals personal conflicts within the military and conflicts between the law enforcers — administrative and military — and those who wanted to flout the law with the practice of trafficking goods or women.

This judicial process also reveals the culture of the written document and report[35] — those millions of written pages that fill the colonial archive, in this case the colonial military archive.[36] It reveals a culture of complaint, both written and oral, for the most diverse array of motives. One of the striking aspects of the document is the array of references to indigenous people who had complained to a state institution, in this case the police station of Luanda, where Castro was the main person responsible. Two of the cases of indigenous complaints are related to money. The complainants appear in the process not as direct protagonists, but because they are complaining of men who are themselves making a complaint against Veloso de Castro precisely because he wanted to punish their actions.

The boy was fourteen years old, an under-age African servant of Manuel Rodrigues de Oliveira, and his entire savings totalled three escudos in silver, which he kept in a small leather purse. When, one day, another employee, no mention of his ethnicity, realised his four escudos in paper had disappeared, all the "pretos" were searched and the young servant's savings were seized as being the stolen money. The boy went to the "administration" crying at having his money taken away when he had not stolen anything. Oliveira, the employer, recognised the boy was right but justified the seizure by his need to replace the other, clearly superior, servant's missing money. Veloso de Castro states that he told Oliveira to refund the boy's money, but the latter refused, alleging that the authorities had nothing to do with this.

At this point, Veloso de Castro realized how irritated he was with Oliveira. Only the fact that the latter was an "old man" and a "European merchant" stopped Veloso de Castro from putting him in prison until the money was restored to the 14-year-old servant. For Oliveira, this mercy — the result of his status, race and nationality — was not sufficient and he made a complaint to the Governor General about what he considered to be Veloso de Castro's arrogance.

The second complaint against Veloso de Castro was made by a certain Batista. Again, Veloso de Castro censured Batista's behavior towards his employees. One day an "indigenous servant" came to the police to complain that his employer owed him more than 20 escudos and had dismissed him without paying his debt. Batista was asked to pay the servant, in order to "avoid problems with the natives", and promised to do so that afternoon. That same afternoon the indigenous servant returned to complain again that Batista had refused to pay him. A "European soldier from the police" accompanied the indigenous servant to the Café Central, where Batista was to be found. But Batista reacted by hitting his former servant and leaving him with "blood running out of his mouth and nose". And this "in front of three Belgians, one of them being the Consul himself!" Veloso de Castro continues his description of the event by stating that he ordered Batista to be arrested, and even punished the soldier for not having done so immediately. Batista resisted and had to be taken to prison by force. However, two hours later, when Veloso de Castro went to the Café Bijou, the members of the Commercial Association begged him to release their colleague, Batista, which Castro did on condition of him paying a fine. Not only did Batista ignore the fine but he also repeated his "ignominious actions". According to Veloso de Castro's statements, Batista hit an old black woman who was begging at the Café Central so hard that she was sent to hospital "flowing with blood".

Here, as in most of his defence, Veloso de Castro redirects the accusations made against him towards his accusers. He himself is the victim, precisely for wanting to stop the unlawful despotism of those who mistreated the most vulnerable. Those who accuse him are the culprits: malefactors who do not like seeing themselves under the rule of authority and justice. The possibility of complaint pervaded the different layers of Luanda's social sphere, one where race was a factor, as was age, profession and administrative position. Our first inclination would be to read into the indigenous servant's easy access to a judicial institution a surprising agency of those more vulnerable and "unequal". This enabled indigenous subjects to make not a written complaint, but an oral one; one that required only the physical effort of taking themselves to an institution where they sought justice and the re-imposition of order. But did this agency, this access to a legal channel, this voice, in short, give those subjects a proportionate institutional response?

Beyond the administrative, military and police buildings, the central urban spaces of white male sociability in Luanda seem to have been the cafés. Veloso de Castro's descriptions constantly refer to the Café Central, the Café Bijou and the Café Biker. These were not only "unequal" spaces of entertainment where the colonising agents could engage with each other, but also spaces of conflict, political and personal, within that community. When defending himself against an accusation from António Ferreira David, the "professor", Veloso de Castro argues that David publicly harassed the Governor and led a "political rally" which started at the Pastelaria Bijou.[37] Veloso de Castro adds to an impression of the tolerance he extended by stating how he allowed this "freedom of political action"; and, in another instance in his defence, he states how "no one was imprisoned or mistreated for reasons of political revenge or persecution", a rebuttal to those who accused him of using his official power to punish those with opposing political views, in this case Republican ideals.[38]

Cafés also appear in the accusations as spaces where gender and ethnicity were subverted - "The women of bad reputation with whom I spent nights at the cafés, do not exist" responds Veloso de Castro to one of the accusations against him. He denies ever talking to any "dubious women" in cafés. He would go there only with one woman, one who was well accepted by all "good people", who knew of her misery and were sorry for her. So, who was this woman? Curiously, and probably not by chance, she is the only person who was not described in terms of their race, meaning that she would have been white and Portuguese. In another section of his defence, Veloso de Castro had mentioned how he had taken this "unfortunate woman, who belonged to a renowned family in Lisbon and had brothers in the colony", to Boma.[39] The woman had lived with David Nunes, a known smuggler and fraudster but had left him for reasons unknown, and Castro began protecting her out of pity, mainly when Nunes, the abandoned man, presented a complaint against her accusing her of stealing his furniture and selling it to military officials who worked for the Governor General. However, the document does not make clear the identities of the other women, those of "low life", who also frequented Luanda's public spaces.

Another urban location which became problematic was the police headquarters itself. This was an official, military, white and male space within Luanda, but Veloso de Castro was accused of bringing into it "a few women every night" and of "transforming the barracks into a *serraglio*", the expression used to designate the sequestered living quarters of women in households in the Ottoman empire, and a word that was also used — in an orientalist and crude fashion — to describe a brothel.[40] For Veloso de Castro these were, however, "untruthful expressions" used to describe "simple facts" which he was "not ashamed to confirm as accurately describing his practice". Because the police headquarters was open all night to people of "all classes and ages and of both sexes" Veloso de Castro had no scruples about receiving in his house, the "people serving me during that time" but only, "one at a time". Clearly, here he is referring to the common practice of Portuguese men living alone, who employed local black women. The word he uses is "serving", as if they were servants. But implied in this role of "servant" was that of sexual partner. He is quite clear, however, about his "scruples" over "touching" those women who ended up in the police barracks for different reasons. His rebuttal of an accusation of "involving honest people" in his soliciting of local prostitutes becomes even more explicit in a subsequent section. This denial hints at a common practice of organised prostitution in Luanda. The women he ordered to be sent to him at police headquarters were those with whom he already had a relationship. If he wanted to have relationships with "those" others, he did not have to involve "honest people" as "there are in Luanda specific agencies who deal with those cases with no significant inconvenience."[41] With this subtle distinction, Veloso de Castro is clearly establishing a moral difference between an involvement with local prostitutes and one with local women with whom a sexual relationship had been established. In another accusation, he seems to have been accused by a group of mothers — black Africans — of having sexually abused their daughters a few years before, during his military posting in Pungo Andongo.[42] He refutes this, stating that he had been fortunate enough to arrange for an adequate "servant" during the whole of his time in that posting. By denying the need for "prostitutes" with the argument that he had a "good servant", Castro is reaffirming the sexual dimension of these employer-employee, male-female, relationships.

There are references to the common practice of the Portuguese military of hiring a "lavadeira" to take care of their clothing. This meant, on one side of the relationship, white men belonging to the nationality and ethnicity of the colonisers, and, on the other, black women and girls, African born and thus native to the territories that were being subjected to dominance. The boundaries of the relationship between these "washerwomen" and single men (or men married to wives who stayed in Portugal, as was Veloso de Castro's case) were clearly fluid. The inferiority inherent in this labour carried out in the domestic space favoured sexual and intimate contacts where violence could easily be perpetrated. With the women out of sight and alone, their vulnerability was reinforced. Any violence that occurred could be sexual, physical, or verbal, or could be present in the labour relationship itself, manifested by a lack of a salary or ambiguous duties. The common practice of black African women working for white Portuguese men should be also approached as part of the rich historiographical perspectives that have analysed forced labour as an intrinsic aspect of the colonial state.[43] This was a widespread colonial practice not limited to the Portuguese context and a rich bibliography has explored it in relation to other geographies.[44]

In the many layers of accusation and counter-accusation present in the document, we can identify that a series of complaints made by many officials and also by Veloso de Castro himself, were directed against the women who acted as labour mediators for female domestic workers. Veloso de Castro had not been an administrator for long when he received a complaint from Diniz, a marine official, who described how he was defrauded by an *alcoviteira*, a Portuguese word used for intermediary that tended to have sexual connotations. Diniz paid the mediator 60 escudos in advance but, when the girl arranged disappeared after only a few days, he demanded his money back, something which the woman refused. Castro had already heard about many similar cases, and when it happened to him, he did not make an undue fuss about it because he was the one who had dismissed the *rapariga* "for not knowing how to do laundry".

Having decided to finish with widespread "exploitation" — here meaning exploitation of officials who were dependent on these domestic tasks for their wellbeing — Veloso de Castro made use of his powers to address the case. The *alcoviteiras*, however, subverted the inquiry by excusing one another in relation to the whereabouts of the money, and all had to be sent to police headquarters. The girl herself also appeared, with her mother. She was 12 or 14 years old, and complained to the police of the inappropriate acts committed by Diniz, the man who had hired her through the mediator. Still, mother and daughter returned the money Diniz had paid to the police — money that they had to borrow. During the inquiry, the *alcoviteira* who long before had arranged the "bad" washerwoman whom Veloso de Castro had had to dismiss also reimbursed him the 20 escudos. The money returned by these women was delivered to a charity, and Veloso de Castro congratulated himself for having stopped both the exploitation perpetrated by these women brokers and also the "expedition" of underage girls to the Belgian Congo".[45] But Diniz was not happy with the decision, wanted his money back, and charged Veloso de Castro for this. In this intricate web of relationships, one in which colonial and ethnic identities are interwoven with gender ones, we can see how people depended on each other and what negotiations they entered into to protect their interests. The girl could run away from the sexual violence perpetrated against her. She could even complain about it to the authorities. But, according to Veloso

Castro's report, she still had to pay back the money to regain her freedom. Veloso de Castro ends his report on this trading of domestic female services with another personal case.[46] Needing a "woman from the *musseques* [slums surrounding the city] for work in conditions of stability", Veloso de Castro contacted and paid a young man who was also an intermediary. When he didn't hear anything more from him, Veloso de Castro sent an "indigenous" policeman to search for him. The young man came with his father, a "policeman", and with the money and the girl. Castro not only refused the money and the girl, but withdrew him his police status as it was "not appropriate" to have "police *alcoviteiros*".

Another dimension that surfaces from the document is the widespread practice of trafficking across colonial frontiers. Veloso de Castro referred to the smuggling of arms, gunpowder and cattle into the Belgian Congo at a time when the law forbade all such exports.[47] But the most striking reference to trans-colonial movement is to the trafficking of women for obvious sexual purposes between Portuguese Angola and the Belgian Congo, a subject that would benefit from a cross-national archival search. As happens in many other instances with this document, women — and the fact that they were subjected to sexual violence — do not emerge as the central issue, but as one that lies beneath. Abílio Valente, one of the owners of the Café Biker, made charges against Veloso de Castro.[48] Again, Castro attributes this vindictiveness towards him to the fact that he had stopped the trafficking of women in which Valente was involved. Charged with fulfilling the role of Agent for Passports, Valente was sending *pretas* to the Belgian Congo "without verifying their identity as part of the process" and Castro compelled him to stop, an action that was consistent with an "attitude I had adopted a long time ago after a scandalous case the administration had to confront". Clearly this was not a new practice.

Finally, there is a further accusation, somehow the most delicate one, of Veloso de Castro having "deflowered a goddaughter aged 12 years", which will be dealt elsewhere, because it needs a deeper and longer analysis.[49] However, here we will just refer to how he contested this accusation by turning it back against the African woman with whom he lived at the time, the only one who is named, Isabel. It was she, Veloso de Castro argued, who had suggested he should have a sexual relationship with the girl, who was not 12 but eight years old, because she had already been with many soldiers. It was he, indignant at the suggestion, who hit Isabel, throwing her to the ground. It was he who, knowing how older women negotiated the supply of young "goddaughters" with the Congo sexual traffickers, sent her away from his home. In this interplay of powers and relationships, we see how identities were adjusted to specific contexts: how some women exercised violence over other women; how violence had many dimensions that were intrinsic to the different dimensions of inequality; and how next to the exercise of violence there often lay the exercise of resistance — even when resistance led to further violence.

The immediate consequence of Veloso de Castro's trial was his dismissal from the post of Capitão Mor of Santo Antonio do Zaire by the Governor of Angola.[50] The charges against him also affected the progress of his military career, as can be seen from the extensive report of the Superior Council of Promotions, published on 26 October 1920. The report referred to the inappropriateness and incoherence of the language he used in his defense causing doubts as to his state of mind. The official in charge of Veloso de Castro's trial regretted how the event "cast a shadow over an official who had worked hard and extended himself on behalf of this Province."[51]

Finally, Veloso de Castro was condemned to three days in prison by the Governor of Angola — clearly merely an exemplary punishment with no real consequence; and even this was finally overturned by an official order. Veloso de Castro used his right of appeal against his three days of prison and in February 1923 his appeal was accepted.[52] One request of his that seems not to have been granted, however, was a claim for compensation, probably for moral damages, although this is not specified.[53] This, however, was not the first or the last time that Veloso de Castro's name appeared in the annals of the Military Court. Two other cases deserve mention. The first was dealt with at the Tribunal Militar Territorial da Província de Angola in 1913, and is revealing as to the violence within the military itself, between those who were higher in the hierarchy and those who were below them, especially those black African soldiers who made a living with the Portuguese troops.[54] "António André, an indigenous soldier" was told by his superior, Veloso de Castro, to tuck his shirt inside his trousers. He did so partially, tucking in only the front of the shirt, but not its back. Challenged by this semi-disobedience, Veloso de Castro punched him in the face, something justified by his military rank and legitimized in court on the grounds of an inferior's disobedience. But something unforeseen happened. The black soldier gave Veloso de Castro a firm push, throwing him to the floor, and leaving him with a cut on his arm that meant he was away from work for 10 days.

The African soldier's punishment was signed by Norton de Matos. Instead of three years in prison, he was exiled to Mozambique as a *degredado*. This legitimate practice of physical violence within the military was based on the premise of inequality itself, since it was the prerogative of only some. What this case also reveals, however, is the possibility of dissension, even if at a high price, for those who chose it. António André resisted twice: by partially disobeying the order on how to wear his uniform; and by reacting to a punch from a, white, superior, for which his punishment was a life sentence.

The last evidence in the Military Archive worth mentioning refers to Veloso de Castro's family, which had always existed but only appeared in documentation when it was on the verge of dissolution. Like so many military men in the colonies, Veloso de Castro had a wife and three young children back in Lisbon. However, when he returned to the metropolis in 1920, he did not go back to his family. His wife, very ill and living in poverty, appealed to the military for the maintenance allowance her husband had never paid.[55] This was not for her, she argued, but for the three children she was now incapable of caring for. The Military Court sent an official to confirm her situation but dismissed her request, arguing that only a civil court could make Veloso de Castro pay the maintenance he owed and provide for his abandoned family. Once again, we see an instance of gender violence within the military archive, and one that refers to a relevant social dimension of the colonial project — the place of women within the distant territories where these military men circulated and interacted.

More than 20 years ago, Patricia Hayes published a very interesting article in the journal *Gender and History* on a commissioner in Ovamboland, in the South of Angola, who had some resemblances to Veloso de Castro.[56] "Cocky Hahn" was another example of those men who practiced a non-professional ethnography whilst occupying a post in a colonial administration. Like Castro, he was the object of a complaint and an inquiry in the 1920s that, like Castro's prosecution, gives us an insight into instances of violence, also gendered, and "issues of domination, control and resistance".[57] This example also deals with issues of illegal trading and trans-colonial transgressions, such as when Hahn was accused of hunting in Angola, and had to justify it by arguing that his official Portuguese counterparts had invited him.[58] Through his prosecution, as through Veloso de Castro's, we grasp how violence could be "regulated and sanctioned" — as when Castro punched his disobedient African subordinate, or Hahn justified flogging natives in a context of upheaval and instability.[59] But violence could also be the subject of denunciation and therefore was not wholly "regulated and sanctioned", as when Hahn was accused of kicking a woman servant "between her legs" or when Batista hit his former African servant in a Luanda café.[60]

Leaving Luanda after the judicial process: colonial propaganda and policy-making from the metropolis Veloso de Castro retired to Portugal in 1920, after 18 years in Angola, shortly after his prosecution, and very probably as a consequence of it. The next traces we have of him, nevertheless, show that the judicial process did not blemish his prestige. In 1923, and therefore not long after returning from Luanda, he was granted a major honour for services to the nation, when he was nominated as *Comendador da Ordem Militar de Aviz*.[61] Nor did his trial prevent him from an active involvement in the creation of a discourse on Portuguese colonialism, from participation in conferences and congresses, from directing and writing in newspapers on colonial subjects, or even from being nominated by the Minister for the Colonies — in 1926 — to membership of a commission in charge of writing a report on colonial activities. The passage from Angola to Portugal, from Luanda to Lisbon, seems to have enabled the creation of a frontier between the before and the after from which only advantages were obtained. The upset and negativity that Veloso de Castro had caused during his time in Luanda appear to have stayed behind, not accompanying him to his new metropolitan identity. Somehow, he managed to bring back home mainly the beneficial aspects of having lived in Luanda — increased knowledge and legitimacy — and erase the problematic and conflictive aspects of his Angolan life. How else would it have been possible for him to access the public benefits he did when in Lisbon, from ministerial invitations to the direction of colonial newspapers?

After living so many years in Angola as an active agent of Portuguese colonial occupation and military power, the second part of Veloso de Castro's adult life was spent in another major sphere of colonial consolidation — that of discourse, information, knowledge, propaganda and policy. The centre of the overseas empire, the metropolis, was the site of many public and governmental initiatives in which the colonies were defined and discussed both in their past and their present state, and their future was planned. Veloso de Castro participated in both these paths of reflection — on the "how it is" and the "how it should be". His almost two decades on the terrain, as well as his military career in so many different hierarchical positions, gave him legitimacy as a specialist, not only on Angola, but on the "colonial" as an overarching project. His work in Angola, his production of knowledge through writing, mapping and photographing, combined with his practical experience of many military expeditions and campaigns, was put to good use in his later metropolitan years, when he directed it into other formats, from conferences to reports and newspaper articles, with his photographs also appearing in the latter. From Luanda to Lisbon, he brought his capital of experience, the history he had witnessed and the knowledge he had gained; and he used the photographs he had taken to illustrate the texts dealing with colonial subjects that he contributed to newspapers.

Veloso de Castro's role in writing on colonial matters in Lisbon, and his service in Luanda, deserve a thorough analysis, but here we will only briefly refer to his most official and public positions. Four years after his return from Angola, he participated in the Second National Colonial Congress, at the *Sociedade de Geografia de Lisboa* (Geographical Society of Lisbon), contributing a paper on "Colonial Campaigns in the Course of Military Operations Undertaken in the Congo, in the Libolo and in the Low Cunene".[62] Two years later, he published this same conference paper as an article in a newspaper of which he was one of the editor.[63] A few years after that, at the Third National Colonial Congress in Lisbon, again at the Geographical Society — an institution whose history and role was inseparable from the Portuguese colonial enterprise — his name appears in the organizing commission.[64]

Finally, Veloso de Castro was chosen to replace one of the members of a commission nominated by the Ministry of the Colonies to produce a major report on "The Value of Portuguese Colonial Activity".[65] Even though the appointment was made by the Ministry of the Colonies, ministers from two other departments signed the official document — the Minister for the Colonies, Ernesto Maria Vieira da Rocha; the Minister for War, José Esteves da Conceição Mascarenhas; and the Minister for Foreign Affairs, Vasco Borges — a trio that demonstrated well the dimensions involved in the colonial project, its national and international aspects, and its intrinsic relationship with the military. The Commission was first formed in February 1926 by the Republican government, with the clear intention of demonstrating to other colonising nations the efforts Portugal was putting into the "physical and economic territories" they possessed. Significant for the understanding of this context is the 1925 Ross Report, the result of an investigation by Edward Ross, an American sociologist, of labour conditions in Angola and Mozambique, which was carried out on behalf of the Temporary Slavery Commission of the League of Nations.[66] The initial commission was made up of Jaime Alberto de Castro Morais, a medical lieutenant commander, who was appointed to head it; a law graduate, José de Almada; a major in the infantry, António Leite de Magalhães; a captain in the infantry, Luís Quirino Monteiro; and a captain in the military administration, Vergílio Pereira da Costa. They were all army men, and probably all of them had been in colonial territories in the course of their military careers.

For six months, the five men were exempt from their usual responsibilities, and were wholly dedicated to the task of working on the report. As the date for the delivery of the report drew near, the government's official publishing body recognised that the period had not been sufficient to "obtain, bring together and coordinate" all the information scattered through a wide array of documents, from "overseas legislation" to "reports, memoires, official correspondence", and use it for the task of producing "surveys to be sent to the colonies".[67] It was only towards the end of September 1926 that Veloso de Castro, identified as a "*major de infantaria de reserva*" was chosen to replace one of the members of the Commission.[68] This time, the document was signed by the future President of Portugal, then the Minister for Foreigner Affairs and for War, António Óscar de Fragoso Carmona, and by João Belo, then Minister for the Colonies. Both men had participated actively in the major political event that had taken place on 28 May that year, a coup d'état which had overthrown the Republican Parliament, replacing it with a military dictatorship which lasted until 1928, when Oliveira Salazar initiated a right-wing authoritarian regime that would last until 1974. With Salazar as a totalitarian prime-minister, Carmona became President of the Republic. Can this major political transformation have had anything to do with the choice of Veloso de Castro for such a prestigious task as writing the colonial report?

The delivery date for the report was extended twice more, until the end of 1927, but after that the project disappears from the sources we have identified so far.[69] Each time there was an extension, a text was published in the official newspaper explaining the reasons for the delay and replacing some of the names of the initial commission members, for reasons not always explained. Suddenly, however, no more notices appear on the project. Therefore, we cannot be sure at this distance whether this major colonial report was ever completed, or whether the transformations of the political regime, from a republican government to a military dictatorship, followed by Salazar's Estado Novo, with its changes in policy, ideologies and actors, may have been a determining factor. One dimension of inequality comes to mind in relation to the status occupied by public men within a particular political context. To be against or outside the political powers could mean not having access to the public sphere of decision-making, and not being able to write in the mainstream print culture, while to be with or within the core could open up wide possibilities, from economic, to professional and public ones. Was this the case for Veloso de Castro, a man within the military orbit, as were the majority of men occupying active roles during this period, both in national and colonial politics? Had the man who, in Angola, had been accused of not aligning himself with Republican ideals now found his recognition within the context of the right-wing military dictatorship?

It was between 1926 and 1929 that Veloso de Castro became very active in writing and running two colonial journals published in Lisbon. In a period when there was a thriving print culture, colonial subjects occupied a major place in this, both in specialised newspapers dedicated to colonial matters and in newspapers covering a range of subjects, where colonial matters were a constant theme. This was not merely a metropolitan endeavour. The number of newspapers written, edited and printed within the colonies themselves made it possible for a multitude of voices to be heard, even critical and dissonant voices.[70]

Veloso de Castro was the editor of the periodical *Gazeta das colónias: semanário de propaganda e defesa das colónias* between 10 September 1926 and 25 November 1926, the latter being its last publishing date (numbers 37 to 41). The newspaper had started in 1924 as a fortnightly publication, but, as frequently happened, its appearances soon started to fall off. Veloso de Castro managed to get it back to being printed every two weeks, while introducing, on the front page, the novelty of a summary of the headlines.[71] But finally, by the end of 1926, and despite editorial and advertising hints about future issues, the newspaper stopped being printed.

The other periodical venture in which Veloso de Castro was a major figure was *Lusocolonial. Revista de defesa e propaganda* (Lusocolonial. A Review of Defence and Propaganda). He became one of the three creators and managers of the colonial journal, which published 18 issues between 1927 and 1929, suddenly coming to a halt just on the eve of his death in 1930, perhaps due to his physical incapacity to pursue the project. We have seen how, on his return to Lisbon and in his reinvention of himself as a specialist on colonial subjects, Veloso de Castro used his Angolan experience in different ways. This also happened with the extensive collection of photographs he had taken while living in the territory. Some of them at least were used to illustrate articles in the newspaper he managed. An editor's note in *Lusocolonial* says that all the illustrations published in the magazine are available for sale.[72] They had been archived by the Army's Photography Section since 1917, and prints could be ordered for various purposes — the text offers some suggestions — "to illustrate books and magazines, to be shown at conferences, or to be looked at by the general public." There is no mention of any requirement to pay a fee for the images; only a requirement to refer to their provenance. Veloso de Castro's Angolan photographic booty kept on being used in new contexts and assuming new meanings in the printed pages of the metropolitan propaganda press.

Conclusion

Much has been written on inequality in colonial relationships and contexts, as inequality is in itself the central paradigm of colonial states. Racial difference, discrimination and inequality — and the conflicts, negotiations and heterogeneous categories these imply — have therefore been an ever-present question in approaches to colonialism. Gender inequality should be added as a pertinent axis of reflection. Gender relationships in colonial spaces, in their entanglements with racial, hierarchical, and colonial relationships, have not been explored enough in historiographical approaches to the Portuguese colonial experience.[73] The evidence of their centrality is explicit in many ways in the textual and visual archive, as well as in the oral one for more recent times. Portuguese historiography, however, has not yet fully embraced them, first and foremost because gender approaches are still not mainstream, as they are in other national scholarly contexts. Another reason lies perhaps in the problematic nature of much of the archival evidence — evidence that traditional historiographies tend to place outside the realm of "historiographically legitimate subjects". To write about gender in colonial territories can imply writing on sexual violence, on rape, on paedophilia, on the sexual trafficking of women and girls, on the mixed race children born out of these intimate relationships, on absent fathers, or fathers not assuming responsibility for their children, on double standards of morality within Christian family values — or families in the metropolis on the one side, and sexual, emotional or affective relationships with African women on the other, where no legal, or moral, responsibility needed to be assumed.

The reasons for this historical unwillingness to see the evidence are multiple, but we could suggest some of them. First of all, there is a remaining patriarchal scholarship which tends to overlook practices which "everyone knows existed", but are not meant to be voiced. This scholarship treats history as a Pandora's box that should not be opened for fear of the unexpected consequences. Secondly, and inseparable from the previous reason, there is an overall hierarchy in historical themes where the political, the military, the decision-making, or the narration of war occupy a higher position than subjects such as sexuality, intimacy, emotions, or women- and gender-related subjects overall. There is much more space for the study of violence as part of war or the imposition of the colonial state, than for the study of sexual violence, which, despite being an intrinsic part of the both the practice of war and colonial state formation, is somehow "naturalised" and therefore de-historized, as if not belonging to the domain of those subjects valued as relevant. The fact that much of the history of the colonial experience has been written by men and within the historical category of "military history", also male-dominated, may likewise contribute to the invisibility of these subjects. Finally, and we would argue, perhaps the strongest, deterrent, though it may be unconscious, could be that of recent Portuguese colonial wars opposing paths towards independence. To think historically on questions of gender relations in the context of colonialism or colonial wars would necessarily imply a confrontation with the very recent history of interactions between Portuguese soldiers and African women. Perhaps it is not by chance that the major approaches to the subject have been those of women, for example of Margarida Calafate Ribeiro, who is also collaborating in this volume.[74]

How can we place sexual violence within this perspective, especially the violence practiced within colonial contexts where the wider inequality between colonisers and colonised was entangled with another layer of inequality — that of the dominant relationships of white men and black women? How can these double asymmetrical relationships of power nevertheless enable us to find in the archive affections, emotional involvement and reciprocity? An inference from this document, and especially from those instances where women appear as individual or generalised actors, is how intimate violence and state violence can be entangled, and how gender approaches can give us a precious insight precisely into those dimensions of intimate violence which pervaded colonial interpersonal relationships. It is an obvious fact, even though it is often taken for granted by historians, that the colonial divide was a gendered one — most of the "colonisers" in Angola at this time were men. On the other side of this determining and fundamental inequality, there were African men and women. This first inequality has many gendered implications in colonial daily life, ones which this document enables us to explore. It is likely not by chance that most of the women mentioned in the document, with only one exception, do not have names — identities — in a clear contrast to the many male names referred to.

Our analysis has far from exhausted the density of a source from which so many threads can be pulled. This source's richness lies also in the ways in which it invalidates divisions between official and non-official dimensions, between the private, the personal and the public, between the military and the civic. These dimensions are entangled in complex negotiations of transgression and acceptance, of what was legitimate and what was not, of what could be practiced with discretion and away from the public view, and what could be publicly displayed. We would argue that military archives are a privileged place to explore those dimensions of the colonial state that not only should not be overlooked — as belonging to the realm of the personal — but also should be acknowledged as a central aspect of the embodiment of colonialism. Intimacy and sexual violence, as well as daily relationships and contacts between different peoples, in colonial spaces, are entangled with military and official relationships, and should also be mixed into historiographical approaches. Violence and inequalities were certainly found not only in war, armed conflict and labour relationships, but also in the daily life of interrelationships where multiple identities — gender, race, social and military status — were at stake. It is not possible to verify all these levels of abuse, as Hayes also argues; but more relevant is what we *can* verify — how what was acceptable and what was not acceptable emerge from this culture of complaints and written conflicts, often referring to physical conflicts.[75] "Colonial power worked simultaneously through the production of knowledge and the exercise of physical force, and both were gendered to the core", as Hayes states; and Castro's case has provided us with the possibility of exploring both dimensions of power, and of inequality.[76]

Through the case of Veloso de Castro and the richness of textual sources linked to his name, the Military Archive became a privileged space for the grasping of subjectivities. One of the challenges for today's historiographies of colonialism, of slavery, and the multiple subjects of labour, colonial, and sexual oppression, is precisely how to go beyond the discourses on them. The archives are full of documents where these subjects are spoken of, written about, represented. How can we go beyond their study as objects of discourse to their study as subjects of discourse — disrupting their representations with their gestures, voices, agencies, affects, creativity, resistance, disobedience? How can we move from the colonised, in its broadest sense, as object, to the colonised as subject? Even if mediated by the written description of the military source, those who had no access to the agency of written tools come to the fore in unexpected disruptions and gestures. Military archives may be one of the privileged sites to search for a multiplicity of subjectivities of the subaltern. Could an historiographical search for the subjecthood of women and men in colonial spaces, or in other spaces where inequality is the major frame of interrelationships, be a strategy to overcome inequality itself? Can history mitigate inequalities by searching for the subjectivities of those who led their lives in the most hidden spaces and circumstances of inequality.

Notes

1 Ministerial order of 12 January 1917, endorsed by the Decree of 13 April 1918. Then, in 1919, there was a reorganization of the section, which had no autonomous funds, and it became part of the Direction of the Graphic Services of the Army (Decree 5:935, 28 June 1919), quoted in Eduardo António Martins Mendonça, "O Cinema Produzido pelo Serviço Cartográfico do Exército nas Campanhas de África (1961–1974)" (degree dissertation, Catholic University of Portugal, 1993), p. 28.

2 AHM, Caixa 2124 and photographic collection AHM/FE/CAVE/VC/A10.

3 *Relatório da Viagem Realizada nos Meses de Julho e Agosto de 1905 pelos Alferes de Infantaria, Eugénio Torre do Valle e José Velloso de Castro para Estudar as Condições de Navegabilidade d'Aquele Rio e Provável Ligação Fluvial de Malange ao Bihé* (Lisbon: Tipografia da Cooperativa Militar, 1913), p. 16.

4 Susan Sontag, *On Photography* (London: Penguin, 1979), p. 14.

5 René Pélissier, *História das Campanhas de Angola: Resistência e Revoltas, 1845–1941*, 2 vols (Lisbon: Editorial Estampa, 1986); on the Luso-Cuamata War of 1907 see 2nd vol., pp. 206–212, and René Pélissier, "Campagnes militaires au Sud-Angola (1885–1915)", *Cahiers d'études africaines* 9, 33 (1969): 54–123, esp. 89–94.

6 Alferes Veloso de Castro, *A Campanha do Cuamato em 1907. Breve Narrativa Acompanhada de Photographias* (Luanda: Imprensa Nacional, 1908).

7 David Martins de Lima, *A Campanha dos Cuamatos: Contada por um Soldado Expedicionário* (Lisbon: Livraria Ferreira, 1908); José Augusto Alves Roçadas, *Conferência sobre o Sul de Angola a Propósito das Operações Militares no Cuamato Feita na Sociedade de Geografia de Lisboa pelo Governador da Huíla José Augusto Alves Roçadas, Comandante da Columna de Operações* (Lisbon: Imprensa Nacional, 1908); *A Campanha d'África ou a Guerra com os Cuamatas: Contada por um Soldado e Vários Oficiais* (Porto: J. Ferreira dos Santos, 1908).

8 *A Campanha d'África ou a Guerra com os Cuamatas*, p. 60; in Veloso de Castro's trial it was stated that he was "seriously wounded in the combat of Mufilo" on 27 August 1907.

9 Arquivo Histórico Militar, Caixa 2124, Processo Individual de José Veloso de Castro. Letter dated 19 October 1919, p. 31.

10 Filipe Ribeiro de Meneses, ed., *Paiva Couceiro. Diários, Correspondência e Escritos Dispersos* (Lisbon: Edições D. Quixote, 2011); Vasco Pulido Valente, *Um Herói Português — Henrique Paiva Couceiro (1861–1944)* (Lisbon: Aletheia, 2006); Vasco Pulido Valente, "Henrique Paiva Couceiro — um Colonialista e um Conservador" *Análise Social* 36, 160 (2010): 767–802.

11 Patricia Hayes, "Vision and Violence: Photographies of War in Southern Angola and Northern Namibia." *Kronos* 27 (2001),: 133–157, 137.

12 Henrique de Paiva Couceiro, *Relatório de Viagem entre Bailundo e as Terras do Mucusso* (Lisbon: Imprensa Nacional, 1892.

13 Henrique de Paiva Couceiro, *Angola: Dois Anos de Governo, Junho 1907-Junho 1909* (Lisbon: Edições Gama, 1948); General Norton de Matos, *Angola — Ensaio sobre a Vida e Acção de Paiva Couceiro em Angola* (Lisbon: Edições Gama, 1951).

14 For this period see also the work of René Pélissier and Valentim Alexandre, *O Império Africano - Séculos XIX e XX* (Lisbon: Edições Colibri, 2000); "The Colonial Empire" in *Contemporary Portugal*, ed. António Costa Pinto (New York: Boulder, 2003), pp. 63-84.

15 Photographic albums *Reconhecimentos Topographicos Exectuados em 1908 pelo Tenente José Velloso de Castro, Primeiro Álbum, Junho e Julho, Calulo, Quissongo*

(Columna Móvel de Policia em Operações no Libolo) and *Reconhecimentos Topographicos Exectuados em 1908 pelo Tenente José Velloso de Castro, Segundo Álbum, Agosto e Setembro, Calulo, Quissongo, Cabezo, Qissala, Gungo, Sanga, Quibala (Columna Móvel de Policia em Operações no Libolo).* Arquivo Histórico Ultramarino (Overseas Historical Archive), AHU/ALB23 and AHU/ALB24.

16 *Reconhecimento do Rio Cambo 1906 (Telatório da Viagem Realisada nos Mezes de Setembro e Outubro de 1905 pelos Alferes de Infanteria Eugenio Torre do Valle e José Velloso de Castro afim de Se Verificar as Condições de Navegabilidade dos Indicados Rios. Malange, Junho de 1906)* (Lisbon: Tip Universal, 1908). The manuscript is kept at AHMUL-MUHNAC, IICT, Arquivo de Fronteiras, caixa preta 3, vol. 10, Angola, Tombo Histórico.

17 *Relatório da Viagem Realizada nos Meses de Julho e Agosto de 1905 pelos Alferes de Infantaria, Eugénio Torre do Valle e José Velloso de Castro para Estudar as Condições de Navegabilidade d'Aquele Rio e Provável Ligação Fluvial de Malange ao Bihé,* (Lisbon: Tip. da Cooperativa Militar, 1913).

18 Filipa Lowndes Vicente, ed., *O Império da Visão. Fotografia no Contexto Colonial Português (1860–1960)* (Lisbon: Edições 70, 2014).

19 Cátia Miriam Costa, "O outro na narrativa fotográfica de Velloso de Castro: Angola, 1908" in *Culturas Populares. Revista Electrónica 7* (Julio–Diciembre 2008), pp. 1–16; *Província de Angola. Álbum de Aspectos, Vida e Costumes do Interior da África Occidental Portugueza. Photographias de Veloso de Castro,* (s.l.; s.n., ca. 1905), b/w, 9,5 x 14,5 cm. Album no 1: "Malange: Aspectos"; Album no 2: "Malange: População"; Album no 3: "Malange: Vida Military"; Album no 4: "Malange: Solemnidades"; Album no 5: "Malange: Arredores"; Album no 6: "Quissol: Centro Commercial"; Album no 7: "Rio Cuanza: do Cuige ao Condo"; Album no 8: "Rio Cuanza: do Condo ao Luando"; Album no 9: "Rio Cuanza: do Luando ao Cunhinga"; Album no 10: "Rio Cuanza: do Cunhinga a Cumanga"; Album no 11: "O Rio Cambo: Catala Canjinga e Dala Murila"; Album no 12: "O Rio Cambo: Dala Murila e Marimba"; Album no 13: "O Rio Cambo: Marimba a Tembo Aluma"; Album no 14: "O Cuano: Tembo Aluma"; Album no 15: "O Cuango: Tembo Aluma ao Utunguila"; Album no 16: "O Cuango: Utunguila ao Luremo"; Album no 17: "Do Cuango a Malange".

20 The album analysed by Hayes is "Album de Vassalagem" (Luanda: Centro Nacional de Documentação e Investigação Histórico).

21 Hayes, "Vision and Violence", pp. 136–37.

22 Maria Pia Di Bella and James Elkins, eds, *Representations of Pain and Suffering in Art and Visual Culture* (New York and London: Routledge, 2013); "Conflict, Time, Photography", exhibition at Tate Gallery, London, between November 26, 2014 and March 15, 2015.

23 Susan Sontag, *Regarding the Pain of Others* (London: Penguin, 2004).

24 Inês Vieira Gomes, one the authors of this article, will dedicate a part of her thesis to the analysis of this extraordinary corpus of images.

25 Patricia Hayes, "'Cocky' Hahn and the 'Black Venus': The Making of a Native Commisioner in South West Africa, 1915–46", in *Cultures of Empire. A Reader. Colonizers in Britain and the Empire in the Nineteenth and Twentieth Centuries* (London: Taylor and Francis, 2000), pp. 329–355, p. 329. The article was first published in *Gender and History* 8, 3 (November 1996): pp. 364–92.

26 AHM, Caixa 2124. Letter dated 19 October 1919, p. 32.

27 Here we mention just some examples in different cities, from Paris to London and Leeds: *Deuxième Exposition Interalliée de Photographies de Guerre*, Paris: Jeu

de Paume, 1917; *New Exhibition of Canadian War Photographs*; *Women's War Services — An Exhibition*, London: Grafton Galleries, 1918; *The British Exhibition of War Pictures*, London: Grafton Galleries, 1917; *Exhibition of Allied War Photographs*, Leeds, City Art Gallery, 1917.

28 Inge Henneman, ed., *Shooting Range. Photography and the Great War* (Antwerp: FOMU, Fotomuseum, 2014).

29 These are the documents where we searched for Veloso de Castro's or for Portuguese participation in the exhibition but found no mention of any: Central Office of Information (formerly Ministry of Information, Part/dates: Pt 1 1917–1945, ref: MA/1/C849/1, A0046, A0359, A0441, and A0057). Victoria and Albert Archive, London.

30 Archive histories determine the fate of documents. At the *Biblioteca da Academia Militar*, we found a typed inventory of the photographic collections of the Army in 1992 which mentions the "Reproductions to the Exhibition of London" (Álbum A, A-3, Data: 1917, Negative - Q.-14, Formato, 9x12, E-M, Arquivo C-29 - 16 a 30. Lack of negative n.º 25). When all army photographs were sorted, those taken from 1976 on remained in the CAVE (Centro de Audiovisuais do Exército), while those taken up to 1975 were transferred to the *Arquivo Histórico Militar*. In the process, the previous references were lost, which prevented us from identifying which of Castro's photographs were sent to be exhibited in London.

31 *A Thousand Photographs of the World War* (London: Victoria and Albert Museum, 1917). (http://www.iwm.org.uk/collections/item/object/31709).

32 *Exhibition of Allied War Photographs 1917.* (Reg. nos. 651 to 662–1917) - A0046, Victoria and Albert Archive. Each page of the album has a different photograph of a room of the exhibition. Under each photograph, glued to the cardboard pages, is a short handwritten text. The first one shows the British section. We found none for the Portuguese section, only finding references to Salonika, India, France, Russia, Italy and Serbia.

33 AHM, Caixa 2124, Processo Individual, Documento da Secretaria da Guerra, 1.ª Direcção-Geral, 2.ª Repartição. Quartel General da Província de Angola.

34 AHM, Caixa 2124. Letter dated 19 October 1919, p. 32.

35 For this we can refer to the powerful argument in the chapter on imperialism in Hannah Arendt, *The Origins of Totalitarianism* (New York: Schocken Books, 1951).

36 Just a few examples of a subject with a very extensive bibliography: Durba Ghosh, "Decoding the Nameless: Gender, Subjectivity and Historical Methodologies in Reading the Archives of Colonial India", in *A New Imperial History: Culture, Identity and Modernity in Britain and the Empire, 1660–1840*, ed. Kathleen Wilson (New York: Cambridge University Press, 2004), pp. 297–316; Antoinette Burton, ed., *Archive Stories: Facts, Fictions, and the Writing of History* (Durham: Duke University Press, 2005); Ann Laura Stoler, *Along the Archival Grain. Epistemic Anxieties and Colonial Common Sense* (Princeton: Princeton University Press, 2009).

37 AHM, Caixa 2124. Letter dated 19 October 1919 p. 10.

38 AHM, Caixa 2124. Letter dated 19 October 1919, p. 12.

39 AHM, Caixa 2124. Letter dated 19 October 1919, p. 9, p. 12.

40 AHM, Caixa 2124. Letter dated 19 October 1919, p. 14.

41 AHM, Caixa 2124. Letter dated 19 October 1919, p. 15.

42 AHM, Caixa 2124. Letter dated 19 October 1919, p. 17.

43 On forced labour see Miguel Bandeira Jerónimo, *The "Civilizing Mission" of Portuguese Colonialism (c.1870–1930)* (London: Palgrave Macmillan, 2015); "The 'Civilisation Guild': Race and Labour in the Third Portuguese Empire, c. 1870–1930",

in *Racism and Ethnic Relations in the Portuguese-Speaking World*, ed. Francisco Bethencourt and A.J. Pearce (New York: Oxford University Press, 2012), pp. 173–199.

44 Hayes, "'Cocky' Hahn", p. 346; Nancy Rose Hunt, "Domesticity and Colonialism in Belgian Africa: Usumbura's Foyer Social, 1946–1960", *Signs* 15 (1990): 447–74.

45 AHM, Caixa 2124. Letter dated 19 October 1919, p. 16.

46 AHM, Caixa 2124. Letter dated October 19, 1919, pp. 16 –17.

47 Analysing a case-study situated between the north of today's Namibia and the south of Angola in the early twentieth century, Patricia Hayes refers to the smuggling between colonial frontiers: Hayes, "'Cocky' Hahn", p. 340.

48 AHM, Caixa 2124. Letter dated 19 October 1919, p. 10.

49 We are working on an article focusing on this case and on Veloso de Castro's relationship with Isabel, a local black woman with whom he lived in Santo António do Zaire and in Luanda, and whom he photographed.

50 AHM, Caixa 2124. Ministério da Guerra, Conselho Superior de Promoções. Acta das sessões do Conselho Superior de Promoções dated 26 October 1920.

51 AHM, Caixa 2124. Acta das sessões do Conselho Superior de Promoções dated 26 October 1920.

52 AHM, Caixa 2124. Ministério da Guerra, Direcção-Geral. Serviço da República. Document nº 641 dated 5 February 1923.

53 "The request for compensation of $180 was dismissed by his Excellency the High Commissioner for the Province of Angola." AHM, Caixa 2124. Ofício da Província de Angola, nº 1096/5163 de 14 de Outubro quoted in a document from the Ministério das Colónias, Direcção Geral Militar, 4.ª Repartição, 2ª Secção, Serviço da República, Lisboa, 10 November 1921.

54 AHM, Caixa 2124. Process nº 17/1913 quoted in the document from the Secretaria do Tribunal Militar Territorial da Província de Angola, Loanda, 31 March 1925.

55 AHM, Caixa 2124. Document dated August 13, 1921; Process n.º 5093, August 25, 1921.

56 Hayes, "'Cocky' Hahn".

57 Hayes, "'Cocky' Hahn", p. 338.

58 Hayes, "'Cocky' Hahn", p. 341.

59 Hayes, "'Cocky'" Hahn, p. 342.

60 Hayes, "'Cocky' Hahn", pp. 344–45.

61 O. E. nº 17 (2.ª série), 5 October 1923. Information from his individual process. AHM, Caixa 2124.

62 José Velloso de Castro, "Campanhas Coloniais, no Decurso de Operações Militares Realisadas no Congo, no Libolo e no Baixo Cunene", in *II Congresso Colonial Nacional, de 6 a 10 de Maio de 1924. Teses e Actas das Sessões* (Lisbon: Sociedade de Geografia de Lisboa, Tip. America, 1924).

63 José Velloso de Castro, "Campanhas Coloniais. Memória Apresentada ao 2º Congresso Colonial Nacional, pelo Major Veloso de Castro" in *Gazeta das Colónias: Semanário de Propaganda e Defesa das Colónias*, 37 (10 September 1926): 25–26; *Gazeta das Colónias* 38 (25 September 1926): 27–28; *Gazeta das Colónias* 41 (November 25 1926): . 23–24 and 27.

64 *III Congresso Colonial Nacional de 8 a 15 de Maio de 1930. Actas das Sessões e Teses* (Lisbon: Sociedade de Geografia de Lisboa, Tip. e Pap. Carmona, 1934).

65 "Comissão para Proceder à Elaboração de um Relatório sobre o Valor da Acção Colonial Portuguesa, Nomeada pelo Ministério das Colónias", Portaria de 12 de Fevereiro, Diário do Governo, n.º 47, 2.ª Série, 26 February 1926, p. 664.

66 Edward Alsworth Ross, *Report on Employment of Native Labor in Portuguese Africa* (New York: Abbott Press, 1925); Francisco Martins de Oliveira Santos, *Reply to the Accusation Addressed to the League of Nations by Mr. Edward A. Ross, Against the Portuguese in Angola* (Lisbon: Sociedade de Geografia de Lisboa, 1930.

67 Portaria de 23 de Julho, Diário do Governo, nº 175, 2.ª Série, 28 July 1926, pp. 2441–2442.

68 Portaria de 23 de Setembro, Diário do Governo, nº 227, 2.ª Série, 27 September 1926, p. 3131.

69 Portaria de 16 de Abril, Diário do Governo, n.º 87, 2.ª Série, April 23, 1927, p. 1264; Portaria de 23 de Junho, Diário do Governo, nº 138, 2.ª Série, 27 June 1927, p. 2148.

70 Gina Guedes Rafael and Manuela Santos, *Jornais e Revistas Portugueses do Século XIX,* 2 vols (Lisbon: Biblioteca Nacional, 1998–2002; Aleixo Manuel da Costa, *Dicionário de Literatura Goesa*, vol. 3 (Macau: Instituto Cultural de Macau; Fundação Oriente, 1997).

71 This information is signed by Pedro Teixeira Mesquita, 12 June 2014, on the Hemeroteca of Lisbon. website: http://hemerotecadigital.cm-lisboa.pt/FichasHistoricas/gazetadascolonias.pdf (last accessed 16 October 2016).

72 *Lusocolonial. Revista de Defeza e Propaganda* 2 (30 January 1928): 25.

73 The majority of studies mixing Portuguese colonialism with gender approaches have been undertaken within the context of literary and anthropological scholarship.

74 Projects which have already started, such as CREPAL – Centre de Recherches sur les Pays Lusophones, Université de Paris Sorbonne Nouvelle (Margarida Calafate Ribeiro is a researcher on the project), or ones that are now starting, such as CROME – Crossed Memories, Politics of Silence: The Colonial-Liberation Wars in Postcolonial Times, coordinated by Miguel Cardina, CES-Coimbra.

75 Hayes, "'Cocky' Hahn", p. 340.

76 Hayes, "'Cocky' Hahn", p. 350.

CHAPTER

14

Managing Inequalities: Welfare Colonialism in the Portuguese Empire since the 1940s

MIGUEL BANDEIRA JERÓNIMO

This chapter focuses on the role played by welfare idioms and repertoires in late colonialism, aiming to identify their multiple genealogies, rationales and intents, from the management of inequalities in colonial contexts to political control of the population and to the supervision of socio-economic and cultural change. It essentially deals with the Portuguese case, although it provides some comparative insights into other colonial empires. In the first section, the chapter points to some of the fundamental transformations of the post-war colonial empires, namely the emergence of a particular type of empire-state, with novel modalities of colonial rule and new demands for imperial legitimation, facing new challenges and prospects, tentatively devising new strategies of resilience. In the next two sections, the chapter deals, in a necessarily succinct way, with two fundamental issues of the period: the rise and institutionalization of welfare colonialism; and its development in the Portuguese case. On the one hand, it addresses some of the main facets of the post-war recalibration of the languages and the projects of welfare colonialism, highlighting their international, inter-imperial, national and, of course, colonial dynamics. On the other, it assesses how some of those languages and the projects were embraced, selectively appropriated and put to use, in similar, although not necessarily equivalent, ways, by Portuguese authorities and experts.

The post-war rejuvenation of imperial projects

Contrary to still-persisting narratives, the post-war moment was one of significant imperial rejuvenation. It entailed a "second colonial occupation", a novel "order" bolstered by initiatives aiming at an "accelerated economic growth", reacting to the multifarious challenges of the post-war world.[1] A "late colonial shift" was noticeable. The outlooks and respective expectations of the imperial and colonial governments, the colonizers and the colonised changed substantially. The *modi operandi* and the prospects of imperial and colonial formations were reconsidered. New governing rationales were pondered, and tentatively adopted.[2] The post-war colonial situations were contexts of institutional, ideological and administrative innovation, policy restyling, engineered societal modernization, and novel modalities for the instantiation and governing of difference. New idioms and repertoires of rule and societal transformation proliferated, some reviving past proposals in different circumstances.[3]

In a process partially related to the political and economic reconstruction of Europe after the war, a constellation of political and economic motivations led European colonial empires to reimagine their imperial and colonial endeavours. Such aspirations led to the reinforcement of imperial and colonial projects which were connected to extensive development plans in Africa and Southeast Asia: the renovation and re-legitimisation of imperial prestige abroad, the preservation of colonial outposts as places for investment of European capital and as "markets and raw material suppliers", the use of the colonies as contributors "to relieving acute balance of payment deficits" and to the generation of "foreign (and especially dollar) exchange", with a view to acquiring the "food and goods vital for metropolitan reconstruction". Not least importantly, colonies figured as privileged spaces for the imagination of new model societies, welcoming new flows of white stock that could potentially trigger social unrest at the metropoles. The imperial endgame and associated colonial disengagement were not contemplated as impending possibilities. On the contrary, imperial projects and colonial schemes blossomed. London, Amsterdam, Brussels, Paris (Vichy) and, later, Lisbon planners considered the preservation of imperial preferences and colonial strongholds as a *sine qua non* for their countries' much-needed industrial renovation, and also a fundamental requirement for the renewal of their international prominence and legitimacy as empire-states. Ideological and geopolitical *global* mindsets and frameworks — for instance those related to early Cold War dynamics — reinforced this path. The Marshall Plan soon included imperial projections, which varied according to the nature of particular imperial formations and specific colonies. European efforts at post-war colonial development and programmes of colonial modernization depended on programmes such as the Economic Cooperation Act (1948), the European Recovery Programme (1949), the Point IV programme (1950) and similar financing schemes associated with the European colonial world (and more broadly with the Marshall Plan agenda).[4] The related capital investment, technological, technical and institutional transfers and assistance, and, of course, the circulation of knowledge and expertise (and experts) became processes fundamental to the transformation, and rejuvenation, of post-war imperial formations and their interests.[5]

It was in these circumstances that a particular type of state emerged, the late colonial state. The establishment of a "proactive or developmental state", replacing the "night-watchman state", governed by principles of economic and sociocultural modernizing intervention, aiming as well to transform the norms and rules of engagement with colonial communities, was partially a response to the evolving geopolitical, metropolitan and colonial contexts.[6] European colonial empires needed to reinvent themselves as reformist and progressive polities, confronting archaic and feeble, although highly coercive and routinely violent, modes of government, and engaging seriously with post-war circumstances.[7] The appeasement of challenges to colonial rule, the attainment of long-term solutions capable of maintaining the colonial status quo and the promotion of economic and social development, partially in order to reconstruct metropolitan societies, were some of the goals. As a consequence, a flow of planners, experts, advisers, and settlers, followed. In multiple senses, colonization gained momentum. Diverse political, economic and socio-cultural developmental idioms and projects proliferated, sometimes reviving past ideas and projects.[8] Those idioms and projects entailed international, transnational and also imperial networks and institutions.[9] Doctrines of institutional perfection and idioms of "good [imperial and colonial] government" were debated; arguments about the advantages of planning and the most effective techniques of productivity enhancement abounded.[10] Some of these issues and dynamics were particularly clear in the Portuguese colonial empire, although still relatively neglected in todays' existing literature.[11]

The rise of welfare colonialism

One of the fundamental aspects of the "late colonial shift" was the emergence and institutionalization of idioms and repertoires of welfare colonialism. The question of welfare in the colonial worlds became, in varying degrees and with distinct materializations, pivotal to the devising of novel imperial political and moral economies. It was as central to political projects and economic schemes as it was to strategies of imperial legitimation, at local, metropolitan and also international levels. It was also promoted as a fundamental demonstration of a novel reformist and progressive, morally rejuvenated, polity, guided by models of planned and managed economic development and social and cultural modernization. Welfare was advocated as the most effective "method" to win "hearts and minds", and a powerful tool to fight social, cultural and economic "backwardness", mitigating the negative effects of "tribal life". Welfare became the core of the "ruling compassions" of late colonialism, aiming to deal with the multifaceted inequalities within colonial societies, but at the same time trying to avoid any political social unrest that might be caused by precipitous social change.[12]

The doctrines of welfare colonialism were diverse, but interrelated, sometimes even overlapping. For instance, in a 1964 volume published in Portugal by the Overseas Research Board, community development, social promotion and rural welfare were taken as synonymous. The same was stated in the preamble to the 1962 Rural Labour Code, a new, overarching code that regulated non-specialized labour and social policies in all Portuguese colonies.[13] These doctrines were all connected, albeit in varying degrees, to the institutionalization of colonial developmentalism and welfarism in the political and academic spheres, and they were all more or less affected by processes of nationalization, that is of *national* appropriations and modulations of existing international doctrines.[14] They actively contributed to the competing developmentalisms that marked the post-war momentum.[15] One example was rural welfare (*bem estar rural*), which started to be promoted by inter-imperial networks, for instance by the Commission for Technical Cooperation in Africa South of the Sahara (CCTA), from the early 1950s on.[16]

Another such doctrine was community development or, in the French version, *animation rurale*. Community development was, as the name suggests, a developmental doctrine (strongly influenced by American contributions) encompassing women's activities, youth services, literacy education, health and sanitary services, and infrastructural development projects.[17] Yet another was social development, which was the introduction of "social policies and programmes" into "an overall strategy of economic development". This was an idea that first grew within the context of the debates about Third World development, and had the Ashridge Conference on Social Development (1954) and the constitution of the United Nations Commission for Social Development (1966) as historical landmarks.[18] One last example was social promotion (*promoção social*), the expression used by Portuguese officials and experts to designate the comprehensive set of policies produced to deal with the social "advancement" of African, mainly rural, communities. For instance, in 1962, the need for a new "harmonious policy of social and economic promotion of the totality of the population", including "traditional rural communities", was strongly emphasised. Social promotion was intimately connected with "community development", seen as a "global" form of development.[19] All these doctrines were connected to discussions of economic planning in colonial societies, to projects of aimed at social betterment and the mitigation of socio-economic inequalities, and also to political and securitarian rationales.[20]

However, the shared concern with colonial welfarism and its multiple idioms and repertoires of action was not merely a by-product of the post-war period. Rather, the genealogies of colonial welfarism were lengthier and more diverse. For instance, in the late 1930s, the British government had appointed a committee to investigate the need for social services in the colonial territories.[21] Nonetheless, the global war brought significant changes in the institutionalisation of these idioms and repertoires. The first local colonial welfare departments were formed; experts — social workers — were sent to those territories. A "professional imperialism" emerged, connected to the post-war assertion and consolidation of an "imperialism of knowledge".[22] Gradually, the "narrow remedial focus" of the early departments and bodies was tentatively transcended. Before the war, social services had essentially been delivered by charities and by missionary bodies and their respective missionary stations. During and after the war, a more socially comprehensive approach and more economic-oriented plans emerged, gradually becoming centred in the colonial state apparatus. On the one hand, this was a result of war-related social disruptions; on the other, it was a consequence of particular transformations within colonial societies, namely the growth of cities and their "slums" and the related growth in social problems such as juvenile delinquency, strikes and occasional revolts and uprisings, accompanied, of course, by new forms of political association. A "developmental social welfare" became an important element of late colonialism, closely related to the momentous transformations in the "scope of activity and scale of operation" of the late colonial states.

The administrative instances that managed the modus operandi of colonial empires expanded and changed in significant ways, partially financed by increases in the revenues of colonial states connected to the colonial economic boom of WWII and the increasing monetization of colonial economies.[23]

In the British empire, a "new deal" entailed the provision of "social development" as a priority. Social welfare in colonial contexts became a central element in the administration's *politics of difference*. In 1944, in her influential report *Welfare in the British Colonies*, the anthropologist Lucy P. Mair pointed to the fact that the three traditional pillars of social policy in colonial contexts — education, labour and health — were now joined by a fourth: social welfare. One year later, a Colonial Office pamphlet entitled *Social Welfare in the Colonies* reinforced this assertion and stated that the transference of techniques of social welfare from the metropoles to the "backward" colonies was mandatory.[24] A series of summer conferences and meetings were created to disseminate many of these ideas and foster the establishment of appropriate administrative structures to enact them. As noted above, the Ashridge Conference on Social Development, convened by the British Colonial Office in August 1954, strengthened the importance of the idioms and repertoires of welfarism in the post-war world, popularizing and spreading the doctrines of community development, for instance. These became a holistic "approach to administration in all its branches".[25] The 1940 and 1945 Colonial Development and Welfare Acts saw some of their welfare guidelines reinforced.[26]

Similar tendencies were noted in the French imperial territories, for instance with the launch in 1946 of the Fund for Economic and Social Development (FIDES) and in 1949 of the Rural Economic and Social Development Fund (FERDES).[27] Techniques of societal intervention connected to ideas of welfare and socioeconomic development were also praised and tentatively promoted. For instance, *animation rurale* was commended as a "non-revolutionary" model of social transformation. A product of "progressive planners, developmentalists, and agricultural experts" acting in Senegal in the late 1950s, *animation rurale* became synonymous with rural welfare.[28] Another example of the centrality that welfare acquired in colonial policies and politics of difference was the Constantine Plan and its provisions that aimed to transform the "condition of men".[29]

The dynamics of colonial welfarism in the Belgian Congo and Rwanda-Urundi were also noteworthy. The 1947 Native Welfare Fund for the Congo, Rwanda and Burundi (FBEI) and the 1949 Ten-year Development Plan were instruments for profound experiments in social change.[30] The novel development schemes, highly professionalized, aimed at social welfare, psycho-social intervention, increased economic productivity and enhanced social control. The role of urban and rural *foyers sociaux*, *centres sociaux* and *paysannats indigènes* were crucial. In the Ten-Year Plan about a quarter (23 percent) of the total budget was allocated to medical facilities, education and housing for African communities. By 1959, there was a 70 percent enrolment in primary school. In all this, community development and *animation rurale* were pivotal.[31]

Similar processes occurred, with different temporalities and dynamics in the Portuguese case, which was naturally distinct given the political and ideological circumstances in which they occurred. Certainly, no equivalent to Lord Hailey's *An African Survey* (1938; revised 1956) or to Lucy Mair's 1944 *Welfare in the British Colonies* emerged; nothing to match the 1943 Advisory Committee on Social Welfare, which placed colonial welfare at the centre of policy concerns, particularly education, labour, health and "social welfare", existed.[32] Nonetheless, similar institutional transformations and ideological drives characterized Portuguese late colonialism, promoting planning and development as crucial cornerstones of the (more proclaimed than actually enacted) political, economic and social reforms overseas. The redefinition of imperial and colonial politics and policies was a matter of fact, even if some longstanding issues persisted, including, for example, rigidly racialized *politics of difference*. In 1951 and 1953, the constitutional revision and the promulgation of the Overseas Organic Law introduced welfare and developmental rationales into the imperial political and juridical frameworks. In 1956, the Center for Political and Social Studies of the Overseas Provinces Research Board was formed, and would conduct numerous investigations, including on rural welfare. The resemblances to the British Colonial Research Service and the French *Office de la Recherche Scientifique Coloniale* were significant, at least on paper. One year later, a ministerial reform that created "study" sections focused on the production of specialized knowledge to address political, economic and sociocultural imperial subject-matters.[33] Created in 1959, a Political Affairs Office at the Overseas Ministry, aiming to centralize a new institutional network of imperial strategic information, became essential to the overall tentative transformation of the colonial apparatus.[34]

The development of welfare colonialism

From the 1950s on, several developmental plans were formulated with a view to significantly transforming the imperial and colonial worlds.[35] The First Six-Year Developmental Plan (1953), entailing the investment of 2,562,007 *contos*, constituted a novel experimental exercise in politico-economic planning and managed change, an effort at rationalization that collided with existing realities, envisioning a profound intervention in metropolitan and colonial societies. About a third of the overall expenditure was allocated to the colonies, mainly to Angola and Mozambique (86 percent).[36] Social dimensions began to be included from the Second Six-Year Development Plan (1959–1964) onwards, although it did not prove possible to replicate what had happened in other imperial formations. The focus on infrastructure and the near absence of social investment was reassessed and mitigated (the expenditure on settlement was not). By 1951, expenditure on social services and social development (health and education) amounted to about 43 percent in the British colonial territories. In Nigeria, in the First Development Plan (1946–1955), 40 percent of the expenditure was allocated to "social services". In the French colonial territories, the figure was 20.5 percent, from July 1954 to June 1957. In the Belgian Congo, it corresponded to 20.7 percent of the expected expenditure in 1950–1959 and 31.8 percent in the second, unfinished, ten-year plan (1960–1969). In the Portuguese case, in the 1959–1964 plan, social features — education, health and welfare — accounted for 14 percent and 6 percent of the overall budget in Mozambique and in Angola respectively.[37] These state-managed development plans aimed at a gradual, comprehensive social change, essentially guided by an economic, productivist reasoning but also including social rationales. For instance, from 1961 to 1971, the budget for education in Angola rose from 33,500 *contos* to 847,200 *contos*. Notwithstanding this enhanced concern with social issues, criticism persisted. In Mozambique, for instance, local authorities questioned the paucity of investment in education, labour, welfare and health. The failure to understand the economic value of such investment was denounced. The literacy levels in the sixties rose only from 9.6 percent to 10.3 percent, while the average lifespan was 37.3 years.[38]

Certainly, in relation to initiatives in an earlier period, manifestations of state-sponsored welfare colonialism became an important reality, coexisting with the more traditional activities of ecclesiastical and missionary structures, catholic and protestant, and some private charities.[39] The revision of the Native Statute — (*indigenato*) — in 1954 transformed this near monopoly: a development that was reinforced with the publication of the Rural Labour Code in 1962, which enabled the creation of provincial institutes of labour and social welfare that had funds for social action. Labour syndicates, mutual assistance societies and private firms added to the number of providers of welfare.[40] The Rural Labour Code was promoted as an instrument of "social justice". The provision of "rational and sufficient sustenance, comfortable and hygienic housing, [and a] fair salary" was to be accompanied by the monitoring of the "psychological evolution resulting from the transformation of the traditional system of life".[41] The 1961 establishment of provincial departments of settlement, the appropriation and spread of doctrines such as community development and rural welfare (*bem-estar rural*), and the creation of peripatetic teams providing psycho-social services — which had a manifest social welfare interventionist rationale in rural areas — were other (interrelated) examples of the late colonial state embrace of international languages and models of welfare colonialism and developmentalism. The peripatetic teams, for instance, aimed at the transmission of new standards in household management, individual and community hygiene, agricultural techniques and schemes for productivity, and education. The instructions provided to the *chefes de postos*, who already had a duty to transmit new agricultural techniques, household management principles and basic sanitary standards, along with labour and tax demands, were distributed to many authorities. Efforts to mitigate (or redefine) inequality on many levels were fundamental in all these efforts.[42] As the Bishop of Mozambique, Sebastião Soares de Resende, wrote in 1962, "also in Africa, our time is one of balancing social contrasts".[43] As João Pereira Neto wrote in the same year, success in the "field of social action in the overseas territories" was a precondition for the "very existence of the Portuguese state".[44]

Various modes of "social", "educational" and "religious" assistance were the means of social advancement for local populations. In the mid-1960s, in Angola and Mozambique, the social aspects of government were still considered "deficient", partially due to the limited effects of peripatetic, ad hoc operations. The "new technique of social and economic promotion of underdeveloped populations", that is community development, was to be mobilized, but within a "permanent" and "intensive programme". However, the proclaimed objectives of a swift and profound managed social change were scarcely met.[45] Similar concerns about social welfare were advanced in other state organizations — such as the cotton institutes (1961), where instruction in agricultural techniques was accompanied by lessons on "sewing, cooking and hygiene", and other activities in social centres and clubs — and on the premises of private enterprises, such as the Cassequel plantations in Angola. The acceleration of critical events in the 1960s and the articulation of international and local dynamics exerted some significant influence on the political and economic embrace of welfare idioms and strategies.[46]

Doctrines, and to a lesser extent repertoires, of welfare and development were commonly advocated. Despite some differences, community development, social promotion, rural welfare and rural development were seen as combining three fundamental aspects. One, related to technical and financial issues, aimed at intervening in socio-economic contexts and infrastructures, and fostering agricultural productivity, but also at introducing new forms of production, particularly cooperativism. The second was related to "social education", that is the education of rural communities in social responsibilities, particularly the embrace of "progress". Finally, the third was connected to social, economic and political integration, that is, the involvement of African communities in development. These purposes, and the doctrines that sustained them, were crucial to a "campaign for social justice" that was claimed to be ongoing. Of course, they also had a "preventative nature". The mobilization of a "scientific and systematic" psychological intervention was seen as a powerful political tool.[47]

Psycho-social interventions were valued, but they were also questioned. The beneficial consequences of the service created in 1961 were doubted, as they scarcely improved the material conditions of rural communities. Their impact was not "profound, long-lasting and widespread". Community development, as a technique, was meant to replace such interventions. Its economic impact was more effective and enduring, its social effect more continuous (once the early peripatetic character was abandoned) and its political utility was more appropriate to international audiences, given the fact that psycho-social interventions were frequently denounced as mere "modern techniques of audio-visual propaganda" designed to "constrain the reflexes of native populations in a way favourable to the Portuguese nation". Community development was not denounced. On the contrary, it was widely praised, and therefore less prone to political interpretations, despite its evident political utility, which would become increasingly valued as conflicts spread throughout the empire.[48] The combination of economic benefits, social impact and political usefulness was what made welfare and developmental doctrines particularly appealing to many different authorities and experts. They were low-cost, enabled the use of more elaborate methods of social control and psychological intervention, and facilitated political rule.[49] With the Third Development Plan (1964–1969), community development became a proper policy, meriting study groups and commissions such as the Centre for Community Development Studies (1963).[50]

These trends were clearly connected with similar tendencies emerging and circulating abroad. The echoes of international and inter-imperial conferences on colonial welfare programmes and the role played by community development in such activities were welcomed in Portugal. Indeed, the debates and arguments engaged in at a 1953 Inter-African Conference on Rural Welfare (and a second such meeting in 1957), at the above-mentioned 1954 Ashridge Conference on Social Development, at the United Nations, particularly at the Economic Commission for Africa (ECA), which held a *Cycle d'études sur le développement communautaire* in Addis-Ababa in 1959 (attended by Alfredo de Sousa and Abel de Santos Baptista), at UNESCO, and at the International Labour Organization were embraced, selectively appropriated, and put to use by Portuguese authorities and experts.[51] At the 1953 meeting, which took place in Lourenço Marques, many of the Portuguese contributions, and many of those from English and French participants, naturally engaged with the evolving international and intercolonial welfarist imagination. "Economic factors of rural welfare", "cotton growing areas and native rural housing" and "credit and social assistance" were some of the topics addressed by the Portuguese. Defined in a preliminary meeting of experts in Lisbon, the three main concerns of the conference — "social structure", "economic factors" and "social services and community organization" related to rural welfare — resonated, and continued to resonate, in many other meetings. The "social consequences of economic development" were selected as the fundamental problem to be thoroughly assessed in Lourenço Marques. The identification of "practical steps to be taken to raise standards of living in a purely material sense", through "controlled central planning" or "self-help", and an emphasis on the "social and human approach to development" were major goals.[52]

All these topics, problems and aims became a recurrent concern for the Portuguese, at least on paper. Some years later, this was clearly recognized in some of the most important volumes covering these issues. The recommendations that came out of the 1953 meeting were so important that they contributed to the creation of a Mission for the Study of the Attraction of Big Cities and of Rural Welfare, in 1957, one year after the creation of a Provincial Commission for Native Rural Welfare, which was already promoting similar guidelines.[53] For instance, a recommendation for the retention of "natives" in rural settings, in order to minimize rural exodus and related social, political and economic problems and conflicts, was the main guideline for a research mission in Angola, particularly in Bailundo (the origin of the main migratory flow to Loanda and the northern districts). The subjects studied varied from migration to the disintegration of traditional social structures, from agricultural issues to education and health, from the role of women to that of *assimilados* (Africans who were also citizens, therefore assimilated), from housing to native settlements and neighbourhoods, from credit to social assistance. All these interrelated issues formed a "major social complex" — entailing "economic, psychological, political, assistance- and education-related dimensions, with additional biological, technical and environmental" ones — to which rural welfare was connected. Methods and techniques such as mass education, community development, "regrouping villages", and *paysannats* (land settlement cooperatives) were assessed, taking examples provided by international or inter-imperial meetings as references. As important as these, rural welfare was like a "polynomial". The former challenges were resolved by a mathematical principle; rural welfare by a "political" one defined by the interests of "national politics". Proclaimed to be essentially technical and scientific, the role of the CCTA, and that of the *Institut International des Civilisations Différentes* (INCIDI), which also dealt with rural promotion in 1953, were nonetheless central to the creation of inter-imperial and international political cooperation, aiming to react to the changing nature of international organizations, and to the definition of national, particularly national political, policies in Africa. The technical and the scientific were clearly assumed to be essentially political.[54]

Social promotion was a key doctrine, connected to, and sometimes overlapping with, community development and rural welfare. The programmes were ambitious, revealing the multiplicity of political, social and economic purposes behind the development of colonial welfare; that is, behind the evolution of welfare idioms and policies. The various proposals entailed interventions that went from the education of women to "biological" and "geographical" miscegenation (political and cultural integration), from civic education on corporatism to religious assistance, and from schooling to techniques for increasing living standards, aiming to promote a modicum of commitment to "upward social mobility".[55] These tenets of socio-economic promotion, always supported by community development and welfare techniques, especially in rural areas, were to be articulated with programmes aimed at a significant "revolution" in the colonial economy, especially in agriculture. The entire process would pave the way for an effective countering of any form of "revolutionary subversion".[56]

These connections became clear when the revision of the Third Development Plan was being implemented, and they were articulated in a report produced by experts drawn from the Office of Social Promotion of the Provincial Settlement Department and also from the Technical Commission for Rural Reordering. A "converging evolution" was necessary, closely connecting social, economic and political aspects. The "quick spread" and "evolution into active stages" of "subversion" made social and economic promotion "urgent and unavoidable". "Underdevelopment" was to be tackled immediately. The close connection between "subversion and underdevelopment" was singled out as a major problem. "Situations" of underdevelopment, and related inequalities, were the most effective "cornerstones" of "subversion". Some such situations, considered structural in Angola, were highlighted: the "unfair valorisation" of products exchanged; the "exploitation" of the people by "canteens" (*cantinas*) and "bush shops"; the lack of supervision by the state, which created the idea that "injustices" were "tolerated" by the administration; the persistence of a "tutelary and paternal" attitude by the authorities; land expropriation and the absence of legal supervision and corrective intervention; low and "unequal salaries based on ethnic distinctions"; practices of coerced labour; and the existence of a "colour barrier" in relation to labour. Rural development and rural reordering and resettlement were the key to counterbalancing this state of affairs. Socio-economic promotion should be a priority.[57]

With the intensification of colonial conflicts, with all their attendant causes of dissension, and the deterioration of imperial legitimacy at international gatherings, welfare colonialism became an important social, economic and political tool. New forms of managing (mitigating or reproducing) inequality, created and reinforced by the logic of the colonial situation, were seen as crucial to the establishment of a modicum of political (and military) success. Among many other instances, the Congress on Settlement and Social Promotion that occurred in Loanda, Angola, in October 1970, highlighted this reasoning. The concluding remarks stated that the mobilization of "all moral and material resources" in order to strengthen "the socio-economic promotion of the more underdeveloped communities" was a matter of "pressing urgency". Moreover, it was "a vital precondition of national survival", and would be decisive for "total pacification". The provision of minimum standards of living, and related tentative efforts to reduce inequalities between the services offered to settlers and those provided to Africans living in urban and rural contexts, gained importance in relation to political-military rationales. The "security of the population" was closely linked to educational, economic and financial purposes. To spread the Portuguese language and the putative Portuguese values, to bolster livestock farming, and to simplify access to credit were as important as social control. Indeed, the former were preconditions for the latter. The 1971 creation of Brigades for Rural Promotion and Development was a clear sign of this emerging "major social complex". The articulation of all these interventions was crucial to social promotion, and social promotion was the "solution to the overseas problem". Therefore, the brigades became pivotal to the enterprise, at least on paper. They would enable the "acceptance of new patterns of technical and social behaviour" that would cause trajectories of "integral development". The 1972 Norms of Rural Resettlement and Population Regrouping, an important politico-military set of instructions, echoed such ideas and goals.[58]

As noted above, the engineering of social promotion and the entire arsenal of idioms and repertoires of welfare colonialism were related to modalities of spatial rural reorganization, some focused on the management of white settlers (e.g. *colonatos*), others on the management of native communities.[59] Rural reordering became an important political strategy, with its own Technical Commission, created in 1962, performing a central role in the combining of developmental strategies with security drives. The formulation of an integrated policy of socio-economic intervention in rural areas had clear political-securitarian intents.[60] As the respective decrees stated, rural reordering or resettlement aimed at the "social advancement, development and settlement" of rural communities, through the "rational intensification and spread of education", as well as through "sanitary-medical, social and techno-economic assistance". All this was seen as having clear security advantages.[61] Native rural resettlement locations, the *aldeamentos*, were one such example. They incorporated welfare and socio-economic rationales connected to political and military goals, and these aimed at finding effective ways to deploy counter-subversion strategies. Population control and security enhancement were related, at least in theory, to a coordinated and rational agricultural production, administration of manpower, management of soil use, dissemination of sanitary practices, cultural change and integration — through education, evangelization and other forms of psycho-social intervention — and also to a continuing and expanding implementation of wage labour and even to the formation of a peasant middle-class. Security, development and welfare became closely related. The securitization of late colonial development and the developmentalization of late colonial security were interdependent.[62] Repressive developmentalism was a major facet of late colonialism. By the end of the colonial empire, close to two million Africans had been regrouped in *aldeamentos* in Angola and Mozambique. These (forced) settlements were proclaimed to be exemplary places of integral social change, balanced social order, and economic potential. Moreover, they were proclaimed to be places for managing the social, political, cultural and economic inequalities produced by the very state that had engineered or at least deepened them.[63]

Conclusion

The related histories of the international, inter-imperial and national constitution and institutionalization of idioms and repertoires of welfare colonialism are yet to be properly studied. Their centrality to the ways in which the late colonial states engaged with, and tried to manage, the political, economic and sociocultural inequalities and challenges that characterized post-WWII colonial situations is manifest. This also applies to the ways in which they marked the ideological and institutional dynamics of the "second colonial occupation" and the realities of the late colonial shift. Understanding of this centrality facilitates new and rewarding insights into late colonialism, into the trajectories of decolonization, and even into post-colonial societies. The productive intersections of development, security and welfare are just one example. Even an assessment that focuses on aspects of the Portuguese case, such as this one, reveals why. With significant differences, and in distinct temporalities, the Portuguese case was nonetheless profoundly imbricated with other imperial trajectories, international processes and colonial dynamics. As in other cases, in Portuguese late colonialism, the idioms and repertoires of welfare were potentially an effective social palliative, an efficient mechanism of political control, and an inexpensive factor in economic dynamism.

There are many issues that need to be tackled in relation to these connections. For instance, we need to know how such novel languages and related possibilities were appropriated or refused, used instrumentally, or even dismissed, by local communities, or by the critics of empire. Like the late colonial shift, the political assertion and institutionalization of welfare colonialism transformed expectations in colonial relationships. There was plenty of room to assess whether the realities in the empire matched the promises. Similarly, much more effort is needed to understand the relationship between the proclaimed motivations and interests behind the doctrines and programmes of welfare colonialism and their implementation in colonial territories. This chapter has sought to provide an initial contribution to the proper contextualization of these problems.

Acknowledgement

This text results from the research project "Change to Remain? Welfare Colonialism in European Colonial Empires in Africa (1920–1975)", funded by the Portuguese Foundation for Science and Technology (Ref: IF/01628/2012).

Notes

1 D. A. Low and John Lonsdale, "Towards the New Order, 1945–1963", in *History of East* Africa, vol. 3, ed. D. A. Low and Alison Smith (Oxford: Clarendon Press, 1976), p. 12.

2 Martin Shipway, *Decolonization and its Impact. A Comparative Approach to the End of the Colonial Empires* (Oxford: Blackwell, 2008), pp. 12–17.

3 Miguel Bandeira Jerónimo, "Competing Developmentalisms: International and Interimperial Dynamics in Late Colonialism, 1940s–1970s" (forthcoming).

4 Nicholas White, "Reconstructing Europe through Rejuvenating Empire: The British, French, and Dutch Experiences Compared", *Past and Present* 210, supp. 6 (2011): 214, 219. See also Frederick Cooper, "Reconstructing Empire in British and French Africa", *Past and Present* 210, supp. 6 (2011): 196–210.

5 For a global appraisal of the Marshall Plan see Daniel Speich Chassé, "Towards a Global History of the Marshall Plan: European Post-War Reconstruction and the Rise of Development Economic Expertise", in *Industrial Policy in Europe After 1945: Wealth, Power and Economic Development in the Cold War*, ed. C. Grabas and A. Nützenadel (Basingstoke: Palgrave Macmillan, 2014), pp. 187–212. For a new overall appraisal of post-war economic transformations see Mark Mazower, Jessica Reinisch and David Feldman, *Post-War Reconstruction in Europe: International Perspectives, 1945–1949* (Oxford: Oxford University Press, 2011).

6 John Darwin, "What Was the Late Colonial State?" *Itinerario* 23, 3–4 (1999): 73–82.

7 See also Crawford Young, *The African Colonial State in Comparative Perspective* (New Haven and London: Yale University Press, 1994) and Martin Thomas, *Violence and Colonial Order* (Cambridge: Cambridge University Press, 2012).

8 Joseph M. Hodge, Gerald Hodl and Martina Kopf, eds, *Developing Africa* (Manchester: Manchester University Press, 2014).

9 Frederick Cooper and Randall Packard, eds, *International Development and the Social Sciences: Essays in the History and Politics of Knowledge* (Berkeley: University of California Press, 1997); Marc Frey, Sönke Kunkel, and Corinna R. Unger, *International Organizations and Development, 1945–1990* (Basingstoke: Palgrave Macmillan, 2014).

10 John M. Lee, *Colonial Development and Good Government: A Study of the Ideas Expressed by the British Official Classes in Planning Decolonization 1939–1964* (Oxford: Clarendon Press, 1967).

11 See Miguel Bandeira Jerónimo, "Ordering Resistance: The Late Colonial State in the Portuguese Empire (1940–1975)", *Political Power and Social Theory,* Vol. 33 (2017), pp. 109–128.

12 Despite originating in the context of British Kenya, these arguments apply to many other colonial situations. Joanna Lewis, *Empire State-Building* (Oxford: James Currey, 2000), p. 15. See also Joanna Lewis, "The Ruling Compassions of the Late Colonial State: Welfare Versus Force, Kenya, 1945–1952", *Journal of Colonialism and Colonial History* 2, 2 (2001): 7.

13 Decree 44309, 27 April 1962; A. Correia de Araújo, *Aspectos do Desenvolvimento Económico e Social de Angola* (Lisbon: Junta de Investigações do Ultramar 1964), p. 137, n1.

14 The shifting meanings and the national appropriations and versions of the idioms of developmentalism and welfarism are two processes that are in need of a proper study, despite the fact that both were recognized by historical actors. See, for instance, Albert Meister, "Développement communautaire et animation rurale en Afrique", *L'Homme et la société* 19 (1971): 121–138.

15 Bandeira Jerónimo, "Competing Developmentalisms".

16 CCTA, Inter-African Conference on Rural Welfare: First session (Lourenço Marques: CCTA, 1953).

17 See Daniel Immerwahr, *Thinking Small: The United States and the Lure of Community Development* (Harvard: Harvard University Press, 2015).

18 See, for instance, James Midgley, *Social Development: The Developmental Perspective in Social Welfare* (Thousand Oaks, CA: Sage Publications, 1995), pp. 51–52.

19 Junta de Investigações do Ultramar, *Promoção Social em Moçambique. Grupo de Trabalho de Promoção Social de Moçambique* (Lisbon: Centro de Estudos de Serviço Social e de Desenvolvimento Comunitário, 1964), pp. 22–23, 45.

20 Miguel Bandeira Jerónimo, "'A Battle in the Field of Human Relations': The Official Minds of Repressive Development in Portuguese Angola", in *Decolonization and Conflict: Colonial Comparisons and Legacies*, ed. Martin Thomas and Gareth Curless (London: Bloomsbury, 2017), pp. 115-136.

21 Lucy P. Mair, *Welfare in the British Colonies* (London: The Royal Institute of International Affairs, 1944). See also "Handbook on Welfare in the British Colonies by Dr Lucy Mair", UK National Archives, CO 875/16/3.

22 James Midgley, *Professional Imperialism. Social Work in the Third World* (London: Heinemann, 1981); Frederick Cooper, "Modernizing Bureaucrats, Backward Africans, and the Development Concept", in *International Development and the Social Sciences: Essays in the History and Politics of Knowledge*, ed. Frederick Cooper and Randall Packard (Berkeley: University of California Press, 1997), pp. 64–92.

23 Midgley, *Social Development*, pp. 53–54. See also Frederick Cooper, *Decolonization and African Society: The Labour Question in French and British Africa* (Cambridge: Cambridge University Press, 1996); Crawford Young, "The African Colonial State Revisited", *Governance. An International Journal of Policy and Administration* 11, 1 (1998): 105–106.

24 Leigh Gardner, *Taxing Colonial Africa: The Political Economy of British Imperialism* (Oxford: Oxford University Press, 2012); Mair, *Welfare in the British Colonies*, p. 101; "Social Development in British Colonial Territories: Report of the Ashridge Social Development Conference, 3–12 August 1954", Colonial Office Miscellaneous Paper 523 (London: Colonial Office, 1954), preparatory notes, pp. 2–5.

25 "Chairman's Opening Address", *Social Development in British Colonial Territories: Report of the Ashridge Social Development Conference, 3–12 August 1954*, Colonial Office Miscellaneous Paper 523 (London: Colonial Office, 1954); H. T. Bourdillon, in *Social Development in the British Colonial Territories.*

26 S. Constantine, *The Making of British Colonial Development Policy* (London: Frank Cass, 1984); M. Havinden and D. Meredith, *Colonialism and Development: Britain and its Tropical Colonies, 1850–1960* (London: Routledge, 1993).

27 Tony Chafer, "Friend or Foe? Competing Visions of Empire in French West Africa in the Run-up to Independence", in *French Colonial Mind*, vol. 1, *Mental Maps of*

Empire and Colonial Encounters ed. Martin Thomas (Lincoln, NE: University of Nebraska Press, 2012), pp. 285–286; Frederick Cooper, "Development, Modernization, and the Social Sciences in the Era of Decolonization: The Examples of British and French Africa", in *The Ends of European Colonial Empires: Cases and Comparisons*, ed. Miguel Bandeira Jerónimo and António Costa Pinto (Basingstoke: Palgrave-Macmillan, 2015), pp. 15–50, esp. pp. 23–25.

28 Jean-Pierre Chauveau, "Participation paysanne et populisme bureaucratique. Essai d' histoire et de sociologie de la culture du developpement", in *Les associations paysannes en Afrique*, ed. J.-P. Jacob and Ph. Lavigne Delville (Paris: Khartala, 1994), pp. 25–60, cit. p. 34; Catherine Boone, *Political Topographies of the African State: Territorial Authority and Institutional Choice* (Cambridge: Cambridge University Press, 2003), pp. 84–85.

29 *Plan de Constantine, 1959–1963: rapport général* (Délégation générale du gouvernement en Algérie, June 1960), p. 33; Muriam Haleh Davis, "'The Transformation of Man' in French Algeria: Economic Planning and the Postwar Social Sciences, 1958–62", *Journal of Contemporary History* 52, 1 (2017): 73–94.

30 Fonds du Bien-Etre Indigène, *A Work of Co-operation in Development. Fifteen Years' Operation by the Native Welfare Fund in the Congo, Rwanda and Burundi, 1948–1963* (Gent: Snoeck-Ducaju, 1964); Guy Vanthemsche, *Genèse et portée du 'Plan décennal' du Congo belge (1949–1959)* (Brussels: Académie Royale des Sciences d'Outre-Mer, 1994).

31 Miguel Bandeira Jerónimo, "Repressive Developmentalisms: Idioms, Repertoires, Trajectories in Late Colonialism", in *Oxford Handbook of the Ends of Empire*, ed. Martin Thomas and Andrew Thompson (Oxford: Oxford University Press, forthcoming 2018).

32 Helen Tilley, *Africa as a Living Laboratory: Empire, Development, and the Problem of Scientific Knowledge, 1870–1950* (Chicago: Chicago University Press, 2011), esp. chapt. 2, "A Development Laboratory: The African Research Survey, the Machinery of Knowledge, and Imperial Coordination", pp. 69–114. For the formation in Portugal of scientific knowledge related to imperial affairs see Frederico Ágoas, "Estado, Universidade e Ciências Sociais: A Introdução da Sociologia na Escola Superior Colonial (1952–1972)" and Cláudia Castelo, "Ciência, Estado e Desenvolvimento no Colonialismo Português Tardio", both in *O Império Colonial em Questão*, ed. Miguel Bandeira Jerónimo (Lisbon: Edições 70, Colecção História & Sociedade, 2012), pp. 317–347 and pp. 349–387, respectively.

33 For a synthesis see Bandeira Jerónimo, "Ordering Resistance". See also Sabine Clarke, "A Technocratic Imperial State? The Colonial Office and Scientific Research, 1940–1960", *Twentieth Century British History*, vol. 18, 4 (2007), pp. 453–480 and Christophe Bonneuil and Patrick Petitjean, "Science and French Colonial Policy: Creation of the ORSTOM: From the Popular Front to the Liberation via Vichy, 1936–1947", in *Science and Technology in a Developing World*, ed. T. Shinn, J. Spaapen, and V. V. Krishna (Dordrecht: Kluwer, 1997), pp. 129–178.

34 Miguel Bandeira Jerónimo and António Costa Pinto, "A Modernizing Empire? Politics, Culture and Economy in Portuguese Late Colonialism", in *The Ends of European Colonial Empires: Cases and Comparisons* ed. Miguel Bandeira Jerónimo and António Costa Pinto (Basingstoke: Palgrave Macmillan, 2015), pp. 51–80. See also Diogo Ramada Curto, Bernardo Pinto da Cruz, and Teresa Furtado, *Políticas Coloniais em Tempo de Revoltas — Angola circa 1961* (Porto: Afrontamento, 2016), pp. 59–125.

35 Planos do fomento: Plano de Fomento 1 (1953–58), Plano de Fomento 2 (1959–64), Plano Intercalar (1965–66), Plano de Fomento 3 (1967–73). For these see Victor

Pereira, "A Economia do Império e os Planos de Fomento", in *O Império Colonial em Questão*, ed. Bandeira Jerónimo, pp. 251–286; Cláudia Castelo, "Developing 'Portuguese Africa' in Late Colonialism: Confronting Discourses", in *Developing Africa*, ed. Joseph M. Hodge, Gerald Hödl and Martina Kopf, pp. 63–86; Bandeira Jerónimo and Costa Pinto, "A Modernizing Empire?".

36 Pereira, "A Economia do Império", pp. 252–253.

37 United Nations, *Economic Survey of Africa since 1950* (New York: Department of Economic and Social Affairs, 1959), table 4–xxii and xxiv, pp. 245–246; William Malcolm Hailey, *An African Survey. Revised 1956. A Study of Problems Arising in Africa South of the Sahara* (London: Oxford University Press, 1957), pp. 1325–1326

38 Bandeira Jerónimo and Costa Pinto, "A Modernizing Empire?", pp. 61–62; Pereira, "A Economia do Império", pp. 280–281.

39 See, for instance, Philip J. Havik, "From Hospitals to Villages: The Organisation of Health Services and Social Medicine in Portuguese West Africa", *Portuguese Studies Review* 25, 1 (forthcoming, 2017).

40 Michael A. Samuels and Norman A. Bailey, "Education, Health, and Social Welfare", in *Portuguese Africa: A Handbook*, ed. D. M. Abshire and M. A. Samuels (New York: Praeger, 1969), pp. 178–201. For the case of labour, including the central role played by international and transnational dynamics, see José Pedro Monteiro, "A Internacionalização das Políticas Laborais 'Indígenas' no Império Colonial Português (1944–1962)" (PhD thesis, University of Lisbon, 2017).

41 Preamble of Decree 44309, 27 April 1962.

42 Francisco Alfredo Fernandes, *O Posto Administrativo na Vida do Indígena* (Lisbon: Europa-América, 1953); Bandeira Jerónimo and Costa Pinto, "A Modernizing Empire?", p. 67.

43 Correia de Araújo, *Aspectos do Desenvolvimento Económico e Social de Angola*, p. 139.

44 João Pereira Neto, "Política de Desenvolvimento Comunitário nas Províncias Portuguesas de África", *Ultramar*, vol. 9 (1962), p. 57.

45 Junta Provincial de Povoamento de Angola, *Plano de trabalhos para 1965* (Luanda: JPP-Angola, 1965), pp. 27–29; Junta de Investigações do Ultramar, *Promoção social em Moçambique. Grupo de Trabalho de Promoção Social de Moçambique* (Lisbon: Centro de Estudos de Serviço Social e de Desenvolvimento Comunitário, 1964), pp. 56–57.

46 Jeremy Ball, *Angola's Colossal Lie. Forced Labor on a Sugar Plantation, 1913–1977* (Boston: Brill, 2015), esp. chapt. 4, pp. 115–138; Samuels and Bailey, "Education, Health, and Social Welfare", p. 195.

47 Amadeu Castilho Soares, *Política de Bem-Estar Rural em Angola* (Lisbon: Junta de Investigações do Ultramar/Centro de Estudos Políticos e Sociais, 1961), p. 17; Correia de Araújo, *Aspectos do Desenvolvimento Económico e Social de Angola*, p. 143;

48 Junta de Investigações do Ultramar, *Promoção Social em Moçambique*, pp. 57–58.

49 Bandeira Jerónimo, "'A Battle in the Field of Human Relations'"; see also Alfredo de Sousa, "Desenvolvimento Comunitário e Desenvolvimento Económico", *Estudos Políticos e Sociais* 2, 2 (1964): 294.

50 Alfredo de Sousa, "Desenvolvimento Comunitário em Angola", in *Angola: Curso de Extensão Universitária do Ano Lectivo de 1963–1964* (Lisbon: Instituto Superior de Ciências Sociais e Política Ultramarina, 1964), pp. 421–440; A. J. de Passos Guerra, "Reordenamento Rural e Desenvolvimento Comunitário", *Trabalho: Boletim do Instituto do Trabalho, Previdência e Acção Social*, vol. 4 (1963), pp. 83–128; see also Bandeira Jerónimo and Costa Pinto, "A Modernizing Empire?", and Curto, Cruz, and Furtado, *Políticas Coloniais em Tempo de Revoltas*, pp. 17–19.

51 CCTA, *Conferência Inter-Africana do Bem Estar Rural: Primeira Reunião (Inter-African Conference on Rural Welfare: First Session)* (Lourenço Marques: CCTA, 1953); "Rapport du cycle d'études sur l'élaboration et la mise en oeuvre des programmes nationaux de développement communautaire: Addis Ababa , Ethiopie 14–25 septembre 1959", UN, E/CN.14/24.

52 "CCTA Preliminary Meeting of Experts" and "Preliminary Draft Agenda for the Conference", in "Conferência de Rural Welfare 1953", Foreign Affairs Archive (Lisbon), 2° Piso, Armário 17, Maço 39. See also Miguel Bandeira Jerónimo, "Competing Developmentalisms: International and Interimperial Dynamics in Late Colonialism, 1940s–1970s" (forthcoming).

53 Decree no. 9515, 7 January 1956.

54 This political dimension was duly recognized, even if in a limited way, by Amadeu Castilho Soares in his *Política de Bem-Estar Rural em Angola*, pp. 12–13, 18–23. For ideas discussed by the CCTA and the 1953 recommendation, see also his "Bem-Estar Rural. Aspectos Sociais", in Centro de Estudos Políticos e Sociais da Junta das Missões Geográficas e de Investigação do Ultramar, *Missão para o Estudo da Atracção das Grandes Cidades e do Bem-Estar Rural. Relatório da Campanha de 1957 (Angola)* (Lisbon: CEPS-JMGIU, 1958), pp. 1–62, esp. 1–2, 62, and 2–3, 61. For the INCIDI, see Institut International des Civilisations Différentes, *Programmes et plans de relèvement rural en pays tropicaux et sub-tropicaux: compte-rendu* (Brussels: Institut international des civilisations différentes, 1953).

55 Júlio Costa, "Promoção Social das Populações", 30 September 1968, *Contra Subversão em Angola, 1968–01–01/1972–01–01*, AHD/MU/GM/GNP/RNP/56.

56 Jorge Serro, "A Promoção Sócio-Económica das Populações na Base dos Problemas da Contra-Subversão", *Contra Subversão em Angola, 1968–01–01/1972–01–01*, AHD/MU/GM/GNP/RNP/56.

57 Alfredo Passos Guerra and Jorge Bonucci Veiga, *Promoção Social. Revisão do III Plano de Fomento. Estudo Apresentado ao Grupo de Trabalho n°7* (Luanda: JPP, 1970), pp. 1–2, 8–11.

58 *Congresso de Povoamento e Promoção Social, Luanda, 4 a 9 de Outubro de 1970* (Loanda: Associações Económicas de Angola, 1970), p. 517, 523; Decree n° 17482, 2 February 1971. See JPP Angola, *Brigadas de Promoção e Desenvolvimento Rrural* (Luanda: JPP Angola, 1971), pp. 3, 5–6, 17, 23; *Normas de Reordenamento Rural e Reagrupamento das Populacões*, Reserved, PT-AHD-UM-GM-GNP-RNP-0163-01091; see also Bandeira Jerónimo, "'A Battle in the Field of Human Relations'".

59 Gerald Bender, *Angola under the Portuguese. The Myth and the Reality* (London: Heinemann, 1978); João P. Borges Coelho, "Protected Villages and Communal Villages in the Mozambican Province of Tete (1968–1982): A History of State Resettlement Policies, Development and War (PhD thesis, University of Bradford, 1993); Cláudia Castelo, *Passagens para África: O Povoamento de Angola e Moçambique com Naturais da Metrópole (1920–1974)* (Porto: Afrontamento, 2007).

60 See, among others, A. J. Passos Guerra, "Reordenamento Rural e Desenvolvimento Comunitário", *Trabalho* 4 (1963): 83–128; Jerónimo da Silva Rôlo, *Reordenamento Rural em Angola (Contribuição para o Seu Estudo)* (Lisbon: Instituto Superior de Ciências Sociais e Política Ultramarina, 1967); Rosa Maria Serrão Ravara, *Contribuição para uma Política de Reordenamento Rural no Ultramar* (Lisbon: Junta de Investigações do Ultramar, 1970); for context and articulations see also Bandeira Jerónimo, "'A Battle in the Field of Human Relations'" and Curto, Cruz, and Furtado, *Políticas Coloniais em Tempo de Revoltas*.

61 The italics are ours. Decrees nº3237, 2 May 1962, and nº3484, 25 April 1964. Alfredo Passos Guerra, "Reordenamento Rural. Promoção Económico-Social das Populações Rurais de Angola", *IV Colóquio Nacional do Trabalho da Organização Corporativa e da Segurança Social* (Luanda: JPPA, 1966), in Overseas Historical Archive-IPAD-08418, cit. at pp. 2, 8, 9.

62 Bandeira Jerónimo, "'A Battle in the Field of Human Relations'".

63 Bandeira Jerónimo, "Repressive Developmentalisms".

The Editor and Contributors

Francisco Bethencourt is Charles Boxer Professor of History at King's College London. He organised in Lisbon, Padrão dos Descobrimento, the exhibition *Racism and Citizenship* (May–September 2017, c. 60,000 visitors). He is the author of *Racisms: From the Crusades to the Twentieth Century* (Princeton, 2013) and *The Inquisition: A Global History, 1478–1834* (Cambridge, 2009). He edited or co-edited *Utopia in Portugal, Brazil and Lusophone African Countries* (Oxford, 2015), *Racism and Ethnic Relations in the Portuguese-Speaking World* (Oxford, 2012), *Portuguese Oceanic Expansion, 1400–1800* (Cambridge, 2007), *História da Expansão Portuguesa*, 5 vols. (Lisbon, 1998–1999). He is a member of the Academia Europaea.

Vinicius Mariano de Carvalho has his PhD in Romance Literatures by Passau University, in Germany. He is Lecturer for Brazilian Studies at Brazil Institute, King's College London and Honorary Professor for Brazilian Studies at Aarhus University, Denmark. His most recent publication is the volume *Literature and Ethics in Contemporary Brazil* (Routledge, 2017), that he edited with Nicola Gavioli. He is chief-editor of *Brasiliana – Journal for Brazilian Studies.*

Tiago Fernandes is Assistant professor of political science at Nova University (Lisbon). He holds a PhD from the European University Institute, Florence and his research interests are revolutions, civil society, and democratization. Recent publications include *Civil Society, Democracy, and Inequality: Cross-Regional Comparisons (1970s–2015)*, Special Issue of Comparative Politics (co-edited with Michael Bernhard and Rui Branco, 2017) and *Memories and Movements: The Legacy of Democratic Transitions in Contemporary Anti-Austerity Protest* (Oxford University Press, 2017) and *Late Neoliberalism and its Discontents: Comparing Crises and Movements in the European Periphery* (co-authored, Palgrave Macmillan, 2016). He has been a visiting researcher at Princeton University, the Juan March Foundation, and the Kellogg Institute for International Studies, University of Notre Dame.

Inês Vieira Gomes, art historian, is a PhD student at the Institute of Social Sciences (ICS) of the University of Lisbon and her thesis focuses on photographical archives and practices in the Portuguese African colonies between 1890 and 1940. She has recently been awarded a dissertation fellowship – 2017–2018 Harry Ransom Center Research Fellowship in the Humanities,

Austin, USA, and, in 2015, a fellowship from the Smithsonian Institution, Washington DC, USA, in the National Museum of African Art.

Miguel Bandeira Jerónimo (PhD King's College London, History, 2008) is a Senior Research Fellow at the Centre for Social Studies-University of Coimbra, Portugal. He has been working on the historical intersections between internationalism(s) and imperialism, and on the late colonial entanglements between idioms and repertoires of development and of control and coercion in European empires. He is the author of *The "Civilizing Mission" of Portuguese Colonialism (c.1870–1930)* (2015), and the co-editor of *The Ends of European Colonial Empires* (2015). In 2017, he co-edited *Internationalism, Imperialism and the Formation of the Contemporary World.*

Celia Lessa Kerstenetzky (Ph.D with distinction in Social and Political Sciences, European University Institute, 1998), is Full Professor of Social Policy in the Economics Institute at the Federal University of Rio de Janeiro, Senior Researcher at the Brazilian National Council of Research (CNPq), and Director of the Center for Studies on Inequality (CEDE–UFF). Her research interests include comparative analysis of welfare systems, the relation between welfare states and development, and Brazilian social policy. She has recently published, with the Fondo de Cultura Económica (FCE–Ciudad de Mexico), the volume *El Estado de bien-estar social en la edad de la razón* (2017).

Hilary Owen is Professor Emerita in Portuguese and Luso-African Studies at the University of Manchester and Research Fellow in the Sub-Faculty of Portuguese at Oxford University. She has worked extensively on Portuguese and Lusophone African women writers and feminist theory as well as researching on contemporary Portuguese and Lusophone African cinema. She is the author of *Mother Africa, Father Marx: Women's Writing of Mozambique. 1948–2002* (Lewisburg: Bucknell University Press, 2007), co-author with Cláudia Pazos Alonso, of *Antigone's Daughters? Gender, Genealogy and the Politics of Authorship in Twentieth-Century Portuguese Women's Writing* (Lewisburg: Bucknell University Press, 2011), and co-editor with Anna M. Klobucka, of *Gender, Empire and Postcolony: Luso-Afro-Brazilian Intersections* (New York: Palgrave Macmillan, 2014). She is currently working on a monograph about race in Portuguese cinema.

Pedro Ramos Pinto is Senior Lecturer in International Economic History at the University of Cambridge, and fellow of Trinity Hall. He has a long-standing interest in historical experiences and trajectories of inequality, and has since 2012 directed the Inequality & History Network. His current research explores the genealogies of social policies under authoritarianism in southern Europe. Amongst other things he has authored *Lisbon Rising: Urban Social Movements in the Portuguese Revolution, 1974–1975*

(Manchester University Press, 2013) and co-edited, with Bertrand Taithe, *The Impact of History: Histories at the Beginning of the 21st Century* (Routledge, 2015).

Margarida Calafate Ribeiro is a senior researcher at the Centre for Social Studies, University of Coimbra and holds the Eduardo Lourenço Chair at the University of Bologna/ Camões (dir. by Roberto Vecchi). She co-coordinates the PhD programme *Cultural Heritages of Portuguese Influence.* She specialises in literature and history of the Portuguese empire, politics and heritage, working in the interstices between literary studies and history. Her recent research has been focused particularly on the memory and post-memory of colonialism and empire, identities and postcolonialism in the Portuguese and European context. In 2015 she was awarded a Consolidator Grant from the European Research Council for the project "MEMOIRS – Children of Empires and European Postmemories" (memoirs.ces.uc.pt/). Her work has been published widely and her seminal study *Uma História de Regressos: Império, Guerra Colonial e pós-colonialismo* (2004) presents the foundations of such interdisciplinary research.

Carlos Farinha Rodrigues is associate professor at Lisbon School of Economics and Management, Universidade de Lisboa. He is also adviser of the Statistics Portugal (INE). He obtained his PhD from Technical University of Lisbon under the supervision of Tony Atkinson. His main research interests lie in applied micro-economics, Income Distribution, Poverty and Inequality, Evaluation of Public Policies and Microsimulation. He was recently involved in the international projects "GINI Growing Inequalities' Impacts" and "EUROMOD – Tax-benefit microsimulation model for the European Union."

Lilia Moritz Schwarcz is Full Professor in Anthropology at the University of São Paulo and Global Scholar at Princeton. Lilia was fellow at the Guggenheim Foundation (2006/2007) and a visiting professor at Oxford, Leiden Brown and Columbia University. She published several books, such as *Retrato em branco e negro* (1987), *O sol do Brasil* (2008); Lima Barreto triste visionário (2017); among them three in English: *Spectacle of Races* (1999); *The Emperors beard: D. Pedro II a tropical king* (Farrar Strauss and Giroux, 2004), and *Brazil: A Biography* – with Heloisa Starling (Penguin, Spain; Farrar Strauss and Giroux and Penguin, UK, to be published in 2018). She was a curator of some exhibitions, including: *Nicolas-Antoine Taunay: A French Translation of the Tropics* (2008), *A History of Brazil: An Interpretation by Photographs* (with Boris Kossoy, 2013), *Mestizo Histories* (with Adriano Pedrosa, 2014). Since 2015 she is co-curator at MASP (Museum of Modern Art of São Paulo).

Laura de Mello e Souza taught at the University of São Paulo (1983–2014) and is professor of Brazilian History at the University of Paris Sorbonne – Centre Roland Mousnier since 2014. She researched on poverty in the gold districts of the Portuguese America (XVIII century), witchcraft, demonology and popular religion in the Portuguese Empire (XVI–XVIII centuries) and on the overseas careers of the Portuguese functionaries of the Empire (XVIII century). She published *Desclassificados do Ouro – A pobreza mineira no século XVIII* (1982), *The Devil and the Land of the Holy Cross – Witchcraft, Slavery and Popular Religion in Colonial Brazil* (2003), *O Sol e a Sombra – Política e administração na América Portuguesa do século XVIII* (2006).

Filipa Lowndes Vicente is a researcher at the Institute of Social Sciences of the University of Lisbon (ICS–UL). In 2000 she completed her PhD in History at the University of London (Goldsmiths College). Amongst the books and articles she has published is *Other Orientalisms: India between Florence and Bombay, 1860–1900* (New Delhi: Orient BlackSwan, 2012). In 2015 she was a Visiting Scholar at King's College London (Camões Fellowship) and, in 2016, at Brown University, Providence, USA (FLAD fellowship). She is now preparing the English edition of two books already published in Portuguese: *Imperial Comparisons: British Travellers in Goa (1800–1940)*, as author, and *The Empire of Vision: Photography in the Portuguese Colonial Context (1860–1960)*, as editor.

Laurent Vidal is Professor of History at the Université de La Rochelle. He is Associate Director of the Centre de Recherche en Histoire Internationale et Atlantique. He has been Visiting Professor at the Federal University of Goiás in Brazil in 2000 and is currently Visiting Professor at the Federal University of Rio de Janeiro. He works on the history of Brazil, relations between urban life and politics, Atlantic migrations, and cultural exchanges between Europe and the New World. He led the international program ANR TERRIAT (2011–2015): "Societies, mobility and movement: the territories of waiting (the case of the Americas past and present)."

Index